D1234263

THE INTERNATIONAL
PSYCHO-ANALYTICAL
LIBRARY
No. 68

EDITED BY
JOHN D. SUTHERLAND
PH.D., F.R.C.P.E.

THE INTERNATIONAL PSYCHO-ANALYTICAL LIBRARY
EDITED BY JOHN D. SUTHERLAND, PH.D., F.R.C.P.E.
No. 68

A PSYCHO-ANALYTIC DIALOGUE

The Letters of Sigmund Freud and Karl Abraham
1907–1926

EDITED BY

HILDA C. ABRAHAM

AND

ERNST L. FREUD

TRANSLATED BY
BERNARD MARSH
AND
HILDA C. ABRAHAM

BASIC BOOKS, INC., PUBLISHERS

NEW YORK

WILLIAM MADISON RANDALL LIBRARY UNC AT WILMINGTON

© Hilda C. Abraham and Ernst L. Freud 1965
Library of Congress Catalog Card Number: 66-11590
Printed in the United States of America

BF173
.F85
.A435

CONTENTS

PLATES

141249

EDITORS' FOREWORD

THIS correspondence between Sigmund Freud and his pupil
and friend Karl Abraham is the fourth volume of letters published in the last few years.[1] It differs, however, in that letters
from both have been preserved. The correspondence contains
492 letters, 220 by Freud and 272 by Abraham. It is complete with the exception of the first few letters by Abraham
and of a few of Freud's letters, lost owing to wartime conditions.
It covers the period from June 1907 until Abraham's death at
Christmas 1925, at the age of 48.

A number of letters have been omitted, and the table on
page xvii gives a survey of the proportion between all the letters
exchanged and of those included in this volume. Shortened
letters are marked by an asterisk above the date.

Omissions and cuts have been made for reasons of discretion
where names and facts might lead to recognition of patients or
their families, or where the people discussed would not be of any
interest nowadays; furthermore to avoid repetition or details
about the various psycho-analytical organisations which were
of purely local interest and, finally, to avoid unimportant personal details about the writers and their families, which do not
contribute to the knowledge and understanding of their personalities and of their scientific work.

When the publication was first planned, it was decided that
differences in style and personality—so obvious in the German
originals—would be more clearly reflected if two people were
to undertake the translation; Freud's letters have been translated by Bernard Marsh and Abraham's by his daughter. We
hope we have been successful in conveying this difference in

---

[1] Sigmund Freud, *The Origins of Psycho-analysis. Letters to Wilhelm Fliess*.
Imago Publishing Company (London) and Basic Books (New York), 1954.
Letters of Sigmund Freud, 1873–1939. The Hogarth Press (London) and
Basic Books (New York) 1961.
Psycho-Analysis and Faith. The Letters of Sigmund Freud and Oskar Pfister. The
Hogarth Press (London), 1963 and Basic Books (New York) 1963.

background, generation and personality, as well as in giving a faithful rendering of the scientific content.

The opening mode of address, which has so many shades of meaning in German, from the most formal to an easy and friendly one, had to be simplified and adapted. Thus the Abraham letters use 'Dear Professor Freud' in the early letters, and 'Dear Professor' from about the beginning of the second year of the correspondence. The same principle is applied to the often elaborate endings – we hope without losing their character and warmth.

Certain psychiatric and psycho-analytic terms were allowed to stand in their old forms for historic reasons. Thus 'dementia praecox' is exclusively used in the early letters, since 'schizophrenia' was not generally introduced until Bleuler published his work in 1911. At times the mode of expression or the turn of phrase may sound old-fashioned, so as to convey the manner of speech in the early part of this century.

All references to Freud's writings are to the Standard Edition, and those to Abraham's work to the *Selected Papers on Psycho-Analysis* and to the *Clinical Papers and Essays on Psycho-Analysis*.

Our thanks are due to Miss Anna Freud, Ll.D., for advising us on the selection of material, to Mrs Hedwig Abraham-Allan and Mrs Lucie Freud for their help in clarifying and editing; and to Dr Hilde Maas for checking the translation of the scientific content. Furthermore we wish to express our gratitude to Mrs Marion Burgner, B.A., for her help in translating the Abraham letters and to thank Dr Edward Glover most cordially for his introduction to this volume.

HILDA C. ABRAHAM
ERNST L. FREUD

London 1964

viii

INTRODUCTION

THE animistic art of biography, like that of embalming, the making of graven or painted images or the carving of lettered tombstones, has many modes. In most cases however the patent intention of the artist-biographer is to re-animate and preserve for the benefit or admonition of posterity the images of those who, by their life and work have gained fame or respectively notoriety, and in one or other of these ways have contributed to the self-esteem, and to that extent the well-being of their fellow-men. The superlative merit of the biography is that it affords its author an opportunity not only of preserving the appearance of his subject, which a graven image might do better, but also of tracing and preserving his mental lineaments.

But here is the rub. A biographer cannot see farther than his insight into himself permits. Diarists and writers of autobiographies have long recognised this flaw. Anxious to secure and by becoming one of their own readers to savour in advance a modicum of the immortality they prize so highly, at the same time distrustful of the capacity of others to render the quiddity of their particular lives, they attempt to solve the dilemma by painting their own portraits. Hence they suffer from a double disadvantage, the limitations of their own insight and their tendency to observe themselves through rose-tinted spectacles.

There is however one form of autobiography that is less handicapped or prejudiced, except in the case of those literary figures who write their private letters with one eye on a posterity of readers. It is to maintain and preserve their correspondence with those who have played a part in shaping their adult life. To be sure, as an autobiographical form, the harvesting of private letters has its limitations; it rarely deals with more than a facet or two of the writer's adult life, and leaves his earlier and often more important illiterate phrases unrecorded. Nevertheless there are times when collected letters shed more light on the human nature of their authors than the most meticulous and painstaking of biographies. This is certainly true of the various collections of letters written by Sigmund Freud, and, as the present volume convincingly shows, it is also true of letters written to Freud by one of the most gifted of his favourite pupils, Karl Abraham. In several respects therefore this is a unique collection of letters. It contains two studies in autobiography, and at the same time an invaluable record of the pioneer phase of psycho-analytical development from the time when in the early years of the century there gathered round Freud a small but enthusiastic group of supporters, down to the middle twenties when psycho-analysis finally established itself as an organised though not too popular psychological science with branches throughout Europe and the United States. The untimely death of Abraham in December 1925 at the age of 48 signalised in fact the end of this pioneering phase.

And let there be no misunderstanding about the connotation of the phrase. This book is not a memorial volume of antiquarian interest inspired by the filial piety of its editors. It is sometimes the habit of modern analytical commentators, born some time after Abraham first wrote to Freud, to speak of 'advances' in psycho-analysis made in recent years, as if to suggest that the works of the earlier analysts are now somewhat *démodé*. This is a view to which I have never been able to subscribe. The striking feature not only of Freud's own works but of the contributions of his earliest supporters is not only their freshness but their continuing fertility. With a few exceptions these early workers were clinicians of outstanding aptitude which is more than can be said of some of our modern theoreticians. The term 'metapsychology' was in fact first used by Freud in 1896, and the earlier writers lived up to the implications of the category, basing their ideas on clinical experience and carefully abstaining from metaphysical elaboration or sophistical manipulation. In short this volume should adorn the bookshelves of psycho-analysts of every degree, from tyro to teacher; it should be read by psychiatrists who have not already sold the pass to neuro-physiology and by any general psychologist who is prepared to learn by what steps the principles and practices of (unconscious) dynamic psychology came to be applied to everyday life and character.

Space does not permit a systematic account of the multifarious contents of this correspondence which would in any case read like the index to a comprehensive textbook of abnormal (and normal) psychology. In the very first year (1907) occurs a fairly detailed exchange of views on the role of sexual trauma in dementia praecox and hysteria respectively, in which Freud, speaking of the aetiological significance of sexual phantasy in unconscious conflict, in effect warns Abraham against repeating his (Freud's) 'first great error', viz. confusing traumatic phantasy with traumatic experience, thereby raising a problem in interpretation which, transference or no transference, continues to perplex even our most experienced and didactically pressurised technicians.

And so throughout the book: exchanges on the prognosis of obsessional neurosis (a subject that still intimidates our modern fainthearts), on flying dreams, dreams and myth, on fetishism and 'partial' repression; on traumatic neuroses, agoraphobia, on depression, impotence, masochism, narcissism, exhibitionism, transference, melancholia, female sexuality and a host of other topics. All of which is given additional point and interest in those letters in which the writers exchange views as to their current writings, books, articles and reviews. (In 1908 for example Freud is writing the history of 'Little Hans' . . .) And so as the letters proceed one gets a first-hand account of the ways and means of the writers, more illuminating than any formal bibliography.

But perhaps one of the most striking and in the historical sense most intriguing threads in the correspondence is spun from the inner history of the administrative politics of psycho-analysis, the gradual unfolding of personal reactions not only between Freud and Abraham, but between Freud and Abraham on the one hand and on the other those personalities who first supported psycho-analysis, some of whom renounced their allegiance and by that means gained a more lasting reputation than they would otherwise have achieved. As in a slow motion film these personalities pass across the screen to the accompaniment of shrewd and sometimes astringent comment from the two principals. Many of the names are still familiar, others nearer to oblivion: Jung, Rank, Riklin, Maeder, Eitingon, Ferenczi, Jones, Pfister, Ossipow, Bleuler, Storfer, Brill, Putnam, Fliess, Adler, Stekel, Sachs, Reik, Sadger, Horney, Andreas-Salomé, Federn, Eder, Jelgersama, Hug-Hellmuth, Jeliffe, van Ophuijsen, Simmel, Forsyth, Boehm, Deutsch, Radó, Coriat, Groddeck and so on to the end of this particular chapter of psycho-analysis.

As is inevitable in political history the names that recur most frequently are those of the most important deviants or schismatics, followed by those who, without withdrawing from psycho-analysis, were from time to time at the centre of internal disputation or uncertainty. Then comes the recurring list of staunch supporters, in particular those who made up the 'Committee' founded to relieve Freud of as many tasks of administration as possible. How important the first two of these groups really were is now difficult to determine. Looking back from the present vantage point it sometimes seems that, for example, too much alarm and despondency were aroused by the prospective defection of Jung. Yet it is clear from this correspondence that Freud himself and to a lesser extent Abraham felt that the integrity of psycho-analysis was seriously threatened thereby.

This was a crisis that has been well documented both by the principals concerned and by a number of devoted adherents on both sides. In the present correspondence it continues to crop up from May 1908 when Freud deplores Abraham's critical reaction to Jung down to April 1914 when Abraham wires to Freud his congratulations on the news that Jung has voluntarily resigned his post of president of the International Psycho-analytical Association. And it is interesting to observe that other early deviants were of less concern to both correspondents. Adler and Stekel are dismissed with a few summary comments. Indeed it is not until 1924 that Rank's position begins to concern both writers. Here again Freud for a time continues loyal to his early analytical protégé, whilst Abraham is uncompromising in his criticism, to say nothing of his psychological diagnosis of Rank's case.

As has been suggested, these are now old stories. But they do serve to raise that somewhat hazardous question, namely, what psychological light does this correspondence shed on the character of the correspondents. This is a difficult matter to assess because of the unusual conditions that operate in psycho-analytical affairs. Whenever two analysts co-operate in the study of the workings of the unconscious mind, states of rapport are evoked between them which go by the names of 'transference' and 'counter-transference'. These have to be distinguished from the more adult forms of friendship or dependence and although vigorous attempts are made to eliminate them it is doubtful whether these are ever fully successful. Reading between the lines of these letters it is clear that they give increasing expression to this professional rapport, mostly though not invariably of a positive nature. From the first, Abraham welcomes the position of pupil to his master Freud: and indeed had every reason to do so. Gradually however this gives place to a riper state of friendship which is maintained to the end. Freud, for his part, is a shade more austere in his expressions of counter-transference, but there is no doubt he was deeply moved by the continued allegiance of his most loyal pupil. As indeed he might well have been.

It is clear however that Abraham was no idolator, that he was sustained by that character trait essential to the successful pioneer, viz. a conviction of the soundness of his own judgement—'a guid conceit o' himsel' as the Scots phrase it. Quite firmly and politely he stands up to Freud whenever he feels the occasion demands it. This is most obvious in the protracted correspondence on *l'affaire Jung*. Except for a short period of wavering judgement Abraham stuck to his guns and in the end proved the better judge of character. This Freud handsomely acknowledges in a letter written towards the end of 1913. Discussing ways and means of coping with the Jung crisis, he writes 'since being taken in by Jung, my confidence in my political judgement has greatly declined'. And again when the lesser Rankian crisis developed in 1924 Abraham proved the better judge. But of course he was not hampered by that sense of loyalty to his early supporters which was a venial and indeed endearing trait of Freud's character. To be sure, like Caesar, Freud, who had infinite patience, subscribed to the tenet that if one gives a man rope enough he will sooner or later hang himself. And when he finally felt compelled to turn down his thumb he was quite uncompromising not only in his professional ex-communication but in his severance of the by then usually frayed ties of personal friendship.

In the very last month of his short life Abraham himself comments on the nature of their differences. Apropos his clash with Freud on the desirability of sponsoring a film on psycho-analysis, a project to which Freud had a rooted objection, Abraham (one of the sponsors) remarks that the only differences he has so far had with his master have centred round judgements of personality. In this case however Freud was in my opinion the better judge. Documentary films in those days (1925) were rather simple minded and this particular film (sponsored also by Sachs, who saw himself as an inspired director) was naïve sometimes to the verge of ridiculousness. And I think too that in his estimation of the scientific merits of Fliess, Freud was shrewder than Abraham. So perhaps after all the honours were easy. On the other hand on matters dealing with psycho-analytical research the scientific rapport between the two men was quite

xiii

remarkable. Freud writing with magistral clarity on the essentials of the science he had founded and yet, when he was unsure of his evidence as modest, tentative and even timid as a young post-graduate; Abraham, optimistic and sanguine as ever, reaching boldly into new territories. This was a partnership that paid rich scientific dividends, the more remarkable indeed that both of the partners had evolved their ideas on the basis of self-analysis. I well remember Abraham telling me in 1921 how step by step he had to overcome resistances to ideas which, stated with complete conviction by Freud, he could digest and apply only after close searching of heart and head.

But when all is said and when this correspondence is systematically assessed, perhaps the most striking feature of it is the simplicity of the relationship between the two men, the almost childlike *naïveté* of the more intimate exchanges and the hallmark which almost every letter carries of what in this country would be described as a late Victorian idiom. A modern generation would almost certainly shrug the matter off with the condescending or indulgent comment that both of them were typical representatives of the professional bourgeoisie; others that the formalities of mid-European manners, including the worship of anyone who achieves the academic dignity of a professorship, have a venial if pseudo-religious flavour; still others that the correspondence manifests that 'closeness' of contact by which the Jewish community is sometimes held to have demonstrated its emotional superiority over the 'Aryan' communities of Northern and Middle Europe (both men exhibited, each in his own way, a profound racial allegiance); and still others that the whole relation was simply an idealised model of the more romantic relationship existing between fathers and sons. That is as may be. But the hunt for psychological motivations even under the best of circumstances frequently misses the target. What stands out in this correspondence is the simplicity and sincerity that are characteristic of great men. For Freud was incontestably a man of genius and Abraham will in future be recognised as one of those men of outstanding ability who helped to fertilise and stir into movement the, till then, paretic science of psychiatry. No mean achievement when one considers the regressive tendencies that plague and interrupt the progress of clinical psychology.

*　　*　　*　　*　　*

But introductions however garrulous must come to an end, and, usually, the quicker the better. It remains only to orientate the reader on two points, the first a biographical consideration and the second a personal one. The life of Freud has been documented with such lavish and devoted detail that one may assume some recognition on the part of the general reader of the salient features of his character and genius. His early sub-lieutenants have not been accorded the same appreciative accolade. To most junior analysts and psychiatrists the name of Abraham is now a unit of bibliographical reference concerned with the history of the libido, the ego and the manic-depressive psychoses. For this reason it is pertinent to add here a brief outline of his career.[1] This runs as follows:

Karl Abraham was born in Bremen on May 3rd 1877 and died on December 25th 1925 at the age of 48. He was the younger of two sons of a Jewish teacher, who later entered upon a business career. The family was an old Hanseatic one. He was educated at the *Gymnasium* in Bremen. At that stage he shewed an interest in linguistics and philology. He commenced the study of medicine (mainly at Würzburg and Freiburg) when he was 19 years of age. Then his interests turned towards embryology and histology, and his doctoral thesis was first published in 1901, the year in which he obtained his first post-graduate post under Professor Liepmann (the brain histologist and pathologist) at the Berlin Municipal Mental Hospital at Dalldorf. Here he remained for nearly 4 years and developed a deep interest in psychiatry. At the end of 1904 he was appointed to the staff at Burghölzi and became assistant at the University Psychiatric Clinic of Zürich. He married 'on the strength' in January 1906 when he became first assistant to Bleuler. Dissatisfied with his prospects, he resigned in November 1907, a month before he first met Freud. He then settled in Berlin and began to expand his interest in the teaching of psycho-analysis and founded the Berlin Psychoanalytical Society in March 1910. In 1914–15 he was seconded to the military reserve and worked as a surgeon first in Berlin and afterwards in Allenstein in East Prussia. In 1916 he was finally allotted psychiatric beds. On this basis he built up a hospital psychiatric unit of his own. At this stage he specialised in giving evidence at courts-martial regarding the mental state of accused soldiers. Returning to Berlin in 1918, he pursued his psycho-analytical career, teaching, training, lecturing, writing articles and reviews, and editing the *Zeitschrift*. In 1922 he became secretary of the International Association and in 1924 was appointed its president. In the period between 1900 and 1925 well over 100 contributions appeared under his name. Four of these were small books. His first psycho-analytical contribution dates from

[1] The best account of Abraham's life, character and work so far extant is to be found in Ernest Jones' Obituary Notice: *International Journal of Psycho-analysis*, Vol. VII, April 1926, part 2, pp. 155–89.

early 1907, and from that time onward his papers covered an increasingly wide range. Of these perhaps the most significant appeared in 1925 on the developmental phases of the libido, based on the analysis of mental disturbances.

Which brings me to my last consideration, a personal one. It is not often that one has the opportunity of paying scientific debts, and so, having been invited to write this introduction, I welcome the opportunity it affords of paying tribute to the younger of the two correspondents. I had very limited opportunity of making contact with Freud until he retired from the scene to make his home in England. On the other hand it was my good fortune to enter into a training analysis with Karl Abraham at the end of 1920. In those days the advancement of oncoming analysts was rather on the lines of mediaeval apprenticeship, and so I gradually acquired the confidence to follow his clinical methods. As a guest of the Berlin Psycho-Analytical Society in the Potsdamerstrasse, I used to observe his skilful operations as president of an omnibus group, liable to explode at any time into a bear-garden of often opposing ideas, Abraham bringing the contestants back time and again to the necessity of applying clinical standards to their speculative lucubrations. (This was a service incidentally which his mentor Freud performed for many years for the Vienna group.) I have even been present when he vetted the ideologies of potential leaders of psycho-analysis in new countries (see the comments in this correspondence regarding Van Ophuijsen). I have observed his cool and diplomatic handling of controversial issues when as president of the International Association he guided the policies of that body. And I had the rare privilege, quite unknown amongst our modern acolytes, of being admitted to his family life—a severe test of allegiance. Some of this our young sophomores will regard as reprehensible technique on his part. But I gained much therefrom and, transference piety notwithstanding, welcome the opportunity of maintaining that in the history of psycho-analysis those clinicians who disciplined their theories by reference to their actual observations deserve well of posterity. No better epitaph could be found for the work of Karl Abraham.

EDWARD GLOVER

TABLE OF LETTERS

Year	Total			Included in this volume		
	FREUD	ABRAHAM	TOTAL	FREUD	ABRAHAM	TOTAL
1907	6	7	13	6	5	11
1908	23	21	44	17	17	34
1909	9	13	22	8	9	17
1910	8	10	18	8	5	13
1911	9	11	20	7	6	13
1912	15	14	29	11	10	21
1913	20	22	42	15	19	34
1914	31	39	70	25	23	48
1915	9	14	23	8	10	18
1916	6	13	19	6	7	13
1917	11	14	25	11	10	21
1918	7	11	18	7	9	16
1919	8	11	19	7	7	14
1920	9	9	18	8	9	17
1921	9	12	21	7	5	12
1922	4	5	9	3	3	6
1923	4	8	12	4	6	10
1924	19	21	40	15	13	28
1925	12	17	29	9	11	20
1926	1	—	1	1	—	1
	220	272	492	183	184	367

Sigmund Freud in 1906

Dear Colleague,

I already knew about your paper,[1] which I have now read with great interest. The complete analogy between the pre-history of these neuroses is really very striking. I have the impression that there is less difficulty in uncovering these experiences in the case of dementia praecox than there is in hysteria, just as paranoia in general is the more transparent so far as the early links are concerned.

I await your communications with great interest. If you consider that remarks by me on your findings might be useful to you, I shall gladly make them. It is particularly gratifying to me that you have tackled the sexual side of the problem, which only very few are willing to approach.

Yours faithfully,
Dr Freud

Berggasse 19,
Vienna IX,
5.7.07

My dear Colleague,

I have read your acute and, what is more important, conclusive observations,[2] with quite special interest. Before I deal with them there is one possibility that I should like to clear out of the way, namely that you should regard remarks of mine such as 'That we knew already' or 'I came to a similar conclusion' as making any claim to priority. Please also consider yourself at liberty to make use of my observations in any way you wish. You have of course been spared the mistake I made of believing the real aetiology of neurosis to be sexual traumas. At that time

[1] Karl Abraham, 'On the Significance of Sexual Trauma in Childhood for the Symptomatology of Dementia Praecox', *Clinical Papers and Essays on Psycho-Analysis*, London, 1955, p. 13.

[2] The reference is to a lost letter of Abraham's.

I

I did not yet know that these experiences were very general, and when I discovered the fact I was fortunately able to turn to the psycho-sexual constitution. Meanwhile it is an excellent thing that work on these sexual traumas should be undertaken by someone who, unlike me, has not been made uncertain by that first great error. For you as for me the compelling thing is that these traumas become the formative factor in the symptomatology of neurosis.

There is one consideration that I must not withhold from you that is certainly valid in the case of hysteria – I do not know whether it also applies to dementia praecox. The hysteric later moves very far away from infantile auto-erotism, he exaggerates his object-cathexis (in this he is the very opposite of the manifest dementia praecox case, who in our assumption regresses to auto-erotism). He accordingly displaces his need of objects back into his childhood, and clothes his real auto-erotic childhood in phantasies of love and seduction. Rather like lovers who cannot imagine that there was ever a time when they did not know each other, and construct earlier meetings and links between each other on the flimsiest basis, that is to say, a proportion of the sexual traumas reported by patients are or may be phantasies; distinguishing them from the so frequent genuine ones is not easy, and the complication of this situation and the relationship of sexual traumas to forgetting and remembering is one of the chief reasons why I cannot persuade myself to undertake a conclusive account of them.

According to my impressions, the age of from three to five is that to which the determination of symptoms dates back. Later traumas are mostly genuine, while earlier ones or those falling within this period are *prima facie* doubtful. So here is a gap to be filled in by observation.

I am also aware of the multiplicity of traumas, in part from lurid examples. This is partly a result of phantasy, but is partly also a consequence of the circumstance that in some environments the conditions for such experiences are very favourable while in others they are meagre. In my cases of recent years which come from very good social circles sexual traumas before the age of five have been far rarer than auto-erotism. From eight years onwards the opportunities of course proliferate in all social classes.

2

The question why children do not report sexual traumas has forced itself on our attention here too, and has been answered by us just as it has been by you: children keep silent when they have experienced a pleasure gain. That was how we explained the puzzle of why maltreatment by nurses and governesses is heard of only a long time after their dismissal, even though the child could have relied on the protection of its fond parents; masochism kept the secret. Moreover, the behaviour of grown-up girls is generally similar, and may have the same motivation. Your remark about the displacement of the sense of guilt is unquestionably quite correct. But why do some children talk all the same? It is hard to ascribe an abnormal organisation to the others, because this abnormal constitution is the general infantile constitution. Perhaps here we are once again faced with a more-or-less rather than with a sharp dividing line, and perhaps the sexual trauma develops its pathogenic effect, releases pleasure and the sense of guilt, where the ground is well prepared for it by strong auto-erotism.

I find the two main points of your exposition, the unconscious intention in the experience of sexual traumas and the abnormal constitution, very convincing, only to me everything seems less clear-cut, *i.e.*, more graded in intensity. In one sense this constitution is, as I said, peculiar to all children, and the same infantile perversities, anal erotism, etc., can be found in the mentally healthy. However, in hysteria in particular the perverse endowment can be assumed to be greater than that in the basically healthy. The situation is confused and conclusions made harder to draw by the fact that later events in their lives so often become the decisive factor and force back infantile experiences into a constitutional role of which use has fortunately not been made. I agree that your interpretation applies completely to a number of infantile personalities, but what you say about the unconscious purpose should, I think, be modified to the extent that the dividing line between consciousness and unconsciousness has not yet been established in early childhood. The child reacts as if compulsively to sexual impulses, as if unconsciously in fact, but without any inner conflict arising in the process.

I think I indicated in a passage in the *Interpretation of Dreams* (or elsewhere? In the *Aetiology* . . .?)[1] that theoretically we can regard the phenomenon of the sexual latency period as providing the fundamental prerequisite for the development of neurosis. The child is not mentally equipped to cope with the stronger sexual impressions, and hence reacts to them compulsively, as if unconsciously–that is the first defect in the mechanism; as a consequence of the somatic increase of the sexual release, these impressions later exercise more powerful effects in retrospect and in the form of memories than they did when they were real impressions, and that is the second psychological defect, because this constellation of retrospectively strengthened unpleasurable memory enables repression to take place which would not succeed in the case of direct perceptions. I have not yet got any further than that, and feel that a thorough examination of the whole question is still necessary. In spite of these reservations, or rather uncertainties, of mine, I agree that large parts of your exposition are captivating and convincing; I am thinking in particular of the material about traumas experienced at a somewhat later age. So do not let yourself be dissuaded from keeping me informed about the progress of your work. I shall gladly tell you all I know or can think of in connection with it, and I apologise for my reactions having been so meagre on this occasion. At all events, you have tackled the problem at the right end and, moreover, at the point where most people are unwilling to touch it. Also I am particularly glad that the approach to dementia praecox by way of auto-erotism seems hopeful to you. But due weight must be given to the normal auto-erotism of childhood, and in dementia merely a return to auto-erotism must be postulated. I am very glad to know that all of you in Zürich are taking this heavy labour out of my hands. Your youthful vigour, and the fact that you can spare yourselves the wrong turnings that I took, all promise the best.

With cordial thanks and in expectation of further friendly news from you, I am,

Yours sincerely
Dr Freud

[1] Sigmund Freud, *My Views on the Part Played by Sexuality in the Aetiology of the Neuroses*, Standard Ed., Vol. VII.

My dear Colleague,

Your letter[2] is the first of scientific content that has followed me here during the holidays. It only increased my enjoyment, because it again provides evidence of the advance of knowledge in the matter of dementia praecox and revives the prospect of the realisation of long restrained hopes. I reply to your rich offerings with only two observations which I have had in store for a long time and which coincide so perfectly with what you say that I can let them merge with them.

(1) It has struck me that patients who turn towards dementia and lose their resemblance to hysterics produce their (sexually infantile) phantasies without resistance, as if these had now lost their value, rather as a man who has abandoned his hope of marriage throws away the souvenirs, ribbons, locks of hair, etc., which have now become worthless. The context in which I should like to place this behaviour is that the essence of the turn to dementia lies in the withdrawal of the libido from the sexual object.

(2) I have always assumed that the individuals generally described as idiopathic who later become obviously paranoid have only inadequately completed the necessary development from auto-erotism to object-love. With a proportion of cases of dementia this factor would supply the predisposition that we have been seeking for the later illness, and that would fit in admirably with the general pathological view that illness always implies a regression in development. (The *evolution* and *involution* of British authors.[3])

This practically corresponds with what you report, and it may strengthen your conviction of the necessity of looking at things in this way.

So allow me to thank you cordially for the reports of your work, in which I wish to encourage you because of the lively interest I take in it.

---

[1] South Tyrolese (then Austrian) resort where Freud stayed in the summer.

[2] Abraham's letter referred to has not survived.

[3] Italicised words in English in the original.

Moreover, let us not forget that withdrawal of libido is generally partial in nature, and that the development of sexual life permits a similar predisposition to be assumed in the case of hysteria. In regard to the obsessional neuroses I do not yet see clearly.

Yours very sincerely,
Dr Freud

Zürich,
9.8.07
Dear Professor Freud,

Once again I have to ask your indulgence for not having replied to your letter any sooner. As both my superiors, Bleuler[1] and Jung,[2] were away at the same time, I have had no opportunity for anything but hospital routine during the last fortnight. I was very glad indeed to hear that you agree with the exposition in my last letter. I would add the following comments to the two main points in your most recent letter: communication of phantasies, delusional ideas, etc. occur without resistance in certain phases of dementia praecox. At the moment I am treating a woman who recounts her most intimate affairs, including her religious, grandiose ideas, as impersonally as one would speak of some commonly known incident. Many mental patients behave like this in a particular phase. At other times, however, it is impossible even to elicit a single word from them about such matters. On yet other occasions, one may get a full report of their delusional constructions and nothing at all about their 'voices'. I find this alternating behaviour hard to understand. When the concept of dementia has been clarified, I would be ready to admit that the exposure of the most intimate secrets is a sign of its onset; so far, however, this has not been done. I believe what in cases of chronic mental illness is called dementia is nothing but the patient shutting himself away from the world, the withdrawal of libido from persons and objects.

[1] Eugen Bleuler, 1857–1939, Professor of Psychiatry at the University of Zürich, Director of the Cantonale Heilanstalt Burghölzli.
[2] Carl Gustav Jung, 1875–1961, at that time Physician at Burghölzli at Zürich.

6

In organic psychoses and in epilepsy, one also speaks of dementia. This is unfortunate since it relates to something completely different. The epileptic becomes demented in a totally different way: in his case the mental impoverishment is progressive. On the other hand, he retains the capacity to react emotionally, which is lost in the patient suffering from dementia praecox. In spite of all the dementia and even with the utmost intellectual deterioration, the epileptic shows definite object-love. He is full of exaggerated praise for the members of his family; his handshake with the doctor is over-cordial; he cannot find enough words to express his emotions; he clings tenaciously to his possessions – all this in complete contrast to the dementia praecox patient. We are then faced with the strange fact that the epileptic becomes demented and keeps his object-libido, while the chronic mental patient becomes demented and loses his object-libido. Therefore, the concept of dementia urgently needs clarification. This particular concept is constantly bandied about in psychiatry. Some regard paranoia (or dementia praecox, or whatever one likes to call it) as a partial mental disturbance involving only certain psychic capacities; others apply the term 'demented' or imbecilic to every absurd delusion. One might just as well regard the thousand apparently meaningless and yet meaningful absurdities of the dream as demented and every dreamer as imbecile. What is called dementia in the chronic mental patient seems to me something reversible in contrast to epileptic, paralytic or senile dementia, all of them irreversible. In dementia praecox we find temporary (though often long-lasting) blocking of thought and emotions. Whether or not this condition is reversible, seems to me to depend on the severity and depth of the 'complex'.[1]

In connection with the second point in your letter, I should like to try and substitute another concept for that of dementia in chronic mental illness. The insufficient development of object-love appears to be an inhibition in the maturation of the personality. Personality is, after all, nothing but the individual's

[1] In the papers published by the Zürich Psychiatric Clinic (especially in the *Diagnostische Assoziationsstudien* published by Jung), the word *Komplex* is used for a constellation of ideas strongly charged with emotion, which has a tendency to split off from consciousness and to be repressed into the unconscious.

way of reacting to the stimuli of his environment. It has become clear to me from your work that the reaction to the environment is closely connected with sexuality. Every acute attack of dementia praecox is an obstacle to the development of the personality and, in severe cases, this development may be halted once and for all. I therefore believe that in chronic mental illness one ought to speak of a standstill in personality development rather than of dementia.

To conclude, I should like to express to you, dear Professor Freud, my sincerest thanks for your interest. It was more than I deserved that you should have concerned yourself with my letter during your holidays. I am sending this to your address in Vienna, since it will most likely be forwarded from there if you are still away. Much as I look forward to hearing further from you, I would ask you to postpone your answer until your return.

With grateful thanks,

Yours,
Dr Abraham

Zürich,
6.10.07

Dear Professor Freud,

Please forgive me for writing to you today without waiting for your reply to my last letter. This time I am not writing about theoretical problems but about my personal affairs. I intend to leave Zürich in about a month and am at the same time giving up my mental hospital work. The reasons are not far to seek. As a Jew in Germany and as a foreigner in Switzerland, I have not been promoted beyond a junior position in the past seven years. I shall therefore try to set up in practice in Berlin as a specialist for nervous and mental diseases. Admittedly, there is no shortage of neurologists in Berlin, but I am building my hopes on two factors: first, the practice of psycho-analysis; and, second, my psychiatric training, which Berlin doctors completely lack. You will already have guessed why I am writing to you. I should like to ask for your recommendation, should you ever have the opportunity of suggesting a doctor to undertake psychological treatment in Berlin. I am fully aware of the difficulties I shall encounter and I should therefore also like to ask your permission to turn to you for advice if necessary. I should be most beholden to you for your kind support in both these respects.

I have unfortunately not yet been able to publish my paper on 'Sexual Trauma in Childhood', since the preparations for the move to Berlin and other matters are keeping me very busy. I hope, however, to be able to finish it this month. After that I shall perhaps have something new to communicate to you.

With respectful greetings,

Dr K. Abraham

Berggasse 19,
Vienna IX,
8.10.07

Dear Colleague,

I quickly suppressed the first impulse of regret I felt on reading your letter. No harm can come to a young man like you from being forced into the open *au grand air,* and the fact that things will be more difficult for you as a Jew will have the effect, as it has with all of us, of bringing out the best of which you are capable. That you have my sympathy and best wishes in setting out on your new path is obvious, and if possible I should like to offer you more than that. If my close friendship with Dr W. Fliess[1] still existed, the way would be levelled for you, but now unfortunately that road is completely blocked. During the past year I have repeatedly been in the position of having to tell patients from Germany I was sorry I knew no-one there to whom I could recommend them, but if such cases recur this year I shall know what to do. If my reputation in Germany increases, it will certainly be useful to you, and if I may refer to you as my pupil and follower–you do not seem to me to be a man to be ashamed of that description–I shall be able to back you vigorously. On the other hand, you yourself know the hostility with which I still have to struggle in Germany. I hope you

[1] Dr Wilhelm Fliess, 1858–1929, Berlin physician and biologist, founder of the theory of periodicity. See also pp. 99, 102 and 103.

will make no attempt whatever to win the favour of your new colleagues, who are primarily like those everywhere else and then a whole lot more brutal on top of it, but will instead turn directly to the public. At the time when the campaign against hypnosis was at its most violent in Berlin a very uncongenial hypnotist named Grossmann quickly built himself up a big practice on the basis of that therapy. So one should have the right to expect that with the aid of psycho-analysis you should do even better.

You indicate that there is something else you would like to send me, and I hope you know that I am at your disposal to the best of my ability. Cannot the journey from Zürich to Berlin conveniently take in Vienna?

I shall look out your last letter and answer it as soon as you again have peace to discuss scientific matters.

With my liveliest good wishes,

Yours sincerely,
Dr Freud

Zürich,
13.10.07

Dear Professor Freud,

Your letter gave me great pleasure and was, at the same time, the best encouragement I could receive. Very many thanks for your warm interest which is apparent in every line. If you would like to call me your pupil, I cannot think of any reason why I should object. On the contrary, I see in this a recognition on your part and can assure you that since I first began to read your works three years ago I have looked upon you as my teacher. I shall take up your invitation to come to Vienna as soon as I can. I hope to be settled in Berlin by the beginning of December and, if at all possible, I should then like to come to Vienna for a few days.

I know my Berlin colleagues well. I was a physician at the Berlin Mental Hospital, Dalldorf[1] for more than three years, until I could bear it no longer. I know how difficult it is to stand up against orthodox opinion in Berlin medical circles. In Zürich

---

[1] This name was later changed to Wittenau.

I have breathed freely. No clinic in Germany could have offered me a fraction of what I have found here. That is why I do not find it easy to leave. But I must think of the future, especially as a married man.

I hope before long to tell you personally something of my plans for scientific work. I fear that my letter about dementia has claimed enough of your attention for the time being and I shall not therefore put anything further before you today.

Incidentally, in spite of the impending move, I am quite ready to exchange ideas.

No less than twenty doctors appeared at the second meeting of our 'Freudian Association' here; some came quite a long distance from hospitals in the country. There is therefore no lack of interest. Next time I shall read a paper on the subject of infantile sexual trauma. I cannot help secretly hoping to effect some gradual propaganda in Berlin.

With kindest regards and grateful thanks,

Yours,

Dr K. Abraham

Berggasse 19,
Vienna IX,
21.10.07

My dear Colleague,

As you are in a humour for disputation, I gladly answer your letter of August 9th.

I am in full agreement with what you say about dementia, that is to say, I came to the same conclusions without having had the evidence to confirm them. I see cases of dementia praecox only very rarely, and other dementias practically never. I can repeat in your own words that the mechanism of the dementia in dementia praecox must be different from that of the senile, epileptics, etc. The misleading use of the term by psychiatrists is a matter of no concern. The dementia in dementia praecox must therefore be (*virtute!*) resolvable, must so to speak be a functional dementia. Its model must be the unbelievable momentary dull-wittedness we observe in analysis when the knowledge being sought for has to work against great resistance. The cathexis of the intelligence simply will not go where we wish to direct it. With the refusal to cathect objects that we assume in dementia praecox the phenomenon must of course be on a much vaster scale. Another model–though not a scientifically usable one–would be the very remarkable stupidity that we are accustomed to seeing in the arguments of our opponents, even of otherwise very intelligent ones. That too is only resistance. But you now propose an inquiry into the concept of dementia itself, and in the case of dementia praecox wish to substitute for it another concept, that of inhibition of the personality. Unimportant as such questions of definition are, in this matter I feel I cannot go with you. What good would it do? Who sees in dementia anything other than a symptom that may occur under the most varied conditions (mechanisms)? It means only that the intellectual cathexis is not available for the work required of it, because either it is not there, or it is being used elsewhere, or the activity in question is forbidden it. That is all that the term dementia means. So far as I am concerned, dreams can be called demented, if it gives anyone any pleasure to do so, but such a term of abuse does not touch on the mechanism that makes them so. It is like a son who in an emergency asks his father for money. If the latter fails to produce it, the reason may be that he has none, or that he no longer likes him and does not want to give him any. To the son it is to a certain extent immaterial what the real reason may be, he can starve or go under just as well in either case.

'Personality', like your chief's concept of the ego, is a loosely defined term from surface psychology that does nothing in particular to increase understanding of the real processes, that is to say, *metapsychologically*[1] it says nothing. But it is easy to believe that one is saying something meaningful in using it.

Yours very sincerely,

Dr Freud

[1] This term was introduced by Freud and first used in a letter to Fliess in 1896.

Dear Colleague,

I have read your admirable paper with gratification and, having previously acknowledged the correctness of your basic idea, this time I wish to commend the exemplary clarity with which you describe the different conceptions of the types of infantile traumas, the relationship between pleasure, silence and guilt feelings, and so on. To your description of the abnormality of subsequently neurotic children (quantitative increase of libido, precocity, proliferation of phantasies) I should like to add as an essential feature the existence of a strong tendency to repression, otherwise we should get, not neurotics, but delinquents. The demonstration of this pair of opposites in separate form and intensified degree seems to me to be the latest finding of analysis to date.

I should like to get as much as possible from your visit to Vienna and therefore ask you to include in your programme a whole Sunday on which you will be my guest. On weekdays I have at best a free hour in the evening, and then of course I am not very good company. It would be very kind if you would let me know a few days in advance on which Sunday I can expect you.

Yours with cordial greetings,
Dr Freud

Berlin,
6.12.07

Dear Professor Freud,

Your appreciative words, as well as your kind invitation, have given me much pleasure. I now intend to come to Vienna at the end of next week, so that I can spend Sunday, the 15th with you. I should be very grateful for a short note from you informing me whether this date would be convenient to you and at what time you expect me.

With respectful greetings,   Yours,
Dr K. Abraham

Dear Professor Freud,

When I got back to the hotel on Wednesday night, I found a little box[1] in my briefcase. The contents and the accompanying words gave me much pleasure. This charming gift is the climax of a most enjoyable visit. Let me thank you cordially once again for all your hospitality and for all the instruction and stimulation I received. I very much hope that the followers of your science may increase in numbers. But if they all come and make as much claim on your time and your hospitality as I did, then you might one day prefer your enemies to your friends! The days that I was privileged to spend in your company and that of your family were most beneficial to me. To be surrounded by so much kindliness and so much culture is a rare joy, and I came away with the feeling of being deeply indebted to you. Maybe I shall eventually succeed in paying some of this debt by my theoretical contributions.

I shall soon present to you something on the question of the withdrawal of libido in dementia praecox. I was consulted today about a young patient whom you examined some time ago in Görlitz. He has suffered from a severe hallucinatory psychosis for a long time; the obsessional symptoms persist. This case, in conjunction with two other previous cases, seems to me a very important confirmation of our views.

I shall conclude for today with kindest regards, also from my wife.

Would you also remember me to the Wednesday meeting.[2]

Yours most sincerely,
Karl Abraham

---

[1] Containing two small Egyptian figures from Freud's collection.

[2] These were the early meetings of psycho-analysts in Vienna, which took place in Freud's rooms.

14

Berggasse 19,
Vienna IX,
1.1.08

Dear Colleague,

I wish you the very best of luck this year, which will see you beginning to build yourself up a position in Berlin, and I am delighted to conclude from all the signs that you have the right companion at your side.

Re the Görlitz patient. His parents, good souls that they are, persuaded me to make the journey to the institution only by concealing something from me. There I found out that he also has auditory hallucinations, and thus oversteps the mark of hysteria and obsessional neurosis. I observed one of his attacks myself, and it was uncommonly instructive, as it represented an act of coitus, or rather his rage at an act of coitus observed by him (obviously his parents). His spitting is sperm–ejaculation. The whole thing is very transparent; tragic for his future, though of extreme interest from our point of view, is the organic accompaniment of and basis for his repudiation of sex–the infantility of his genitals. It was because of this last that I was able to hold out so little hope of a cure to his parents; meanwhile they will be very pleased with improvements. There is no doubt that the case must be regarded as dementia praecox; but the relationship of the latter with hysteria and obsessional neurosis was undeniably evident.

I am eager for further news from you, whether the young woman came to you, and many other things.

My family thank you for your greetings and your wife's in particular.

With best wishes for 1908,

Yours very sincerely,
Dr Freud

Berlin,
8.1.08

Dear Professor Freud,

First of all, many thanks for your letter. I am glad that you are keen to hear 'much' from me, for I have a lot to tell you. I am quite pleased with the beginnings of my practice. Oppen-heim[1] has sent me two cases of obsessional neurosis. In one of them, where all other methods had been tried in vain, Oppen-heim has in fact asked me straight out to try your method! This case, a severe form of compulsive brooding, worries me a lot. The patient suffers, first, from compulsive praying; second he has to look at every object carefully and to brood over its origin and, in so doing, he passes over to cosmic problems in the way we know so well. The patient spontaneously produced a very nice screen memory:[2] as a boy of seven, he once chanced to see a woman during a quarrel with neighbours pull up her skirts and show them her bare buttocks. The patient told the maid at home about this, and she said that he was very naughty and threatened a policeman would come and fetch him, etc. There-upon he became very frightened, began to pray and soon could not free himself from the compulsion to pray, to cover scraps of paper with all kinds of prayer formulae so as to omit nothing, etc. I gradually succeeded in recovering a number of analogous memories from repression: how as a boy of four he slept with his former wet nurse and pulled her nightdress up over her but-tocks (here he probably equated breasts and nates). Later on, when his mother took him into bed with her, he did the same thing, whereupon she scolded him for being indecent. The in-cident with the neighbour happened around the same time. Here the patient was only a witness of an exposure. In the other cases he actively brought it about. That is why this scene is re-membered and covers the more embarrassing ones. Repressed memories followed of how he later shared a bed with his eldest brother and handled his genitals, and also of several other inci-dents, such as locking himself in with a girl of his own age and touching her buttocks. In short, up to his eighteenth year there are analogous experiences. The praying has persisted up to the present, apart from temporary remissions, and is easily ex-plained by self-reproaches about his sexual activities. There is

[1] Herman Oppenheim, titular Professor, founder of a well-known clinic in Berlin; as a Jew he was not eligible for a Professorship at a University Clinic. He was related to Abraham by marriage.

[2] Karl Abraham, 'A Screen Memory Concerning a Childhood Event of Apparently Aetiological Significance', *Clinical Papers and Essays on Psycho-Analysis*, London, 1955.

no doubt that the looking at female buttocks is connected with compulsive looking at different objects. I have noticed that the patient always turns objects round when looking at them so that their reverse side is facing him. This is as far as I got in two sessions without too great resistances. But now I am stuck. I am searching in vain for similar events in his later life. The patient has for some years been almost entirely free from his compulsive symptoms. On the other hand, five years ago, and again one year ago, the old symptoms became very acute again. Can one make any general inferences as to the cause of these exacerbations? Furthermore, I am sure I have only uncovered part of the repressed material, but I cannot see how to get deeper. Maybe you know from similar cases how to find a way to these deeper layers. Finally, I should like to know whether one can draw any conclusions from the thematic content of the brooding. My patient worries himself to death about the origins of objects, the material they have been made of, etc. Is there any definite explanation for this? The general interpretation of brooding is well known to me, but can one draw any conclusions from the type of problems the patient sets himself?

The case of G. seems very important to me for our concept of dementia praecox—that is, its differentiation from neurosis. There is a far-reaching similarity with obsessional neurosis. I consider the following points diagnostically decisive, leaving aside those crude psychotic symptoms which appeared during the last few years. Firstly, the patient transferred strongly on to his mother in early childhood, wanted to keep her all to himself, was jealous of his father and brother, idolised his mother and was wildly demonstrative in his tenderness towards her. All this lasted up to the moment when she placed him in boarding school. In a neurotic, one would now have expected a strong emotional reaction to set in; his longing would become unbearable, etc. In G. there followed a sharp turning away of libido. From then on he 'cut' his mother, did not mention her in his letters, treated her with cold formality. Even now he pays no attention to her visits and destroys the presents she brings him. Secondly, there was early negativism, representing sexual rejection, which is characteristic of dementia praecox. The mother says: at the age of two he was already *Der Geist der stets*

17

verneint.[1] Thirdly, there was early automatism, for instance screaming fits. As a very small boy he was once reprimanded for this, and replied: 'it screams on its own, daddy.' The case is similar in all respects and in every detail to the two cases of obsessional symptoms in dementia praecox in early childhood, of which I told you. In one of these cases it is the grandmother who plays this remarkable role. In G.'s case I have the following hypothesis, on which I should like to have your opinion. According to your analysis, the patient was present during the parents' coitus. Might he not have displaced this experience from his, at that time much-loved and jealously guarded, mother on to the great-grandmother whom he barely knew? He also has a compulsion to utter obscene words, especially those referring to the female genitals. I suspect that he wants to separate these painful ideas from his mother and link them with another female person, whom he has only seen once or twice. I could say much more about this case, but would rather like to get on to some other matters today.

I should like to know whether the incomplete interpretation of the first dream in the *Interpretation of Dreams* is intentional– ('Irma's injection'). I find that trimethylamin leads to the most important part, to sexual allusions which become more distinct in the last lines. After all, everything points to the suspicion of syphilitic infection in the patient: the spot in her mouth is the plaque representing the infection, the injection of trimethylamin which has been carelessly given, the dirty syringe (!!). Is not this the organic illness for whose continued existence you cannot be made responsible, because syphilis or a nervous disease originating from it cannot be influenced by psychological treatment?

I have still not finished! I am just reading the *Interpretation of Dreams* once again and find that I have some questions to ask. I will confine myself today to the flying dreams. The infantile source seems clear to me but I believe I have found an actual one as well. I refer to a dream an acquaintance had. The lady dreams that she is floating in the sky as a small pink cloud. Then a large hand comes after her, comes nearer and finally

[1] Quotation from Goethe's *Faust*; Part I (ii) where Mephistopheles says: 'The spirit I, that endlessly denies' (Penguin Classics translation).

grasps her. I find the following interpretation for this aesthetically beautiful dream. Two sisters of the dreamer have been married for some considerable time. A third became engaged shortly before the dream. She alone is left, is no longer young, has been getting very fat for some time and is obviously afraid of being left on the shelf. In the dream she is as light as air instead of fat and a male hand finds her desirable. Might not the flying in the dream also mean: I should like to be lighter? Perhaps you have had some experience with regard to this.

In the *Interpretation of Dreams* you regret that concerning the dreams of normal persons you are completely restricted to self-analysis. If you should like to have some good examples of analysed dreams of healthy people for the new edition, I could tell you several of mine and of my wife's. The Psychiatric Conference in Berlin is on April 24th–25th. Bleuler has now officially announced a paper. I hope that Salzburg[1] will not clash with it. I am sufficiently egoistic to want to be present at both. You will already have heard from Jung of the changes in Jena. They show that things are on the move. I have heard in recent months of several doctors who are intensely interested in your work. Maeder[2] in Zürich has published a short paper on the *Psycho-Pathology of Everyday Life*. Life gradually becomes a real joy.

Finally, my wife and I wish to thank you for your kind and appreciative remarks about her. But how do you arrive at this opinion? With kindest regards from house to house and please remember me to the Wednesday meeting.

With grateful thanks,

Yours,

Karl Abraham

P.S. The young woman you asked about has not yet turned up.

---

[1] The first Psycho-Analytic Congress took place at Salzburg.
[2] Dr Alphonse Maeder, Swiss psycho-analyst.

Berggasse 19,
Vienna IX,
9.1.08

Dear Colleague,

I write hurriedly, formlessly, impersonally, to enable you to make use of my technical information as soon as possible. I am sorry you are afraid of getting stuck. That does not happen to me all the year round. I must get out those technical rules of mine soon.

Your compulsive case is bound to be very instructive. The technique is rather harder than in hysteria, the means of repression rather different, it is a different dialect, but not more.

You found confirmation of the activity at once; a great sense of guilt, and masochistic and homosexual tendencies (beating the buttocks), are to be expected in your patient. The brooding is a direct continuation of the earlier sexual curiosity which is certainly still aware of problems to the present day.

The compulsive periods correspond of course to times of increased libido, that is to say, whenever the patient is in love or his specific condition for loving (jealousy) is touched on in life. His curiosity about the origin of things is equivalent to the question: Where do babies come from? Anthropogenesis. You should associate the cosmic by way of the heavenly bodies with the anatomical. In the case of a young person, a great deal can be done by giving enlightenment as soon as it is asked for.

The chief rules are: (1) Take your time, in the words of the Salzburg motto. Mental changes are never quick, except in revolutions (psychoses). Dissatisfied after only two sessions? At not knowing everything? (2) A problem like: Where shall I probe now? should not exist. The patient shows the way, in that by strictly following the basic rule (saying everything that comes into his head) he displays his mental surface from moment to moment.

Syphilis is *not* the subject-matter of the examples you refer to.

Sexual megalomania is hidden behind it, the three women, Mathilde, Sophie and Anna, are my daughters' three godmothers, and I have them all! There would be one simple therapy for widowhood, of course. All sorts of intimate things, naturally.

The actual meanings of flying dreams are of course very numerous. Yours is a very fine case, I should like it for the second edition. But other things can equally well be made of the material, as I shall show from examples.

I gladly accept your offer of your own dreams. Your optimistic view of the situation cheers me greatly. We must still expect to have hard work in front of us. My opinion of your wife is based on so-called instinctive knowledge of mankind. I shall write to you about other things another time. I am posting this at the main post office.

Yours very sincerely,
Freud

*

Berlin,
15.1.08

Dear Professor Freud,

Very many thanks for your prompt reply which was most welcome. I now feel a little ashamed that I turned to you for help instead of ploughing on by myself for a few more sessions. It can, however, be explained by the circumstances. I particularly wanted a quick analytic triumph in this case which was referred to me by Oppenheim, and I was therefore annoyed when I could make no headway, especially as the first session went so well. It is true, though, that I am dealing with a very difficult case. Forty-seven years old and with strong repressions. The following incident serves to show how good he is at hiding his secrets. In one of the next sessions after I wrote to you, I took up the hypnotic treatment the patient had previously had. He told me that hypnosis had harmed him. On further questioning, it transpired that something painfully embarrassing had occurred to him in the first hypnotic session which he had not talked about and which he had not remembered on waking up. On his way home in the tram the thought returned, and he immediately felt compelled to say certain formulae in an undertone, became excited about this, was afraid of being noticed by other people in the tram, got out and walked the streets for a long time repeating these formulae, before going home. So far

I have not succeeded in getting at this thought in spite of strenuous efforts. The only result was that in the same session the patient ceased to respond to my lead. He obviously transferred on to me the grudge he had then felt against the hypnotist. He was late for the next session and completely negative in his affective reaction. Characteristically superficial talk and jumping from one theme to another were all he produced. At the same time, he showed a false euphoria, described his compulsive obsessive symptoms as not very important and said that he would overcome them by his own will-power. Very clearly: I do not need your treatment! In the following session his superficial talk gradually subsided, and I had little difficulty in confirming my assumption that his investigations into the origin of all things were really founded on sexual curiosity. I hope that I shall now continue to make progress, although the case is unfavourable in several respects. I hope to gain greater confidence with practice. It consoled me today to find in a note at the end of the Case of Hysteria (Dora)[1] that you yourself were no better off at first in a similar situation. I have yet to acquire the technique and am therefore very grateful for the hints that you gave me in your letter.

I am so glad that you can use the flying dreams. Today I am sending you one of my dreams and two of my wife's. Please use them as you wish and alter them as you like. We do not of course want to be mentioned by name. The dreams are written in direct speech, the interpretations are given impersonally, as if the dreams came from a stranger. The first long dream of my wife's does not seem to me to be interpreted as fully as it should be. Possibly a shared complex has prevented it. The Godiva dream seems to be useful as an example since it is so condensed.

My letter was interrupted at this point by my obsessional patient. Today I made good progress and found various sources from which, after a long remission, compulsive praying and brooding have reappeared. I shall report to you later on this. My enclosures today will give you enough reading matter. One more request, though. Would you let me know some time how you explain the change-over from compulsive praying to com-

[1] Sigmund Freud, *Fragment of an Analysis of a Case of Hysteria*, Standard Ed., Vol. VII.

pulsive denial of God's existence (followed again by increased praying)? I have a suspicion concerning my patient in this respect.

With kindest regards and grateful thanks,

Yours,

Karl Abraham

*

Berggasse 19,
Vienna IX,
19.1.08

My dear Colleague,

If I may give you some advice based on age and experience, conduct the psycho-analysis of the Oppenheim patient without a lot of 'sexual displacement'[1] and without any ambition to impress O. by a rapid success. For in the first place it will go better like that, and in the second the case is not suitable to be developed into a show-piece. Such a long-standing obsession in a man nearing the fifties is technically very difficult and therapeutically rather unfavourable. Obsession must be dealt with early, in persons who are still young, and then the treatment is a triumph and a pleasure. But do not allow yourself to be discouraged, and keep the man as long as possible; such patients generally become easily attached, and are often satisfied when the physician is not. So far as details are concerned, I shall always tell you what I can divine from a distance, and thus try to fill in the gaps left by my failure to publish detailed technical rules. The switch from prayer to atheism is characteristic (typical) of these obsessional neuroses. From the beginning they have to express both contradictory voices, generally in immediate juxtaposition. Hence also their vacillation, because of the equal weight of both sides of the motivation. A patient, for instance, sees a stone lying in the roadway and has compulsively to remove it. But it leaves him no peace, and he has to put it back again. The explanation is that the girl he is in love with is going away that day, and will be passing along that street in a cab. The cab might jolt over the stone, so he has to remove it.

[1] Freud here means 'without excessive involvement'.

23

But his next thought is: No, let the cab overturn, with her inside it. So he has to put it back in its place. In his unconscious he simultaneously combines excessive affection for his beloved with hatred of her.

Back to technique. You are right, that was the most taxing of all to acquire, and that is why I want to spare those who follow in my footsteps part of the grind and – part of the cost.

Yours very sincerely,

Freud

*

Berlin,
29.1.08

Dear Professor Freud,

Your last letter has once again given me some very important insight. It always seems to fit in so incredibly well with my patient! I recently had yet another opportunity of confirming the fact that I would be unable to understand most cases of neurosis without knowledge of your theories. I saw on the same day two cases of anxiety neurosis, both men; it was as if they had conspired together to give me a demonstration of the main aetiological factors of their illness. In one case coitus interruptus and, in the other, frustrated sexual excitement were found to be the main factors of the illness. In both cases my questions led me to the root of the matter, and my own confidence quickly gained me theirs. In both, treatment is progressing very satisfactorily. I may perhaps report to you at a later date on the very interesting symptoms of one of them. Just one small detail about the other one. I spoke to his wife privately and reassured her about her husband's impotence. Hardly had I said to her that potency could be restored, when the lady, who had hitherto held her handbag quietly by its chain, began opening and shutting it.

The patient with obsessional symptoms, about whom I asked your advice the other day, improved a little and then lost patience. I had to break off the analysis which had been very uphill work.

I have received an invitation to Salzburg from Jung. As I

hope to be able to take part in the meeting, I have sent in the title of my paper: 'Psycho-Sexual Differences between Hysteria and Dementia Praecox'.[1] Some new aspects of this theme have occurred to me which fit in well with the theory of auto-erotism. I hope you like the subject. Since you have previously acknowledged that in my earlier work I approached the problem from the most important angle, that of sexuality, I thought it important to stress at this, our first Congress, that sexuality forms the nucleus of the problem.

I have just had from Juliusburger[2] a review of his paper, 'Contribution to the Theory of Psycho-Analysis'. If you have not yet received it, I could send it to you.

Just one more question for today. In your first paper on anxiety neurosis, you say that the affect in the problem of anxiety neurosis cannot be tackled by way of psycho-therapy. Do you still hold the same opinion? This interests me in connection with one of my two cases.

My practice is going well; at any rate better than that of most beginners. I often attend Oppenheim's Out-Patients' Department, but unfortunately there is no understanding of psychic mechanisms there. In the last few days, for instance, some particularly strange cases of tic in boys were completely passed over in the crowd. The diagnosis is registered and arsenic, hydrotherapy and gymnastics are prescribed.

I could tell you of another scientific project which is very much occupying me these days, but I would prefer to wait until it has become more tangible in order not to bother you too much. It will be something truly Freudian.

Yours,
Karl Abraham

---

[1] Karl Abraham: *Selected Papers on Psycho-Analysis*, London, 1927.
[2] Dr O. Juliusburger, psychiatrist in Berlin and a follower of psycho-analysis for a number of years.

My dear Colleague,

After the end of a rather stormy period and the approximate recovery of the domestic patients I take advantage of a peaceful Sunday to answer your letter of January 29th.

The news that you are satisfied with the beginnings of your practice came as no surprise to me, but was as gratifying as the confirmation of an expectation always is. I look forward with pleasure to seeing you again at Salzburg. I am of course in full agreement with your proposal to put the libido in the foreground. I have not received the Juliusburger précis, or the paper itself, and I shall be glad if you will get him to send it to me.

As for the reducibility of the anxiety in anxiety neurosis, you will find full information in Stekel's book on anxiety hysteria[1] (expected in April). I myself still regard the old position as theoretically unassailable, but I see that pure cases of anxiety neurosis are great rarities and perhaps once again only abstractions, and that the not actually typical phobias permit and call for psycho-analytic resolution. I 'fancy' there is nearly always an element of hysteria in them. In practice what happens is that actual therapy is first attempted, and resort is then had to psycho-analytic therapy to deal with what turns out to be resistant. Forming one's own opinion experimentally is certainly justified in every case. True, when the actual therapy is omitted or cannot be undertaken, the emptied forms are again and again filled with new material, so that one never comes to an end of them.

The new scientific project you mention makes me very curious. Will it be ready to be disclosed at Salzburg?

The series in which the study of Gradiva appeared (Vol. 2, Riklin,[2] *Fairy-tales*, Vol. 3, Jung, Content of the Psychoses)–in which we should be very glad to publish something by you some time–is now published by F. Deuticke. My little paper[3] from

[1] Dr Wilhelm Stekel, Vienna nerve specialist and psycho-analyst.

[2] Dr Franz Riklin, Swiss psycho-analyst and psychiatrist.

[3] Sigmund Freud, *Hysterical Phantasies and their Relation to Bisexuality*, Standard Ed., Vol. IX.

the new *Zeitschrift für Sexualwissenschaft* must have reached you by now.

Among the small novelties – there are no big ones at present – you will be most interested by *Character and Anal Erotism*,[1] which I gave to Bresler* for his little weekly. It tries to advance into new territory and so will be off-putting enough.

My wife's journey is off for the time being.

Yours very sincerely,

Dr Freud

* Editor of the *Psychiatrische Neurologische Wochenschrift*.

*

Berlin,

23.2.08

Dear Professor Freud,

The project I hinted at has come nearer to fulfilment. It had been my intention to send you the finished manuscript and to ask you to accept the paper for the *Sammlung*,[2] but you forestalled me by asking for a contribution. The title is to be 'Dreams and Myths', or something like that. I want to deal with the symbolism of language and of myths, and especially with the numerous analogies between dreams and myths. I do not know how far Riklin goes in this respect; according to a short paper in the *Psychiatrisch-Neurologischen Wochenschrift*, he appears to confine himself to demonstrating wish-fulfilment. I should like to develop a number of other aspects, such as infantilism, condensation, censorship, repression, identification, etc., and to prove that these concepts are important, not merely for individual psychology but also for folk psychology. As an example I shall take first of all the myth of the Descent of Fire, as interpreted by Adalbert Kuhn,[3] and try to show that the most important aspects of this interpretation resemble those of dream interpretation. Other myths will be briefly dealt with and the various statements concerning them will be elucidated. If all goes well, I hope to finish in about six weeks. I believe the

[1] Sigmund Freud, *Character and Anal Erotism*, Standard Ed., Vol. IX.

[2] *Schriften zur Angewandten Seelenkunde.*

[3] Adalbert Kuhn, 1812–81, Indo-Germanic scholar.

topic is suitable for the *Sammlung*. Perhaps you would indicate to me the minimum or maximum length that would be acceptable. A lot of interesting questions arise in the course of the work, but I am confining myself today to this outline of the basic scheme and shall leave the details till later. I very much hope that you will approve of my project.

Many thanks for your paper on Hysterical Phantasies. Like every single one of your papers, it comes as a relief to me insofar as things which I would not yet have dared to tackle are made clear to me. I am even more curious to see the next. Anal erotism will have the effect of a small bomb. The lack of understanding is so great that this work, too, will not bring anyone into our camp. Anyway the conspiracy to kill us by silence is at an end. However full of misunderstanding Friedlaender's[1] collective review in the *Journal für Psychologie und Neurologie* may be, it goes to show that the ideas are being discussed. I find from conversations with my colleagues that indifference is increasingly giving way to enmity. This, however, does not always mean a poor prognosis. I have brought two of my colleagues to the point where I can argue with them, and one of them even gets me to interpret his dreams. I hope that the establishment of a Freudian Society, like those in Vienna and Zürich, is not too far off.

I have great hopes of Salzburg. I have received a very valuable confirmation for my paper. At a party I made the acquaintance of a poet of great talent but undoubtedly suffering from dementia praecox, and found in him auto-erotism in a sublimated form. He starves himself for days, as Indian fakirs do, in order to bring on visionary states; then he experiences a condition of supreme ecstasy which he describes as an infinite enjoyment of the self. The external world remains far behind him; nothing interests him except his own self; he revels in the feeling of being detached from the world and from human beings. He considers this to be the highest and most dignified form of enjoyment of life, which he obtains completely from himself. The turning away of the libido from the external world could not be more beautifully illustrated.

[1] A. A. Friedlaender, psychiatrist and titular Professor in Berlin.

With kind regards to you and your family, also from my wife, I am, with many thanks,

Yours,
Karl Abraham

*

Berggasse 19,
Vienna IX,
1.3.08

My dear Colleague,

Your project interests me greatly. I await the work with much interest and shall publish it as Vol. V. The fourth in the series deals with a similar theme, the myth of the birth of the hero (Cyrus, Romulus, Moses, etc.), which is given a completely psychological interpretation. The author is our young secretary, Herr Otto Rank,[1] and a little of it will be mine. But I think you ought to tackle the astral significance of myths, which now, since the discoveries of Winckler[2] (Jeremias,[3] Stucken[4]) about the ancient oriental world system can no longer be ignored. We were confronted with the same task. I believe there is also room for a psychological explanation, because in the last resort the ancients only projected their phantasies on to the sky.

The *Anal Erotism*, which I expect daily, will not be very effective in winning people over, in that you are right. But if we can only master the matter. The others will come over in the end, whether in my life-time or not, I have no misgivings about that. At Salzburg we shall strengthen each other; that is the main thing.

I hope your practice is making progress and yielding the raw material from which inspiration springs.

With cordial greetings,

Yours,
Freud

---

[1] Dr Otto Rank, 1886–1939, psycho-analyst in Vienna, later New York.
[2] Hugo Winckler, 1863–1913, orientalist, professor in Berlin.
[3] Alfred Jeremias, 1864–1935, Assyriologist and professor in Leipzig.
[4] Eduard Stucken, 1865–1936, author of *Astralmythen*, 1896–1907.

Dear Professor Freud,

Very many thanks for your letter and for returning the dreams. I had not actually expected you to send them back. You mention having mislaid them and, if this means you wish to keep them, I shall be glad to let you have them again.

As usual, I have some questions to put to you. I have noticed in two psychotic women a symptom that is familiar to me from other cases: they both complain of a tense, puckered feeling around the mouth, as if it were constricted. In one of them this sensation gradually leaves the mouth and moves to cheeks and forehead. It is obvious that this is a displacement upwards. I know that both patients have an aversion—in one of them repressed—to their husbands. One of them hardly tolerates any sexual intercourse and even reacts at times with physical symptoms of revulsion and disgust. Could the constricting sensation round the mouth stand for displaced *vaginismus?* The latter is, after all, only an expression of revulsion. Have you come across a similar phenomenon in other cases?

Now a question about the *Interpretation of Dreams.* On p. 217 you speak of the expression of logical relation, *inter alia* of the 'either-or'.[1] I have seen a very instructive case in this connection. We had a visit from a friend of ours, a lady who is of Jewish descent on the paternal side and who had become engaged to a young Jew. It was to be expected that both families would be strongly opposed to the match. They were secretly engaged for years until they decided to marry. The lady came to stay with us at a time of complicated arguments with both the families. She had a dream on the first night of her visit which I was able to interpret immediately. This interested her greatly, and on the following morning she said to me, 'Last night I had five dreams.' She could relate them all very clearly; she had obviously dreamt them with the wish that I should interpret them. All five dreams were naturally concerned with the marriage, but each dealt with the subject from a different point of view. Thus, the five dreams presented the following five

[1] Standard Ed., Vol. IV, Chapter 6, p. 317.

Karl Abraham about 1904

possibilities. One, they could live together unmarried. Two, they could marry in a register office without having to give up their respective faiths. Three, *he* could be baptised. Four, *she* could become Jewish, but with only a civil marriage both in this case and in the previous one. Five, *she* could change her faith and they could marry according to Jewish rites. In each of the dreams the couple were represented by relatives or friends who fitted the case. Each time the interpretation was easy, and I was able to see the five dreams as an expression of all future possibilities. I find this manner of expressing an 'either-or' very remarkable, and I should like to know whether my interpretation is correct.

Please accept for yourself and your family kindest regards from my wife and myself,

Yours,
Karl Abraham

Berlin,
4.4.08

Dear Professor Freud,

This time you have had to wait a long time for my reply. I deliberately delayed my letter until the manuscript of 'Dreams and Myths' was finished. It was finally sent off today by registered post and should reach you in a few days. The work on myths gave me great pleasure, especially since it revived my former philological interests. The material certainly merits much fuller treatment and I should some time later like to undertake work on a specific cycle of myths. First of all, though, I wait to hear your opinion. My expositions are, of course, based entirely on yours and I very much hope that you will agree with the conclusions I drew about myths from the *Interpretation of Dreams*. I am naturally interested to know whether the paper will appear soon. Or have I to wait until Jung and Rank are published? Rank's subject is certainly very fruitful. If you haven't come across it yet, I should like especially to draw your attention to the Samson legend and to Steinthal's[1]

[1] Heyman Steinthal, 1823–1899, philologist and philosopher, Professor at Berlin University.

paper on it ('Die Sage von Simson', *Zeitschrift für Völker-psychologie und Sprachwissenschaft*, Bd. 2, 1862). Riklin's paper reached me just as I had finished mine. It is a pity that the style is so irritating; it does not do justice to the content.

Now I must thank you for the two reprints. A few days before I received the 'Sexualmoral',[1] I heard a paper on 'Medizin und Ueberkultur' by our new clinician, His,[2] which is the complete opposite of your paper. Not one word on sexuality in the whole of it! Yet it was a most learned paper and drew on all sorts of material not directly connected with medicine. *Summa summarum*, only a spate of words as a cover for sexual repression. Soon after that I read *your* paper. 'Wie anders wirkt dies Zeichen auf mich ein!'[3]

I had already found the paper on Anal-Erotism in the *Journal* a few days before your parcel arrived. It will arouse a lot of head-shaking.[4] The description fits one of my relatives exactly–a peculiar bachelor. Furthermore, it fits a case of hysteria analysed by Jung with which you will be acquainted from his description. The loving interest in their defaecation displayed by men who have early exhausted their sexuality certainly belongs in this context, as a way of returning to anal erotism. Would not the following also belong here? Before puberty, lavatory humour plays the same role as sexual humour does later. There are people who never rid themselves of the first kind, whose greatest pleasure is to make jokes referring to defaecation in the most unsuitable surroundings. Aren't such people anal erotists? It seems to me as if old men as well, after their potency disappears, return to lavatory humour.

I am analysing a nice case at the moment–compulsive ideas of having committed sins of omission, obsessional washing, swear words compulsively appearing in prayer, etc. I am very well satisfied with the success of the first sessions. Now a question as usual. Do you know a psychological cause for the so-called

---

[1] Sigmund Freud, *Civilized Sexual Morality and Modern Nervous Illness*, Standard Ed., Vol. IX.

[2] Professor Wilhelm His, 1863–1934, holder of a Chair of Medicine at the University Clinic in Berlin (Charité).

[3] Quotation from Goethe's *Faust*: Part I (i), where Faust says: 'How differently this sign strikes me.'

[4] A jocular quotation from Wilhelm Busch's *Jobsiade*.

'Ictus Laryngis' (Charcot)?[1] I saw a case in Oppenheim's Out-Patients' Department, in an apparently healthy man, attacks of coughing over the last twenty years with dyspnoea and increased pulse rate. There must be something psychological behind it.

There was a lively Freudian discussion the other day at a party at Professor Liepmann's,[2] where only doctors and their wives were present. In the course of the battle it so happened that two groups formed in two different rooms. While I defended the wish-fulfilment theory of dementia praecox in one room, my wife in the other room had to defend the theory of repression. Otherwise there is little opportunity for propaganda. I am planning before very long to arrange a course for doctors in order to discuss the theory of neuroses and dreams. What do you think about this?

You write in your last letter that you are now reassured about my paper. Did it originally not appear on the programme? I hope that all your family are well again, and add my kindest regards to all of you.

Yours, with grateful thanks,
Karl Abraham

Bergasse 19,
Vienna IX,
3.5.08

My very dear Colleague,

I am very glad that you regard Salzburg as a gratifying event. I am in no position to judge, as I am in the thick of it, but I too am inclined to regard this first gathering as a promising experiment.

I can answer your question straight away: the congress is not to be publicly mentioned at all; and thus not under the title of your forthcoming publication.

In connection with the latter, I wish to make you a request

---

[1] Jean Martin Charcot, 1825–1893, Professor of Psychiatry, University of Paris (Saltpétrière).

[2] Professor Hugo Karl Liepmann, 1863–1925, neurologist and brain anatomist at Berlin University (Charité).

on the fulfilment of which all sorts of things may depend. I recollect that your paper led to a slight conflict between you and Jung, or at any rate that is what I concluded from something that you said to me afterwards. Now, I believe rivalry between the two of you to be inevitable and also, within certain limits, to be innocuous; in dealing with the question at issue I did not hesitate to say that you were in the right and to attribute Jung's sensitiveness to his vacillation. But I should be most unwilling to see serious dissension arising between you two. There are still so few of us that disagreements, based perhaps on personal 'complexes', ought to be excluded among us. Another thing that should weigh with us is that Jung should find his way back to the views that he has now abandoned and you have stood by so consistently. I believe that there are prospects of this; also Jung says in a letter to me that Bleuler is very much influenced and is almost inclined again to drop the view that dementia praecox is organic in nature.

Thus you will actually be doing me a great personal favour if you inform him in advance of what you are going to write and ask him to discuss with you the objection that he then made, which you wish to take into account. Such an act of courtesy would certainly nip dissension in the bud, would give me great pleasure, and would show me that we are all capable of drawing practical benefit for ourselves from the practice of psycho-analysis. Do not make too heavy going of the small self-sacrifice demanded.

Please be tolerant and do not forget that it is really easier for you than it is for Jung to follow my ideas, for in the first place you are completely independent, and then you are closer to my intellectual constitution because of racial kinship, while he as a Christian and a pastor's son finds his way to me only against great inner resistances. His association with us is the more valuable for that. I nearly said that it was only by his appearance on the scene that psycho-analysis escaped the danger of becoming a Jewish national affair.

I hope you will do as I ask and send you my cordial greetings.

Yours,
Freud

My dear Colleague,

Not yet having received an answer to my request, I write to you again to reinforce it. You know how gladly I put what I have at the disposal of you and others, but nothing would be more painful to me than sensitivity about priorities arising among my friends and colleagues. That will be avoided if everyone plays his part. I hope that both for my sake and that of the cause you will be persuaded.

With cordial greetings,

Yours,
Freud

Berlin,
11.5.08

Dear Professor Freud,

I was just about to write to you when your letter of May 9th reached me. In the interests of the work I did not reply to you sooner. When I read your first letter, I was not entirely in agreement with you and therefore let it rest for a few days. By then I was able to read it *sine ira et studio* and I convinced myself of the validity of your arguments. After that I delayed no longer in writing to Zürich, but did not send the letter off immediately. I wanted to make sure after some days had elapsed that there was not something hidden somewhere that might turn the *rapprochement* into an attack. I know it is difficult for me to avoid polemics altogether, and my subsequent reading of the letter proved me right. Yesterday I re-wrote the letter in its final form. I hope it will serve the cause. I did not want to write to you, dear Professor, until I had completed the letter to Jung. You will surely forgive my silence. Now that I look upon this matter calmly, I have to thank you for your intervention and at the same time for the confidence that you placed in me. You have no need to fear that the matter will leave a feeling of discord behind as far as I am concerned. I hope that the way

I acted will have the desired effect and I shall certainly keep you informed of further developments.

As a matter of fact I became involved quite innocently in this conflict. In December I asked you whether my subject might not bring me into collision with Jung, as you had communicated your ideas to him as well. You dispelled my doubts at the time. My manuscript for Salzburg contained a remark which would certainly have satisfied Bleuler and Jung; on a sudden impulse I omitted to read it out. I deceived myself momentarily by a cover-motive, that of saving time, while the true reason lay in my animosity against Bleuler and Jung. This was caused by their latest and far too conciliatory publications, by Bleuler's Berlin paper, which made no reference to you, and by other slight incidents. The fact that I omitted to name Bleuler and Jung obviously means: 'They turn aside from the theory of sexuality, therefore I shall not cite them in connection with it.' It naturally did not come into conscious thought at that moment that this omission might have serious consequences.

According to your wish, the publication of my paper will not contain any mention of the Congress.

I hope that everything is now put right as you want it. As far as I am concerned, the harmony will not be disturbed. I should like to ask you most sincerely to criticise me frankly in future. I shall always try to follow your views. As with so many theoretical questions where at first I could not follow you but later became convinced of your ideas, I hope I shall also succeed here. I freely admit that I find it easier to go along with you rather than with Jung. I, too, have always felt this intellectual kinship. After all, our Talmudic way of thinking cannot disappear just like that. Some days ago a small paragraph in *Jokes*[1] strangely attracted me. When I looked at it more closely, I found that, in the technique of apposition and in its whole structure, it was completely Talmudic. In Zürich, by the way, I was always pleased that Bleuler and Jung so successfully overcame the resistances based on their different personality structure. This makes the change in them all the more painful.

[1] Sigmund Freud, *Jokes and their Relation to the Unconscious*, Standard Ed., Vol. VIII.

The suggested alterations in 'Dreams and Myths' are already partly completed and the others will be done in the course of the week. I called on Dr Hirschfeld[1] and gained an impression which is far better than his reputation. Among other things he asked me to collaborate with him in the revision of a questionnaire which he says he showed you. Some days after my visit to him, he sent me a homosexual patient for psychoanalysis.

With kind regards,

Yours,
Karl Abraham

Berggasse 19,
Vienna IX,
15.5.08

My dear Colleague,

I thank you, and shall not forget that you have allowed me to influence you in this matter. I hope that you too will be satisfied.

I await your paper in its revised form and shall duly submit it to the publisher.

Our *Jahrbuch* is assured favourable conditions, and is to appear in two parts; the decision between Deuticke and Marhold has still to be made. The first issue will contain a survey of published psycho-analytical works. Jung will deal with the Zürich section, Maeder with the French, Jones[2] with the British, and the purely negative and hostile literature will, I think, be surveyed separately. For the Vienna publications, mine included, and the contributions from Germany Jung has suggested you, so that I can now inquire directly of you whether you will accept. If undertaking my publications is too much of a burden to impose on you, I can shift the load to Rank,

---

[1] Dr Magnus Hirschfeld, 1868–1935, sexologist.

[2] Dr Ernest Jones, 1879–1958, founder of the British Psycho-Analytical Society and author of Freud's biography (*Sigmund Freud: Life and Work*, 3 vols., Hogarth Press, London, 1953, Basic Books, New York, 1953).

who is very well attuned to me, though his matriculation is just ahead. The reviews will of course be paid for, 50 marks a signature. I shall be contributing a case history in each half-yearly issue.

With cordial greetings and thanks,

Yours,
Freud

Dear Professor Freud,

By the time you receive this letter your wife will already have given you our regards. My wife and I were so pleased with her visit and regretted that there could only be this one short meeting.

My reaction to the suggestion in your last letter can only be one of glad acceptance. I shall be able to say whether or not I can manage on my own the work allotted to me when I know more precisely what it involves and also how much time I shall be allowed for it. I assume that I would first have to give a collective review of all your papers. As far as I know, I have them all. On the other hand, I do not have exact knowledge of all the other papers contributed from Vienna. Could I have a list? I assume that the Psycho-Analytic Society is in possession of all the papers. Perhaps Rank would be kind enough to draw up such a list for me. Could I also borrow from the Society's library those papers that I cannot obtain here? The German literature contains very few positive contributions and these I can find myself.

First of all, then, I should like to see how much work is involved and how much time I may take over it. Then I can easily judge whether I can manage by myself or whether I would have to ask Rank for his help. I am looking forward to this task. I cannot give you any news about the Jung affair as I am still waiting for a reply.

The elaboration of the Soma myth is taking up more time than I had expected as Kuhn only gives an incomplete inter-pretation on this point. I have therefore to think it out for

myself and, consequently, must be doubly careful. The inter-
pretative work is most interesting though and yields the same
layers and the same wish-fulfilments as in the Prometheus
myth. I am most grateful to you for your advice to include this
myth.

In connection with *Jokes*, I have arrived at some further
understanding of the psychology of mental illnesses, especially
the behaviour of the so-called persistent paranoid querulant.[1]
I shall tell you about this on some future occasion. I have
promised Dr Hirschfeld a contribution to his Journal ('On the
Sublimation of the Sexual Instinct'). There is enough work to
last me for some time.

My practice is doing fairly well. The analysis of the homosexual is making quite good progress and shows noticeable
results. It is still doubtful whether I shall succeed in making
him potent in his marriage. He is almost forty years old and
has been married for eight years.

With kind regards from house to house,

Yours,
Karl Abraham

Berggasse 19,
Vienna IX,
7.6.08

Dear Colleague,

On this rainy Whitsun day I have read your revised paper
for the *Schriften zur Angewandten Seelenkunde*, and as your first
reader I shall not withhold from you my thanks and full appreciation, particularly as I do not know whether you will
get these from other quarters. It is all so clear, well based and
constructed, full of conviction and free of misunderstanding
and misunderstandability. I like the piece very much. You are
right, it is not an essay but a treatise, but that after all is what
you chose to make it, and perhaps the persuasiveness of the
whole has only gained thereby.

[1] In German the word *Querulant* describes a patient with predominantly
paranoid ideas and litigious tendencies, now covered by the term *paranoid
querulant.*

I was very much struck by the fact that you found such far-reaching agreement with our theories and statements among the great ethnopsychologists.

May I make one or two small suggestions to you? You might make use of one more conclusive detail in connection with Moses's staff when he appears before Pharaoh. The transformation from stiff wood to flexible snake is nothing but an unconcealed (reversed) representation of erection, which is in a way the most striking phenomenon encountered by man. Also you might care to mention what I say about myth in the paper 'Creative Writers and Day-Dreaming',[1] which fits in very well with what you say. The vitalising effect of semen is to my knowledge directly expressed in Indian erotic literature. There is one reference in Fuchs,[2] *Das erotische Element in der Karikatur*, pp. 29–30. Further, the legend of the Soma potion contains the highly important presentiment that all our intoxicating liquors and stimulating alkaloids are merely a substitute for the unique, still unattained toxin of the libido that rouses the ecstasy of love.

Herr Rank is getting together the literature for you. I shall send off your work to be printed before the beginning of the holidays; I must allow the publisher a few weeks' peace.

Personally (that word 'peace' was the cue) I am counting the weeks till I get some myself. We have booked at Berchtesgaden, where part of the family will be going at the end of June and I shall join them on July 13th. Literary work there is nothing but a pleasure in comparison with the hard professional grind.

Hoping that 'cleaning up neurotics' will soon be as disagreeable to you as it has become to me, I send you my cordial greetings and remain

Yours very sincerely,
Freud

---

[1] Standard Ed., Vol. IX.
[2] Eduard Fuchs, author of *Geschichte der erotischen Kunst*, 1908.

Dear Professor Freud,

Your appreciative words gave me great pleasure. I only hope its propaganda value will bear out your prognosis. I shall put your suggested additions into the proofs. If I write another contribution for this collection, I may perhaps succeed in adopting a style more to your taste. I am, incidentally, becoming more and more convinced that a paper can be useful to our cause only if the author unreservedly identifies himself with our findings. I believe that the reviews in the *Jahrbuch* should also allow the reviewer's opinion to emerge clearly. I have started on this work. The *Three Contributions* are finished and I am now engaged on *The Psychopathology of Everyday Life*.

Yesterday I received an invitation from Moll[1] to collaborate in a new journal. He tells me that you have agreed to contribute. I have done likewise and shall have a further discussion with Moll on this matter.

I intend to hold a course for doctors in the autumn and the reviews serve as a kind of preparation for this. Or do you believe that such a course is too ambitious a venture *in partibus infidelium?*

You will certainly be waiting to hear something about the outcome of the affair with Jung. To my very great regret, I cannot tell you anything since, after more than a month, I still have not had a reply.

The subject of the Soma potion is one that I should like to take up again at some later date in order to investigate the psychology of intoxication; but some other subjects attract me first.

With kind regards and grateful thanks, I am,

Yours,
Karl Abraham

[1] Dr Albert Moll, Berlin psychiatrist specialising in criminology.

Berlin,
9.7.08

Dear Professor Freud,

Your card pleased me very much. I take it that I may expect *Myths* to be published in the autumn. Gaupp[1] will publish the Salzburg paper on July 15th. A little while ago I gave Hirschfeld a short paper on the 'Psychological Relationship between Alcoholism and Sexuality'.[2] A further paper is being prepared and will deal with the Psychology of Marriage between Relatives.[3] This has been regarded for many years as a cause of nervous illness. I want to prove the reverse: namely, that neurotically disposed persons have a preference for marrying blood relations because they cannot detach their libido from its earliest object—father or mother—and can most easily find an object with similar qualities within their own families. I have collected some very interesting material but will not trouble you with it just now before the holidays.

The practice, though numerically small, is at least therapeutically satisfying. I have achieved very good results in a case of severe anxiety hysteria. The patient, an extremely intelligent doctor of philosophy, showed excellent insight and is, moreover, interested in our theories. The wife, who also had anxiety symptoms, has got rid of them. This couple is at the same time an excellent example of my theory about intermarriage between relatives.

I do not want to say anything about Zürich today. You will draw the right conclusions about it for yourself. Oppenheim, on the other hand, shows signs of coming round. He asked me recently, in the Outpatients' Department *coram publico* to investigate a boy psycho-analytically! His earlier resistance seems to be changing into tolerance. Perhaps we shall yet live to see

[1] Dr Robert Gaupp, Professor of Neurology and Psychiatry in Tübingen. Editor of *Zentralblatt fuer Nervenheikunde und Psychiatrie.*

[2] Karl Abraham, 'The Psychological Relations between Sexuality and Alcoholism', *Selected Papers on Psycho-Analysis*, London, 1927.

[3] Karl Abraham, 'The Significance of Intermarriage between Close Relatives in the Psychology of the Neuroses', *Clinical Papers and Essays on Psycho-Analysis*, London, 1955.

'signs and wonders'.[1] But I do not rush anything and can see that reticence gets me further than propaganda.

I wish you a very pleasant holiday. I myself am staying in Berlin and shall write the reviews for the *Jahrbuch*.

With kind regards,

Yours,
Karl Abraham

Berggasse 19,
Vienna IX,
11.7.08

Dear Colleague,

Please do not make too heavy going of the survey for the *Jahrbuch*. It should be as brief as possible. Have I drawn your attention to Warda's papers?[2] One is in the *Archiv für Psychiatrie*. It would be best for you to ask him for them.

I have little news from Zürich, that is to say, from Jung, and have heard nothing concerning you. I greatly deplore your quarrel. If I have an opportunity of talking to Jung in the autumn, I shall take thorough soundings. I am afraid that, with the exception of what you did recently for my sake, there is a lack of desire for a satisfactory harmony on both sides. I must reconcile you for the sake of the cause; you are both too valuable to me.

Your idea about marriage between close relatives is certainly correct and worth describing. It has already been mentioned in our group, but you need of course take no notice of that. A girl cousin very often takes the place of a sister. I believe the prognosis in such marriages to be generally very favourable. Your reserve in relation to Oppenheim is very appropriate. Let us do as we do in relation to associations in analysis; not run after anyone who refuses himself.

On the 15th I am leaving for Dietfeldhof, Berchtesgaden;

---

[1] Quotation from the Bible: Exodus VII, 3.
[2] Dr W. Warda, psychiatrist, later a member of the Berlin Psycho-Analytical Society.

I feel in great need of the holiday. At your age things were different with me too.

With cordial greetings,

Yours,
Freud

P.S. I have just read the flood myths and traced them back.

Dear Professor Freud,

I really ought to leave you in peace just now at the beginning of your holiday, but I must reply to some points in your letter. My brief reference to Zürich in my last letter did not refer to my personal disagreement with Jung, but to the general attitude at present adopted in Zürich. To deal with the former first, I have not the slightest wish for an estrangement from Zürich. My letter to Jung was as accommodating as possible (I could send you a copy). His failure to reply is rather inconsiderate. But if the good relationship can be re-established now or later, either through your mediation or in some other way, I shall certainly not object. On the contrary, I should like to keep in touch with the Burghölzli. Even though a number of unpleasant things happened before I left, I brought so many agreeable memories away with me that I should certainly not wish to disturb the peace.

The matter goes deeper. Jung's behaviour to me is, after all, only a symptom. I believe all the gentlemen from Vienna had the impression at Salzburg that not much more could be expected from Zürich. I had news from a reliable source about the latest developments, and it was under the impact of this that I wrote to you last time. I do not wish to worry you with details. But the sudden fading-out of the Freudian evenings, so well attended until April, is striking. Jung seems to be reverting to his former spiritualistic inclinations. But please keep this between ourselves. However, if Jung gives up for this reason and for the sake of his career, then we can no longer count on the Burghölzli. Bleuler alone, however efficient he may otherwise be, will do nothing. He is a very complex personality, a mass of reaction formations. His external simplicity and often exaggerated modesty cover strong grandiose tendencies. Salzburg was no help to the latter. The others are of little account. Riklin is Jung's creature. Only Maeder can be relied on; he is both intelligent and independent. Eitingon[1] is hardly suitable for active collaboration, although he shows the greatest understanding. My remark referred to these matters and not to my personal affairs.

I will make the reviews as short as possible, but they must not be too short. There is no sense in selecting only a few findings from your papers. The most important lines of thought which lead to the conclusions and to our present point of view must be made clear. In any case, a short review is no less work than a long one. The review of *Jokes*, which I am just writing, will be approximately one and a half pages long. Rank has sent me everything I wanted. I shall take Warda's papers into consideration.

I have received the first proofs from Deuticke. May I ask you to reply to my recent question? I should like to know whether you agree with my plan of organising a course for doctors.

I hope you will have very pleasant days at Berchtesgaden, and my wife and I send best regards to you and your family.

Yours,
Karl Abraham

Berchtesgaden,
20.7.08

Dear Colleague,

I like your work better with each signature. Please permit me to point out that the secondary elaboration (p. 46) is not quite correctly described, but this can easily be corrected in accordance with the *Interpretation of Dreams*. It is restricted too much to the last part, the distortion that takes place in the telling, while the essential point is the false distribution of emphasis in the whole dream content.

[1] Dr Max Eitingon, 1881–1943, psycho-analyst in Berlin, later in Jerusalem.

I shall write to you about Burghölzli more fully next time; I am thinking of going to Zürich at the end of September; I think a great deal more favourably about Jung, but not about Bleuler. On the whole it is easier for us Jews, as we lack the mystical element. Forgive me for not answering your question about the course for physicians. I should be very glad of it, but make sure of Oppenheim's feelings in the matter; I should not like to see you coming to any harm.

With cordial greetings,

Freud

Berchtesgaden,
23.7.08

Dear Colleague,

Thank you very much for your paper on dementia praecox and hysteria,[1] which arrived today. I value so highly the resolute tone and clarity of your writings that I must ask you not to think that I overlook their elegance. May I say that it is consanguineous Jewish traits that attract me to you? We understand each other.

You also know what it is that mars my pleasure in your paper. It makes manifest your latent quarrel with Jung. You certainly had every justification for writing in that way, but it would have shown greater delicacy of feeling not to have made use of it. At the time I gave the same idea to each of you, and had no intention other than that each should take it up and work on it independently. By adopting it you are to an extent forcing him into opposition.

When I go to Zürich as arranged at the end of September I shall try to make good what can be made good. Please do not misunderstand me; I have nothing to reproach you with; I nurse a suspicion that the suppressed anti-Semitism of the Swiss that spares me is deflected in reinforced form upon you. But I think that we as Jews, if we wish to join in, must develop a bit of masochism, be ready to suffer some wrong. Otherwise there is no hitting it off. Rest assured that, if my name were Oberhuber, in spite of everything my innovations would have met with far less resistance.

[1] See footnote, p. 25.

46

I prefer not to share your unfavourable prognosis in regard to the co-operation of Burghölzli. The dropping of the evening discussions struck me too; but I do not know whether it is final. Bleuler I surrender to you; at Salzburg he struck me as very odd, the situation cannot have been comfortable for him, and you seem to me to have summed him up as I did. But Jung is a different matter, there is a personal liking between us on which I count, and he writes to me about his chief—just as you did, and in fact in the same words. Moreover, he can hardly back out, he could not repudiate his past even if he wanted to, and the *Jahrbuch*, of which he is the editor, is a tie not to be broken. I hope that he has no intention of breaking the tie with me, and that you, because of a competitiveness that has not been overcome, do not see the situation correctly.

I am busily writing the case history of the boy of five[1] which I hope will interest you greatly. Meanwhile I am correcting the second edition of the *Interpretation of Dreams* and reading the galleys of *Dreams and Myths*. I am more and more convinced that you are right and that we share the honour of explaining mythology. Good luck!

Why cannot I harness Jung and you together, your precision and his *élan*?

With cordial greetings,   Yours,
                                                                        Freud

Berlin,
31.7.08

Dear Professor,

I am very sorry that not only my work but also my personal affairs are taking up your time and attention. But since the subject of Zürich has been broached, I must add something further to it. You think that I should have used more tact in formulating my paper. I myself believe that some things look more aggressive in print than they sound when spoken. I did not have any intention of hurting but, while writing it, my feelings towards Zürich were far from friendly. Shortly before

---

[1] Sigmund Freud, *Analysis of a Phobia in a Five-year-old Boy*, Standard Ed., Vol. X.

going to Salzburg, I received Jung's Amsterdam paper and Bleuler's and Jung's reply to E. Meier,[1] and heard Bleuler's paper at the Congress here. These three efforts did, I admit, strike me unpleasantly. I then came to understand Jung's defeat in Amsterdam. In his paper Bleuler avoided anything relating to psycho-analysis (and how much he could have said!) and, as to their joint publication, I found that really incredible. The sub-division into primary and secondary symptoms as the only result of years of analysis of mental patients! And hair-splitting about toxins, etc. Shouldn't they have stated that the problem was presently to be approached on the basis of the theory of sexuality? Not a word about Freud or the theory of sexuality. But Meier! (He has a Chair at Königsberg, and is known to both authors as a complete nonentity). On the journey to Salzburg, Eitingon told me of this change and also that Jung's paper on dementia praecox would contain nothing Freudian. I had long before written to Jung to let him know how I intended to tackle my subject and that I had added some new points of view to those formerly discussed. One would have thought from his paper that he had never heard of such things as, for instance, auto-erotism. We talked at cross purposes. You yourself have put the reason for Jung's subsequent ill-humour in the best possible way. There was universal surprise at the behaviour of the Zürich contingent. Everyone saw it as a secession. Can one then say that I anticipated Jung in using an idea which we both got from you? In my opinion, the matter is as follows: I used the idea, and Jung deliberately suppressed it. I cannot help seeing it that way. Later events confirm it. I received the following comment some weeks ago from someone who knows nothing of my conflict with Jung: 'At the Burghölzli, Freud seems to be an idea that has been superseded'. Why do people who are not involved arrive at this viewpoint? And how could all the tact in the world on my part have helped? I have had no reply to my letter in which I expressly referred to your wish. In my opinion, Jung should not have ignored this letter, if only for your sake.

I have been hesitating all this week whether or not to write all this to you. I have tried to make your opinion my own. I am

[1] E. Meier, Professor at Königsberg University.

48

afraid I cannot be optimistic in this matter. Nobody could have been more pleased than I was about Jung's initial behaviour. That is why the change gives me so much pain. Your last letter, dear Professor, is so kind and appreciative that it makes it difficult for me to write this one. But it is just those personal sympathies you mention that force me to do it. If you are successful in Zürich in September, I shall be very pleased. If Jung wishes, he can be of extraordinary service to our cause and I fully understand your wish to keep him. It would also be unpleasant if our opponents were able to say that the only hospital supporting us had now left us. But if this conclusion is to be avoided, it is necessary for them to produce something positive soon.

The prognosis for Berlin is not too bad. Favourable signs are increasing.

I should be glad to talk to you sometime about traumatic neurosis. For the present, however, we seem to be restricted to correspondence. As soon as I find the time, I shall put the main points together. A great number of other subjects are crowding in on me. The proofs of Myths are finished, and therefore nothing will prevent publication in September. My short paper will appear in Hirschfeld's journal[1] in a fortnight.

With kind regards,

> Yours,
> Karl Abraham

*

Berlin,
21.8.08

Dear Professor,

Things are moving! On the 27th the Berlin Psycho-Analytic Society will meet for the first time. For the time being, the following physicians will take part: Hirschfeld, Ivan Bloch,[2] Juliusburger and Koerber[3] (Chairman of the *Monistenbund*).[4]

[1] See footnote 1, p. 37.
[2] Dr Ivan Bloch, 1872–1922, sexologist in Berlin.
[3] Dr Heinrich Koerber remained a member of the Society.
[4] The *Monistenbund* was a cultural and philosophical movement founded by Professor Ernst Haeckel, 1834–1919, a follower of Darwin.

I believe there will soon be others. Dr Juliusburger in particular is very keen; he is a senior physician in a private institution and is introducing psycho-analysis in spite of his chief's opposition.

My paper on Sexuality and Alcoholism has just appeared but I have not got the reprints yet. Meanwhile, the psycho-analysis of a colleague has taught me many interesting things about the sexual basis in the use of sleeping draughts. In this patient the narcotic serves as the substitute for masturbation which had been given up with difficulty. The analogy holds good down to the smallest detail. The weaning from sleeping pills meets with great resistances. Today he brought a neat confirmation of my views: after two nights without drugs he suddenly felt a return of the infantile urge to suck!

The practice is very quiet now during the summer but gives me much satisfaction, both scientifically and therapeutically. I have had very satisfactory results with a married couple and may tell you something about this some time.

With kind regards to you and your family,

Yours,
Karl Abraham

*

Dietfeldhof,
24.8.08

Dear Colleague,

I congratulate you on this beginning. Berlin is difficult but important soil, and your efforts to make it cultivable for our purposes are highly appreciated. Of the members probably only Juliusburger will be a pure gain, because the others have other guiding interests, but even if they are only touched by components it will still be valuable.

Your paper on alcoholism will certainly have given you confirmation of the Soma interpretation. Your observation on the substitution series: auto-erotic satisfaction in phantasy before going to sleep–sleeplessness–sleeping drugs is of course conclusive.

Apart from working on the second edition of the *Interpretation of Dreams*, I have written the article for the *Jahrbuch*, a paper on infantile sexuality that is to appear in the *Sexual Problems*, and a short article, '*Some General Remarks on Hysterical Attacks*'[1] for Moll's new *Zentralblatt*. I shall let you know whether I shall be going to England on September 1st, because if I do so my movements will be uncertain until then, and I shall not be reachable until I go to Zürich.

With cordial greetings and best wishes for the thriving of your undertaking,

Yours most sincerely,
Freud

Berggasse 19,
Vienna IX,
29.9.08

Dear Colleague,

Having arrived here early today from Lake Garda, I am writing to you at once in spite of the fatigue of the journey, as I found an inquiry from you waiting for me and owe you some amends.

First about business matters. I could not write to you from Zürich; I was never alone until late at night; we spent up to eight hours a day walking and talking. So let me recapitulate. Part I of the *Jahrbuch*, apart from my paper, Binswanger's[2] analysis, and your review, is to include only a number of short reviews. Opponents' works will be dealt with separately and briefly. You can find out directly whatever you wish. I think it unnecessary for you to send your review to me, unless you especially wish to do so because of some point or other. That can also be done at the proof stage.

Now to the chief thing. I am glad to say that you were only partly right, that is to say, only about Bleuler. As for Jung, he has overcome his vacillation, adheres unreservedly to the cause, and also will continue to work energetically on the dementia praecox question on our lines. That is highly gratifying to me, and I hope it will be pleasing to you also. But nothing will come of Bleuler, his defection is imminent, and his relations with Jung

[1] Standard Ed., Vol. **IX**.
[2] Dr Ludwig Binswanger, psychiatrist at Kreuzlingen.

51

are strained to breaking-point. Jung is giving up his position as physician, but remains head of the laboratory and will work completely independently of Bleuler.

It was a great satisfaction to me that Jung did not make it difficult for me to prepare the ground for the reconciliation with you that I wish to bring about. His high regard for your scientific work was of great assistance. He spoke only in hints, but I was able to conclude that he thinks you have had ideas about him put into your head by others that do not correspond to reality, and regrets it. I do not want to stand between you, but I hope that in direct communication with each other you will soon find it possible to resume the friendly and harmonious tone which alone befits colleagues who respect each other. So I left Burghölzli the richer for this valuable expectation.

Now for my transgression against you. I actually was in Berlin for twenty-four hours without having called on you. I could not, because I crossed from England with my aged brother[1] to see my sister who lives in Berlin,[2] and between the two camps of fond relatives I saw as little of Berlin as I did of you.

For certain reasons I gladly confess to you that Jung found the way the day passed incredible–in retrospect I do not know how I spent it myself. I remember only that I could not leave the hotel before eleven a.m., and that at eleven p.m. my train left, so that the twenty-four hours were reduced to twelve. But I do know that because of my brother and sister I shall soon be going to Berlin again, and I hope that until then you will forgive me the appearance of unfriendliness.

So today there can be only cordial greetings from

Yours most sincerely,
Freud

Berlin,
4.10.08

Dear Professor,

I am very glad to hear that your holidays finished up so well in Zürich. I am grateful for the trouble you have taken on my

[1] Freud's half-brother Emmanuel Freud, 1834–1915.
[2] Marie (Mitzi), married to Moritz Freud.

behalf. I have had two cards from Jung which clearly show your influence and I am very pleased indeed that the unpleasant situation has been brought to an end. You may rest assured that in my correspondence with Jung I shall not refer in any way to what is past. Admittedly, I see some things at the Burghölzli differently from you. In three years of daily contact one gains insight into a great deal. But I welcome it as a valuable result of your Zürich visit that Jung is actively working with us again. I am sending the reviews directly to him.

I must beg you, dear Professor, not to imagine that I took offence because you did not visit me when you passed through Berlin. If you reproach yourself for this reason, there is a simple way to make amends. When next you come to Berlin, please give my wife and myself a good deal of your time.

I am sending you *Dreams and Myths* together with this letter. You mentioned some time ago that you had analysed the Flood myths. I have also been working on this and am quite certain that it is a symbolic representation of pregnancy. That is your opinion too, I take it? There are amazingly fine symbolisms contained in it, and I regret that I was unable to include the legend in my book.

I understand that a first paper on psycho-analysis has been published in Italy. I have only read a review. The author, Baroncini, is favourably inclined towards psycho-analysis.

I have chosen for my paper in the Psychological Society the title: 'Childhood Phantasies in the Mental Life of the Adult.'

With kind regards from house to house,

Yours,

Karl Abraham

Berggasse 19,
Vienna IX,
11.10.08

Dear Colleague,

I thank you for so amiably accepting everything mentioned in my last letter, but I do not expect too much self-suppression from you and prefer to note that I owe you a debt that will one day be paid off.

You know it was not easy for me between the two of you. I wish to dispense with neither of you, and I can tell neither how much liking I have for the other. It will be a great relief to me if you can make friends, or at any rate get on with each other. Just because I get on most easily with you (and also with our colleague Ferenczi[1] of Budapest), I feel it incumbent on me not to concede too much to racial preference and therefore neglect the more alien Aryan. I ask both to make sacrifices, not to me personally but to the cause that matters.

Dreams and Myths[2] are now about to serve that cause. We shall see what people say about it. Your interpretation of the Flood myths is of course correct, but you were not able to grasp the whole because you did not approach it by the right path. This leads by way of the myths 'of the birth of the hero' (the exposition at birth of Romulus, Cyrus, Moses, etc.), with which Rank is to deal in the next volume. The same themes are at work in both cases. I do not mind your having reserved the interpretation of the Flood myths for this context.

On Friday evening – your chief[3] and his wife were our guests here. They were very kind, in so far as his unapproachability and her affectation permit. He had not yet read *Dreams and Myths*. They both tried to take me by storm and persuade me that I should not talk of 'sexuality', but should find another name for what does not coincide with sexuality in the popular sense. All resistance and misunderstandings would then cease. I replied that I had no use for such household remedies; and besides, they could not suggest another name for it themselves.

There is little scientific news. The second edition of the *Interpretation of Dreams* is ready and is to appear in November. The 'Case of Hysteria'[4] is also to undergo a resurrection in some form or other.

Does your little society still meet regularly, and what form

[1] Dr Sandor Ferenczi, 1873–1933, founder of the Hungarian Psycho-Analytical Society.

[2] See p. 27.

[3] See footnote 1, p. 6.

[4] Sigmund Freud, *Fragment of an Analysis of a Case of Hysteria*, Standard Ed., Vol. VII.

is its activity taking? No doubt I shall hear about your lecture as soon as possible.

With cordial greetings to yourself and your wife,

Yours,
Freud

Berlin,
10.11.08

Dear Professor,

I have postponed my reply longer than usual because I wanted to tell you without delay what happened yesterday evening. I spoke to the *Berliner Gesellschaft für Psychiatrie und Nervenkrankheiten* on Intermarriage between Relatives and Neurosis.[1] To sum up: the evening was quite successful on the whole. The subject proved suitable for this first attack because I did not need to touch on certain points most likely to raise people's temperatures. I chose a few remarks of Oppenheim's as a starting point and stressed the fact that certain of his observations on neurotic children were in agreement with your views. I avoided mentioning several important points (for instance, the connection with homosexuality) because these would have aroused unnecessary opposition, but stood very firm on all my references to sexuality. I think you will also agree that it was best not to mention your name too often. It acts like a red rag to a bull and, in any case, people knew what I was aiming at. The audience remained attentive to the end and, in spite of the late hour, a discussion followed. First of all Oppenheim, very appreciative in several respects. He was fully convinced on some new points. It was only against the Freudian view of infantile sexuality that he felt obliged to take a 'most determined and resolute stand'. Ziehen[2] came next. While Oppenheim had on the whole remained factual, Ziehen rode his academic high horse. 'Wild assumptions', 'what Freud has written is all nonsense', and so forth. Then two speakers (Schuster, Rothmann),[3] who made factual contributions. And

---

[1] *Clinical Papers and Essays on Psycho-Analysis*, London, 1955, p. 21.
[2] Theodor Ziehen held the Chair of Psychiatry in Berlin (Charité).
[3] Neurologists in Berlin.

finally the high spot. A very pushing member, B., whose conversion to Christianity has proved only partially successful, assumed a moralising tone more suited to a public platform. I had, *inter alia*, mentioned Konrad Ferdinand Meyer (as has Sadger) as an example of love for the mother. That was unheard of. German ideals were at stake. Sexuality was now even attributed to German fairy tales, etc. It was very gratifying that authorities such as Ziehen and Oppenheim had taken such a determined stand against Freud. The whole Association should express their disapproval of this new trend. Liepmann replied in a very reasonable and dignified manner, declaring himself actually opposed to Freud but deprecating the arrogant tone of the previous speaker. I avoided all acrimony in my final summing up in order not to damage our cause. I only hit out at Ziehen, since he had been so very rude. I stood in lonely opposition to the well-attended gathering. Juliusburger, who would certainly have seconded me, was prevented from coming at the last moment. After the meeting, quite a number of members told me that they had enjoyed hearing something new as a change from the eternal demonstration of anatomical preparations. I had the impression that quite a few of them went home at least half convinced. At any rate, the ground has been prepared and perhaps I might advance in the second half of the winter with heavier artillery. The advice you gave me a year ago has proved useful. I waited almost a year before coming forward and was then more moderate than I in fact care to be. I think it was just the crudity of some people's opposition that swung the mood of the meeting in my favour. Oppenheim, whose good opinion is very important for me, expressed his appreciation in private. Admittedly he did not want to hear anything about infantile sexuality, but he agreed with me in many respects and even suggested publication in the *Deutsche Zeitschrift für Nervenheilkunde* (of which he is co-editor!). You see one can get on without making concessions as long as one does not put forward too many new things at once.

Our psycho-analytic meetings are shaping quite nicely. I hope that more physicians may soon be interested enough to join. We meet every two or three weeks.

You may already know that I sent yesterday's paper, in a

somewhat extended form, to Jung for the *Jahrbuch*. I believe that the *Jahrbuch* will come out under favourable auspices. Stekel's[1] book has been widely read in Berlin. It was very suitable for propaganda, and I know of a number of doctors whose interest in further publications has been aroused. The new editions you mention are surely another good sign.

The *Gesellschaft Deutscher Nervenaertzte*, which met recently in Heidelberg for the second time, plans to have its next Congress in Vienna. Should one? What do you think? Wouldn't you like to try and participate once again? Moll's recently published book (*Sexualleben des Kindes*) shows a greater lack of understanding than I have yet come across. I was very interested in your report on Bleuler's visit.

With many thanks for all the personal things you wrote in your letter, and kind regards to you and yours, also from my wife,

Yours,
Karl Abraham

*

Berggasse 19,
Vienna,
12.11.08

Dear Colleague,

Your account of the evening at which you read your paper was very interesting. Things are really not easy for you, but I think you are applying the right technique – treating people like patients under psycho-analysis, calmly ignoring their denials, and continuing one's explanation without telling them anything that too much resistance makes inaccessible to them. After the clarity and resolution of *Dreams and Myths* no one will accuse you of making excessive concessions.

The resistance to infantile sexuality strengthens me in the opinion that the *Three Essays*[2] is a work of similar value to that

---

[1] Wilhelm Stekel, 1886–1940, psychiatrist and psycho-analyst in Vienna; *Conditions of Nervous Anxiety and their Treatment*.

[2] Sigmund Freud, *Three Essays on the Theory of Sexuality*, Standard Ed., Vol. VII.

of the *Interpretation of Dreams*, the second edition of which you will, I hope, be receiving next week; the book is out, but I have no copies yet. Moll's piece is as pitiful as it is dishonest. You see that I am in form today. I did not know you had sent Jung your paper.

Unless the most improbable changes take place in the meantime, I shall not myself attend the congress in Vienna, and shall also prevent my hotheads from taking an active part. If you wish to attend and speak, that is a different matter. You possess the necessary self-control and detachment. But you will not derive much pleasure from it, and I shall not grant my dear Viennese the pleasure of a battle in which we should be shouted down. On the other hand, our absence will annoy them, and that suits me. As an opportunity to have you with us again here, this time with your wife, the congress would suit me very well, however.

I am now working on a 'General Method of Psycho-Analysis'. Where it is to be published is not yet settled, but in any case it will appear–perhaps exclusively–in the second volume of my papers on the theory of the neuroses.[1] Unfortunately I have so little time that it is making only very slow progress. A pleasing event in my family, my daughter's engagement to the young man of her choice,[2] also does not exactly increase leisure time. But one is not only a literary and medical beast of burden.

With cordial greetings and thanks,

Yours,
Freud

Berlin,
23.11.08

Dear Professor,

I read with great pleasure your news about your eldest daughter's engagement. I sent her my congratulations direct some days ago and I am now repeating them to you. At the

[1] It was later used in the papers on the technique of psycho-analysis.
[2] The engagement of Freud's eldest daughter Mathilde to Robert Hollitscher.

same time, I should like to thank you most sincerely for the *Interpretation of Dreams*. It is rare for a book with a poor initial sale to go into a new edition after so many years. Interest must be growing. I am eagerly looking forward to all that you are going to write in the next few months.

I, too, have always taken the resistance against the *Three Essays* as a sign of its importance. I might add that I prefer this work to all the others because it contains so very many ideas that will require detailed elaboration, while the *Interpretation of Dreams* is so well rounded and finished that there remains nothing for any of us to do. Besides, what I like in the *Three Essays* is its compactness; every sentence seems to contain several ideas.

Something might be done later, I suppose, about the Congress in Vienna. And how about *our* Congress? It would be nice if it came off again.

The psycho-analytic case you mention would be very welcome since I do not have a suitable patient at the moment. In the case of one woman I was successful with a partial analysis which, for external reasons, I had to combine with another type of treatment. Unfortunately, I am always short of young and new cases. At the moment a psychotic woman takes up hours of my time every day. A number of reports on court cases also keep me busy. I am well satisfied with the result of my first year's practice. The income surpasses my expectation but is naturally still far behind my expenses.

In the mentally ill patient I just mentioned one can observe the formation of delusions at an early stage, and the mechanism of the so-called melancholic delusions is also clearly recognisable. I am always hoping that I may one day get to work on the psycho-genesis of the various forms of delusions.

With kind regards,

Yours,
Karl Abraham

Have you read the nice *lapsus linguae* in the *Reichstag*? *Rückgratlos* instead of *rückhaltlos*.[1] The following slip of the pen is

[1] The German slip is untranslatable; the nearest might be *spineless* instead of *unreservedly*.

also very neat: a lady has to undergo painful treatment by a woman dentist with whom she is obviously in love. Reporting this to her family she writes—'I have just returned from this wonderful *creature*' (instead of *procedure*).

*

Berlin,
18.12.08

Dear Professor,

You must not assume that I expect you to reply letter for letter. The reprint you sent was in itself a sign of life that gave me much pleasure.

I have high hopes of the psycho-analysis of a case that I began a week ago. It is that of a seventeen-year-old boy belonging to the Jewish aristocracy. He suffers, among other symptoms, from an obstinate localised backache which has persisted for five years, and also from sexual neurasthenic symptoms. He was in the hands of orthopaedic surgeons for practically five years; then under Oppenheim, who treated him with radium and who finally referred him to me. It would make a great deal of difference if I were successful in this case, which has been given a very unfavourable prognosis by everyone. The beginning looks promising. I am writing the case up in exact detail because it is of the greatest interest, especially concerning the appearance of certain symptoms within one family. No other analysis has yet given me so much pleasure. The patient, whom Oppenheim described as very inaccessible, is keenly interested and happy to have been free from his nightly anxiety attacks and pollutions since his second session with me.

A strange endemic cluster of Freudians has been in existence for about a month in Charlottenburg. One of my first patients was a very intelligent philologist, a teacher at a new school in Charlottenburg. He is very grateful and shows an excellent understanding of analysis. As the result of a certain incident with some pupils at the school, he gave your writings and mine to the headmaster. The headmaster pored over them for the last four weeks and then demanded of the school doctor that he immediately familiarise himself with the whole of the theory of sexuality on which he subsequently examined him! The teachers had to do the same. My informant says that those who do not know these works are considered old-fashioned by the headmaster, and what teacher wants to be behind the times? By the way, I was told by a bookseller that the *Interpretation of Dreams* is selling very well.

There are also, of course, some less pleasant incidents. Some months ago I sent an English translation of my earlier publications on Sexual Trauma to Morton Prince[1] (*Journal of Abnormal Psychology*). I had written to him in advance informing him of its subject. He asked me to send him the manuscript so that he could look at it and added that he did not really like to publish things that had been previously printed elsewhere. This looked very much like an excuse, since a complete translation of one of his own papers was published just at that time in a German journal. After a long delay, I received an evasive reply and finally a rejection slip from the assistant editor. I am enclosing it. The reasons given are good enough. The manuscript was returned at the same time, enriched by many grease spots.

I found a communication from Jung even more disagreeable. Only now, after the *Jahrbuch* has gone to press, does he tell me that he has postponed publishing my reviews which he has had for over two months. He says that, for reasons of propaganda, he wanted to make the first issue as varied as possible. I can scarcely be wrong in assuming that at the last moment he substituted a paper of his own for my reviews. I find it extremely inconsiderate to have this put to me as a *fait accompli*. He could have seen to the variety of the contents somewhat earlier. I have written to Jung in a calm and factual manner and suggested that, in the circumstances, I should withdraw the reviews on the German and Austrian literature, but have urged him to print the reviews of your papers now. I know that many colleagues are very interested in an objective, collective review of your writings, and the natural place for this is surely the first issue. I assure you that I would have preferred not to permit the publication of all three manuscripts so as to show Jung that his arbitrary behaviour must have its limits. I believed, however, that you would prefer it if I were as moderate as possible in my requests.

[1] Morton Prince, American psychiatrist.

61

I am enclosing a picture (you do not need to return it), which will undoubtedly interest you. It corresponds exactly to Jensen's[1] description of how Gradiva steps from stone to stone. One might perhaps be able to get some interesting information from the deaf-mute sculptor.

With kind regards,

Yours,
Karl Abraham

Berggasse 19,
Vienna IX,
26.12.08

Dear Colleague,

I reply without delay to your interesting letter, which contains pleasing and unpleasing news side by side, as happens indeed in life itself.

In the first place, many thanks for the woman of Pompeii. It would be really interesting to know whether the sculptor knew Gradiva or worked independently. Unfortunately I have not even a trace of foot worship, and that is why I am so completely at a loss about the whole problem. Now for the painful part. I am really very sorry that you are again at loggerheads with Jung. At Zürich I tackled him vigorously and found him amenable, and only recently he wrote to me saying he was glad he had established good relations with you. This time I cannot agree that you are in the right. Jung made a decision that is obviously within his rights as editor, and I believe that anyone who undertakes office and responsibility is entitled to a certain amount of elbow-room. There is certainly nothing hostile to you in what he did; you are, so far as I know, represented in the first half-yearly volume by your paper on inter-marriage between close relatives, and the postponement of your review until the second cannot be regarded as a snub to you. I fear you have a rather excessive mistrust of him, a trace of a persecution complex. I should be very sorry indeed if you were to do anything that seemed to justify in retrospect his earlier behaviour towards you. I have deliberately refrained from exer-

[1] Wilhelm Jensen, 1873–1911, German writer, author of *Gradiva*.

cising any influence on the contents of the *Jahrbuch*, and I believe you can do the same without doing yourself any injustice. I should also like to remind you that your prognostication of Jung's future behaviour in relation to us did not turn out to be correct. You see from this how important it is to me that in these affairs in which each of you forms an opinion of the other both of you should turn out to be wrong and I to be right. I cannot tolerate that 'two such fellows'[1] both of whom are so close to me should not be able to get on with each other.

The hostility by which we are surrounded bids us hold together. Morton Prince, who has always been a kaleidoscopic character, is this time really lamentable. Where do the Americans expect to get with this fear of public prudery? Unless you specifically forbid me, I shall warn Brill[2] and Jones, who are being continually bombarded with requests from him to expound our theories in a series of articles for the *Journal of Abnormal Psychology*. He always begins by over-compensating for his cowardice and then withdraws into it. In fact he intended to come to Salzburg.

My warmest congratulations on that patient of yours whose analysis gives you so much pleasure. Radium has raised my spirits for hours today, it is really a miraculous element. There is only one worry in my mind that I should like to mention. It has often been my experience that just those cases in which I took an excessive personal interest failed, perhaps just because of the intensity of feeling. When such a *'test'*[3] case succeeded, however, I found that the previously constituted jury by its silence withheld its approbation. The opportunity of demonstrating our skill comes eventually, even if it should fail in this particular case. Do not lose heart. Our ancient Jewish toughness will prove itself in the end.

At Christmas I am expecting our colleagues Stein[4] and Ferenczi; we all grew very fond of the latter at Berchtesgaden. If Dr Abraham of Berlin joined us, it would be a splendid little

---

[1] This is a quotation from Eckermann: Gespräche mit Goethe, May 12th, 1825.

[2] Dr A. A. Brill, Freud's first follower in the United States.

[3] This word in English in the original.

[4] Dr George Stein, Hungarian psycho-analyst.

assembly, and a great refreshment in this period of hard work. Because of the consumption of energy in my practice I am not managing to get on with the 'General Method of Psycho-Analysis', which has been stuck for weeks on page 36. The slightest extra load turns the scale, and physical complaints also contribute to this state of affairs. That is what things are like when 'all is well'.

The Charlottenburg endemic is priceless. There seems to be a similar centre of infection in Munich, and it seems to have affected the craziest artists and people of that kind. No doubt one day there will be a great deal of noise, if the appropriate impulse is given. But that is nothing to look forward to. Every theory sacrifices something valuable when it becomes popular.

I already have the manuscript for the next number of the *Schriften zur Angewandten Seelenkunde*. *The Myth of the Birth of the Hero* will certainly interest you greatly as an advance that continues your own. I expect a huge defensive din to arise from the case history of the boy of five which is to be the first article in the *Jahrbuch*; I have the proofs here for correction. German ideals threatened again! Our Aryan comrades are really completely indispensable to us, otherwise psycho-analysis would succumb to anti-Semitism.

With cordial greetings,

Yours very sincerely,
Freud

Berggasse 19,
Vienna IX,
10.1.09

Dear Colleague,

I told you not long ago that I owed you some amends. I remember that as I write to you today, though your long silence points to your feeling seriously offended by the criticism in my last letter. You know that that criticism is consistent with the friendliest feelings towards you, or rather derives from those feelings, because it was from my liking for you that I deduced the right to draw your attention to a wrong emotional turning along which I saw you making your way. Permit me to hope that you are not capable of taking frankness amiss for long, and show this soon

To your cordially devoted
Freud

Berlin,
12.1.09

Dear Professor,

You are indeed wrong. The reason for my silence was illness. During the last few days since I have been up again, I have had no time to write to you because a lot of work has accumulated, particularly reports on court cases. My sincere thanks for your kindness, and I hasten to assure you that there is no question of my taking offence. If possible I shall write more fully later today.

With kindest regards and many thanks,

Yours,
Abraham

*

Berlin,
13.1.09

Dear Professor,

You will by now have received my brief note of yesterday which will have convinced you that I am in no way offended. Your last letter reached me just before Christmas. Just then, I went to visit my parents for a few days and, on my return to Berlin, I had to go straight to bed. The influenza epidemic did not spare me. Your card, with Stein's and Ferenczi's greetings, reached me in bed. After I got up, there followed, for the first time in my practice, a somewhat overwhelming influx of patients, and I also had to write some psychiatric court reports in a hurry. In short, I did not find the desired leisure to reply to your letter which gave me particular pleasure in every way. It was perhaps wrong of me not to send you at least a few lines as an interim reply, but I hoped from day to day that I should at last be able to get down to answering it properly. And now, dear Professor, once and for all my assurance: I shall never take

65

offence at your criticism of me. Nor do I think there is anything for which you have to make amends. I am, after all, aware of your personal interest in every one of your letters. The most recent one demonstrates it yet again. I would therefore have no reason to sulk and, besides, I don't react in this way. The whole matter does, however, offer one comfort; I am not the only one who occasionally goes wrong in interpreting motives.

I should have been so glad to accept your invitation to come to Vienna at the same time as our colleagues from Budapest. The card from the Café Riedl[1] awakened many memories. I think it will be possible to meet soon. I assume from your remarks that you will shortly be visiting Berlin, and after that it will be time for our spring meeting at Salzburg or elsewhere. It will presumably take place?

The psycho-analytic case I wrote you about last time is progressing well; unfortunately, family circumstances may intervene to make its further course unfavourable. Radium, too, still keeps interfering. Oppenheim sees the patient at infrequent intervals, but the patient does not prove accessible to these 'rays'.

I have reason to be pleased with the result of my first year's practice. The new year has also started well, so that the hope of being able to earn my living in this way no longer seems so far off. During the past months I have had a number of court and other reports to write, mostly through the good offices of Dr Hirschfeld, who altogether takes the kindest interest in me.

I look forward to the *Jahrbuch* and Rank's paper.

With kindest regards and many thanks,

Yours,
Abraham

Berggasse 19,
Vienna IX,
17.1.09

Dear Colleague,

I am delighted to have been wrong, and I am always willing to be wrong if I can be so to such advantage. But you will find that I tend to acquire prejudices which turn out to be very resistant to opportunities for shaking them.

[1] Meeting place of psycho-analysts after Freud's lectures.

I gladly answer your questions. There is to be no congress this year, but it will take place again next year, to make it easier for our gallant Americans to attend. Also the accumulation of material worth communicating can be only desirable. Jones is in Toronto, Canada, 35 Chicora Avenue, from where he writes very interesting, sarcastic letters in which his countrymen come off badly. He thinks we shall come to grief there on Anglican prudery.

You will certainly have read Strohmeyer's good and certainly effective paper,[1] which is very pleasing. I was also pleased to see from the proofs of the *Jahrbuch* that Jung has given your contribution first place after the analysis of little Hans.

No 5, with Rank's work, is already at the printer's. During the period when you were missing I received an invitation to deliver four to six lectures at the twentieth (!) anniversary celebrations at Clark University, Worcester, Mass., in the first week of July, and they offered to pay my fare. I had to decline, as I am not rich enough to be able to sacrifice three weeks' earnings in Vienna. But I was sorry, and at least the invitation can be talked about here in Europe.

The news of your practice is excellent. Hirschfeld is certainly an agreeable colleague because of his well sublimated homosexuality. Perhaps you will gradually be able to convince him of the incorrectness of his theoretical assumptions about the origin of homosexuality, if he is sufficiently uninvolved.

I have no news of Moll's new journal, and I had to write to him recently because my intended contribution to it is now to appear in the second series of the Collected Papers on Neurosis.[2]

Things are moving everywhere. Hold out valiantly, and write to me soon again, pending an opportunity for a more extensive exchange of ideas.

Yours most sincerely
Freud

---

[1] Dr Wilhelm Strohmeyer, neurologist at the Kraepelin clinic at Munich: 'Über die ursächlichen Beziehungen der Sexualität zu Angst und Zwangzuständen', *Jahrbuch für Psychiatrie und Neurologie*, 1909.

[2] Sigmund Freud, *Sammlung Kleiner Schriften zur Neurosenlehre*, Vol. I, Vienna, 1906.

Berlin,
31.1.09

Dear Professor,

You are probably busier than usual owing to the forthcoming family celebrations.[1] All the same, I should like to ask your help concerning a few psycho-analytic difficulties. Please do not trouble to reply for the time being to anything else contained in this letter.

The young patient, about whom I have already written to you, has suffered from anxiety since his childhood. He is particularly frightened of speaking or eating in the presence of a stranger. He will eat in front of the family; he just manages in the presence of friends if he is alone with them. However, as soon as strangers join the family circle (or a stranger sits at the family table), he cannot eat or talk. Nor can he ever speak to several members of his family at once, but only to one person at a time. If someone else joins in, he becomes silent. (He has, incidentally, become much more accessible since he started analysis.) His fear of strangers is certainly partly based on a repressed scopophilia which is, by the way, only directed towards the male members of his family and towards male strangers. I cannot find a suitable explanation for his inability to eat. There is no nausea whatsoever. (He only feels aversion towards certain dishes – for instance, fish, and certain fluids such as white wine, champagne and coffee.) I have tried in various ways to explain his fear of talking but cannot make any headway. Perhaps you could advise me a little on this point. The patient shows strong unconscious homosexual masochistic trends. His main symptom (the one for which he came to me) is pain in a certain spot beneath his right shoulder blade. It is linked with his anxiety. Pain and anxiety are both tied up with a 'sensation of dread' which is both frightening and sensuous. He also experiences this feeling in certain anxiety dreams (especially in dreams of falling). But it is particularly connected with the relationship he had up to his thirteenth year with his elder brother, who showed strong sadistic tendencies. (Lying

[1] This refers to the wedding of Freud's eldest daughter Mathilde to Robert Hollitscher.

on top of each other in bed, kissing, biting, licking and then hitting each other – in all this the patient was usually the passive partner.) I have uncovered a lot of important material concerning the origin of the pain, but so far its localisation remains puzzling. (I only know that the 'sensation of dread' has moved from the perineum to that region, but why does it stop just there?) The last fortnight the patient spent with his brother, before the latter was sent away and soon afterwards committed suicide, is subject to an almost complete amnesia. I suspect that this is where the most important clues are to be found, for the pain first appeared after the brother's departure. I cannot give you all the other related details. The case is extremely complex because other pains later supervened which the patient took over from his sister, while she in turn took over certain pains from him. His backache once disappeared for ten days – after his first successful coitus – but it returned. Apart from anxiety and pain, he has from early infancy suffered from feelings of exhaustion and somnolence which do not seem to me to be sufficiently accounted for by masturbation. I hope that this will give you a rough outline and that you will be able to let me have some hints along which lines I should search further.

As for the aversion to fish, I have just had an interesting illumination from another patient and I should like to know whether it has general validity. The patient, bisexual and referred to me by Hirschfeld for analysis, has gone through the typical transference on to his mother and the subsequent turning away from her. He lost his father at the age of six, and thereafter shared his mother's bedroom and felt repelled by the menstrual smell. The smell of fish, especially smoked and salted herrings and such like, reminds him of this. Have you come across similar instances?

I shall save up the rest for another time. So, for today, my thanks in advance and kind regards,

Yours,
Abraham

Berggasse 19,
Vienna IX,
2.2.09

Dear Colleague,

I thank you for showing me so much consideration and hasten (relatively) to reply. Your patient obviously treats eating and talking as sexual activities. The course to follow is to search for the conditions in which his inhibitions become meaningful; and I hope you will find the problem readily soluble if you bear in mind the 'displacement upwards' that you generally apply so skilfully and refer back to anal activity the oral activity (including speech) on which there is so much emphasis in this case. With the key of anal erotism, which is constitutionally reinforced in all homosexuals, you will be able easily to unlock the closed doors.

Little work has been done on food fads, but they very often have the same root as in your second patient. In the course of time you will increasingly fall in with the inevitable trend to trace back more and more to sex, to genital and functional details.

I eagerly await further news from you.

With cordial greetings,

Yours,
Freud

*

Berlin,
14.2.09

Dear Professor,

First of all, many thanks for your advice. It proved perfectly correct. I was able with the help of anal erotism to explain my patient's fear of eating and other of his symptoms. An embittered resistance lasted throughout two sessions, which were then followed by associations in plenty. I believe that I am dealing with a particularly difficult case with whom the proven method —to let the patient bring associations freely and without selection—fails. He is quite intelligent but obstinately declares himself to be stupid and, when I ask him to bring me his associations in the usual way, he asserts that he is overcome each time by the fear of saying something stupid as well as by his aversion to speaking. I hope that this will change when I have found, in anal-erotism, the explanation of the latter symptom. The idea of his stupidity is mainly derived from his sadistic elder brother who constantly showed him – the masochist – up as the stupid one. The desire for physical and mental ill-treatment by the brother (who has since committed suicide) pervades his whole illness.

Unfortunately it is so difficult to discuss these things by letter. Are you coming to Berlin soon? I take it that family reasons have kept you in Vienna up till now. Since there is to be no Congress this year, it would be very pleasant indeed to see you some time in Berlin. Our scientific meetings have been quite stimulating on the whole, but were largely concerned with general sexual topics. All the same, there has been a lively interest in psycho-analysis.

I am planning to read another paper next term in the *Berliner Gesellschaft für Psychiatrie und Nervenkrankheiten,* as I did this term. I think six months is about the right interval but would like to have your opinion. I do not want to bore people – that would do more harm than good.

A Russian journal has invited me to contribute a short article on psycho-analysis and I shall probably take this up.

Some time ago I wrote to you of my wish to write on traumatic neuroses. This is something I would like to discuss with you. I consider it a very important subject because it has so far always been used to disprove the sexual basis of neurosis. I am now certain that it is, in fact, also a sexual neurosis. I shall, as soon as the opportunity arises, look for further material in Oppenheim's Out-Patients' Department. Do you agree that this piece of work needs doing? I have, for some time past, been very much attracted by another subject, a psycho-analytic study of Giovanni Segantini,[1] whose personality and works can be understood only with the help of the theory of sexuality. I should also like to discuss this with you personally. It is extraordinary how great a role is played here by the sublimation of

[1] Giovanni Segantini, 1858–99, Swiss painter.

71

component instincts, the repression of incestuous phantasies and the transfer on to non-human objects.

To conclude, just one more question concerning foot fetishism. I am familiar with the symbolic significance of foot and shoe, but it does not seem to go far enough. I have just come across the case of a six-year-old girl where the foot was of great significance. The sister and brother practised mutual masturbation by touching each other's genitals with the foot. Do you happen to know whether this is a frequent practice?

Now I have again troubled you a great deal, dear Professor. I conclude with kind regards to you and your family.

Yours,
Abraham

*

Berggasse 19,
Vienna IX,
18.2.09

Dear Colleague,

The fact that it is very uncertain whether we shall see each other so soon in Berlin does not relieve me of the pleasant obligation of writing to you. You know of course that for nine and a half months of the year I am the slave of money, which is to be earned only in small amounts and therefore does not permit any real lavishness or freedom of movement.

First, your questions. I agree that six months' interval is enough, and that one can gradually get bolder. Consideration for Oppenheim will do little good, for he will surely go deeper and deeper into opposition. I believe traumatic neurosis to be hard to tackle and, apart from a remark in the 'Sexual Theory,' I have no suggestions about linking it with our theories. If you have a definite idea or expectation in connection with it, you are of course perfectly justified in testing it. Scientific work, like psycho-analytic technique, must follow the path of least resistance.

In stereotypes like those of your patient who will not talk for fear of saying something stupid, the difficulty can be got over by exercising rather more patience than usual without changing the technique, which always leaves a feeling of uncertainty behind. The aversion to talking is ultimately based on other intended (sexual) uses of the mouth, and that can be stated, and repeated a few times.

As it happens, I am in a position to give you some guidance about foot fetishism, thanks to some findings of the past few days. The use of the foot (heel or knee) for masturbation is not uncommon either as a solitary or mutual practice. But that explains only one factor in the situation: the appearance of the foot in the symptomatology, but not the fetishism. (In one of my cases a paralysis was the comprehensible consequence.) Fetishism comes about as follows: it is the result of a special kind of repression that could be described as partial; part of the complex is repressed and in compensation for that another part pertaining to it becomes idealised. (A historical parallel is provided by the mediaeval contempt for women and the simultaneous exaltation of the Virgin Mary.) In our case we have an original olfactory pleasure in the smell of a dirty foot (which the pervert always prefers to a clean foot). This olfactory pleasure is repressed, while the foot that provided the pleasure is elevated into a fetish. We then hear no more of its smell. I know clothes fetishists in whom the connection is even closer. They are former voyeurs, watchers of undressing scenes, to whom clothes were once very much in the way. The normal clothes fetishism of women is also connected with the passive wish to be seen, with exhibitionism. I am still waiting for numerous examples before publishing this conclusion, and in the meantime I shall be delighted if you are able to solve any problems with this key.

If you are serious about your study of Segantini, I want to claim it at once as an ornament for the *Angewandten*, for *Dreams and Myths* has made an excellent impression on everyone who has mentioned it to me, and these testimonials to your many-sidedness make me very proud of you.

A reprint from Moll's first number is going off to you by the same post. Apart from that I do not think our relations with him will develop very amicably. The review of 'A Case of Hysteria' makes me suspect that Moll means to oppose us in this journal, and that he uses a show of impartiality as a trimming to his rather underhand character. Several passages in the

73

Sexual Life of the Child really merit a charge of libel, but they are best answered with–prudence and silence. In any case, *hic niger est, hunc tu Romane caveto.*

With cordial greetings,

Yours very sincerely,
Freud

Berlin,
5.3.09

Dear Professor,

This time I have to thank you for a long letter which contained so much that is pleasing to me personally, and also for the reprint and the *Kleine Schriften.*[1] Your discussion of the hysterical attacks which is concise and to the point and which I find particularly illuminating, gave Oppenheim the opportunity of attacking you yesterday while examining a hysterical woman in his Out-Patients' Department: it was simply unheard of, etc. Only yesterday one of his assistants suggested that one might ask the out-patients a little about their sexual life, but he rejected this with considerable affect. You are therefore quite right in your opinion of Oppenheim. Psycho-therapy in Berlin is altogether in a nice way! The enclosed cutting shows you how an obviously psychogenic case of migraine is treated here.

I shall not start work on the traumatic neuroses yet. It is not opportune just at present to involve patients in Oppenheim's department in discussions of their sexual life. I shall therefore start on Segantini. If my paper is good and extensive enough to appear as a monograph, then the *Angewandte*[2] is the only place where I should like to see it published, and I am grateful for your invitation to include it there. I have seen no mention yet of *Dreams and Myths*, apart from one short paragraph in a newspaper. I am all the more pleased that you have heard favourable reports. You will have received a short paper of Wulff's[3]–a fairly good, but not very thorough analysis.

[1] Sigmund Freud, *Sammlung Kleiner Schriften zur Neurosenlehre*, Vol. I, Deuticke, Leipzig and Wien, 1909.

[2] *Schriften zur Angewandten Seelenkunde.*

[3] Dr M. Wulff, psycho-analyst in Odessa, now in Israel.

My analysis of a bisexual with a great preponderance of homosexual tendencies will soon be finished and has been very successful. The case of hysteria, about which I recently asked your advice, will also soon be concluded; that is to say, the greatest resistances have been resolved and the therapeutic results are already quite far-reaching.

I hear that a collective review of your publications has appeared in the journal edited by Stern[1] in Breslau. There is no other news today.

With kindest regards,

Yours,
Abraham

*

Berggasse 19,
Vienna IX,
9.3.09

Dear Colleague,

Jung is coming on a visit on the 19th inst. He writes that a Dr Häberlin[2] in Basle has announced a 'course of lectures' on 'Freud's interpretation of dreams'. He is a lecturer on psychology and runs a school.

And now for the big news. I have accepted the repeated invitation of Clark University, Worcester, Mass., near Boston, to give a series of lectures there in the week beginning September 6th on the occasion of the university's twentieth anniversary celebrations; and I shall be leaving at the end of August. My brother, and probably also Dr Ferenczi of Budapest, want to come too. I am very curious about what will happen there and about the outcome of these lectures. The trip may certainly be mentioned, it is as sure as anything human can be. Perhaps it will annoy some people in Berlin as well as in Vienna. That cannot do any harm.

[1] Dr William Stern, 1871–1938, Professor of Psychology in Breslau, later in Hamburg, editor of the *Zeitschrift für Angewandte Psychologie*.
[2] Dr Paul Häberlin, Swiss psycho-analyst.

I know you will be pleased about it, and send you my cordial greetings.

Yours,
Freud

*

Berlin,
7.4.09

Dear Professor,

The eagerly awaited *Jahrbuch* has now been in my hands for a few days. It only became available in Germany a week ago. I read your analysis[1] at one sitting and I am still completely under the impression it made. I have not heard any other opinions about it yet. I am not at all curious since I know them in advance. It is certainly very gratifying to find what we have learned from adult analyses so clearly manifested in the child. There is proof in every line and that is at least some compensation for the lack of understanding on the part of our colleagues.

It is striking that the remaining contents of the volume all come from the Zürich school. Maeder's paper[2] seems very valuable to me. I had heard a great deal beforehand about Jung's contribution[3] and had therefore expected something completely original. I am afraid he disappointed me because he does not seem to shed any new light on the question under discussion. Are you, incidentally, also of the opinion that the father is so predominant? It is definitely the mother in some of my analyses; in others, one cannot decide whether it is the father or the mother who plays the more important part. It seems to me to depend very much on the individual circumstances. Binswanger[4] is unfortunately rather too long-winded. How much more of him will there be in the next volume? I think it

---

[1] See footnote 1, page 47.

[2] A. Maeder, 'Sexualität und Epilepsie', *Jahrbuch für Psychoanalytische und Psycho-Pathologische Forschungen*, Vol. I, 1909.

[3] 'Die Bedeutung des Vaters für das Schicksal des Einzelnen', *Jahrbuch*, Vol. I, 1909.

[4] Dr. Ludwig Binswanger 'Versuch einer Hysterieanalyse', *Jahrbuch*, Vol. I, 1909.

technically wrong to report the second part of an analysis after an interval of six months. Those who read the first part now will scarcely be able to follow the second part after such a time lag.

I am delighted that the American trip is coming off after all. The people whom I told about it at your suggestion have unfortunately not taken sufficient umbrage. Are you passing through Berlin either on your journey there or back? That is what particularly interests me.

I have, interestingly enough, tracked down a symptomatic action in myself. While I am analysing and am waiting for the patient's reply, I often cast a quick glance at the picture of my parents. I know now that I always do this when I am following up the patient's infantile transference. The glance is always accompanied by a certain guilt feeling: what will they think of me? This is of course connected with my breaking away from them, which was not too easy. Since explaining this symptomatic action to myself, I have not caught myself at it any more. Another observation of our little girl, aged two years and four months. On two occasions I have had to give her a glycerine enema. Since then she has told me every day that she does not want another injection, but she says this without real affect and, on most occasions, even with a rather arch smile. She does not show any other anal-erotic tendencies.

That's enough for today.

With kind regards,

Yours,
Abraham

Berggasse 19,
Vienna IX,
27.4.09

Dear Colleague,

I was very glad to receive a letter from you after a longish interval. My reply has been delayed by all sorts of disturbances, such as conjunctivitis and my daughter's falling ill again. She has had an operation which, however, has finally disposed of the matter, I hope. She is now fully convalescent.

First of all, let me say that everything you tell me in confidence will be treated confidentially, personal matters in particular. I willingly grant you the preponderance of the Zürich school, to which you belong yourself. My comments on the problem Jung deals with are similar to yours. I have previously believed the parent of the same sex to be more important for the person concerned, but can reconcile myself to greater individual variations. Jung has taken a part out of the whole, but he has done so very effectively.

I am sailing for America on August 21st from Trieste, but the return journey will be by way of Hamburg and Berlin and will make possible a brief meeting with you. If the trip does not annoy the Berliners, there is really nothing to be done with them.

Jung and his wife were here at the end of March, Dr Pfister[1] was here during the last few days. Half an hour before him Moll was here, and the interview ended badly. It came to hard words, and he left suddenly, with a great deal of rapidly secreted venom. I almost had the impression that he thought he was patronising us, and at that I let myself go a little. Probably you will now feel the repercussions. Never mind.

I have now to prepare the third edition of the *Everyday Life*, but because of pressure of medical work cannot get round to it. Also my health has left something to be desired during these past few months. Perhaps it is a good thing if you young people take over.

Rank's paper will have been of special interest to you because of its mythological content, and I very much want to hear your comments. The mistakes in the *Interpretation of Dreams* referring to it have already been explained, but I have forgotten the explanation. But it was not caused by any special resentment against Rank.

With cordial greetings from

Yours,
Freud

---

[1] Oskar Pfister, Zürich pastor and psycho-analyst.

Dear Professor,

I hope by the time this letter reaches you the various illnesses you mentioned some weeks ago will be things of the past. I have not answered your letter till today because I wanted to write to you about my paper in the Psychological Society under Moll's chairmanship. It is not a professional association but a rather mixed group. I spoke about 'Infantile Phantasies in the Mental Life of the Adult'.

What gave me most pleasure in your letter was the hope of seeing you here in the autumn. May I now ask you to be generous in apportioning your time? I am so much looking forward to our meeting—in the course of time such a lot has accumulated that I want to discuss with you.

My practice, which from the outset has developed more favourably than I had dared hope, has recently surprised even me by its progress. I am busy for the greater part of the day with long-term treatments. I have nine patients tomorrow, six of them psycho-analytic cases. A year and a half ago I would not have dreamt of this. Admittedly I am not yet sought out by the public. I owe most of the cases to other doctors or to personal contacts. For several months I have had no support from Oppenheim who has either been ill or away but, in spite of this, my practice has not declined. I now see that psychotherapy can be a very exhausting business and, if it remains like this, there will not be much free time left for writing. If finances permit, I should like to go away for some weeks in mid-summer with my wife and our little girl. Have you decided yet where you are going? Maybe there will be a chance to meet during the holidays after all.

I liked Rank's book[1] very much. I am only sorry that he has not dealt more fully with the Flood. It has so many connections with the birth legend. Besides, at least in the biblical form, it is a particularly good demonstration of the effects and working of repression. The subject might well deserve treatment on its own.

Do you agree that it might be worth while some time to work

[1] See p. 54.

on a special study of agoraphobia? I am just dealing with several such cases that very nicely demonstrate the fixation on mother or father. I should like to know your opinion on several points. I find in these patients that during their anxiety states they feel very small, would like to crawl on all fours and have the impression at the time that other people are terribly big. Here the phantasy of being a child who is unable to move is transparent. Some such patients, however, describe a feeling as if they were shrinking and sinking into the earth. I assume that this stands for the wish to be an embryo, to return to the mother's womb. Do you approve of this interpretation? It fits my cases very well. Of course there is no hurry about answering this question. There are other matters in my practice that I should like to put before you, dear Professor, but every letter must come to an end. I therefore conclude, with kindest regards,

Yours,

Karl Abraham

*

Berggasse 19,
Vienna IX,
23.5.09

Dear Colleague,

I am delighted at your good news, not least at your independence of O., who is a hopeless proposition in any case.

Now to the most important matter, our next meeting. On the outward journey I shall probably be travelling direct from Muinch to Bremen (I am sailing on August 21st in the *George Washington*, Norddeutscher Lloyd). On the way back I shall stop briefly at Hamburg and then break the journey in Berlin, where I have a very jealous and incredibly youthful and energetic seventy-five-year-old brother from whom I shall conceal my presence for half a day in order to have the chance of talking to you and catching a glimpse of your hospitable home. The rest we shall see. Probable date, towards the very end of September. The tracing back of agoraphobia to infantile spatial impressions is known to me, and is certainly important. You will never miss the father-mother fixation in any future case.

The specific factor in agoraphobia seems to be disappointed and abandoned ambitious phantasies. More when we meet.

I am of course too tired to work, but am otherwise well again. My wife and my second daughter are at Karlsbad.

With cordial greetings to yourself and your family.

Yours,
Freud

Berlin,
10.11.09

Dear Professor,

Now comes my abreaction. The day before yesterday there was a battle in the Neurological Society. The 'Dream States'[1] met with a far worse reception than I had expected. Admittedly, Ziehen as Chairman had, in the most infamous way, done all he could to make my paper fall flat. While I was speaking, I was confronted by a row of faces wearing those well-known supercilious smiles. Ziehen refused any discussion, only allowing himself time to deliver a short but furious attack on my 'hotch-potch'. I have never in any neurotic patient seen such crude and poorly disguised resistance. I merely replied that, in view of Ziehen's prejudice, I did not wish to sum up. Very characteristic: the only colleague who took an objective view was, as I heard privately, a surgeon who had strayed into the meeting by mistake. This man is able to find an outlet for his aggression with the scalpel and does not, like the neurologists, need to air it in petty animosities.

Otherwise I am very well, and I sincerely hope that this is so with you too by now. My wife and I were very sorry that in the circumstances we could offer you so little hospitality. But I must once again thank you very warmly for the hours you gave us.

As regards my practice, I can report that the public is gradually finding its way to me under its own steam. In the course of the next few months I shall also have to appear as an expert in several big lawsuits. Among others, I shall probably have

[1] Karl Abraham, 'Hysterical Dream States', *Selected Papers on Psycho-Analysis*, London, 1927.

to give evidence concerning a spiritualist medium, about whose unmasking there was a great deal in the press. I am amused to see that two other nerve specialists have recently moved right into my neighbourhood and that a third will soon follow. Whatever success one achieves cannot be due to psychoanalysis–this time it's due to the district!

A Russian doctor by the name of Wulff, who has been Juliusburger's assistant in a private mental hospital for some time, is now going to settle in Odessa. He is very interested in psycho-analysis and, because of this, lost his last job in Berlin after only a few weeks. I know him to be a hard-working and reliable man who is unfortunately in very difficult financial circumstances. Perhaps you or one of your colleagues in Vienna might be able to send him some patients. I expect he will write to you personally as he has asked me for your address. Juliusburger also tells me that Wulff would like to do translations into Russian.

With kind regards, also to your family,

Yours,
K. Abraham

*

Berggasse 19,
Vienna IX,
23.11.09

Dear Colleague,

Only the necessity to use all my leisure to draft the Worcester lectures has made such a bad correspondent of me and caused me so long to delay thanking you for putting in an appearance with the 'Dream States'. Shall we be getting it for the *Jahrbuch*? You are just the man to take as little notice of the general opposition as I did in Vienna at the time, and to find sufficient compensation in our interest alone.

I thank you for your kind reception and your wife for her hospitality. You remember how rushed I was, and that only the train journey gave us an hour for the unhampered discussion for which we had been waiting so long. Our colleague Eitingon will long since have told you the news from here and given you the bad photograph, which at least shows how heavy were the demands that America made on me physically.

I am well again now, except for the usual complaints from overwork.

The practice was never so busy as in these last two months, though never so dreary and scientifically arid; and the flow of would-be patients that usually enabled me to pass on cases to younger colleagues has so far not materialised.

Publication of the second semi-annual volume of the *Jahrbuch* is imminent, and it is to contain all sorts of things. You will also be shortly receiving from me the third edition of the *Everyday Life*. The next job is the second edition of the *Sexual Theory*. It will be some time, I think, before a short paper on Leonardo da Vinci that so far only Eitingon knows about enriches the *Contributions to Applied Psychology*.[1] I should like to scc your Segantini there. Then there would be two advances into biography writing as we see it.

I am now giving my lectures in the form of a seminar, and I shall soon be having a report and discussion on one of your papers, probably that on the differences between hysteria and dementia praecox.[2]

In the hope that this delay will not have frightened you off, and with many good wishes to your little family.

Yours very sincerely

Freud

*

Berlin,
24.11.09

Dear Professor,

I should have written at once to thank you when Dr Eitingon brought me your picture some days ago, but he told me that there was a letter to me lying on your table which I would shortly be receiving. Now I can thank you for both at the same time. I was particularly delighted with the picture. It

[1] Schriften zur Angewandten Seelenkunde.
[2] Karl Abraham, 'The Psycho-Sexual Differences between Hysteria and Dementia Praecox', *Selected Papers on Psycho-Analysis*, London, 1927.

most faithfully mirrors your appearance seven weeks ago. It now stands in a particularly suitable frame, and surveys the birth of the 'Dream States' with a critical eye. This will be published in the next half-yearly volume. Your new plans, of which Eitingon has already told me, arouse my curiosity. It will be a little embarrassing for my Segantini to be so near your Leonardo. But it will certainly be written as soon as possible. The letters and writings of Segantini, for which I have been waiting, have just been published and I hope I shall be able to start work in a week or two.

To characterise our enemies, I have something to add to my previous report. I heard from a reliable source that Ziehen told a colleague that he gave such a bad reception to my paper in order to demonstrate to guests from abroad what people in Berlin think of Freud (my informant would not like this to be spread around).

What you say about your seminar interests me, partly because of the discussions of my paper but mainly because of a course of lectures I am planning for January. I am still very uncertain about the form this will take. The one you have chosen seems to be suitable only for an advanced audience.

With my own and my wife's kindest regards to you and your family,

Yours,
Karl Abraham

*

Berggasse 19,
Vienna IX,
20.I.10

Dear Dr Abraham,

A patient, a sister of one of your latest patients, has shown me an advertisement in a Berlin paper announcing the beginning of your course. That reminded me of how long it is since I last wrote to you.

You are no doubt following how eagerly the Americans are now taking up psycho-analysis. Jones is very active, and

Putnam[1] is just publishing a series of articles on our visit to Worcester in the *Journal of Abnormal Psychology*. Stanley Hall[2] is to devote the whole April number of the *American Journal of Psychology* to us. Both of them recently thoroughly discomfited the confused and dishonest Boris Sidis[3] at a meeting of American psychologists.

Our congress at Nuremberg is fixed for March 30th and 31st, thus to follow on Easter. The invitations will be going out very soon. We Europeans will, I hope, be present in full force. This time the subject will be primarily questions of principle and organisation.

We have been extending hospitality to L. Binswanger and his wife since Sunday, in so far as it is possible to be hospitable in Vienna in these days of hard work. My wife obviously prefers the memory of another psycho-analytic couple who have so far been only partly our guests. But please do not repeat this.

I cannot do any work at all now. Routine jobs such as the preparation of the second edition of the 'Sexual Theory' and the German edition of the Worcester lectures,[4] letters, the seminar, the Wednesday meetings, that is all. Not a line on Leonardo for weeks. I gladly yield precedence to Segantini. I send you my cordial greetings and hope that you and your little family are well.

Yours very sincerely,
Freud

Berlin,
22.2.10

Dear Professor,

I have submitted a paper on fetishism[5] for Nuremberg. You told me in September that you might put your notes on an

[1] James J. Putnam, 1846–1915, Professor of Neurology, Harvard University.

[2] Granville Stanley Hall, Professor of Psychology and President of Clark University, Worcester, Mass.

[3] Dr Boris Sidis, American psychologist.

[4] Sigmund Freud, *Five Lectures on Psycho-Analysis*, Standard ed., Vol. XI, p. 3.

[5] Karl Abraham, 'Remarks on the Psycho-Analysis of a Case of Foot and Corset Fetishism', *Selected Papers on Psycho-Analysis*, London, 1927.

analytic case at my disposal. If it is no trouble to you, I should now like to ask you for them; but rather than take up too much of your time with this request, I would prefer to restrict myself to my own analytic work. Perhaps you would contribute your experience of such cases if a discussion should follow. This one case has naturally not given me complete understanding, but I can put forward a number of new viewpoints.

I give you below the text of an advertisement which you may consider a favourable sign. Several colleagues asked me to arrange another course.

In March, I intend to arrange another four weeks' course on Freud's Theory of Neuroses (including the Theory of Sexuality and Dream Analysis), twice weekly, from 8.30 to 10 p.m., date to be announced later. It will start on Monday, 28th February at 8.30 p.m. at my flat. Fee: 30 marks. Applications and written or verbal enquiries to: Dr K. A. etc.

Did you happen to see the article on dream interpretation in the *Frankfurter Zeitung*? The author is one of my patients. The article is very intelligently written. Resistance only appears at the end – against wish-fulfilment, of course. You will probably receive a copy direct from the author.

With kind regards from house to house,

Yours,
Abraham

*

Berggasse 19,
Vienna IX,
24.2.10

Dear Colleague,

I am uncommonly pleased at being able to help you in something. Unfortunately it is only very little, but please make any use of it you wish.

I have investigated only one case in detail; of others in which the subject of fetishism was instructively touched on I have only the results, not the notes. The case was that of a highly educated, elegant and sophisticated man of twenty-five, who carefully adjusted the creases in his trousers before lying down for the first time on the psycho-analytic couch. He turned out to be a clothes fetishist in the better sense of the word, attached great importance to elegance and taste in his own clothes, and found women 'impossible' if they did not dress in accordance with his ideal demands. He suddenly lost all interest in a girl who had greatly attracted him when she turned up for an appointment unsuitably dressed.

He was psychologically impotent, and analysis showed a fixation on his mother, who for years had made him the spectator of her dressing and undressing, at any rate up to the penultimate point, was completely in love with him, and was still inclined to such intimacies to the present day, in spite of his withdrawing from them. (During the treatment he achieved excellent potency, but remained psychologically anaesthetic.) He was also a shoe fetishist, though not of the crudest kind. His childhood was full of unusually intense coprophilic activity. At the age of from eight to ten, for instance, he managed to keep a hard sausage hanging from his rectum from which he kept breaking off little bits in the course of the day. His sense of smell had always been over-sensitive. In the years of puberty he was a voyeur, and his masturbation began with his spying on some American girls undressing in a Swiss hotel.

I have learnt from other cases that shoe fetishism goes back to an original (olfactory) pleasure in the dirty and stinking foot. This indeed recurs in the positive perversion. I regard coprophilic olfactory pleasure as being the chief factor in most cases of foot and shoe fetishism. Also it must be emphasised that the female foot is apparently a substitute for the painfully missed, prehistorically postulated, female penis. The plait too must be a substitute for this. Cutting off plaits thus stands for castration of the female, 'making' female, since it is by castration that females are 'made'. I have not analysed glaring cases of fetishism.

I am now writing Leonardo[1] *at odd times*;[2] from next week onwards there will be a decrease in my practice, and then at last I shall be able to get on with it. Otherwise I have nothing in store for the *Sammlung*. I am rejecting as flat and boring an essay by Riklin on Goethe's 'beautiful soul'.

[1] *Leonardo da Vinci and a Memory of his Childhood*, Standard Ed., Vol. XI.
[2] These three words in English in the original.

As an epilogue to the American trip I shall probably be going to Karlsbad on July 15th to take the cure. Otherwise I am keeping pretty well. So far work has been hard, opposition great, and friends far away. What did me most good was Ferenczi; I went to see him in Budapest and he came to see me one Sunday in return. I received the clever article in the *Frankfurter Zeitung*, and did not really believe the assurance that it was written before reading the book.

Have I already mentioned to you that Stanley Hall is producing a number of the *American Journal of Psychology* that is to be filled exclusively with our papers, etc.?

With cordial greetings to you and to your wife,

Yours,
Freud

Berlin,
28.4.10

Dear Professor,

I assumed that you returned from Nuremberg feeling completely satisfied. The greatest pleasure for me was the mood in which all participants left the Congress. I travelled back with Eitingon, Hirschfeld and Koerber, and during the whole of the nine hours' journey we never stopped discussing our impressions. Tomorrow I shall open the proceedings of our local Society with a report on the Congress.

Meanwhile, you have once again given me new cause for gratitude. So far I have only read the first of the five Lectures[1] and glanced through the others. They arrived just at the right moment to introduce psycho-analysis to the many people who have recently become interested. The Americans were indeed fortunate to hear all this in the spoken word!

Psycho-analysis has recently been flourishing in my consulting room. I have started four new treatments in quick succession, three of them in a strange way. One of your former patients—I think his name is F.—has introduced analysis here to a small circle of neurotics. First of all a very intelligent young woman arrived; she is doing very nicely in her treatment, and

[1] See footnote 4, page 85.

soon sent her best friend; then some days ago she sent another friend who once discussed treatment with you in Vienna. These three are all most interesting patients; among them is one case of actual parent-incest. From this one, and from one other case which Hirschfeld sent me for analysis, I have learned a great deal about the question of exogamy, mixed marriage,[1] etc., which I intend to publish soon.

Official opposition in Berlin is stronger than ever.

With kind regards from house to house,

Yours,
Karl Abraham

Berggasse 19,
Vienna IX,
5.6.10

Dear Dr Abraham,

Apart from illness and work, my long silence has been due to the postponement from week to week of the appearance of *Leonardo*. It has at last appeared, and my digestion is improving under medical care, but I have still to go on working for another forty days. At any rate my eldest is very much better. My wife and second daughter returned from Karlsbad today.

Your good news pleased me very much. Otherwise you are just the man to stick things out. Attacks still do not disturb my equanimity. Our latest *coup d'état*, the foundation of the *Zentralblatt*, will soon turn out to be biologically advantageous. Privy Councillor F. recently spent four hours with me one evening – I kept him for such a long time in order to study him. As a result of the examination I ask you to believe (there is no need for discretion) that he is a liar, rogue and ignoramus.

Yesterday I had a much more pleasing visitor, Ossipow[2] from Moscow, who has a good mind and is a convinced follower. He asked for and received permission to publish the Worcester lectures in Russian in his journal.

---

[1] Karl Abraham 'On Neurotic Exogamy: A Contribution to the Similarities in the Psychic Life of Neurotics and of Primitive Man', *Clinical Papers and Essays on Psycho-Analysis*, London, 1955.

[2] Dr N. Ossipow, Russian psycho-analyst.

If your small group should be showing signs of despondency, you can comfort them with the news that the third edition of the *Interpretation of Dreams* is to appear this winter, that is to say, only a year after the second. The interval between the first and second editions was nine years. *Nonum prematur in annum.*

I have of course been able to do only little work. I am preparing a trifle on love life for the *Jahrbuch*.[1] We shall use the Nuremberg lecture in the first number of the *Zentralblatt*.

Jung is having great difficulties in Zürich at present. The *Jahrbuch* is delayed through Deuticke's fault, the organisation is moving very slowly. There are such times, but the hold-up is only apparent.

Is your domestic news limited to your moving house?

With my best wishes to you and your family,

Cordially yours,
Freud

My greetings to the members of your group.

*

Berlin,
6.6.10

Dear Professor,

One anxiously approaches every new work[2] of yours wondering whether it will be a further advance on your earlier ones. This suspense has now been resolved. The analysis is so delicate and so perfect in form that I do not know anything quite like it.

I can best express my thanks for the book by getting on quickly with my Segantini. But the material overwhelms me by its diversity and I am only making slow progress.

With sincere thanks and regards,

Yours,
Abraham

---

[1] Presumably *A Special Type of Choice of Object made by Men*, Standard Ed., Vol. XI.

[2] See page 87, footnote 1.

Berggasse 19,
Vienna IX,
3.7.10

Dear Dr Abraham,

Many thanks for the good news from your group, which is small but perhaps particularly distinguished by reason of its homogeneity and unity. In Zürich there really are difficulties, with Bleuler at the centre of them. They do not want to join the society, and attend its meetings only as guests. I cannot imagine how this will work out at the next congress. Of course I am not fully informed about these things. I hear from Jung that Binswanger, who is now the leader, is sympathising with the dissidents.

I have received the first review of the Leonardo, Havelock Ellis[1] in the *Journal of Mental Science*, he is friendly as always. It pleases all our friends and I hope will disgust all outsiders.

In the year that is now turning towards its end America was the chief thing. Let us now seek some rest and refreshment against the troubles of the next.

With my best wishes for your wife and cordial greetings,

Freud

Noordwijk,[2]
22.8.10

Dear Friend,

I must take your latest piece of work as an opportunity to congratulate you on all your contributions to the cause of psycho-analysis. I do not know of anything to place beside them for clarity, solidity and power of carrying conviction. I am convinced that that is the impact on all readers on our side. The others, with Ziehen at their head, will have to see how they deal with them.

My stay here, where I have not been able to work at all, is nearing its end. Dr Jones, who was my guest for two and a half days, shook me out of my lethargy a little. I heard from him,

[1] Havelock Ellis, 1859–1939, British sexologist.
[2] Dutch seaside resort.

and by letter from Putnam, that the American group is coming into existence. Ferenczi, with whom I shall be travelling during September, arrives here on the 27th. We want to see a few towns in Belgium, and then travel by way of Basle and Rome to Sicily. We shall do plenty of psycho-analytic work at the same time. I am greatly looking forward to it, because I am already taking idleness badly. Please send me the expected domestic news by way of my wife, who is staying in Holland until about September 15th. On October 1st I go back to work, to which one becomes reconciled after a long break.

On the whole, I think, our cause is going very well, and is no longer restricted to my four eyes only.[1] Advances will now be more difficult, the surface has been creamed, the final results are perhaps not yet plainly visible, and defence is required not only against enemies but also against rash fellow-workers. But perhaps it is merely I who feel the necessity to slacken my pace while the younger generation is vigorously pressing forward.

With greetings to you and your family,

Cordially yours,
Freud

Noordwijk,
30.8.10

Dear Friend,

I am still in time myself to send you my hearty congratulations on the birth of a son and the completion of your fatherhood,[2] and my best wishes for the young mother's rapid recovery. I am off early tomorrow to Paris to have a look at the Leonardo,[3] and then on to Italy.

Yours very sincerely,
Freud

---

[1] A play on the then current German saying that a secret should be restricted 'to four eyes only'. (Originally from the Hebrew.)

[2] Freud means that Abraham now had both a son and a daughter.

[3] Leonardo's *St Anne with Two Others* in the Louvre.

Rankestrasse 24,
Berlin W.,
18.10.10

Dear Professor,

I have left your kind congratulations on the birth of our son and the various postcards from your journey unanswered till now. It has been a somewhat unsettled time for us. Now we are established in the new flat and I can think of other things apart from the worries of moving in. There has unfortunately been a break of several weeks in my writing. Segantini will therefore be rather late–I hope not very late.

The two Congresses are fortunately over, one as unproductive as the other, the only difference being that the neurological one was rather more vicious. Oppenheim's review on anxiety did not contain one word that could not be found in any popular article. It was in fact merely the frame for a long-repressed, affective outburst. Oppenheim went so far as to call for a boycott of those sanatoria which make use of psycho-analysis. Hoche,[1] who followed, was simply boring. The discussion mainly consisted of a number of directors of sanatoria getting up and solemnly declaring that they did not practise psycho-analysis. At their head, Mr Friedlaender, your special friend! Only Raimann from Vienna stood out, proposing that, since Freud was evading a discussion, the enemy should be sought out in his own camp (*sic!*) and every failure of psycho-analytic treatment should be publicised. Boycott and denunciation. I find the unpleasant signs are mounting up in a most gratifying way. We, the heretics in attendance (Koerber, Warda and myself), remained silent. I need hardly mention that the after-dinner speeches at the banquet had, on the whole, just one target.

Now I must tell you about Bleuler who spent hours with me in order to abreact. You are familiar enough with his complexes. He does, of course, make various excuses to justify his staying away from the Society but, even with a lot of help, he is unable to get to the real underlying reasons. All the same,

---

[1] Alfred Hoche, 1865–1943, Professor of Psychiatry at Freiburg.

I have a number of things to say in his favour and should like to ask you, dear Professor, whether it would not be appropriate to meet him half-way, in order to make up for certain mistakes and to help our cause. I have discussed many psycho-analytic topics with Bleuler and I must say that he shows a keen interest in them. During the Congress he had many discussions with Kraepelin,[1] Aschaffenburg[2] and others, and they all considered him, as I personally heard, a really convinced partisan. I believe his service to our cause in this respect more than outweighs the occasional harm he may have done to it by being too reserved. And, finally, the main point: both before and at the time of the formation of the Zürich Society, Bleuler was obviously severely snubbed. You know that I have always been very critical of him. But if one makes it a principle in psychoanalysis not to challenge complexes, why should one behave differently towards Bleuler? He would welcome a *rapprochement*. He is at odds with himself and suffers from it. Is there no way to better understanding?

And now a happy sign. I think it was Aschaffenburg who told me that on a journey through America the first question asked by all the physicians was: 'What do you think about Freud?'

I find the first part of the second *Jahrbuch* excellent. Incidentally, more and more topics are accumulating which I should like to discuss with you. One ought to be able to go beyond 'The Antithetical Meaning of Primal Words'.[3] In particular, the question of bisexuality in language would have to be investigated.

But I don't want to write any more about theoretical matters today. With kind regards from house to house,

Yours,
Karl Abraham

---

[1] Emil Kraepelin, 1856–1926, Professor of Psychiatry and Neurology at Heidelberg and later at Munich.

[2] Gustav Aschaffenburg, 1866–1944, Professor of Neurology and Psychiatry at Heidelberg, later in Cologne, and then in U.S.A.

[3] Sigmund Freud, *The Antithetical Meaning of Primal Words*, Standard Ed., Vol. XI.

Berggasse 19,
Vienna IX,
24.10.10

Dear Friend,

You have made up for the long interval by an unusually substantial letter. All good wishes for the new home. How is your son thriving?

I am sorry for Oppenheim, who is a good but inept man. I wonder why he has to select the subject of anxiety to establish his position in the eyes of a later generation. Surely there are many other points on which psycho-analysis is assailable.

Now to Bleuler. I had decided to get in touch with him ('to make nerve contact with him'[1]) even before your letter, and since then I have been in continuous correspondence with him, the individual items running to from eight to ten pages.

Things are as you say. His arguments are vague and intangible, everything is full of alleged imponderables, and yet he seems unshakable. I have agreed to go to Zürich over Christmas if he will give me a chance to compose matters. I have of course no intention of sacrificing the society. Its foundation was too well justified. Incidentally, it was he, Bleuler, who first expressed the wish for a personal discussion.

The *Zentralblatt*[2] arrived here yesterday. I hope it will be a success, though the editors may not yet have discovered all the tricks of the trade. There is already an abundance of material for the next few numbers, so we are forced to make contributors wait.

I am in the thick of work, and have penetrated somewhat more deeply into paranoia along the path that you trod.

I shall keep you informed about the progress of the Bleuler affair as we go along. He has asked me to read his *Apologie* in

---

[1] A quotation from Daniel Paul Schreber's *Denkwürdigkeiten eines Nervenkranken*, Leipzig, 1903.

[2] The *Zentralblatt für Psychoanalyse*, edited by Alfred Adler and Wilhelm Stekel.

proof so that I might suggest changes that suited me, but I am naturally declining.

With cordial greetings to your new home and full house,

Yours,
Freud

*

Berlin,
14.12.10

Dear Professor,

Eitingon brought me your greetings today. He did not need to remind me that I owed you a letter. I postponed writing to you because I wanted to send you a letter together with the Segantini. This latter, however, is very resistant to analysis—hence the delay. Since I cannot, after all, send you the manuscript before Christmas, I am at any rate sending you a sign of life. The subject is really unusually difficult but I believe I have by now solved all that is accessible to solution, and I have only the last two chapters to write.

I hear that you will be meeting Bleuler quite soon and I am calmly awaiting the result. A pity your journey does not take you through Berlin. A great number of questions have accumulated that I should like to discuss with you.

As regards professional matters, I only want to tell you today that I have got quite a long way in the analysis of two cases of so-called cyclothymia which, with one other investigated previously, provide very good insight into the character of this illness. Unfortunately, I have only seen all three patients in their depressive phases and know of the exalted phases merely from their subsequent descriptions. All the same, I believe I have come near to the understanding of the manic flight of ideas.

With kind regards from house to house.

Yours,
Abraham

Dear Friend,

I am delighted to have heard from you again, particularly such good and promising news. Among the latter I include your Segantini,[1] which I should very much like to read over the holiday. But do not rush yourself over it. I am hardly having a rest; except for the two days of Christmas every day will be the same, and only Sunday a real holiday. In any case I should not be able to send it to the printer immediately, because he already has the German translation of Jones's study of Hamlet,[2] and after that I have accepted a legal paper (the first) by a talented young Züricher named Storfer.[3] But your Segantini will of course follow as quickly as possible after that.

A meeting with Bleuler has been arranged in Munich, at any rate so far as I am concerned; his reply has not yet reached me. He is a strange customer. I am waiting to read his apology this week in the *Jahrbuch*.

Our *Zentralblatt* would gladly publish a splendid contribution from you.

A paper of my own that I have just finished deals with Schreber's book and uses him as a point of departure to try and solve the riddle of paranoia. As you can imagine, I followed the path shown by your paper on the psycho-sexual differences between hysteria and dementia praecox. When I worked out these ideas at Palermo I particularly liked the proposition that megalomania was the sexual over-estimation of the ego. In Vienna I found that you had already very trenchantly said the same thing. I have of course had to plagiarise you very extensively in this paper.

I also think that I am able to clear up the difference between dementia praecox and true paranoia.

[1] Karl Abraham, 'Giovanni Segantini, a Psycho-Analytical Study', *Clinical Papers and Essays on Psycho-Analysis*, London, 1955.

[2] Ernest Jones, 'A Psycho-Analytical Study of Hamlet,' *Essays in Applied Psycho-Analysis*, London, 1923.

[3] Albert Josef Storfer, *Zur Sonderstellung des Vatermordes, eine rechtgeschichtliche und volkspsychologische Studie*, Vienna, 1911. Storfer was the first director of Freud's publishing house, the Internationaler Psychoanalytischer Verlag.

I should be delighted to discuss all these things with you again, but there is no respite from the necessity of earning money. In America things are going very well. Brill has now translated the 'Sexual Theory' and Putnam provided an excellent introduction. That old gentleman is a magnificent acquisition. Your wife and progeny are very well, I hope?

Cordial greetings,

Yours,
Freud

*

Berggasse 19,
Vienna IX,
20.1.11

Dear Friend,

Your Segantini is very welcome. Its position is as follows: The translation of Jones's 'Hamlet' is to appear very soon, followed two months later by a paper on parricide by a Zürich lawyer, and then comes Segantini's turn. I cannot expect Deuticke to accept more than five or six volumes a year.

Dr Bjerre[1] was in Vienna for a week, and at first made things difficult for me by his taciturnity and stiffness, but then I worked my way through to discovering his serious personality and good mind. I advised him to join the Berlin group, and I hope he will do so. Scandinavia is after all your natural hinterland.

Have I already told you that I spent Christmas in Munich with Bleuler and then with Jung? No, I certainly have not, evidently my brain is weakening. With Bleuler things went well, I was so tired that I was perfectly natural with him, and that worked. We parted as friends, and he has since joined the Zürich group. So the schism there has been healed. I discussed the congress with Jung; as a result I think it will be postponed until September, because of the Americans; and perhaps it really will take place at Lugano. The most important event of the moment, Bleuler's apology,[2] is already in your hands.

---

[1] Dr Paul Carl Bjerre, Swedish psychiatrist.

[2] E. Bleuler, 'Freudsche Theorien, Vortrag gehalten auf der 4. Jahresversammlung der Gesellschaft deutscher Nervenärzte', Zentralblatt, I, 1911.

The *Zentralblatt* would very much like to publish something by you. Juliusburger has done a very good thing with his quotations from Schopenhauer,[1] but my originality is obviously on the wane.

With cordial greetings,

Yours,
Freud

*

Berlin,
11.2.11

Dear Professor,

The Segantini manuscript goes off to you together with these lines. I send it to you with the request for your criticism which seems particularly necessary to me this time, since it is a piece of work with some personal complexes behind it. Besides, I should like to have your opinion about a question of lay-out. Would it be useful to include some of the main pictures, since they are not as generally known as some of the works of Boecklin[2] and other modern painters? I would suggest one of the pictures belonging to the mother-complex and one of the mystical ones, 'The Wicked Mothers'. If you are in favour of illustrations, would you discuss this with the publisher?

Bleuler's paper is gratifying on the whole. But the second half is much less good. I am glad that unity has been re-established in Zürich, at any rate outwardly. In the last few days I heard of certain matters which must have made it very difficult indeed for Bleuler to meet us half-way. But now for peace.

At the moment I find myself in a dilemma. The other day I mentioned to a colleague that I had, in a case of circular psychosis, been struck by the appearance of masculine and feminine periods. She spoke of this to Fliess, with whom she is friendly, and a few days later told me of Fliess's request that I should visit him. On the one hand, I should not like to be discourteous; on the other, I find it unpleasant to have to force

---

[1] O. Juliusburger, 'Weiteres von Schopenhauer', *Zentralblatt*, Vol. No. I, 1911.

[2] Arnold Boecklin, 1827–1904, Swiss painter.

myself to adopt as much reserve as would be necessary in this case.

To conclude, a little satire from Ziehen's clinic: a demonstration of a case of obsessional neurosis. The patient suffers from the obsessional idea that he must put his hands under women's skirts in the street. Ziehen to the audience: 'Gentlemen, we must carefully investigate whether we are dealing with a compulsive idea with sexual content. I shall ask the patient whether he also feels this impulse with older women.' The patient in answer to the question: 'Alas, Professor, even with my own mother and sister.' To which Ziehen says: 'You see, gentlemen, that there is nothing sexual at work here.' To his assistant: 'Note in the case history—patient suffers from a non-sexual but senseless obsessional idea.'

With kind regards from house to house,

Yours,
Abraham

*

Berggasse 19,
Vienna IX,
13.2.11

In haste

Dear Friend,

I am replying by return of post because of what you say about Fliess, and am taking the liberty of giving you my advice unasked, that is, telling you my attitude in the matter. I cannot see why you should not call on him. In the first place you will meet a remarkable, indeed fascinating man, and on the other hand you will perhaps have an opportunity of getting scientifically closer to the grain of truth that is surely contained in his theory of periodicity, a possibility that is denied to me for personal reasons. He will certainly try to side-track you from psycho-analysis (and, as he thinks, from me) and to guide you into his own channel. But I am sure you will not betray both of us to him. You know his complex, and are aware that I am the centre of it, and so you will be able to evade it. You know in advance that he is a hard man, which I took many years to discover. His talent is one of exquisite exactitude, for a long time he had no idea of psychology, at first he accepted everything literally from me, and he will by now of course have discovered the opposite of it all.

I am eagerly awaiting the things you are sending me. Could you not make up your mind to let me use the priceless story about Ziehen in the *Zentralblatt*? Ziehen has no claim to mercy. Please reply by postcard, but without obligation.

With cordial greetings to you all,

Yours,
Freud

Berggasse 19,
Vienna IX,
23.2.11

Dear Friend,

Your Segantini is very fine, it goes deep without causing offence, and it is evidently also discreet. I was very much struck by the similarities of character with Leonardo (anarchism because of absence of paternal authority, fixation on the mother, influence of the chance events of childhood, but different results because of the death of the mother, jealousy of the brother). On a second reading I shall of course get even greater pleasure from it. The manuscript is now with Deuticke; the two illustrations have been agreed to without any difficulty, and you will no doubt get in touch with him to arrange the matter. Your work is being printed at the same time as a legal article by a young Swiss named Storfer which will be ready before yours because it is shorter.

Things have been happening in the society here; there have been agitated discussions about Adler's theories. Adler[1] and Stekel have resigned, and I shall probably have to take over the presidency. Putnam's article will certainly have given you pleasure too. In due course I shall be sending you some reprints for distribution. Brill reports that he has founded a

[1] Dr Alfred Adler, 1870–1937, Vienna nerve specialist, founder of Individual Psychology.

branch society in New York with sixteen members of which he is the president. Our enemies are rather quiet at the moment.

With cordial greetings to you and your family,

Yours,
Freud

*

Berlin,
26.2.11

Dear Professor,

Thank you for the trouble you have taken with my *opus*; I am pleased that it could go straight into print. You remark that the work is guarded on some points. This is quite true, particularly concerning the question of the homosexual component. The material was too inadequate here. The similarities to Leonardo had struck me right from the beginning–perhaps I might insert a note about this in the proofs.

Now I must tell you about Fliess. I had a very friendly reception. He refrained from any attacks on Vienna; he has closed his mind to the new results of psycho-analysis since the conflict, but showed great interest in all I told him. I did *not* get the fascinating impression that you predicted. Fliess may have changed in the last few years but, nevertheless, I did get the impression of a penetrating and original thinker. In my opinion he lacks real greatness, and this is borne out in his scientific work. He starts off with some valuable ideas, but all further work is concentrated merely on proving their correctness and on their more exact formulation. He met me without prejudice, has meanwhile visited me in turn, and I must admit that he made no attempt to draw me over to his side in the way you feared. I have learned many interesting things from him, and am glad to have made his acquaintance–perhaps the most valuable I could make among colleagues in Berlin.

I am so sorry about the inner conflicts of your Society, the more so since, up till now, everything has been progressing most pleasantly here.

I am writing an article on blushing[1] for the *Zentralblatt*. I

[1] Probably never published.

shall let you have it soon together with some short communications.

With kind regards, also to your family,

Yours,
Abraham

*

Berggasse 19,
Vienna IX,
3.3.11

Dear Friend,

I have to inform you that I have taken over the presidency of the Vienna group again after Adler's and Stekel's resignation. Adler's behaviour was no longer reconcilable with our psycho-analytical interests, he denies the importance of the libido, and traces everything back to aggression. The damaging effects of his publications will not take long to make themselves felt.

Please allow me to ask you once more to make the little scene in Ziehen's clinic available for the *Zentralblatt.* It is too priceless.

You must not think Fliess so crude as to betray any intention in the first hour. Unfortunately he is the opposite, subtle or even cunning. You will certainly come across his complex. Do not forget that it was through him that both of us came to understand the secret of paranoia ('The Psycho-sexual Differences').[1] What you say about the nature of his work strikes me as remarkably true; I once loved him very much and therefore overlooked a great deal.

Stekel's dream book[2] appeared a few days ago. There will be a lot to be learned from it, a lot that will be missing, and a good deal to criticise.

Let me draw your especial attention to the last number of the *Journal of Abnormal Psychology.* Jones is correct and understanding.

Cordially yours,
Freud

[1] See footnote 2, p. 83.
[2] W. Stekel, *Die Sprache des Traumes*, Wiesbaden, 1911.

Dear Professor,

Many thanks for your further remarks about Fliess whom I have not yet seen again, and also for the Putnam reprints. I hope to get the new publications you write about before long. I have already had part of the Segantini proofs. Deuticke is in touch with the Photographic Union in Munich about the paintings.

As regards the Ziehen affair, I wrote to Dr Maier[1] at the Burghölzli and received the enclosed letter from him. I must admit he is right. It was fortunate that I wrote to him first, for publication would surely have upset Zürich–that is to say, the Burghölzli. After all, the rift has only just been mended. We shall just have to pass the story on by word of mouth.

I cannot really regret Adler's resignation. In spite of one's respect for his good qualities, he was certainly not the right man to be at the head of your group. His more recent papers are not at all to my liking. It is true that I would not trust myself to give a more definitive judgement because I cannot detach myself from an antipathy to Adler's style and exposition. I am therefore in danger of rejecting certain ideas rather than making the effort of adapting myself to his style. I do not think, however, that I do him an injustice if I find the 'aggressive drive' too one-sided. The giving up of the concept of libido, the neglect of all we have learned about erotogenic zones, auto-erotism, etc., appear to me as a retrograde step. The pleasure principle is entirely lost. On top of that, he relapses into superficial psychology, such as 'over-sensitivity', etc. The one-sidedness of his interpretation is very evident wherever he gives an example. The fundamental fact of over-determination is completely neglected as, for instance, in the remark in his Nuremberg paper in which he disposes of erythrophobia. The 'masculine protest' seems to me to be a valid point of view in certain cases. I do not, however, find anything basically new in it. I would say that it is an idea already contained in your *Three*

---

[1] Dr Hans Maier, later Professor of Psychiatry in Zürich and Medical Director of the Burghölzli.

Essays (about the masculinity of the libido), exaggeratedly stressed and pushed to the extreme. The 'masculine protest' must have its roots in his unconscious. In spite of all these objections, one always finds something valuable so that one tends to regret it is all so sketchy, fragmentary and based on insufficient evidence.

With kind regards to you and your family, also from my wife,

Yours,
Abraham

*

Berggasse 19,
Vienna IX,
14.3.11

Dear Friend,

Your opinion of Adler coincides completely with mine, and particularly with what I thought of him before the discussions. Since then I have grown more severe. A great deal of confusion is concealed behind his abstractions; he dissimulates a much more far-reaching opposition and shows some fine paranoid traits.

I am glad to hear that your practice is doing so well, your success at your difficult post deserves all respect and reward. I have had a less busy week and am therefore feeling very refreshed.

With cordial greetings,

Yours,
Freud

*

Berlin,
14.5.11

Dear Professor,

You congratulated me four weeks ago on Segantini's birth, but I did not receive the reprints until a few days ago; you will meanwhile have received one. Very many thanks for your proofs. Unfortunately, I have not yet found the time to read the two papers at leisure, but even a cursory reading has given me particular pleasure. The postulation of the two principles[1] is unusually illuminating and helpful; it seems indispensable to me for the understanding of the development of the libido. I should like to go into it in greater detail when I have read the paper once again.

You have succeeded wonderfully well in the Schreber analysis[2] and in further developing the theory of paranoia. There is a great deal in this paper that I should like to discuss with you in more detail. Could you possibly reserve some time for me in the autumn just before or after the Congress? So much has accumulated that is difficult to discuss in letters. I must thank you for the incidental pleasure I have gained from several of your comments!

If your time permits, I should like to ask you to comment briefly on a passage in the *Three Essays*[3]–on the last paragraph of the second essay ('The same pathways . . .'). I was questioned about it a short while ago, but was unable to give a satisfactory reply.

With kind regards from house to house,

Yours,
Karl Abraham

Berggasse 19,
Vienna IX,
18.5.11

Dear Friend,

It is true that I received the first copy of your Segantini weeks ago. Opinions of your work in my immediate circle are extremely favourable, and I hope even our opponents will speak of it with respect.

I shall be very glad indeed to meet you for an undisturbed private talk before or after the congress, and very much look

---

[1] Sigmund Freud, *Formulations on the Two Principles of Mental Functioning*, Standard Ed., Vol. XII.

[2] Sigmund Freud, *Psycho-Analytic Notes on an Autobiographical Account of a Case of Paranoia (Dementia Paranoides)*, Standard Ed., Vol. XII.

[3] Sigmund Freud, *Three Essays on the Theory of Sexuality*, Standard Ed., Vol. VII, p. 206.

forward to the rare opportunity. It would make things much easier for me if you would choose the later of the two dates for Weimar; I could then spend the previous day with you and go to Zürich on the following day for the visit of inspection I have had in mind for a long time. For private family reasons[1] September 16th is a very inconvenient, practically impossible, date, though I am loth to arrange the date of the congress according to my personal requirements.

The passage in the *Sexual Theory* had to be delivered oracularly, because no clear idea lay behind it, only a hypothesis. There are unknown paths by which sexual processes exercise an influence on the digestive system, blood formation, etc. The disturbing influences of sexuality travel by them, and thus formative and other usable influences probably normally travel by them too. Thus I can really give you only a paraphrase of a dawning suspicion.

With cordial greetings and many good wishes to your wife and children,

Yours very sincerely,
Freud

*

Berlin,
28.8.11

Dear Professor,

Many thanks for your lines from Klobenstein.[2]

I have submitted the title of a paper—on the Psycho-Sexual Basis of Manic and Depressive States[3]—and I believe I shall be able to present some ideas that are new, or at any rate not yet published. My Segantini has caused quite a stir. Servaes[4] wrote to me unfavourably about it, and advised me at the same time of an article which has now appeared in the *Frankfurter Zeitung,*

---

[1] Freud's silver wedding day was celebrated on 14.9.11.

[2] The letter referred to here is missing.

[3] Karl Abraham: 'Notes on the Psycho-Analytical Treatment of Manic Depressive Insanity and Allied Conditions', *Selected Papers on Psycho-Analysis*, London, 1927.

[4] Franz Servaes, German writer and biographer of Segantini.

of which he promised me a reprint. The article appeared, but not the reprint. In another paper a local colleague expressed violent indignation and called on all the neurological saints. And a poem '*Wissenschaft und Stumpfsinn* [Science and Stupidity] appeared in the *Jugend*.[1]

Otherwise, the summer's peace has only been interrupted by seven new papers by Jones. I will not disturb yours any further. Your kind regards, and those of Dr Ferenczi are most sincerely reciprocated by my wife and myself,

Yours,
Karl Abraham

*

Berlin,
29.10.11

Dear Professor,

I have not written to you since Weimar.[2] You will see from the enclosures that there has since been some conflict within our Society. Hirschfeld sent in his resignation and has stuck to his decision in spite of all I said. In accordance with his wishes, I am sending you his letter. There are resistances in him which link up with an external cause—Jung's behaviour towards him —but this is by no means the real basis. At a lengthy members' meeting, during which Weimar was discussed, he displayed an ignorance about psycho-analysis which was truly appalling; as it has turned out it was not interest in analysis that made him join us. It was most probably only the emphasis on sexuality that made analysis attractive to him, especially at a time when his own investigations into sexuality met with hostility. Hirschfeld's defection is really no loss to us and for the work of our group it is rather a gain. On the other hand, I regret his decision for personal reasons. The Congress also aroused much discontent in Koerber and Juliusburger, but this has virtually died down by now. In order to prevent our meetings this winter from becoming too superficial, I have suggested that we should work through the *Three Essays* in the form of reports and discussions, and this suggestion has been accepted.

[1] Munich weekly.   [2] Third Psycho-Analytic Congress.

I recall the days in Weimar with great pleasure. I have followed up the private discussion we had on the last day and found out a number of interesting facts about totem animals. I shall report to you when my observations are more complete. I have sent two small communications to Stekel for the *Zentralblatt*. Now I am occupied with writing up my Weimar paper, and this will soon follow. After that, a short essay[1] on a strange ceremonial is to come: it deals with women who every evening before going to bed dress up as brides prepared for death as the phantasied marital partner. I had the opportunity of analysing such a case in detail, and am now treating a similar one.

I have undertaken one issue of a new publication called *Beitraege zur Forensischen Medizin*. It is to be entitled 'The Child's Instinctual Life and its Relation to Delinquency'. Some other time I'll write about the various plans that were furthered by the hours I spent with you.

I was gratified to hear that our third journal[2] will not have the title originally intended. I am very much looking forward to its appearance.

Bleuler's *Dementia Praecox*,[3] which I recently read, is as contradictory as the man himself. In many ways the book is excellent; yet, at the same time, it contains half truths such as abounded in his Weimar paper.

With kindest regards,
                                                              Yours,
                                                              Abraham

                                                    Berggasse, 19,
                                                    Vienna IX,
                                                    2.11.11

Dear Friend,

I too think back with pleasure to the days at Weimar and face a relatively unsatisfactory present. It is a great pity that we have no psycho-analytic institution here in which I could place

[1] Karl Abraham, 'A Complicated Ceremonial Found in Neurotic Women', *Selected Papers on Psycho-Analysis*, London, 1927.

[2] *Imago, Zeitschrift für die Anwendung der Psychoanalyse auf die Geisteswissenschaften.*

[3] *'Dementia Praecox'* by Professor E. Bleuler, published by Franz Deuticke, 1911.

all my four assistants and train new ones. But Vienna is not soil in which anything can be done.

What gave me most pleasure in your letter was the number of the projects you have in mind the source of which you trace back directly to Weimar. I too am using a period of relative leisure to go more deeply into the matter I mentioned to you. I already anticipate the chief conclusions, but reading and collecting evidence is very tedious, and the end is nowhere in sight. Anything in the nature of pleasure gain can only arise at the stage of final formulation, and God alone knows when I shall arrive at that.

To maintain the parallelism still further, let me tell you that I have completed the purge of the society and sent Adler's seven followers packing after him. The decrease in numbers is immaterial, and work will be much easier but, with the single exception of Rank, I have no-one here in whom I can take complete pleasure. Perhaps Sachs,[1] the second editor of the still unborn journal, will fill the bill. My spirits have not been improved by the fact that its publication has been rejected in three (really four) quarters. Perhaps our member Heller[2] will rise to the occasion.

Yours most sincerely,
Freud

Berggasse 19,
Vienna IX,
2.1.12

Dear Friend,

Having filled the holidays with the writing of two papers (which I do not like) and all sorts of private discontents, I at last come round to sending my best wishes for the prosperity of your wife, your children and yourself that you so well deserve and the fulfilment of which will give me so much pleasure. Shared interests and personal liking have brought us so close that we have no need to doubt the genuineness of our good wishes for each other.

[1] Hanns Sachs, 1881–1947, Dr. jur., psycho-analyst in Vienna, Zürich, Berlin and at Harvard University.

[2] Hugo Heller, Vienna bookseller and publisher.

I know how difficult your position is in Berlin and always admire your unruffled calm and confidence. The record of our undertaking is perhaps not always pleasing, but that is probably true of most records; nevertheless it will make a fine chapter of history. The latest favourable signs, strangely enough, come from France. We have won a powerful ally in Morichau-Beauchant at Poitiers (see his article in the *Gazette des Hôpitaux*, 1911, p. 1,845[1]), and today I received a letter from a pupil of Régis[2] at Bordeaux written on his behalf apologising in the name of French psychiatry for its neglect of psycho-analysis and announcing his willingness to publish a long paper about it in *Encéphale*.

For myself I do not have any great expectations; gloomy times lie ahead, and recognition will come only for the next generation. But we have the incomparable satisfaction of having made the first discoveries. My work on the psycho-analysis of religion is going ahead only very slowly, so I should prefer to remove it from the programme altogether. I have to write something in the nature of a preliminary communication for the new journal *Imago*, something from the psycho-analysis of savage peoples. Reik's[3] work is too long for the *Sammlung*, and I have just heard from the author, who is a member of ours, that it is to appear in book form.

Farewell, and do not write too seldom to

Yours sincerely,
Freud

Berlin,
11.1.12

Dear Professor,

Only a few lines today to thank you sincerely for your kind wishes and encouraging words. The latter have helped me a lot.

I have just completed the preparatory work on my paper for the new journal. I know that its theme will interest you: it is

[1] R. Morichau-Beauchant, 'Le rapport affective dans la cure des psychoneuroses'.

[2] Dr Emanuel Régis, Professor of Psychiatry at Bordeaux.

[3] Dr Theodor Reik, psycho-analyst in Vienna, later Berlin, now in the United States.

about Amenhotep IV and the Aton cult.[1] The subject has a particular attraction for me – to analyse all the manifestations of repression and substitute-formation in a person who lived 3,300 years ago. The Oedipus complex, sublimation and reaction formations – all exactly as in a neurotic of the present day. I did the preparatory work in the Egyptian department of the Berlin Museum, and was reminded more than once of the first introduction to Egyptology that I enjoyed in Vienna in December 1907.

That is all for today. In accordance with your wishes, I did not want to keep you waiting too long for news. With kind regards to you and your family from my wife and myself,

Yours,
Abraham

Berggasse 19,
Vienna IX,
14.1.12

Dear Friend,

Just think of it, Amenhotep IV in the light of psychoanalysis. That is surely a great advance in orientation. Do you know that you are now included with Stekel and Sadger[2] among the *bêtes noires* of psycho-analysis against whom I have always been warned? That has been apparent since your Segantini, and what will it be like after Amenhotep? But you will not let it worry you. The reason why I am in such a good mood is that I have just finished a paper for *Imago* on the incest ban among savages.[3] What is so splendid is not that I think it good, but that it is finished.

The work to which I referred above is 'On the Psycho-Analytical Theories of Freud and Related Views', by Arthur Kronfeld, of Berlin, published as No. 3, Vol. II, *Papers on Psychological Paedagogics*. Its tone is quite decent, but it proves

[1] Karl Abraham, 'Amenhotep IV. Psycho-Analytical Contribution towards the Understanding of his Personality and of the Monotheistic Cult of Aton', *Clinical Papers and Essays on Psycho-Analysis*, London, 1955.

[2] Dr Isidor Sadger, Vienna psycho-analyst.

[3] Sigmund Freud, 'Some Points of Agreement between the Mental Lives of Savages and Neurotics', *Totem and Taboo*, Standard Ed., Vol. XIII.

philosophically and mathematically that all the things that give us such a headache simply do not exist, because it is impossible that they should exist. So that's it.

After a short pause I am going to have to write a short English paper on the *unconscious*[1] in psycho-analysis[2] which has been asked for by the Society for Psychical Research, or read Bleuler's manuscript[3] on autistic thinking, which I received today. Reading is even worse than writing.

With my cordial greetings to you and your wife,

Yours,
Freud

*

Berlin,
25.2.12

Dear Professor,
I wish to begin my long overdue letter with the pleasant news that I am up to my neck in psycho-analytic work. Since January the practice has been overwhelming, never less than ten hours a day. This has brought about the desired effect that I am no longer dependent on Oppenheim's support, particularly as at present referrals from him are scarcely worth mentioning. I remain very much in his debt but the present state of affairs, with its full independence of action, is far preferable. I had recently to refuse a few cases because I could not take on any more, and passed one on to Eitingon who occasionally accepts a patient. The lack of a fellow-worker is gradually making itself felt, and I do not know where to look for one. It is true that I can hardly expect my work to go on at this rate right through the year, but it would nevertheless be desirable to have someone else with me. I am also very pleased with the type of patients I am getting, almost all of them intelligent

[1] This word in English in the original.

[2] Sigmund Freud, 'A Note on the Unconscious in Psycho-Analysis,' Standard Ed., Vol. XII.

[3] E. Bleuler, 'Das Autistisch-undisciplinierte Denken in der Medizin und seine Überwindung', *Jahrbuch für Psychoanalytische Forschungen*, Vol. IV, 1912.

people with very individual forms of neurosis, so that the work is never monotonous.

I have very little time for writing just now. The Egyptian research for *Imago* progresses at a snail's pace. I always wonder how you manage to write so much in addition to your practice. Many thanks for the reprints.

A theoretical comment: one of my more long-standing patients recently went through a hysterical twilight state of several days' duration, during which he developed a persecution mania. I succeeded in understanding it, in part during the twilight state and in part after the patient had recovered and gained insight. It is rare to have such an opportunity of observing delusion formations *in statu nascendi*, and of analysing them after full insight has been reached. Here I was able to demonstrate with remarkable clarity everything that you deduced in the Schreber case. I want to publish the whole thing when I find time.

Our small Berlin group leads an uneventful existence. At our last meeting we enjoyed a report from Dr Horney[1] about sexual instruction in early childhood. For once, the paper showed a real understanding of the material, unfortunately something rather infrequent in the papers of our circle.

Just one request. Would you, dear Professor, write me a few words some time on the prognosis in cases of impotence in neurotics with a strong tendency towards fetishism? These cases seem particularly unfavourable to me.

With kind regards from house to house,

Yours,
Abraham

*

Berlin,
28.4.12

Dear Professor,

There has not been anything particular to report lately, and so I have not taken up your time with correspondence. Your letter, received some days ago, gives me an excuse for writing.

[1] Dr Karen Horney, psycho-analyst in Berlin, later in New York.

I am quite glad that the Congress is not to take place until next year, but spring would suit me far better than autumn. There is not much news from our group but public interest in psycho-analysis is on the increase in Berlin. In any case, you will be interested to hear what I was told happened after the meeting of the Kant Society at Halle. There was an unofficial discussion on psycho-analysis, during which many people showed themselves to be well-informed and where the general feeling was favourable rather than not. Have you read the '*Die Intellectuellen*' by Grete Meisel-Hess? Stekel recently stated in the *Zentralblatt* that it was inconceivable that a woman would commit suicide as a consequence of undergoing a psycho-analysis. Since then I have seen both the authoress and the heroine – who was supposed to have committed suicide – sitting together quite happily, a fact that reassured me enormously.

One of the visitors to the Weimar Congress, Mrs Lou Andreas-Salomé,[1] has just spent some time in Berlin. I have come to know her very well and must admit that I have never before met with such deep and subtle understanding of analysis. She will visit Vienna this winter and would like to attend your meetings.

My *Dreams and Myths* was recently published in a Russian translation, and will shortly be published in English in the *Journal of Nervous and Mental Diseases in America*.[2]

I hope you and your family are well, and I send kindest regards, also from my wife,

Yours,
Abraham

[1] Lou Andreas-Salomé, 1861–1937, friend of Freud, Nietzche, and Rainer Maria Rilke, who became a psycho-analyst and practised in Goettingen. Author of *In der Schule hei Freud*, published 1958.
[2] *Nervous and Mental Disease Monograph Series*, No. 15, New York, 1913.

Dear Friend,

Many thanks for your good news. I was very pleased to hear about the English and Russian translations. Your domestic news was less pleasing, but fortunately does not go beyond what one is prepared for.

Imago is eagerly awaiting your Amenhotep. Will you not want to include a portrait of the interesting king? On the strength of your recommendation Frau L. A.-Salomé will be very welcome; she is said to have sent Jung a paper[1] for the *Jahrbuch* which has been promised me for a reading too.

Imago has on the whole had a good reception; only in Vienna is the interest slight. There are now some innovations in the *Zentralblatt*: A 'debating society' and a 'children's corner' are to be organised, the former for the exchange of ideas and for internal criticism. Your 'bride-of-death' ceremony is priceless and in many respects overwhelming. You are right to identify the father with death, for the father is dead and death himself—according to Kleinpaul[2]—is only a dead man. The dead are universally thought of as coming for their own.

At the society yesterday we had discussions on the last two numbers of the *Zentralblatt,* and we are to make our psycho-analytical literature the subject of regular discussions. Your paper on melancholia[3] was very intelligently criticised by Federn,[4] and all sorts of things dawned on me which may lead further. We are still only at the threshold.

At home things are going well, but I am over-worked, that is to say, dim-witted, and the work on taboo is going very badly. The 'totem' will have to wait for a long time.

With cordial greetings and wishes for the recovery of your wife and children,

Yours sincerely,
Freud

[1] Lou Andreas-Salomé, 'Vom frühen Gottesdienst', *Imago*, 1913.
[2] R. Kleinpaul, 1875–1918, German historian of ideas.
[3] See footnote 3, p. 107.
[4] Dr Paul Federn, psycho-analyst in Vienna, later in the United States.

Dear Professor,

Following your suggestion, I shall add two photographs to the 'Amenhotep' manuscript, which is now with Rank, one of the king with his consort, and the other of his mother. I hope Heller will have no difficulty in obtaining permission to reproduce the two pictures from Breasted's *History of Egypt*.

On the question of melancholia, to which you referred in your letter, I can report that I have for some time past had a particularly instructive case of cyclothymia under observation. In this patient everything is unusually close to consciousness and she is particularly aware of her own inability to love. Physically as well as psychologically she presents an 'intermediate' stage, very masculine in physical appearance, manner, voice, movements, etc., as well as in her thinking and feeling. The mixture of male and female in her is such that she is too masculine to love men, and also unable to achieve full object-relationships with women. Thus she never reaches a satisfactory relationship with either a man or a woman. As a reaction to this she has a vivid phantasy life serving substitute gratification (prostitution phantasies) as well as masturbation, both of which are however not sufficiently satisfying. Hence, frequent bouts of depression alternating with outright manic exaltation. I am not making much progress with this case. The patient lacks the type of transference usually met with in neurotics.

The patient I described in some detail in my paper[1] is at present giving me more trouble. He did quite well for approximately four months, then went through a depression lasting some time which, though not as severe as some of his earlier ones, continued for about six or seven weeks. I have the impression that I have not got to the bottom of this case. You hint that you have some new ideas about this. I should be very grateful for any suggestions, as I would like to make a fresh effort with the poor man.

I have recently analysed in two patients a disturbance which is an exact counterpart of Schreber's ability to stare into the

[1] See p. 107, footnote 3.

sun without flinching. The photophobia proved to be directly connected with the father. One of the cases, a dementia praecox, forces one to assume that photophobia is based on an unconscious phantasy of grandeur. If the patient firmly focuses both eyes under closed lids, he has a visual hallucination of two eyes which suddenly merge into one sun. Thus he himself is a sun, just as good as his father. I suspect that Schreber's idea has the secondary meaning that he himself, that is, his eye, is a sun more radiant than the paternal sun. Thus the latter cannot possibly blind him. Of course, I see this merely as a possible complement to your own explanation.

I spoke briefly the other day in a discussion in the *Berliner Gesellschaft für Psychiatrie und Nervenkrankheiten,* less for the sake of propaganda than in order to show up some of the speaker's (Kohnstamm's) psychological absurdities.

With kind regards from house to house,

Yours,
Abraham

*

Berggasse 19,
Vienna IX,
3.6.12

Dear Friend,

I have read your Egyptian study with the pleasure that I always derive both from your way of writing and way of thinking, and should like to make only two criticisms or suggestions for alteration. In the first place you express the view that when the mother is particularly important the conflict with the father takes milder forms. I have no evidence of this, and must assume that you have had special experiences in regard to it. As the matter is not clear to me, may I ask you to have another look at this passage? Secondly, I have doubts about representing the king so distinctly as a neurotic, which is in sharp contrast with his exceptional energy and achievements, as we associate neuroticism, a term which has become scientifically inexact, with the idea of inhibition. We all have these complexes, and we must guard against calling everyone neurotic. If we have

118

warded them off, we should be spared the name. Perhaps nothing of value will have been sacrificed if you call your work a character study and leave the neurotic as an object of comparison in the background. I cannot judge from my knowledge of the literature how positive is the evidence of real neurotic symptoms in Amenhotep IV. If you have such evidence, you should quote it in full.

In cyclothymic cases you should go on quietly digging; you will see more another time. The difficulty is not in finding the material but in linking up and classifying it correctly. It is true that I also have the impression from your extremely valuable work that the formula is not assured and the elements not yet convincingly linked. If I knew more, I should not withhold it from you, but you will learn more from the cases themselves.

I am now resting from more serious work. The *Taboo*[1] is to appear in the next number of *Imago*. You will have seen the last technical paper[2] in the *Zentralblatt*. The society has adjourned for the summer. Jones is expected here in the middle of June.

With cordial greetings to you and to wife and children,

Yours,

Freud

*

Berlin,
9.6.12

Dear Professor,

I had already heard from Rank about your two objections to my paper, and immediately asked him to return my manuscript. I shall revise it as soon as I get it back. I shall only compare Ikhnaton with the neurotic patient, as I did with Segantini. I shall investigate the other question further with the help of my case historics. Part of my statement is correct, but I used too general a formulation and this makes it untenable. I hope something useful will emerge in the end.

Imago certainly comes at the right moment. Interest in Germany is rapidly increasing, except in medical circles.

[1] See footnote 13, p. 112. The reference here is to Part II.
[2] Sigmund Freud, *The Dynamics of Transference*, Standard Ed., Vol. XII.

Many thanks for the reprint. I enjoyed every word of the paper. I am longing for the holidays. Ten hours' analysis is ample in this heat. What a pity that our holiday destinations are so far apart. I hope during that time to do some preparatory work on a philological subject.

For today, kind regards to you and your family, also from my wife,

Yours,
Abraham

Berggasse 19,
Vienna IX,
3.7.12

Dear Friend,

It is excellent that you should so soon have reached the limits in your practice, but you must now turn over a new leaf and defend yourself against the blessing. The first step to be taken, if the flow continues, must be to increase your fees, and you must find time to work and rest. The answer to your question how I manage to write in addition to coping with my practice is that I have to recuperate from psycho-analysis by working, otherwise I should not be able to stand it.

Your admirable contributions to the *Zentralblatt* please me very much for the reader's sake, and I look forward with special personal eagerness to the recently announced contribution on paranoia. It would be nice if we were right about it, and theoretically important. But *Imago*, which is my youngest and favourite child, must not be neglected, if only for the sake of the editors.[1] I am working with my last, or penultimate, ounce of strength on my article on taboo, which is to continue the theme of the ban on incest. Incidentally I hope to have contributed to the analytic understanding of guilt-feelings and of conscience, but this will appear only later.

I have no special experience of impotent fetishists. Your prognosis is probably correct, but each case behaves differently. I have had little success with masochists.

[1] Otto Rank (see footnote 3, p. 29) and Dr. Hanns Sachs (see footnote 1, p. 110.

Kronfeld's paper[1] is creating a lot of feeling against us. I can find nothing in it but a notably decent tone, but its 'logic' is not worthy of the name.

Could not Eitingon take patients off your hands to a greater extent? He has sent me a case on which he began incredibly correctly.

With cordial greetings to you and your family,

Yours sincerely,

Freud

*

Kurhaus Stoos, ob Brunnen,
9.8.12

Dear Professor,

Since writing my last postcard I have been ill with bronchitis for some time, which has indeed improved my holiday! In practice, however, it made little difference as it has been raining so hard for the past week that it was impossible to go out of doors. I hope you are having a pleasanter time and that the cure has had the expected results.

I have heard quite a lot about Zürich in the last few weeks. Details had better be left for discussion when we meet. My own prognosis is not too unfavourable. Jung's resistances are reminiscent of Adler's in their motivation but, since we are dealing with a person without a paraphrenic tendency, it may all change again, just as it did four years ago. Unfortunately, he wavers between the rejecting attitude of recent times and an uncompromising recklessness. I believe the latter has cost us more than the former, and I do not only have Bleuler in mind. I am glad that we are not having a Congress just now; I think everything will have been smoothed out by next year.

The theoretical points I hinted at recently are very varied in character and are therefore hardly suitable for a holiday letter. I only wish to mention briefly one question that has occupied me for some time. It concerns a case of hay-fever which I recently treated successfully by psycho-analysis, and the theoretical conclusions to be drawn from it. The patient

[1] See p. 112.

was in treatment last spring for a neurosis. During the first month of analysis he also suffered from severe hay-fever and particularly from hay-asthma. I did not discharge him without first looking for the psycho-sexual roots of the hay-fever. I have recently heard from him that he has generally been much better this year and has also remained free from hay-fever.

With kind regards to you and your wife,

Yours,
Abraham

Karlsbad,
11.8.12

Dear Friend,

I am replying immediately in order not to miss you in this migratory period. As you say, our meeting will have to take place in Berlin on the way back, or somewhere on the way. What would be most delightful would be your joining us in London between September 10th and 18th or thereabouts.

I am glad your prognosis in the matter of Jung is good, I know you are not exactly an optimist about him. But it is not the same as four years ago. Then the vacillation took place behind my back; when I found out about it, it was over. This time I have felt obliged to react to the changed behaviour towards me and in so doing to lay down the armour of friendship and show him that he cannot at his pleasure assume privileges to which no-one is entitled. How he will take this I cannot foresee. So far he has expressed a firm determination not to stage an outward defection.

The last week of our stay is being spoiled by the appalling weather. We hope to be at the Hotel Latemar, Karersee,[1] on the 16th inst, from where you will hear from us.

With cordial greetings to you and your wife and thanks for your congratulations.

Yours sincerely,
Freud

---

[1] Lago di Carezza.

Berlin,
13.10.12

Dear Professor,

The last weeks have been a sorrowful time for us. A fortnight ago my father-in-law died from a stroke after being unconscious for nine days. Now that we have got back into calmer waters, I can at last reply to your news and greetings from Italy. I hope that you and your family have all come back refreshed from your holiday.

Owing to the upsets of the last few weeks, I have scarcely found the time to read the new papers in the *Jahrbuch*, etc., with the exception of your short paper,[1] which I have studied with pleasure and admiration.

I too should like to publish something on impotence before long. During this year I have treated two men with *potentia coeiundi* but who, over the course of many years, have never had an emission. Both have been cured by psycho-analysis. One, whose marriage was childless, is now looking forward to becoming a father. I cannot find anything about this symptom in the literature, but merely mention of delayed emission in contrast to premature ejaculation. I assume that you have also come across such cases and would ask you, if it is not too much trouble, to let me have a few words about them some time.

I very much regret that our meeting never took place. There is so much from the various scientific fields that I should have liked to talk over. I have been wondering whether I could make a short trip to Vienna during the winter. Could you, dear Professor, tell me now when I would disturb you least—just before Christmas or between Christmas and the New Year?

With kind regards from my wife and myself to you and your family,

Yours,
Abraham

---

[1] Sigmund Freud, *Contributions to the Psychology of Love: On the Universal Tendency to Debasement in the Sphere of Love*, Standard Ed., Vol. XI.

Berggasse 19,
Vienna IX,
21.10.12

Dear Friend,

I like your Amenhotep in its revised form very much better, it is an ornament of our *Imago*, which continues to count on you.

I have heard in quite a number of my cases of a failure to achieve ejaculation as a mental disturbance, but at the time of the analysis the disturbance was over and had given way to a common anaesthesia with excellent motor potency. I have not had cases like yours.

Now to what troubles me. I do not like to think that perhaps we get on so well only because we meet so rarely. (Ferenczi and I get on just as well, though we see each other frequently.) So I should most willingly agree to your suggestion that you should come to Vienna, were it not for my daughter's engagement,[1] which is already known to you, to the young man from Hamburg, which would limit me just at the time you have in mind. We are expecting him to visit us at Christmas, before the wedding which has been arranged for February. There is, however, a consolation, as in future I shall be going at least once a year to Hamburg to see the child, and that will provide an excellent opportunity to see you in Berlin.

I am now busily engaged with the continuation of 'Some Points of Agreement'[2] and with technical papers for the *Zentralblatt*. You will soon be receiving a reprint of the *Taboo*. We are kept busy with political worries, but I take them coolly. Jones, whose friend I now have under treatment, has become personally very attached recently. He is now in Italy.

With my cordial greetings to your whole family,

Yours sincerely,
Freud

---

[1] The engagement of Freud's second daughter Sophie (b. 1893) to Max Halberstadt, a photographer at Hamburg.

[2] See footnote 3, p. 112.

Dear Friend,

Just a brief note to inform you officially that I am no longer editor of the *Zentralblatt* and that Stekel is going his own way. (I am so delighted about it; you cannot realise how much I have suffered under the obligation to defend him against the whole world. He is an intolerable person.) The occasion for the split was not a scientific one, but presumption on his part against another member of the society whom he wished to exclude from the reviews in 'his paper', which I could not permit.

I am of course planning to start a new journal to take the place of the *Zentralblatt*, and ask you to withdraw your name from the latter and no longer to direct papers from your group to it. In the next few days a circular letter will ask you to take these steps and to co-operate with the new organ. I had in mind offering you the editorship of the latter, but was deflected only because of the happy circumstance that your practice already keeps you busy to the point of excess. I have therefore asked Ferenczi, but should very much like to hear your views on the matter.

Whether the editor is you or Ferenczi, at a time when psycho-analysis is threatened with a split, and discussion with followers comes on top of the struggle with the outside world, such a journal means a great deal to me, and it is a blessing to have got rid of such a doubtful character as Stekel.

I shall keep you informed of how things develop with the publisher, etc.

Meanwhile I remain, with cordial greetings,

Yours,
Freud

Dear Professor,

I am deeply distressed that you should once more have to suffer from lack of consideration from a person who owes you everything.

I had the following idea after receiving your letter today. If Ferenczi takes on the editing, I might be able to help in some other way. If he declines, then I am at your disposal. Should the proposal be finally put to me, I would find it most pleasant to collaborate with Ferenczi if that is technically feasible. If this turns out to be the case, my other work would not be a reason for declining the offer. I have, by the way, already talked to Eitingon who says he is ready to help in any way possible. At the moment I am not clear what is to happen to the *Zentralblatt,* or whether the new journal will be the official one. I shall probably learn that from the circular letter.

It is so difficult to discuss all this by letter. If you, dear Professor, should wish for a verbal discussion, I could manage it on a Sunday (for instance, on November 24th). The journey to Vienna does however take up a great deal of time and I cannot easily leave my practice for a period of several days. Perhaps we could meet half way, in Prague or Breslau. We could travel on Saturday afternoon, have the whole of Sunday and travel home during Sunday night.

That's all for today. I am in a hurry and shall therefore not go into your letter of October 21st, for which many thanks.

With kind regards,

Yours,
Abraham

Berggasse 19,
Vienna IX,
21.11.12

Dear Friend,

So I can expect to see you sooner than intended, on the 24th inst. in Munich. Meanwhile a bitter cup has passed you by. Ferenczi and Rank have undertaken the editorship of the new journal. Because of your very great kindness and willingness to undertake the task I owe you an explanation of the choice. I had begun negotiations with a Berlin publisher which seemed promising, and if they had come to anything I should have asked you to undertake it, with Eitingon's help. But the Berlin publisher let me down and, as I had to decide on Heller, the publisher of *Imago*, I could only choose the editor in the neighbourhood. I know that you will not take this amiss.

I have had a great deal of worry and trouble over the affair. All our inside and outside colleagues have come with us, only Jung (!) and Juliusburger, who does not seem to be informed and therefore does not wish to sever his connection with the *Zentralblatt*, have declined. Apart from that, one other Viennese has made certain reservations. But the blessing of having got rid of Stekel is worth some sacrifice.

I hope there will be time in Munich for an intimate exchange of views, and send my greetings to you and your whole family.

Cordially yours,
Freud

*

Berlin,
1.12.12

Dear Professor,

Now that a week has passed since our discussion in Munich, I hope that you too will have come to the conclusion that the end result was a favourable one. Being rid of Stekel has the advantage of narrowing the rift between Vienna and Zürich. If, as I hope, I come to see you in a few weeks, we can talk more of this than the short time at Munich permitted.

Now a request. While Ziehen held the Chair here, I could not carry out my long-standing plan of joining the Faculty. The present Professor, Bonhoeffer,[1] is a much pleasanter person, and I have a very good recommendation to him from Professor Liepmann. I now learn from your report that Kraus is becoming increasingly sympathetic to our work. If both Bonhoeffer

[1] Professor W. Bonhoeffer, 1868–1948, Professor of Psychiatry at Berlin University.

and Kraus supported me, my chances would not be too bad. (The anti-semitism of the Faculty does, of course, remain an obstacle.) My request is this: would you send a few words to Kraus[1] about me, so that if Bonhoeffer approaches him he will know what it is all about?

Although I had already buried this project, two considerations induced me to take it up once again: apart from the probable usefulness to my practice, there is the hope that I might be able to awaken interest in our cause among the students—something I have not managed to do so far among qualified doctors. I thank you, dear Professor, in anticipation of your kindness. I am saving up everything else to tell you personally.

With kindest regards to you and yours,

Yours,
Karl Abraham

*

Berggasse 19,
Vienna IX,
3.12.12

Dear Friend,

I shall very gladly give you the warmest recommendation to Kraus, and as soon as you wish. I only fear that nothing will come of it, because that would be too good. I do not know Kraus personally and, apart from the acceptance of two chapters for his book, I have had no relations with him whatsoever. But we shall try it, particularly if you promise that in the event of success you will greatly increase your fees.

I shall be delighted to see you here before Christmas. You must of course include a Sunday.

With cordial greetings,

Yours,
Freud

P.S. I received a very kind letter from Jung shortly after returning from Munich, but have not yet had any news about the outcome of his trip to Wiesbaden.

[1] Friedrich Kraus, Professor of Medicine at Berlin University.

128

Berggasse 19,
Vienna IX,
12.12.12

Dear Friend,

The letter to Kraus has long since reached its destination. But has it attained its object?

Come and see us when you can. I shall actually be able to give you much time only on Sunday, but then in plenty. Let me know when I can book a room for you at the Hotel Regina.

Tell your wife that we do not want you to get indigestion anywhere but with us. Otherwise all at last is quiet.

I look forward to seeing you again.

Cordially yours,
Freud

*

Berlin,
27.12.12

Dear Professor,

It is only today that I find time to send you a sign of life. The indisposition that began in Vienna worsened somewhat in the next few days. Now I am rather better and must no longer delay in sending you my thanks. It is difficult to mention everything and it is almost impossible to put into words my gratitude for the warm reception in your home and for all your personal interest. If a recent criticism made of you is justified–that you treat your followers like patients–then I have to reproach you with several grave technical errors. First, you spoil your patients and it is well known that one should not do so. Second, you have given presents to the patient, which might give him a completely wrong idea of treatment. And finally, before my departure from treatment, you secretly went to my hotel to pay the bill. 'If you had been a psycho-analyst', you would not have done such a thing since, at the end of the treatment, the patient should know as much about his own case as his physician. You, however, kept a secret from me. And you know after all how easily a feeling of guilt can lead to hostility. But since I was in general satisfied with the 'treatment', I shall not make any complaint, and can only thank you once more for all you did. Please give the enclosed lines to your wife.

There is not much else to say today. I shall if possible despatch 'The Grandparents'[1] within the next few days. After that, a short article[2] about a screen-memory is to follow.

With kind regards, also from my wife,

Yours,
Karl Abraham

*

Berggasse 19,
Vienna IX,
1.1.13

Dear Friend,

Thank you for your friendly lines. The hospitality we are able to provide in Vienna, and what I in particular am able to do in that respect, is so little.

Now accept my cordial good wishes for the New Year, which will certainly not be an easy one for us. The past year did some good for us on the very last day with a letter from Kraus, from which I gather that he asked you to call on him and is by no means disinclined to your cause. He also counts on Bonhoeffer's approval, and confirms that you have a good reputation even among our opponents. The letter was very decent, unusually so for someone who is soon to become a privy councillor. You will of course be keeping me informed about developments.

Cordially yours,
Freud

[1] Karl Abraham, 'Some Remarks on the Role of Grandparents in the Psychology of Neuroses', *Clinical Papers and Essays on Psycho-Analysis*, London, 1955.
[2] Karl Abraham, 'A Screen Memory Concerning a Childhood Event of Apparently Aetiological Significance'. *Clinical Papers and Essays on Psycho-Analysis*, London, 1955.

Berlin,
5.I.13

Dear Professor,

Many thanks for your letter and good wishes which I heartily reciprocate.

Kraus asked me to go and see him just before the New Year. In the course of my visit he told me that he has made enquiries about me and that the replies were favourable, and he advised me to submit a thesis for the post of University Lecturer. He promised to do what he could for me and asked for a list of my earlier, non-psycho-analytic papers. This at least shows a friendly interest. His influence within the Faculty is very great, although Bonhoeffer would have the final say in my case. I shall choose the most innocuous theme possible and I shall then have to mobilise my old contacts. Bleuler might be able to influence Bonhoeffer favourably; it is also important for me to win over one or two other members of the Faculty. Keibel,[1] my former teacher in Freiburg, could give me a useful recommendation to one of the two anatomists; one of them—Waldeyer[2]—has a lot of influence. In 'prehistoric' times I did several years of microscopic work[3] under Keibel. In spite of all this, I am not too optimistic about this matter.

Time permitting, I shall send some small contribution to Ferenczi in the near future.

With kind regards,

Yours,
Abraham

---

[1] Franz Keibel, 1861–1929, Professor of Embryology and Histology at Freiburg and later in Berlin.

[2] Wilhelm von Waldeyer, 1836–1921, Professor of Anatomy and Histology at Freiburg and later in Berlin.

[3] Abraham wrote his doctoral thesis on an embryological subject: 'Entwicklungsgeschichte des Wellensittigs' [The Developmental History of the Budgerigar].

Dear Professor,

Everything should now be running normally again after last Sunday's event,[1] and I am therefore writing to you today about some political and scientific matters.

Following Stekel's unofficial paper—and possibly at his suggestion—a committee, with a great deal of resistance at its disposal, was set up in order to establish an Association for Sexual Science. I was invited to the preparatory meeting. This development will certainly not do us any harm and it may even be of limited use in overthrowing various prejudices. I only mention it because I saw an interesting letter from Stekel which seems to suggest that the *Zentralblatt* is about to collapse. Stekel offers his publication to the new Association and wants to extend it to a *Zentralblatt für Analytische-Seelenkunde mit besonderer Beruecksichtigung der Sexualpsychologie*,[2] with which the publisher is said to be in agreement. He recommends this new title as 'excellent' with the profound reason that 'every unravelling of an illness is an analysis'. The offer has, however, been gratefully refused. This attempt to join forces with an Association which is as yet unborn proves how incapable the *Zentralblatt* is of continuing. There is a particularly nice postscript with which Stekel tries to entice the sexual researchers: 'The gentlemen's names will all be on the cover.' One would like to say with Adler—a unique opportunity for being on top!

It gave me great pleasure to receive the first number of our *Zeitschrift*[3] today. Contents, typography and general appearance are excellent. It makes a much better impression than the *Zentralblatt*. I assure you of my further active collaboration.

I took down verbatim the following sentences from an analysis of a paranoid patient: 'I at first try to come closer to everyone, but am prepared from the very beginning to break off the relationship.' 'I am prepared from the very beginning to find in everyone I meet nothing but bad intentions directed against me.' I find that these statements fit in extremely well with the

[1] Wedding of Freud's second daughter.
[2] *Journal for Analytical Psychology with Special Reference to Sexual Psychology.*
[3] *Internationale Zeitschrift für Psychoanalyse.*

opinions you put forward in your Schreber paper. There are certain reasons why I cannot publish anything from this particular analysis for the time being.

On the other hand, I would ask you to make use of the following, if you wish. In Vienna you discussed with me the deification of the murdered father. One of my patients brought me the following neat confirmation of this theory. Over a period of time he had a number of Oedipus dreams concerning the possession of his stepmother and his father's death. A series of these dreams was followed by one in which the patient ascends to heaven where he finds God in his majesty, looking like his father. The ascent to heaven obviously has two meanings: first, coitus with his stepmother and, second, the patient ensures that his father is in heaven—that he is really dead—whereupon he deifies him.

Nothing new to report in the matter of my thesis. I shall shortly start on this and shall probably undertake some association experiments in cases of senile dementia. This should be a sufficiently innocuous topic.

With kind regards from house to house,

Yours,
Abraham

Berlin,
6.2.13

Dear Professor,

Please forgive me for being importunate and writing again so soon. I am sending the enclosed paper[1] direct to you instead of to Ferenczi because it is a contribution to a special question put by you. As noted in the introduction, the case does not fully conform to your demands. I do not know therefore whether you will be able to use it.

This time only kind regards,

Yours,
Karl Abraham

[1] Karl Abraham, 'Mental After-Effects produced in a Nine Year Old Child by the Observation of Sexual Intercourse between its Parents', *Selected Papers on Psycho-Analysis*, London, 1927.

Dear Friend,

I have to thank you for your two valuable contributions, and I do so so belatedly because again I have had to use all my time for drudgery.

The infantile dream, which is clinically particularly interesting, is already with the International Journal.[1] The dream about God is being saved up.

Dr Spielrein[2] has told me of a striking defence of psychoanalysis by Kraus. So there is ground for hope for you.[3]

Sincerely yours,
Freud

*

Berlin,
3.3.13

Dear Professor,

First of all, many thanks for your letter and for the reprint. I am amazed at all the new ideas and views put forward in this new series of papers. I have also received the two reprints from the *Internationale Zeitschrift*; I should like some time to make a few small additions to the paper on technique.

I shall have to let my psycho-analytic pen rest for the time being, as I am now occupied with preparations for my thesis. I have for that reason sent several small contributions to the *Zeitschrift* for them to draw on. *Imago* must wait for a while. I am working on associations in normal old age and in mild cases of senile dementia. It will be a good old Prussian piece of work, exploring well-trodden paths. If only it would also open up the path to the University! In fact, things do not look quite so bad for me as I first thought. Kraus has become very interested. For two days running he discussed psycho-analysis in some detail in his Clinic. But the best is the following. I had

---

[1] The *Zeitschrift*.

[2] Dr Sabina Spielrein, Vienna psycho-analyst.

[3] A reference to the university appointment for which Abraham hoped.

asked Professor Liepmann, the man who did the research on aphasia apraxia, to speak to Bonhoeffer about me. Liepmann wrote to me at the time that Bonhoeffer's reaction had been quite negative. Subsequently, while talking to Liepmann, I asked him to tell me about the matter in detail, and I then discovered that Bonhoeffer had actually said that if I wrote a good paper he would not oppose me on principle. Liepmann's strange contradiction, which throws interesting light on the reliability of witnesses, is due to the fact that, in spite of his recognised ability, he himself never got the Chair he ardently hoped for. He has already been suggested four or five times for different universities. He has become very pessimistic and despite his good intentions toward me, has carried this complex into my affairs.

Meanwhile, the Association for Sexual Science has been founded. It will not interfere with us. Otherwise, there is nothing much happening here. I heard by chance that Jung is soon going to America again for some months. I am afraid that this will once more make for difficulties in preparing the Congress. It would be a good thing if someone were to take over and do whatever is necessary.

Just one small theoretical comment. In the footnote on page 5 of the new article[1] in *Imago*, you mention the biblical commandment against making images, which refers in particular to the worship of images. I have found in a few psychoanalytic cases that patients set up an analogous 'prohibition' referring to their parents. The patient is capable of recalling the features of all his relatives and friends with great visual clarity; it is only his parents' features that he cannot recall, despite the fact that he may just have parted from them. The most pronounced case was that of an obsessional neurotic with very severe compulsive brooding. The repression of scopophilia had led to the most fantastic obsessional symptoms: for instance, brooding about the appearance of invisible things—what the conscious and the unconscious looked like in the brain, what his neurosis looked like, etc.; he wanted to see everything. (For example, also his own birth. He envied Pythagoras for having

[1] Sigmund Freud, 'Ueber einige Uebereinstimmungen im Selenleben der Wilden und der Neurotiker', Part 3, *Imago*, Vol. II, No. 1, 1913.

experienced his own birth three times. Severe incestuous fixation of his scopophilia could, of course, be demonstrated.) Might not the biblical prohibition of worshipping God as an image be connected with the repression of scopophilia? He who looks on God is in fact threatened with death or blindness.

As soon as I find a little time, I shall send the *Zeitschrift* a very interesting observation[1] about oral erotism in a case of hebephrenia. It is about a patient who at the age of fourteen had to wean himself from sucking milk from a bottle and who attributed his masturbation–at least consciously–to the fact that at night he could not get any milk to drink. This is the same patient of whose 'mouth pollutions' (dribbling saliva while dreaming) I spoke to you in Vienna.

It is a pleasure to see how keenly the editors of the new *Zeitschrift* are setting about their work. The first number was excellent and can easily compete with the inferior 'organ'.

I assume that *Dreams and Myths* will have reached you.

Of course I do not expect a reply to this letter, dear Professor, I know how heavily burdened you are with correspondence and would only ask for a few words about Breslau[2] some time.

Kind regards to you and yours, also from my wife,

Yours,
Abraham

Berggasse 19,
Vienna IX,
27.3.13

Dear Friend,

Your Easter greetings from Weimar reminded me that I have made use too long of the permission you gave me not to reply. Having returned yesterday from Venice, where I went with my single little daughter,[3] the only one still left at home, and feeling slightly more rested, I hasten to converse with you.

[1] Karl Abraham, 'The First Pregenital Stage of the Libido', *Selected Papers on Psycho-Analysis*, London, 1927.

[2] See footnote 1, p. 139.

Anna Freud, b. 1895, psycho-analyst.

First, let me say how pleased I am that things do not stand so badly in regard to your lecturership. I should welcome it very much; Kraus's letter to me has made me rather hopeful.

Next I should like to suggest that you finish your comments on the ban on graven images for the *Zeitschrift*. It would cost you only an hour, and would be very valuable to us.

On the question whether you should attend the congress you refer to, I can really advise you only on secondary grounds. Perhaps the answer should be yes, so that we could have a report on it in the journal with some strong words in it, and you could get two days' relaxation. You have not mentioned whether you have actually done anything about increasing your fees. I am afraid that that is the only point in which you—wrongly—refuse to follow me.

Jung is in America, but only for five weeks, that is, he will soon be back. In any case he is doing more for himself than for psycho-analysis. I have greatly retreated from him, and have no more friendly thoughts for him. His bad theories do not compensate me for his disagreeable character. He is following in Adler's wake, without being as consistent as that pernicious creature.

I am pretty overworked, but in the months from now until the holidays have to finish the *Totem* job of which you remind me. Gradually one becomes depleted.

I send my cordial greetings to you and your wife and look forward to good news of you both.

Sincerely yours,
Freud

*

Berlin,
5.5.13

Dear Professor,

If one only considers external events, then the outlook for psycho-analysis is again very grim. The enclosed reached me when I was just about to write to you. Any lingering desire I had of attending the Congress left me when I read Bleuler's contradictory stuff. It is best to stick to our old ways and to keep to ourselves. As far as I know, only Wanke[1] has announced a paper. He is honest and will certainly stand up for our cause, but he will not make any impression. I shall ask him to write a summary of the Congress.

I am now busy with preparations for my thesis. That is to say, I visit the old age institution to take down associations of patients suffering from senile dementia. Otherwise, every day brings ten hours' work. I can however reassure you, dear Professor, on the question of fees. Last autumn I started putting up my fees from 10 to 15 marks and recently made the jump to twenty marks for the first time. As soon as I have established the increase in fees, the best time for which is after the holidays, I shall cut down my working day by one hour in order to have more leisure for scientific work. So much is ready and only waiting to be written down. The thesis is also a hindrance at the moment.

You ask me to work on image prohibition. I shall do this. But I would prefer not to do it on its own and would rather place it in a larger context. I should like to speak at the Congress on the transformation of scopophilia.[2] You will undoubtedly be content if I leave this small item unpublished until then. I should be very glad to know whether your work on totem will be published before Munich, as I should like to refer to it in my paper. I would ask you, if possible, to let me see the proofs, as you did once before.

I am sorry to have to endorse what you write about Jung. All the same, I do not believe that 'Adlerism' has come to stay in Zürich.

With kind regards to you and yours,

Yours,
Abraham

---

[1] Dr Georg Wanke, psychiatrist who practised psycho-analysis as medical superintendent at a sanatorium in the Harz mountains.

[2] Karl Abraham, 'Restrictions and Transformations of Scopophilia in Psycho-Neurotics; with remarks on Analogous Phenomena in Folk-Psychology', *Selected Papers on Psycho-Analysis*, London, 1927.

Berggasse 19,
Vienna IX,
13.5.13

Dear Friend,

The totem job is finished, apart from the revisions and appendices from the literature. It is going to the printer's on June 15th, and I shall send you the galleys as soon as I have them. It is to appear before the congress in the August number of *Imago* and will serve to cut us off cleanly from all Aryan religiousness. Because that will certainly be the consequence.

I am very much in agreement with your proposed course of lectures and economic reforms. Your admission to the faculty seems to me particularly important at this moment; as we must now count on the secession of Zürich and Munich, a school in Berlin would be the only proper compensation.

For all its ambivalence, Bleuler's essay[1] plainly shows his regressive trend. He actually accepts far less than he did two years ago. Also he used to add the modest flourish that, when he contradicted me, subsequently he so often found that I was right after all, etc. . . . .

I have discovered with great satisfaction that you are corresponding with Rank about our affairs. Politically I am crippled, and see all hope for psycho-analysis as we understand it in the unity of the four or five who are closest to me, among whom you seem to count yourself.

With my cordial greetings to you and your wife,

Freud

*

Berlin,
23.5.13

Dear Professor,

Nothing but vague rumours have reached me here about what is happening in Zürich, but I can well imagine it. I do not know whether, as you indicate, the breach is unavoidable.

[1] E. Bleuler, 'Kritik der Freud'schen Theorien', paper read at the congress of the German Psychiatric Society, Breslau, 1913.

As far as it lies in my power, Berlin will offer compensations. No further developments have taken place concerning my admission to the Faculty, except that I am working on my thesis. I have to assemble the material gradually, hope to finish it in the summer and to submit the paper in the autumn. After that it is in the lap of the Faculty gods. I am as sceptical about this as I have always been. If I fail, something else will have to be attempted.

Breslau was grim. According to Eitingon who was there, Bleuler behaved most unpleasantly. Eitingon will tell you about this personally. Only Stegmann was present from our group. He appears to have behaved very nicely and correctly. Hoche won the audience over by his jokes; however, I have talked to several people who, though not supporters of psycho-analysis, felt greatly repelled. It is a good thing that after the neurologists (in 1910) the psychiatrists have now also given vent to their wrath. Our cause will prosper all the more after this. I notice with amazement how interest in psycho-analysis has grown in Germany. One thing is certain: no topic in the realm of medicine and psychology is at present so widely discussed in professional circles as psycho-analysis, and no doctor's name is mentioned as often as yours even though the speaker crosses himself three times as he says it. It is just the same in lay circles.

I received a letter from Jung, addressed to our group, enquiring whether the subject for discussion chosen in Munich (The Function of the Dream) still stands. I see no reason against it. If there are any objections to this subject on the part of the Vienna group, I should like to hear particulars. In that case I would ask you to get Rank to let me know.

I am at present reading Hitschmann's[1] *Schopenhauer*[2] and am glad that the journals are going so well, while the *Zentralblatt* sinks to a lower level with each number.

With kind regards from house to house,

Yours,
Abraham

[1] Dr Edward Hitschmann was a very early member of the Vienna Society who died recently in the U.S.A.

[2] Dr. E. Hitschmann, 'Schopenhauer, Versuch einer Psychoanalyse des Philosophen', *Imago*, Vol. II, 1913.

Berggasse 19,
Vienna IX,
1.6.13

Dear Friend,

You will already know by now that we are to meet in Munich on the day before the congress (early on Saturday, Sept. 6th). Jung is crazy, but I have no desire for a separation and should like to let him wreck himself first. Perhaps my *Totem* paper will hasten the breach against my will. You will of course receive the galleys as soon as I have them (from the middle of the month onwards). I shall be reading it to the society on Wednesday; now I have grave doubts about it, the reaction after the exhilaration.

Jones is off today for two months' analysis with Ferenczi. I reflect with pleasure that your marriage shows that psycho-analysis does not necessarily lead to divorce.

Bleuler has regressed remarkably. I suspect that the final impulses were the psycho-analytic paper on the gynaesthesias, which raised tremendous resistance in him (see the *Zeitschrift für Psychologie*, last number). Perhaps it shows that in this matter Pfister and Hug were really right after all.

With cordial greetings to yourself and your wife,

Yours,
Freud

*

Berlin,
29.6.13

Dear Professor,

I have now read the Totem paper through twice, always with increasing enjoyment and growing conviction of the correctness of your point of view. I do not want to go into details today. I intend to express my gratitude by the paper which I shall read at the Congress and which will make some additions—not inconsiderable ones, it seems to me—to the subject. Today I only want to say that I find rich confirmatory material in my psycho-analytic cases. Only yesterday I discovered something

I never knew about till now: a perfectly obvious tree-totemism in a case of neurosis. So far I have only encountered animal totemism. It is evident in this case, just as in the totems of primitive peoples, that this is not so basic and primordial as animal totemism.

Last week there was, for once, an opportunity to speak in public in Berlin about psycho-analysis. In the *Aerztliche Gesellschaft fuer Sexualwissenschaft* a bad paper by Rohleder[1] was followed by a discussion on masturbation, in which first Koerber and then I emphatically put forward the psycho-analytic viewpoint. The preceding week brought me a few unpleasant days as an expert at court in the case against the *Anthropophyteia*.[2] I said whatever I could in its favour but unfortunately had to conclude that some of the authors were scientifically very poorly qualified, and that serious objections could be raised against Krauss himself. Bjerre from Stockholm came to see me today on his way to the Tyrol. He is very well informed and a really serious and reliable man. He has arrived at a perfectly sound assessment of Jung and Adler all on his own.

With kind regards from house to house,

Yours,
Abraham

*

Berggasse 19,
Vienna IX,
1.7.13

Dear Friend,

Your opinion of the totem paper was particularly important to me, as after finishing it I had a period of doubt about its value. But Ferenczi, Jones, Sachs, Rank, have expressed opinions similar to yours, with the result that I have gradually recovered my confidence. The way in which all of you try to show me the value of the work by supplementing and drawing conclusions from it is of course the most marvellous. I am prepared for vicious attacks, which will of course not disturb me

---

[1] Dr Hermann Rohleder, German psychiatrist.

[2] Friedrich Krauss, folklorist and ethnologist, editor of *Anthropophyteia* until 1927 (11 vols.)

in any way. The gap between ourselves and the Swiss is likely to be substantially widened.

I am counting the days till the beginning of the holidays, and see that there are still twelve of them left. But I have stopped work–apart from the eleven hours a day of my practice.

Frau Lou Salomé has, in her own words, 'laid a small egg' for *Imago*.[1] At all events it is very welcome. Of the papers for the congress I know of Tausk[2] on narcissism, van Emden[3] (who is here now) on the analysis of a pseudo-epilepsy, Jones on the technical behaviour of the analyst on questions of sublimation, Ferenczi on a subject still to be decided. I shall not speak.

It would be a good thing to arrange our meeting in Munich a long time in advance. Shall we both stay at the hotel or elsewhere? I still have no information about the place.

I send you my cordial greetings and hope you and yours enjoy your well earned holiday.

My address at Marienbad will be the Villa Turba, but my Vienna address can also be depended on throughout the holidays.

Yours,
Freud

*

Berlin,
20.7.13

Dear Professor,

I do not want to disturb your holidays with a long letter but would only like to revert to one point in your last letter, now that you have had a week's rest and may therefore be more receptive to persuasion.

You wrote that you would not be speaking in Munich. I hope you only said this under stress of the last working weeks

---

[1] Lou Andreas-Salomé: *Zum Typus Weib, Imago III*, 1914.

[2] Dr Victor Tausk, Vienna psycho-analyst.

[3] Dr Jan van Emden, Dutch physician and psycho-analyst.

in Vienna. If this were your last word, it would not be a proper Congress. I think I am speaking for the group which will assemble on September 6th if I ask you most sincerely to ensure the importance and effectiveness of the Congress by giving a paper. Who knows how much unpleasantness might occur, and nothing would be more effective in counteracting this. You will remember the effect you had in Munich in November, and on that occasion you only gave a report on troublesome internal politics. The effect of a scientific paper would be even more favourable in the present situation. I do not want to pursue it further; Eitingon, who is visiting you today, will surely succeed in persuading you to change your mind. My best wishes go with him.

That is all for today.

With kind regards to you and yours,

Yours,
Abraham

Pension 'Ozon',
Noordwijk aan Zee,
29.7.13

Dear Professor,

Eitingon told me your views about a possible paper, and I then wrote to Jung to find out his intentions regarding the discussion. I reminded him of the suggestion made in Munich that only the main paper, and not each individual paper, should be followed by a discussion. I enclose the reply which I have just received. Unfortunately it does not coincide with your wishes. But I do not think this need be decisive. After all, we are having our preparatory talk on September 6th. It would be so simple if one or two of us were to undertake any necessary replies to unpleasant remarks in discussion, so that you would not have to bother with them. You would only have to make a short summing-up.

I still hope that you are prepared to make the Congress into a real Congress by reading a paper. I do not wish, dear Professor, to plead with you any further on this point. I would only remind you that there will probably be quite a number of young people present this time and the Congress would lose its greatest attraction if you were there as a silent listener.

With kind regards from my wife and myself to you and your family,

Yours,
Abraham

*

Marienbad,
31.7.13

Dear Friend,

Early today there arrived a letter from Jung urging the announcement of a paper and simultaneously complaining about misunderstandings and making some supercilious remarks that I find it difficult to follow. In view of these everlasting misunderstandings, I can only regret that the Zürichers have lost the gift of making themselves intelligible.

This afternoon your letter arrived, from which I see how much you want me not to make a demonstration by abstinence. This repetition of the request transmitted by Eitingon was decisive for me, in spite of the unfavourable arrangements for speaking at the congress. So I shall make a short communication on the problem of the choice of neurosis.[1] You will see that I am not afraid of discussion, though I wish to avoid it.

It pleases us to think that you are now enjoying our beautiful Noordwijk. Above all the sunsets were magnificent. I did not like the wind and the dunes. The small towns are delightful. Delft is a little gem. You have to go a long way to find an Egyptian collection as fine as that in the museum at Leiden. Also the Attic steles are outstandingly beautiful.

With cordial greetings,

Yours,
Freud

[1] Sigmund Freud, *The Predisposition to Obsessional Neurosis*, Standard Ed., Vol. XII.

145

Noordwijk aan Zee,
6.8.13

Dear Professor,

I could not have hoped for better news than that contained in your letter. Since you tell me that it was the result of my repeated requests, I want to thank you sincerely for your decision. You will of course not be subject to the time-limit. We also had a time-limit of half an hour on papers at our previous Congresses; yet I still remember with great pleasure the two hours taken up by your paper at Salzburg. I am quite sure that no one will notice when the first twenty-five minutes are up! I would ask you not to restrict yourself to a short communication, especially since Eitingon has made me very curious about your new ideas on the question of choice of neurosis. But I shall gladly content myself with what I have achieved by my previous letter.

With all good wishes to you and your family for your journey to the Tyrol, and my own and my wife's kindest regards to you all,

Yours,
Abraham

(Picture postcard of the Arch of Titus, Rome)

13.9.13

The Jew survives it!
Cordial greetings and *coraggio, Casimiro*![1]

Yours,
Freud

[1] This refers to the following event: Two guides with whom Abraham had climbed a mountain took some raw meat with them to eat. By the time they reached the hut and set about cooking it, it had gone bad, and one of them encouraged the other to eat it with the words: '*Coraggio, Casimiro.*' Freud and Abraham subsequently continually quoted this remark.

Berlin,
17.9.13

Dear Professor,

From your encouraging postcard, for which I thank you very much, I take it that you are extremely happy in Rome and that you have thrown off the unpleasant memories of Munich. I may say for myself that in some ways I now feel better than before the Congress – the open discussion came as a relief.

I am back at work again, and the day is already almost fully occupied. I am also toiling at my thesis, and then for a respite I turn to the paper, part of which I gave at the Congress.[1] I have obtained such rich new material that I shall extend the subject. I shall have to split it up for publication in the *Zeitschrift* (I do not care for the *Jahrbuch* any more) into several small sections which can then be published as a series, like your papers on technique.

Deuticke informed me that *Dreams and Myths* is now being translated into Dutch by Staercke.[2]

I often think back to the pleasant days I spent in your family circle at San Martino. The enclosed card of the Pyramids near Eusigne in the Vallais will certainly interest you.

Yours ever,
Abraham

Eden Hotel,
Rome,
21.9.13

Dear Friend,

Many thanks for your friendly words and your good news, and in particular for the promise to work for our journal, which we must now keep going entirely on our own resources.

In the incomparable beauty of Rome I quickly recovered my spirits and energy, and in the free time between museums,

[1] Karl Abraham, 'Restrictions and Transformations of Scopophilia in Psycho-Neurotics; with Remarks on Analogous Phenomena in Folk-Psychology', *Selected Papers on Psycho-Analysis*, London, 1927.

[2] Dr August Staercke, a member of the Dutch Psycho-Analytical Society.

churches and trips to the Campagna finished a foreword to the book on totem and taboo, an expansion of the congress paper, and the sketch of an article on narcissism,[1] as well as a proof of my propaganda article for *Scientia*.[2] My sister-in-law,[3] who warmly returns your and your wife's greetings, sees to it that the real Rome work is kept within bounds. She has put up unexpectedly well with all the inevitable exertions, and it is a pleasure to see her succumbing increasingly every day to enthusiasm for Rome and Roman comfort.

I received yesterday from Maeder a letter retrospectively assuring me of his admiration, with the addendum: Here I stand, I can do no other (which is appropriate in the case of someone taking a risk, but is ill suited to someone withdrawing from one). He will get a cool, not very communicative reply.

The whole Roman setting will alas! be laid aside in a week and give place to a more sober and familiar one.

I send you my cordial greetings and hope to hear continuing good news from you and your family.

Sincerely yours,
Freud

*

Berlin,
27.9.13

Dear Professor,

I must particularly thank you for writing to me at such length from Rome. At the same time, I want to tell you how glad I am that you–and, according to your report, psycho-analysis as well–are so indebted to Rome. When you get this letter you will probably have just returned to your *lares and penates*.

My work is already back to its ten-hour schedule. I soon hope to be able to refer some patients to my new colleagues. We had our first meeting yesterday. I gave a report on Munich, and the schism was then discussed. It is a good thing for our small group that Juliusburger is turning back to us. I do not

[1] Sigmund Freud, *On Narcissism: an Introduction*, Standard Ed., Vol. XIV.

[2] Sigmund Freud, *The Claims of Psycho-Analysis to Scientific Interest*, Standard Ed., Vol. XIII.

[3] Minna Bernays (1865–1941), who had lived with the Freuds since 1892.

think he will give Stekel any more contributions. It looks as if life within our group will pick up this winter. The *Aertzliche Gesellschaft für Sexualwissenschaft* provides us with an increasing number of contacts from a wider medical circle.

In conclusion, I only wish you an easier winter with shorter working hours. With my own and my wife's kind regards to you and your family.

Yours,
Abraham

*

Berggasse 19,
Vienna IX,
8.10.13

Dear Friend,

Thank you for your letter on the occasion of my arrival in Vienna which, because I was immediately overwhelmed, I am answering only today.

I came back from Rome feeling fine and with the draft of the paper on narcissism. Here I promptly caught a cold, like all the Viennese, and have not yet been able to take it out of the drawer again.

The group in London is said to have been founded, we have had no more news from Switzerland, and we had our own first meeting today, at which I gave a very straightforward account of Munich.

It is a quarter to one in the morning. Reason to wish you and your wife the finest days ahead.

Sincerely yours,
Freud

*

Berlin,
10.10.13

Dear Professor,

I am eagerly looking forward to *Narcissism*. I found the last two numbers of the *Zeitschrift*, which I have just read, very satisfying, though of course not all the contributions equally so. Today I sent Ferenczi a short paper on 'The Ear as an Erotogenic Zone'.[1]

Simultaneously with my thesis and the paper on scopophilia, I am working on a few more short articles. A brief essay will deal with 'Neurotic Exogamy',[2] along the lines of your *Imago* paper.[3] Our group here has already had its first meeting.

Many thanks for the *Scientia* article,[4] and with kind regards, also from my wife.

Yours,
Abraham

Berggasse 19,
Vienna IX,
26.10.13

Dear Friend,

The letter to Kraus has resulted in my receiving a reply from Brugsch, which I enclose. It is a rotten reply, which nevertheless makes possible a continuation of negotiations. I was already thinking I had hit on a special university technique for treating undesirable elements and would be granted no answer at all. The best thing in the whole business seems to be Kraus himself.

I shall not make up my mind about the next step until I have heard from you and have your approval. You are so very much affected that you must have the first say.

These are gloomy times in other ways too, or perhaps only a time when gloomy moods predominate. I shall have to say *coraggio Casimiro* to myself.

Rank and Sachs are excellent, and great supports for the cause. Ferenczi yesterday sent in a trenchant criticism of

[1] Karl Abraham, 'The Ear and Auditory Passage as Erotogenic Zones', *Selected Papers on Psycho-Analysis*, London, 1927.

[2] Karl Abraham, 'On Neurotic Exogamy: A Contribution to the Similarities in the Psychic Life of Neurotics and of Primitive Man', *Clinical Papers and Essays on Psycho-Analysis*, London, 1955.

[3] Sigmund Freud, *The Return of Totemism in Childhood*, Standard Ed., Vol. XIII.

[4] See footnote 2, p. 148

Bleuler's negative article in the *Zeitschrift für Psychiatrie*.[1] Your criticism of Jung's theories will appear with it in the *Jahrbuch*, we declined to have it reviewed by Eder.[2] The question now is the extent to which Jones will be able to steer the new London group into our channel; all further 'political' steps depend on that.

At the first lecture yesterday I was struck by the complete analogy that can be drawn between the first running away from the discovery of sexuality behind the neuroses by Breuer and the latest one by Jung. That makes it the more certain that this is the core of psycho-analysis.

I send my cordial greetings to you and your whole family and await your decision.

Yours,
Freud

*

Berlin,
29.10.13

Dear Professor,

Once again there is very little to report. Brugsch's letter confirms that Bonhoeffer is behind the whole thing. My chances depend mainly on Bonhoeffer. It seems to me that whatever stand you take with Kraus and Brugsch will have little effect on my prospects, and I am therefore glad that I need not ask you for any special consideration.

Brugsch's diplomatic letter has the advantage of leaving the matter open. If only one knew whether he means everything he says. Could you not take him at his word and offer to deal with the other theories of hysteria as well? That would dispense with Kutzinski. I think one of our colleagues in Vienna could undertake this piece of work as a critical and historical introduction to your paper. (I do not know whether this suggestion is useful; it just occurred to me as I was reading Brugsch's reply.)

[1] Ferenczi's review appeared in the *Internationale Zeitschrift für Psychoanalyse*, Vol. II, 1914.
[2] Dr M. David Eder, British psycho-analyst.

When I recently went to Bremen at the week-end, I took Jung's work with me for careful perusal once again. I shall soon start on the detailed review.[1]

I am returning Brugsch's letter with many thanks for sending it to me.

With kindest regards from house to house,

Yours,

Karl Abraham

Berggasse 19,
Vienna IX,
2.11.13

Dear Friend,

Two questions:

(1) Jung, with a display of injured innocence, has resigned the editorship of the *Jahrbuch*, evidently with a view to securing sole control after getting rid of the editorial board. Our friends here are unanimously of the opinion that we should not abandon this position, and I am prepared to keep the *Jahrbuch* if you are willing to undertake the editorship. You can have Hitschmann as your assistant, with special reference to all negotiations and work in Vienna. The *Jahrbuch* would be reduced in size to from fifteen to eighteen signatures, it would appear only once yearly, its title would be simplified, all boring laboratory papers would be declined and it would be a real psychoanalytic year book, that is, it would contain, apart from some selected original papers, critical accounts of the literature, a survey of progress in the various fields, and reports of events in the psycho-analytic movement. Thus it would become an essential tool to those interested in psycho-analysis. Please let me know whether you will accept.

(2) We think the time has come to think of a severance of all ties with Zürich and thus to dissolve the International Psycho-Analytical Association. As the best way of bringing this about we have in mind forwarding to the central office a resolution proposing dissolution, signed by the three groups in

[1] Karl Abraham, Review of C. G. Jung's *Versuch einer Darstellung der Psycho-analytischen Theorie* (Attempt at a Representation of Psycho-Analytical Theory), 1914, *Clinical Papers and Essays on Psycho-Analysis*, London, 1955.

Vienna, Berlin and Budapest. If Jung does not accept this, these three groups can then resign and promptly form a new organisation. We do not want to begin by resigning, because that would again mean abandoning a position to them and Jung would remain president. Similarly, in the event of our resignation the new organisation would have to elect me as president to put an end to the falsifications of the Zürichers.

We therefore ask you for your views on the attitude to be adopted, as on the question of the resolution to be submitted to the head office and the foundation of a new organisation, and hope you are in full command of your group.

The matter is urgent. We are already in communication with Jones about the prospects in America. Please keep the matter secret for the time being.

With cordial greetings and in haste,

Yours,
Freud

Berlin,
4.II.13

Dear Professor,

I am answering you by return and therefore in haste, without giving your second question sufficient and calm consideration.

Your first question can be quickly answered. If you are willing to entrust me with the editing, I would undertake it (with Hitschmann's collaboration) and be glad to do so. Jung's resignation from the editorship is a good thing for us, and one must definitely not leave the *Jahrbuch* in his hands by your giving up your claims to it. I fully approve of the programme as you are planning it. I believe that if all three journals are edited in the same spirit, this can only benefit psycho-analysis. Unfortunately, we know nothing of Jung's real motives. He will certainly not give up his position, unless he has some other plan.

The question of the dissolution of our Association is a most delicate one. Our rules do not contain a paragraph dealing with this contingency. On going through them, I notice that the President is elected for a term of two years. We could not, therefore, elect a different President in the autumn of 1914.

This is an uncomfortable state of affairs but I do not see that it has changed much since Munich. Unfortunately I hear very little here about it all. If nothing has happened since, I wonder whether it is wise to choose this moment to adopt a new policy. The proposal made by three groups can too easily come to nothing. We would then be forced to secede, and I would consider this a great mistake. The existing Association, known, as such, must remain a truly psycho-analytical one, and you in particular must not leave it. What is of more practical importance is that I cannot be certain of Berlin. Of our eighteen members, only nine are in Berlin. How are we to come to a decision? It could not be done in one meeting, as we would then be making our decision over the heads of those who live elsewhere. It would be a precarious move to inform these members by letter. They are either unreliable or would offer well-meant peace proposals. The group would suffer a schism due to these special circumstances. I must add the following points in the interest of our group. Two colleagues have recently settled here, one of whom – Stockmayer – is very much under Jung's influence, or at least is still close to him. I had great hopes for our group from these two members, both of whom are keen and whom I am sure of gradually winning over. Berlin may become very important in future, and it would be a pity if political differences were to occur in our circle just now when it is beginning to develop.

At any rate, the result of a vote in our group would be doubtful. That is why I cannot unreservedly urge you to this action. Nevertheless, I do not at present have any better suggestion. What a pity that we cannot meet to talk things over. I shall give this matter further thought and shall let you know if I think of something.

If I have come to a wrong judgement due to insufficient information, you could ask Rank to let me have further details. I have only expressed my doubts from my particular viewpoint. As soon as I am certain of the rightness and inevitability of your suggestion, I shall of course do everything to ensure its success.

With kind regards,

Yours,
Karl Abraham

Berggasse 19,
Vienna IX,
6.11.13

Dear Friend,

My heartiest thanks for your acceptance of the task. Jung obviously gave up the *Jahrbuch* only in order to gain sole control of it after my withdrawal. Deuticke is inclined towards him, and it is probable that he will succeed; at the present moment Deuticke has two offers, the Jungian and ours, and he will shortly have to decide between them. If he turns us down, we shall remember that Heller is very anxious indeed to have the modified *Jahrbuch*, and we shall probably do it with him. An imprudence on my part which Deuticke rapidly exploited encouraged his coming to an understanding with Jung. Relations between Deuticke and Jung have developed with uncanny speed.

On the second question, I know that all your misgivings are correct. On the other hand, however, there is something oppressive about the situation, and both affectively and practically it calls for a solution. Under the terms of the contract we can, for instance, do nothing if Zürich requires us to publish all its rubbish in the *Korrespondenzblatt*, or to publish special papers. Formally the difficulties are slight. The passage in the rules which says that the purpose of the society is the cultivation of Freudian psycho-analysis gives us a smooth handle to call for its dissolution, as a statement by me that the Zürichers do not do this can hardly reasonably be set aside. Of course Jung would make difficulties. In the event of the secession of our three groups we should be obliged to found a counter-organisation, and our groups would lose about a third of their membership. In the last resort that risk would have to be accepted. We cannot have regard for our external members here either. If the dissolution came about from Jung, all difficulties would be removed. But it would have other disadvantages.

I shall circulate your letter to our friends. Then you and all the others must consider the most advisable course. I feel very uncertain in the matter and must not give in to my inclinations, which would certainly be a very unambiguous guide.

Unfortunately all these affairs disturb one's energy for work, besides wasting one's working time.

With heartfelt thanks and in expectation of hearing from you further.

Yours,
Freud

Berlin,
7.11.13

Dear Professor,

Your letter, which reached me a few hours ago, has quickly converted me to a more radical point of view. I consider it unethical for the President of an Association to negotiate with a publisher behind our backs, as Stekel once did, in order to lay his hands on the *Jahrbuch*. I need not go into the reasons for my views. In my opinion the Association cannot tolerate such underhand activity. Since, however, we cannot shake off Jung in any other way, I am in favour of taking extreme measures, but I could not decide on this until I knew of the most recent developments.

The main thing now is to bring about this change without friction and with the least possible loss of membership among the seceding groups. The following method seems to me the most practicable. The three groups should plan a preconcerted action. A circular letter would serve this purpose best, to be signed by the Presidents of the three groups and sent to all members; it should contain a factual statement of our action. Subsequently, each President would have to call a business meeting to arrive at a decision – these meetings should, if possible, occur simultaneously and the result should be immediately forwarded to Zürich. The letter would have to state our point of view incisively and take a stand against all false rumours. Sachs seems to me the right man to draft it.

I think we shall have an almost unanimous vote at our meeting. The objections raised in my last letter referred to members outside Berlin, and particularly those from other countries. We are likely to lose some of them. On the other hand, Berlin as well as Vienna might expect some additional members from the secession of the Zürich group (Binswanger, Oberholzer,[1] Ginzburg,[2] Pfister?).

Are you, dear Professor, definitely going to Hamburg at Christmas? If you are, any editorial matters concerning the *Jahrbuch* could be discussed then. I am completely at your disposal. If, for instance, you do not have enough time for Berlin, I could travel with you part of the way. Should you not be going away at all, I could come to see you in Vienna if necessary.

For the rest, we will do as Casimiro. With kind regards from house to house, and also to your loyal colleagues,

Yours,
Karl Abraham

*

Berggasse 19,
Vienna IX,
9.11.13

Dear Friend,

The situation has changed so rapidly that a great deal of what you suggest no longer applies. Under the impact of your letter, and a very similar one from Jones, Rank and Sachs have agreed to a postponement of the operation against the Association, and Ferenczi, who has been the hothead in the whole business, will no doubt agree to it too. You know that in these matters I gladly let myself be advised by my friends, as since being taken in by Jung my confidence in my political judgement has greatly declined. I enclose Jones's letter.

So the *Jahrbuch* remains ours. Deuticke was simply over-hasty, he seems to have made no secret agreements, and at first had misunderstood me. I shall be sending you soon the detailed plan for the volume I should like to bring out on about July 1st, and shall myself take a substantial part in the work. I shall tell Hitschmann on Wednesday and ask him to get in touch with you. We shall all put our best efforts into making the new *Jahrbuch* a testimonial to what we are capable

[1] Dr Emil Oberholzer, Swiss psychiatrist and psycho-analyst, later lived in the U.S.A.
[2] Dr Benjamin Ginzburg, Swiss psychiatrist and psycho-analyst.

of, and you will automatically find yourself in an extremely influential position. True, the material benefit will be slight. I already see that the whole situation depends on our squeezing every ounce out of ourselves. There is the cause, and we shall sacrifice ourselves for it without complaint. C. C.[1]

On the way back from Hamburg I propose to spend the afternoon and evening in Berlin (Sunday, December 28th from midday to the night train), when we shall be able to discuss everything.

I send my heartfelt good wishes to your whole family, and am delighted to be able to regard you officially as what you have always been, one of my best helpers.

Sincerely yours,
Freud

*

Berlin,
13.11.13

Dear Professor,

I am glad that we are not going to be concerned with politics for the time being. I find Jones's exposition most acceptable. I hope we shall make good use of our energies for creative purposes in the near future. Despite heavy pressure, I am looking forward to my work for the *Jahrbuch* and sincerely thank you for your kind remarks on this occasion. I always have the feeling that I cannot really do enough for our cause, since my obligation to you is too great in every respect. I feel this with every new stimulus I receive either from you or from psycho-analysis, and even more so on account of the increasing success of my work.

I am not quite certain whether I shall be in Berlin on December 28th, as there are several other things happening around that date. Should I not be here, we would have to make another arrangement. As soon as I know more definitely, I shall write further.

As with everything else you have sent me, I welcomed *Totem and Taboo* with great pleasure. It looks very good in this edition and will certainly arouse wide interest. Many thanks.

[1] For *coraggio Casimiro*.

I am returning Jones's letter, and send best wishes from my wife and myself to you and your family,

Yours,
Abraham

*

Berlin,
8.12.13

Dear Professor,

What a great and unexpected pleasure it was to receive your picture today. The reproduction is excellent. It is only the lateness of the hour that limits me to a few short words of thanks!

I am glad to be able to reciprocate with the enclosed gift[1] which I have just completed. This copy is meant for you, Rank and Sachs. Ferenczi and Jones will receive one each. I have put a lot of work into this unpleasant review but I do not regret it, because only by doing it have I come to recognise the complete sterility of the Jungian 'School'. What I have always guardedly called an incorrect exposition, actually deserves a different name.

Now I must apologise to you, dear Professor, that in a paper on Agoraphobia[2] which I recently sent to Ferenczi, I committed an unconscious plagiarism. I refer to the remarks on railway phobia which I found, to my amazement, in the *Three Essays* when I was reading them for the purpose of the Jung review. I shall make the necessary amendments in the proofs.

Many thanks for the reprints which I have not yet read, and with kind regards from house to house,

Yours,
Abraham

---

[1] See p. 152, footnote 1.
[2] Karl Abraham, 'A Constitutional Basis of Locomotor Anxiety', *Selected Papers on Psycho-Analysis*, London, 1927.

159

Berggasse 19,
Vienna IX,
10.12.13

Dear Friend,

As today is Wednesday, I shall not be free to study your paper in the evening, but I have skimmed through it and seen that it would deserve a civic crown if such distinctions were awarded in science. It is, in short, excellent, cold steel, clean, clear and sharp. Moreover, heaven knows that it is all true. I shall pass it on to Rank and Sachs and, if any comments seem to be called for, I shall make them to you. You cannot imagine what pleasure the co-operation of five such men[1] gives me.

It makes no difference to me whether I stop in Berlin on the way there or the way back, and it can be left undecided until a few days beforehand. I shall bring the plan of the first volume of the *Jahrbuch* with me.

My cordial greetings to your wife and children, whom I shall thus soon be seeing.

Sincerely yours,
Freud

*

Berlin,
14.12.13

Dear Professor,

Your opinion of my review gives me great satisfaction. Jones has meanwhile returned his copy with comments. I hope that, after using all the additional ideas which I get from Vienna and Budapest, something will emerge that will not fail to make an impression.

Your suggestion about Thursday, 25th December, suits me extremely well. I have unlimited leisure then, so that the best use can be made of these few hours. I do not know whether you have any other business in Berlin. If time runs short, I

[1] The reference is to Freud's closest collaborators (Abraham, Ferenczi, Jones, Rank and Sachs), who had formed themselves into a 'committee'.

could accompany you part of the way to Hamburg. Just to make sure I would add that you will, of course, be our guest for lunch.

With kind regards,   Yours,
                                                    Karl Abraham

Berlin,
7.1.14

Dear Professor,

My correspondence with the reviewers for the *Jahrbuch* went off well. I am spending every free moment on the scopophilia paper.[1]

Your communications about the genesis of masochism have, in the last few days, led me on to a trail which seems promising. It is concerned with the problem of exhibitionism (as a perversion and does not refer to general exhibitionistic tendencies of neurotics). The connection with castration anxiety seems quite striking to me. It would stand for the exhibiting of that part of the body which causes anxiety due to several converging motives.

First: compulsive anxiety—the patient exhibits himself but experiences anxiety because of the threatened castration and, like the masochist, obeys his unconscious impulse and wish to be castrated.

Second: defiant exhibitionism—in spite of the threat, I still have the penis.

Third: the wish to impress the woman, or to frighten her. The attempt to incite the woman to similar activity, as his diminished sexual activity (castration anxiety) does not allow for any other mode of behaviour – impotence is usually to be found in these cases.

According to the analysis, this exhibitionism is originally directed towards the mother; an attempt to compete with the father.

It is late and I would therefore ask you to excuse this sketchy presentation.

[1] See p. 147, footnote 1.

161

My wife thanks your daughter Anna very much for her letter. For the rest, kind regards from house to house and best wishes for 1914.

Yours, as always,
Karl Abraham

Berggasse 19,
Vienna IX,
12.1.14

Dear Friend,

So we all vote for Dresden. Our meeting is on the 14th.

Your remarks about exhibitionism (for which your son provided the impetus) seem to me to be very pertinent. I think matters will turn out to be similar in the case of all the perversions, and new viewpoints for therapy and understanding are opened up thereby.

I am writing the history of the psycho-analytic movement,[1] and am completely absorbed in it. It will be vigorous and plain-speaking. For the time being I should like your help with the following points:

(a) When did Eitingon first come to me in Vienna?
(b) When did the Freud society in Zürich first become active?
(c) When did interest in psycho-analysis in Bleuler's clinic first begin?

With cordial greetings and thanks,

Sincerely yours,
Freud

Berlin,
15.1.14

Dear Professor,

In reply to your questions:

1. Eitingon, according to his own statement, visited Vienna for the first time at the end of January 1907.

[1] Sigmund Freud, *On the History of the Psycho-Analytic Movement*, Standard Ed., Vol. XIV.

2. The 'Freudian Association' must have had its first meeting approximately half-way through the year 1907. I myself read a paper at one of the first meetings (on the Significance of Sexual Trauma), which was published in November 1907. It must have been presented late that summer.

3. The third question is hard to answer. When I came to the Burghölzli in December 1904, interest in psycho-analysis already existed. The following years saw a rapid increase in this interest. The listed events definitely preceded this.

(i) Jung's *Occult Phenomena* (1902), in which your *Interpretation of Dreams* is quoted (p. 102).

(ii) Jung's attempt at an analysis of the patient B.St., published in the appendix to the *Psychology of Dementia Praecox*.

(iii) Several of the studies on association had already been published.

(iv) A case of hysteria had been analysed by Jung (definitely 1904).

I should say that interest began to increase during 1903, or possibly not till 1904.

In haste, with kind regards,

Yours,
Abraham

*

Berlin,
11.2.14

Dear Professor,

Everything seems to be going smoothly with the *Jahrbuch*. I hope the reviewers will all send their work in on time. Sadger's review has already arrived. I myself am still busy on the scopophilia paper but hope to finish in a week or two, and will then write my review.

We had a very satisfactory meeting of our group a few weeks ago with four reports concerning the Jung affair. The meeting was very harmonious.

Today there was one real ray of light among the gloom. Renterghem[1] sent me a newspaper carrying a detailed report of

---

[1] Dr A. W. van Renterghem, neurologist and psychiatrist in Amsterdam.

the inaugural address on the Unconscious given by the Leyden psychiatrist, Jelgersma.[1] As you may not have heard about it yet, I shall report to you briefly that J. (incidentally the most distinguished psychiatrist in Holland) fully accepts the dream and neurosis theories, calls them a great achievement, also supports sexuality, and ends by speaking of the enormous impression which the re-discovery of the Oedipus complex made on him. All in all, a very comprehensive review and wholehearted appreciation without any reservations. I immediately sent a short excerpt of the Holland report to Ferenczi with the suggestion that Jelgersma's permission should be sought for a translation of his paper for inclusion in the *Zeitschrift*.

In haste, with kind regards from house to house,

Yours,
Abraham

*

Berggasse 19,
Vienna IX,
15.2.14

Dear Friend,

Jelgersma really seems to be an event. I had already received his pamphlets and the copy of the newspaper through Renterghem before your letter arrived. Next day I received a letter from him that corroborated all your information and was really very kind. So here is an official psychiatrist who swallows psychoanalysis hook, line and sinker. Whatever will happen next?

I shall send you his letter as soon as I have it back from Ferenczi and it has been read to the Wednesday meeting. Heller intends writing to him and arranging a German edition. I do not think it is anything for the *Zeitschrift*, as it does not go one word beyond the *Interpretation of Dreams*. I finished the rough draft of 'On the History of the Psycho-Analytic Movement' an hour ago. It is now on its way to Budapest, from where it will reach you as my first contribution to the *Jahrbuch*. It was hard work. I have nothing to say to you about

[1] Professor G. Jelgersma, Professor of Psychiatry at Leyden University. *Unbewusstes Geistesleben*, published 1914.

it but the celebrated words *coraggio Casimiro*. If you have any comments or amendments to suggest, I promise to be very grateful for them. Ferenczi will be doing the same.

Our summer plans are still entirely inchoate. We are no longer a family, only three old people. Even my little daughter wants to go to England by herself this year, as your wife still recalls. What sort of revolution the expected guest[1] in Hamburg will bring about is also still unknown.

With cordial greetings to you and yours,

Sincerely yours,
Freud

Berggasse 19,
Vienna IX,
27.2.14

Dear Friend,

I think of you a great deal, because I am writing the paper on narcissism. The 'History of the Psycho-Analytic Movement' has been with Ferenczi for a week, and you no doubt will have received it too. Please send your critical comments separately and order three copies of the proofs from Deuticke so that I may secure the comments of Rank, Sachs and Jones as well.

Hard work is being done to make up for time lost because of the strike. I hope two numbers will be finished by the first week of March.

I shall be very grateful to you if you can do anything for Reik. We must not leave our fellow-workers in the lurch. Perhaps he can help you in some way in your work.

We have begun a joint research and discussion-project in the society on the Oedipus complex in the child. The first meeting passed off very well. Might it be possible for your group to take part or to co-operate in the publication (No. 3 of the Discussions)?

All are well here and I hope the same is true with you, and send you my cordial greetings.

Sincerely yours,
Freud

[1] Freud's daughter Sophie was expecting her first child.

165

Berlin,
9.3.14

Dear Professor,

A small parcel will be posted to you tomorrow containing a long overdue gift in return for your picture. Some time ago I received a request from Stanley Hall to present my photograph to the psychological seminar at Worcester. I am sending you a copy of the photograph I had taken on this occasion.

Your manuscript has been with me for a week and I have read it several times. I have no factual comments to make except that I am in complete and absolute agreement with every word. It is a relief that for once everything has come out into the open and the way you have done this is particularly satisfactory. I shall only mention a few very minor points:

1. On p. 21 you relate how Rank joined you, but his name is omitted. I do not know whether this is intended, but wished to draw your attention to it.

2. On p. 27 there seems to be an omission: 'Havelock Ellis, who had followed its development sympathetically.' Are the words 'from the beginning' missing here?

3. Might the adjective you assign to Hoche not lead to disagreeable consequences? You are certainly right about him, but would it not be better to omit it?

That is all I have to say, except that I enjoyed my editorial privilege of reading the manuscript before anyone else. It compensated me for the hard work of the last few months.

My scopophilia paper has just been finished and my review must now be completed in record time. I hope to receive all the contributions in the course of this month.

I am enclosing Jelgersma's letter which Jones sent me. I am very pleased with it. You will have heard that I am in frequent correspondence with all the members of the Committee. I am doing everything possible for Reik but it isn't easy to find anything for him.

I shall ask our group whether they are prepared to take part in the research on the Oedipal phase in childhood, and shall let you know.

With kind regards,

Yours,
Abraham

Berggasse 19,
Vienna IX,
16.3.14

Dear Friend,

Tomorrow I am sending you the 'Narcissism', which was a difficult birth and bears all the marks of it. Of course I do not like it particularly, but it is the best I can do at the moment. It is still very much in need of retouching. (You see what my thoughts are lingering on.) Please look out yourself the passage where I have to mention your first (Salzburg) paper; I shall be grateful to you for this, as for any other criticisms. Your comments on the 'History' will be taken into account at the proof stage.

Your proposal of aggressive action against Jung will be discussed tomorrow evening with Rank and Sachs. What I am most curious about is the reply from London, where difficulties could easily arise.

In Hamburg I gather things are going very well, my daughter seems to be behaving bravely and intelligently. She already has milk, but the little creature is not yet sucking properly. Strange that these vital instincts should awaken with such difficulty. I have always thought that Mephistopheles's speech to the student *So nimmt ein Kind der Mutter Brust im Anfang widerwillig an*[1] – was wrong. It is perfectly correct, however, and so, I hope, is the continuation: *Doch bald ernährt es sich mit Lust.*[2]

Your picture will return tomorrow from the framer's, and will then take the place of Jung's. It does not quite do you

---

[1] 'So does a child take unwillingly to the mother's breast', a quotation from Goethe's *Faust.*

[2] 'But soon it feeds with pleasure.'

justice, but I thank you very much for it. Deuticke has developed a very healthy respect for your work as editor. We have really all been putting the last ounce into the work. I must also mention how excellent your locomotor paper[1] is. In the 'Sexual Theory' I found no better argument for 'muscular erotism' than the analysis of the abasias, which culminate in the phantasy memory of the first attempts to walk on the maternal body (the earth).

With cordial greetings to you and your wife,

Yours
Freud

*

Berggasse 19,
Vienna IX,
25.3.14

Dear Friend,

I enclose Jones's letter. It is quite remarkable how each one of us in turn is seized with the impulse to kill, so that the others have to restrain him. I suspect that Jones himself will produce the next plan. The usefulness of co-operation in the committee is very well illustrated by this. We shall discuss all this. The critical number of the *Zeitschrift* has now appeared, and will perhaps spare us a lot of decisions.

You do not mention when you are going on your well-earned little journey.

Since finishing the 'Narcissism' I have not been having a good time. A great deal of headache, intestinal trouble, and already a new idea for work, which is an added difficulty for the summer, because it precludes staying at a hotel and requires a quiet place where one can work. So far our plans for the summer are utterly obscure.

With my cordial greetings to you and to your wife,

Sincerely yours,
Freud

---

[1] Karl Abraham, 'A Constitutional Basis of Locomotor Ataxia,' *Selected Papers on Psycho-Analysis*, London, 1927.

Berlin,
2.4.14

Dear Professor,

Firstly, your two manuscripts. I have already written to you about the 'History'. I have read it over and over again and have increasingly come to see how important a weapon it is. After giving it much thought, I have also come to the conclusion that everything personal should stand as it is. There is only one expression which I would like to have changed. You say about Adler how much he complained of your persecution, and I am afraid this word might cause harm. Adler will protest against being called paranoid. An expression with less pathological implication, such as hostility, would be preferable.

I cannot understand why you should be dissatisfied with 'Narcissism'. I find the work brilliant and completely convincing throughout. I do not wish to go into details of your train of thought, but will only emphasize one point: namely, the particularly successful analysis of the delusion of being watched, its relation to conscience, etc. Your description of the ego-ideal is especially valuable for practical purposes. These expositions had been in my mind for some time, and with every sentence I read I was able to guess what was coming next. In particular, the distinction between ego-ideal and true sublimation is something that I have always explained to my patients, but without putting it in so precise a form. Might I add a suggestion here? I think this is where the contrast between Jung's therapy and psycho-analysis can be most pointedly stressed. The life task and all similar concepts—including the 'prospective tendency' of the unconscious—is in fact nothing but an appeal to the ego-ideal and thereby a path that by-passes all real possibilities of sublimation (with the unconscious intention of avoiding them). Perhaps a paragraph referring to this might be useful?

I am looking forward to 'Moses',[1] but do not quite understand.[2] Do you not think that the lion's paw will be recognised in any case?

[1] Sigmund Freud, *The Moses of Michelangelo*, Standard Ed., Vol. XIII.

[2] This refers to Freud's intention to publish the work anonymously; the author's name was not revealed until 1924.

In May our group will have a meeting on the subject of the Oedipal relationship in infancy. I hope at least some of the contributions will be worth publishing.

Pollak's[1] etching arrived a few days ago. I like the pose very much. It takes some time to get used to the facial expression, but one comes to like it in the end. The whole composition, especially the distribution of black and white, is very well done.

I recently came across your work on Cocaine (1885) in a second-hand bookshop and read it yesterday.

I hope, dear Professor, that your health has improved in the meantime. Your grandson, too, I hope, is making good progress and no longer fails to recognise the gratification of sucking. By the way, we had this difficulty with both our children.

With kind regards from my wife and myself to you and your family,

Yours,
Karl Abraham

*

Berggasse 19,
Vienna IX,
6.4.14

Dear Friend,

Hitschmann telephoned this morning to say that the patient from Berlin[2] had arrived, thus putting an end to a minor worry. Your manuscript was considered overdue, and we did not dare to imagine the situation that would have arisen if disaster had overtaken it.

Do not let yourself be put out by Sadger, and insist on the elimination of everything irrelevant or spiteful. S. is seldom tolerable without censorship. Also providing publicity for Stekel is really superfluous.

'Persecution' is the term used by Adler himself. I shall replace it in accordance with your suggestion, and instead of the 'filthy' spirit of A. Hoche I shall insert 'evil' spirit.

Your acceptance of my 'Narcissism' affected me deeply and binds us still more closely together. I have a strong feeling of

[1] Max Pollak, Viennese artist.
[2] The 'patient' was Abraham's manuscript for the *Jahrbuch*.

its serious inadequacy. I shall incorporate the comment you would like on the by-passing of sublimation in the Zürich therapy. The 'Moses' is anonymous partly as a pleasantry, partly out of shame at the obvious amateurishness which it is hard to avoid in papers for *Imago*, and finally because my doubts about the findings are stronger than usual, and I published it only as a result of editorial pressure.

Your opinion about the etching coincides with that of many here. I have heard more severe and more enthusiastic opinions.

The short work on dreams[1] appeared yesterday in an English translation by Eder.

Otherwise all is quiet. Perhaps the calm before the storm.

I send my cordial greetings to you and your wife, and hope there will be a quick recovery from the inevitable childish complaints, which are best got rid of sooner rather than later.

Yours,
Freud

Postscript

The first number of the *Zeitschrift für Sexualwissenschaft* has reached me. I decided to make my contribution to it dependent on the attitude to psycho-analysis that it displayed. This turns out to be not very alluring. There is an extremely shabby reference in Eulenburg's article (p. 9), and a review by Saaler that regards Stekel's work on fetishism as representing the present status of psycho-analysis. This strengthens my intention to go on maintaining reserve.

The society is designed to achieve recognition for Fliess. Rightly so, because he is the only mind among them and the possessor of a bit of unrecognised truth. But the subjection of our psycho-analysis to a Fliessian sexual biology would be no less a disaster than its subjection to any system of ethics, metaphysics, or anything of the sort. You know him, his psychological incapacity and his logical consistency in the physical field. Left hand = woman = the subconscious = anxiety. We must at all costs remain independent and maintain our equal rights. Ultimately we shall be able to come together with all the parallel sciences.

[1] Sigmund Freud, *On Dreams*, Standard Ed., Vol. V.

Berlin,
19.4.14

Dear Professor,

I am replying today to your detailed letter of the 6th, assuming that you are now back in Vienna. I hope the short trip has given you the rest you needed.

Jung's *Jahrbuch* is rather mediocre. I think our new one will be far superior and I am glad it will appear as early as June. I hear from Hitschmann that you have somewhat qualified what I said in the preface concerning the exclusion of case material–I entirely agree. Some time ago Sadger sent me a paper for the *Jahrbuch* containing both case material and some basic theories on inversion. I rejected it at the time. Should we accept it after all?

I should like to remind you to let me know which days you and the Vienna members suggest for the Congress. Jung suggested September 4th and 5th on account of the subsequent International Neurological Congress in Berne.

The new *Zeitschrift für Sexualwissenschaft* does not greatly impress me. Eulenburg, incidentally, is quite senile. That is why I have spared him in recent discussions.

In May our group will meet and discuss the Oedipus phenomena in infancy. I myself must resume work on my thesis which has had to rest throughout the winter. I would much rather turn to a few subjects which interest me more. Perhaps I can combine both.

One of the last numbers of *Simplicissimus* contained a joke which brilliantly illustrates your essay on Narcissism, especially with regard to the significance of hypochondria–I therefore enclose it.

Kind regards from my wife and myself to you and yours,

Yours,
Karl Abraham

Telegram

Berlin,
22.4.14

Sincere congratulations on the Zürich news.[1]

Abraham, Eitingon

*

Berggasse 19,
Vienna IX,
24.4.14

Dear Friend,

You were certainly just as surprised as I was at how meticulously Jung carried out our own intentions. But our reserve has now indeed borne fruit; somehow we shall get rid of him, and perhaps of the Swiss altogether.

I immediately assumed the role of summoner of the conference of presidents, and arranged for Rank to send out a circular letter which will make possible a decision by correspondence, thus saving travel. Action is being taken in two phases, first among our friends and only when these have reached agreement, steps will be taken officially by all the presidents of societies (*i.e.*, two more). Please support the proposal that you should become president of the congress.

I enjoyed Brioni[2] very much, but had to struggle with an indisposition I could not account for, which broke out on my return as a severe tracheitis-laryngitis. I am by no means well, and in particular I am quite inactive intellectually. Perhaps it is also the intoxicating spring which one feels in one's bones.

Hitschmann says that he already has too much material for the *Jahrbuch*, so Rank and Sachs have withdrawn their contribution. Sadger can be accepted and put in store.

Last week I talked to two members of the American group from Ward's Island (the most serious of them), and they assured me that Jung's influence is quite unimportant with them. He appears to have strong support in Jellife.

[1] This refers to the news of Jung's resignation from the presidency of the International Psycho-Analytical Association.

[2] Island in the Adriatic.

With cordial greetings to you and your wife and good wishes for the new Jungless era,

Yours,
Freud

*

Berggasse 19,
Vienna IX,
7.5.14

Dear Friend,

You are now our president. We have the Association in our own hands and shall not let go of it so quickly.

Maeder agreed in a very gracious fashion; and Seif[1] did so laconically. The official announcement of the result of the vote will probably be sent out by Rank tomorrow.

I now suggest to you the preparation of a *Korrespondenzblatt*[2] which can be printed in the fourth number of the *Zeitschrift*. (The third is as good as finished.) In the preamble to your proclamation please do not omit to mention that the previous headquarters ceased all activity after Munich and did not even produce a congress report.

I am still unwell and without energy for work, and am waiting for the proofs of the *Jahrbuch*, which fail to arrive in spite of all reminders. There is a good deal that I shall say more sharply, and several things that I shall soften.

I still have no idea what we shall be doing in the summer.

Heller is complaining vigorously about the bad state of the subscription list of both our journals. Certainly the printers' strike did us a lot of harm. But we must see it through.

I hope your children have now fully recovered, and that you and your wife are as well as is appropriate to your youth and harmony.

I was fifty-eight yesterday.

With cordial greetings,

Yours,
Freud

[1] Dr L. Seif, psycho-analyst in Munich.

[2] A bulletin containing news of the activities of the branches of the International Psycho-Analytical Association.

Dear Professor,

It gives me great pleasure and satisfaction that you, dear Professor, and our closest friends, wish me to be President and I sincerely thank you all for your confidence. I had already stated my readiness to take over temporarily, but you seem to want me as permanent President. I have given this much thought. I am not reverting to my earlier proposal (Jones) because I realise that London is too far away from the centre and it would be particularly difficult to direct the *Korrespondenzblatt* from there. The most important objection to my being President really comes from you. If a splinter group misuses the name of psycho-analysis, then you personally should be at the head of the legitimate movement so that everyone is aware which is the Freudian Association. That was your own view when we discussed it in the winter. On the other hand – and I have talked about this with Sachs during the last few days – you ought not to be troubled with new burdens. I have therefore thought of a solution and I hope you will find it feasible. The actual presidential duties will be taken over by myself, or whoever else is finally elected; however, my suggestion would enable you to stand officially at the head and to lead the scientific part of the Congress. I think we ought to follow the practice of other scientific associations and make you a permanent Honorary President. As far as I am concerned, I shall not say too much about my feelings of inadequacy, for I feel confident that I can do better than my predecessor. Thinking back to the first Congresses, I realise that the harmonious atmosphere, and much else besides, was due to your leadership. With the best will in the world, none of us others can restore the atmosphere which the Congress lost in Munich. The business report and the chairing of the business meetings would be the President's job, as well as all business during the year. You would assume office only on the two Congress days and could even be relieved then if it proves too much for you – but that is unlikely. Sachs immediately approved of this suggestion, and I should be very happy if you agreed as well.

I thought the printing of the *Jahrbuch* was proceeding well as I received the proofs of Federn's paper a long time ago. I hope there will be no delay.

Reik gave a very nice paper in our last meeting about the male 'puerperium'.[1] He wants to expand this paper and submit it for the *Jahrbuch* under the title of 'Father Rites'. Staerke has sent me a long manuscript with eighteen illustrations which had previously been in Jung's hands. I am looking through it very carefully but it is unlikely that we shall be able to accept it, not even parts of it as Staerke now suggests.

I believe that, by the time we meet in the summer, the Swiss affair will have been decided. Your 'History' in the *Jahrbuch* will result in the resignation of Jung and his followers, and we shall then be able to enjoy the Congress.

I am preparing a paper for *Imago* on forms of greeting.[2] If the Congress turns out as we plan it, I should like to give a talk about the psycho-analytic therapy of mental diseases.

Kind regards to you and yours, also from my wife,

Yours,

Karl Abraham

Berggasse 19,
Vienna IX,
13.5.14

Dear Friend,

Many thanks for your rich letter. Meanwhile I have been ill again myself, and have been having a bad time in general, as if worry and work were at last wearing me down.

My last bout of intestinal trouble caused my specialist[3] to take the precaution of carrying out a rectoscopy, after which he congratulated me so warmly that I concluded that he had regarded a carcinoma as highly probable.

So this time it is nothing, and I must struggle on. Our summer is still not settled. If, as Rank suggests, you manage to have

[1] Theodor Reik, 'The Couvade and the Psychogenesis of the Fear of Retaliation', *The Ritual*, Psycho-Analytic Studies.

[2] Apparently never published.

[3] Dr Walter Zweig, lecturer in gastro-intestinal diseases at Vienna University, jestingly described by Freud as his '*Leibarzt*'.

September 20th–21st (Sunday) accepted as the date of the Congress, we can have our private meeting beforehand on the 19th, I shall be able to deliver my lecture at Leiden on, say, the 23rd, and then go and see my daughter and grandson in Hamburg. My daughter in England can cross over and join me in Holland, and then there will be more time for us in Berlin than the interval between two trains.

Meanwhile I firmly accept your promise of a visit after your tour of the Dolomites. Perhaps we shall travel to Dresden together.

It is true that it is my personal wish to see you as our definite president. I know what to expect of your energy, correctness and conscientiousness (in most agreeable contrast to your predecessor). From other quarters it is pointed out that relations with America and regard for capturing the young London group speak in favour of Jones. In these circumstances I wish to leave to all of you the decision that will have to be made at our pre-congress. To decide now would be premature. We do not know whether the Swiss will really resign after the appearance of the *Jahrbuch*, and this must necessarily influence the choice of president. I myself would like to be excluded, or alternatively held in reserve for some extreme emergency. Your suggestion that I should become honorary president does not appeal to me; in the first place there is a flavour of retirement about it, and in the second the present bad and crisis-ridden times do not seem to me to be appropriate for anything honorary. But I must not refrain from heartily thanking you for the friendly idea. In quiet, successful times I should gladly have accepted. For the time being the institution of a president and vice-president seems to me to be indispensable, and the sharing of the two functions between you and Jones at brief (two-yearly) intervals advisable. However, as I mentioned, I am positive that the committee will itself be able to settle this question without being disturbed by personal ambition.

What really upsets me is my lack of desire or incapacity for work, which has persisted since Easter. This week I at last finished the proofs of the first third of the 'History of the Psycho-Analytic Movement', the part in which there was practically nothing to alter. I have only added a motto, *fluctuat nec mergitur*, and inserted Rank's name in a passage of previously anonymous praise. I propose to change a great deal in the third section.

I welcome all your work projects. I expect to hear about you and Berlin from Sachs tomorrow.

Do not take amiss the low level of morale in this letter and accept the most cordial greetings from

Yours,
Freud

*

Berlin,
15.5.14

Dear Professor,

In my last letter I did not enquire in any detail about your ill-health since I thought it was not serious. This is what happens if one is narcissistically restricted by one's own complaints. I now hasten to join your doctor most sincerely in his congratulations. I hope to hear from you as soon as you have a chance to write that you are once more fully satisfied with your health and your achievements—this would be the most reassuring news in view of the demands you make upon yourself. Meanwhile, you might perhaps apply to your own health the motto you mentioned, since there seems to be no reason for pessimism.

As regards the matter of the Presidency, I fully agree with you. I cannot however see why my suggestion concerning your Honorary Presidency should put you in mind of retirement since it would, on the contrary, make you once again the active leader of our Congresses. It goes without saying that I should like most of all to see you as full President. The best solution to the problem will probably be found within the circle of our close friends.

This letter, dear Professor, needs no reply. Do not trouble yourself unnecessarily just now. I should like to add to what I wrote in my last letter—I am working on a short paper about the relationship between the oral and sexual drives.[1] The

[1] Karl Abraham, 'The First Pregenital Stage of the Libido' (1916), *Selected Papers on Psycho-Analysis*, London, 1927.

Zeitschrift should not be completely without contributions from me.

More about plans for the summer as soon as I know something myself. I should like to know some time when your holidays begin – the middle of July or later?

With kind regards and good wishes,

Yours,
Karl Abraham

*

Berggasse 19,
Vienna IX,
5.6.14

Dear Friend,

I read your paper for the *Jahrbuch* yesterday, and cannot refrain from congratulating you on it. I think it the best clinical contribution that has appeared in any of the five volumes, unequalled in assurance, correctness, many-sidedness and interest. *Vivant sequentes.*

Rank will have told you about the immediate political affairs that are engaging our attention. I do not share your confidence that the Zürichers and their Munich appendage will resign before the congress. In any case the uncertainty remains and disturbs our preparations for it, for if they attend it is bound to be different from what it will be if we are left peacefully among ourselves.

One way out would be for you (at the right time) to ask Maeder and Seif outright whether their groups propose to attend or not, your motivation being the necessity of settling the subjects for discussion.

I am thinking of making them 'The objects and aims of a psycho-analytic society', in order to justify the association's existence, rebut the objections relating to restrictions on scientific research, and give some parting counsel to the Swiss, should they be present. In the event of our being undisturbed by them the subject could still stand. I am not concerned about the effect on the American groups, who in any case are unable to join us as an organised society. London will, I hope, remain with us.

I thought it very noble of you not more specifically to have attacked the Zürich slovenliness in your *Korrespondenzblatt*, and defended you for this against Rank. But at the congress you need not mince your words.

With cordial greetings,

Sincerely yours,
Freud

*

Berggasse *19*,
Vienna IX,
14.6.14

Dear Friend,

Having read practically all the galleys of the new *Jahrbuch* today, I must express my thanks for the tremendous pains you have taken in the interests of our cause. It will be an impressive demonstration by our little community, about whom there will be no lack of obituary notices in the near future.

Most of the reviews are very good, and some outstanding. I have no need to stress which. The homogeneity of outlook that runs through them all is very pleasing. Perhaps some of the very good ones are too short, there is a lack of uniformity in the allocation of space.

I should like to ask you to phrase rather more cautiously the passage about my question in the Schreber analysis whether the concept of the libido should be changed, so that it does not seem to justify Jung's misinterpretation. I asked it purely dialectically, in order to be able to answer it in the negative, as Ferenczi correctly saw. But I have no other misgivings to add.

We are now of course awaiting the effect of the 'bombshell' which has not yet been laid. Deuticke has promised to do his utmost to hurry things. As for myself, I have to report that I feel quite well again. In accordance with these times of emergency, I am working from eight in the morning until nine at night.

With cordial greetings and thanks,

Yours,
Freud

Berggasse 19,
Vienna IX,
25.6.14

Dear Friend,

So the bombshell has now burst, we shall soon discover with what effect. I think we shall have to allow the victims two or three weeks' time to collect themselves and react; also I am not sure they will respond to the blandishments bestowed upon them by resigning.

Rank has shown me that the familiar demon has played a small trick on me. So I am sending you a correction for the last page of the *Jahrbuch*; perhaps you yourself will have something to add from other papers.

With cordial greetings,

Yours,
Freud

*

Berlin,
5.7.14

Dear Professor,

I have heard nothing yet from Zürich or Munich. I shall send off the letter to Maeder and Seif next Sunday, unless you wish otherwise.

Last Friday, at the end of the summer term, I read a paper in the *Gesellschaft für Sexualwissenschaft* on 'Incest, Marriage among Relatives and Exogamy'.[1] I met with more understanding and appreciation than I had anticipated.

Now I must ask for your advice. I wrote to you some time ago that I would talk at Dresden on the treatment of psychoses. I have meanwhile come to feel that it would be preferable to have some further experience before presenting the subject to the public; perhaps this subject could be the main theme of the next Congress. I am now preoccupied with another topic. Several analytic cases which I have treated during this last year

---

[1] Paper read in the *Aerztliche Gesellschaft für Sexualwissenschaft* on July 3rd, entitled 'Eigentümliche Formen der Gattenwahl, besonders Inzucht und Exogamie'.

have, I believe, enabled me to explain the symptom of *ejaculatio praecox* almost completely—back to its earliest roots in the first two years. I should like to put the results to the Congress and should be glad to know whether you think the subject suitable. Furthermore, I would mention that I should have to go into castration anxiety in some detail, and that what you told me at Christmas on the journey to Berlin has not yet been published. The most pleasant solution would be, of course, if you yourself would speak about these matters at Dresden and if I could then demonstrate their application to a specific problem. This derivation from castration anxiety is, incidentally, only one of the results I have arrived at.

Your holiday is now approaching. If I have no opportunity to write to you before you leave, I wish you and your family a pleasant journey and a good rest. I should also like to have your address in Karlsbad. My wife leaves with the children tomorrow for the Baltic.

With kindest regards from both of us to you all,

Yours,
Abraham

P.S. A reply to the above question is not urgent.

*

Berggasse 19,
Vienna IX,
10.7.14

Dear Friend,

I have the two hardest weeks of the year behind me, and have withstood them well. I note that the bit of sympathy that my friends have been showing me on the occasion of the 'bombshell' has done me a lot of good. No reaction from Zürich yet. Did I suggest to you that you should wait with your circular letter until the 20th?

Lou Salomé has sent me an exchange of letters with Adler that shows her insight and clarity in an excellent light and does the same for Adler's venom and meanness, and with such trash, etc. Sometimes even Casimiro loses heart.

The *Interpretation of Dreams* arrived today and will soon be with you.

It will be possible to do something about the papers for Dresden only when we are sure of the non-Swiss. In those people's presence we shall say nothing. In that case 'premature ejaculation' would seem to me to be a very suitable subject. Do not hesitate to deal with the castration question in so far as it is useful to you. For me the time for publication has not yet come. The question has magnified and grown more complicated, and thus the solution has receded, so that I must also ask you for restraint in the interests of prudence.

I have had some insight into the basic structure of human early sexuality with which I shall bother you later. But after a fortnight of twelve or thirteen hours' work daily I am incapable of any synthesis, and am panting for the holidays.

Hoping that you and yours will enjoy yourselves on the Baltic,

Yours most sincerely,

Freud

Berlin,
16.7.14

Dear Professor,

How nice that our letters did not cross again. I look forward with great satisfaction to the prospect of the Swiss members' early resignation. Bleuler's letter which I received from Jones today, reminds me of my last months at the Burghölzli. Jung's secession from the Association may well serve as a bridge for Bleuler's return to us. Did you note the concluding sentence? I think Bleuler would like to be asked to take over the leadership in Switzerland again. We shall invite him to the Congress and see what happens. If he were to rejoin us, this would make good any harm the secession may have caused us outside. On the other hand, dear Professor, I take a completely opposite view from yours about Pfister.

I am very curious about the latest on infantile sexuality. Another ten or twelve days and then I shall be off.

Kindest regards to you and your wife,

Yours,
Karl Abraham

Villa Fasolt,
Karlsbad,
18.7.14

Dear Friend,

I cannot suppress a cheer. So we have got rid of them. We shall print their demonstration of indignation in the next number of the *Korrespondenzblatt*, in which I hope you will make a statement on the matter as our definite president.

I enclose two letters, a statement by Putnam and also a letter from Maeder, which remains unanswered, like that to you. The *Zeitschrift* will be glad to get rid of Riklin, Seif and the rest as well as Maeder. So my bombshell has worked well. It is good that your circular letter has already arrived. So once more we shall have a good congress.

Come whenever you like. I shall have to see how to fit it in with work. Also I do not know whether I shall have any desire for work. Saying no to you was made difficult by the circumstance that I originally proposed that we should spend the whole summer together at a time when I was not yet thinking of work during the holidays. The postponement of the meeting is connected with a plan to show my wife Lake Maggiore at the beginning of September.

Do not be afraid of disturbing my cure more often. Such news is good for me.

With cordial greetings and thanks,

Yours,
Freud

*

Berlin,
23.7.14

Dear Professor,

I have now also reached the point where I am groaning under the burden of the last few working days. On Sunday morning I am off on holiday (address: Brunshaupten i/Mecklenburg, Hotel Dünenhaus). The two letters are being circulated. Putnam might have said more; nevertheless, his statement is valuable because it proves that our organisation in America is in no way endangered. Maeder's letter is at any rate courteous in tone. His reference to differences in types, meaning differences in race, does not become more intelligent by repetition. It is easy to withdraw to this position since it is unassailable. The manifesto announced by Maeder has not yet arrived. Seif has not even replied to my letter, sent off a fortnight ago. We should still be without direct proof that the Zürich contingent does not intend to come to the Congress, had we not received some characteristic reactions to our invitation. No reply has as yet been received from Zürich, but I did of course send out their invitations two days later.

The publication of a French work on psycho-analysis is a good sign, and an even better one is the new edition of the *Interpretation of Dreams*. Many thanks for sending me a copy, and also my congratulations. I hope to be able to read it during the holidays.

I called on Mrs A. at her hotel. She speaks of staying in Berlin. I was surprised to learn from her that she is the subject of the 'Predisposition to Obsessional Neurosis'.[1]

I shall be staying with my wife and children in Brunshaupten until August 3rd; from there to Bremen, and back here on August 7th, when Eitingon and I will send off the final Congress programme. On August 9th or 10th we leave for the Tyrol.

After this extensive interruption of your cure, I can only add my kindest regards to you and your wife. I should be glad to learn in your next letter how your sister-in-law is getting on.

Yours,
Karl Abraham

*

Karlsbad,
26.7.14

Dear Friend,

Simultaneously with the declaration of war, which transformed our peaceful spa, your letter arrived, at last bringing the

---

[1] Sigmund Freud, *The Predisposition to Obsessional Neurosis*, Standard Ed., Vol. XII.

liberating news. So we are at last rid of them, the brutal, sanctimonious Jung and his disciples. I must now thank you for the vast amount of trouble, the exceptional clear-sightedness, with which you supported me and our common cause. All my life I have been looking for friends who would not exploit and then betray me, and now, not far from its natural end, I hope I have found them.

I can now satisfy your recently expressed wish and tell you what my subject is; it is aspects of psycho-analytic technique. Please put me in somewhere when the people have warmed up.

It will not be difficult to comment on the motivation of the Swiss refusal with regard to the programme of the International Psycho-Analytical Association.

It is of course impossible to foresee whether conditions will now permit us to hold the congress. If the war remains localised in the Balkans, it will be all right. But the Russians are unpredictable.

However, for the first time for thirty years I feel myself to be an Austrian and feel like giving this not very hopeful Empire another chance. Morale everywhere is excellent. Also the liberating effect of courageous action and the secure prop of Germany contribute a great deal to this. The most genuine symptomatic actions are to be seen in everyone.

I wish you undisturbed enjoyment of your well-earned holiday.

Yours most sincerely,
Freud

Karlsbad,
29.7.14

Dear Friend,

Where are you and what are you thinking of doing? Did you expect your rest *re bene gesta* to be like this? Can you perhaps tell me whether in a fortnight's time we shall be thinking half ashamedly of the excitement of these days, or whether we are close to the turn of destiny which has been threatening us for decades? Do you know whether we shall be able to meet in an intimate congress this year?

Nobody knows, and the abundance of uncorroborated news, the ebb and flow of hope and fear, is bound to have an unsettling effect on us all.

We are here, alone, waiting for letters that arrive late and writing letters which leave irregularly. We hope to be able to leave Karlsbad on Monday, the 3rd, as traffic with Germany remains open, and after some hold-ups to get to Seis[1] after all by way of Munich. We are overjoyed that none of our sons or sons-in-law is personally affected, and yet really ashamed of this in view of the multitude of victims all round us. The weather is as appalling as if it were merely a projection of the state of mind of mankind at this time. Eitingon wanted to come and see me, but the war alarm intervened; our telegrams took twenty-four hours, and so I asked him to give it up. The great struggle would stifle all interest in the minor one which we have now happily ended.

I am glad to have finished two technical articles while it was still quiet, one on transference love and the other entitled 'Recollecting, Repeating and Working Through'.[2] I think my way of writing has changed, since the showdown I have become more honest, bolder and more ruthless. I cannot now imagine myself beginning anything new.

First a change of scenery.

For your amusement I quote verbatim what Jones writes to me today: *I had a long talk with Mrs E. last week, who has just had a month's analysis with Jung. . . . You may be interested to hear the latest method of dealing with Übertragung.*[3] *The patient overcomes it by learning that she is not really in love with the analyst but that she is for the first time struggling to comprehend a Universal Idea (with capitals) in Plato's sense: after she has done this, then what seems to be the Übertragung may remain.*[4]

Risum teneatis, Casimiro.

Eagerly looking forward to your news,

Sincerely yours,
Freud

---

[1] Seis-am-Schlerm (now Siusi) in what was then Austrian South Tyrol.
[2] Sigmund Freud, 'The Dynamics of Transference' and 'Recollecting, Repeating, and Working Through', Standard Ed., Vol. XII.
[3] Transference.
[4] Passage in italics in English in the original.

Ostseebad Brunshaupten,
29.7.14

Dear Professor,

Your letter of the 26th reached me here on the day after my arrival. I should like to respond to your gratitude by doing everything I can to ensure that the Congress will fully compensate you and us all for Munich. You can surely have no doubt that the small circle of the five[1] will do everything possible and give of their best, both at the Congress and also in the future. I shall schedule your paper for the best available time and I believe we shall have a full and varied programme.

Here too everyone is solely preoccupied with the question of war. I do not think any of the powers will start a general war. But there is a strong universal feeling of alarm, in spite of a very friendly attitude towards Austria. We cannot yet tell what will happen to our plans. Rank wrote to me yesterday strongly advising me against going to the Dolomites. It would be a great pity if our meeting were to fall through. If the worst came to the worst, we could meet in Switzerland. The Congress, too, has become somewhat problematical. I hope the next few days will bring a quick decision.

Our *Jahrbuch* arrived yesterday from Deuticke. I am very pleased that we managed to get it ready within six months, despite all the difficulties. I shall start preparations for the next one as soon as I return to Berlin. It should certainly appear in the spring of 1915.

Kind regards from us both to you and your wife,

Yours,
Abraham

Brunshaupten,
31.7.14

Dear Professor,

I am replying straight away. We know nothing here. It is possible that we shall leave today or tomorrow. There are strong indications that general mobilisation will take place

[1] The same Committee referred to in the letter of 10.12.1913, p. 160, footnote 1.

tomorrow or Sunday. It is out of the question to remain here if war breaks out. One cannot make any further plans and so we shall probably wait in Berlin. I must not be far away if war comes, since I am liable for hospital service;[1] otherwise, I have no duties.

This place is already half empty; officers on the active list and men on leave have already been recalled. If you were to stop in Munich, it might be possible for us to meet, but who knows?

One tends to assume that none of the powers wants to start the war. All the same, things look very serious. The papers are only allowed to print half of what is going on.

All I can promise you today is to keep in regular communication with you. Your letter postmarked the 30th has, incidentally, reached me very quickly. This letter brings you best wishes from all of us. I am looking forward to your new papers with as much anticipation as is possible at the moment.

With kind regards,

Yours,
Abraham

Did you not receive my last letter?

Karlsbad,
2.8.14

Dear Friend,

Your letter received today (dated July 31st) has been overtaken by events, so I am writing to you again to Berlin. I thank you for your promise to keep me amply provided with news, and I shall try to do the same with you. We shall probably stay here for another week; travelling to Vienna during the period of mobilisation is hardly practicable, and to Munich it is impossible. Our Ernst[2] is at Salzburg with his brother Martin,[3] and will probably be unable to return for the time being.

[1] Because of an emphysema of the lungs in childhood, Abraham had not done his military service and was therefore only on the reserve.

[2] Ernst, b. 1892, Freud's youngest son.

[3] Jean Martin, b. 1889, Freud's eldest son.

We can dismiss from our minds all worry about the congress, etc. All interest now lies elsewhere. At the time of writing the great war can be regarded as assured; I should be with it with all my heart if I did not know England to be on the wrong side.

I should very much like to get to work on a worthwhile topic that has begun to plague me, but I am still too tense and too distracted. I must wait for definite news, a *fait accompli*. Meanwhile I still feel ashamed at enjoying all the refinements of the spa at charming Karlsbad with my wife while the world is quaking like this. No more white bread is being baked in Vienna. What is perhaps more worrying is that savings and other banks are not paying out deposits over 200 crowns. We shall see to what extent it is possible to do even without money in ordinary life.

We cannot fall out of the world,[1] that is the great consolation.

I hope that you and your family have arrived safely and that your war service will not take you too far from home.

With a cordial shake of the hand,

Sincerely yours,
Freud

Berlin,
3.8.14

Dear Professor,

We got home last Saturday after a very exhausting journey. What are you and your family doing? I shall probably do some locum work for the time being. There is no question of our meeting unless you can come here.

Kind regards,

Yours,
Abraham

[1] A quotation from *Steinklopfer Hans* by Ludwig Anzengruber, 1938–89, Austrian dramatist.

Berlin,
14.8.14

Dear Professor,

I take it that you are now back in Vienna. Unfortunately, I have had no news from you for some time and do not know what may have happened to you all in the meantime. Did your sons have to join the reserve? What has happened to Rank, Sachs and Ferenczi? Our lively correspondence has come to a complete standstill. I have to stand by as a reservist and volunteer physician. I shall probably be employed in this capacity quite soon but know no particulars yet.

The first great victories have done very much to raise morale here. We have had no news since the day before yesterday from the battle-fronts. There may well be great things happening just now and we are in a state of utmost tension. The practice has, to my surprise, somewhat increased this week. This was supposed to have been the holidays and we were to have met in the Tyrol just now. But, in times like these, one has to give up holidays for the sake of a little more financial security. I am working three or four hours a day. I am still too restless to get down to any writing. We are living from one newspaper to the next and are scarcely satisfied with one lot of news before demanding more.

In the hope of receiving good news soon (postcard or open letter) and with kindest regards from house to house.

Yours,
Abraham

Berggasse 19,
Vienna IX,
25.8.14

Dear Friend,

If I expected this open letter would ever reach you, I should tell you that at last I have heard from you (your last letter was dated August 2nd). Since then I have written to you repeatedly, obviously in vain. I have heard from Eitingon in Prague that you are probably remaining in Berlin.

Our news is as follows. We returned here from Karlsbad on August 5th, my sister-in-law, who is at last recovering, was back before us, as her sanatoria had closed. Oli[1] turned up a few days later, and for twelve days we were unable to find out whether Ernst had managed to get back to Munich from Salzburg, to which he had made an excursion. Eventually he reached Vienna from Munich as a passenger of the Austrian consulate there with 1 mark, 55 pf travelling money, but here he was returned with thanks[2] and since then he has been living with us. Annerl[3] is so-to-speak a prisoner-of-war in England; after some long, anxious days we managed to get in touch with her *via* the Hague through Dr van Emden. She remains unmolested at her boarding school on the coast, and is in contact with our friends in London, who will certainly look after her in case of need. She is said to be well, and to be behaving very pluckily. Living in an enemy country cannot be completely without its difficulties.

Martin completed his court practice at Salzburg before the outbreak of war. When the storm broke he volunteered, proved that he had fully recovered from his broken thigh, and managed to be posted to the unit in which he once did his year of military service (41st Regiment of Field Artillery). His reason, according to what he writes, is that he did not want to miss the opportunity of crossing the Russian frontier without changing his faith.[4] He was expecting to remain at Salzburg for several weeks' training, but today we heard that he has left. We do not know of course where he has gone, whether south or north.

My son-in-law in Hamburg has received his calling-up papers for September 7th.

Now for the others. Rank and Sachs are here. Rank is as cheerful as ever and, as we are all for the time being incapable of scientific work, has found himself a job arranging and cataloguing my library. Ferenczi has been called up; he is awaiting employment as a medical officer, and will be coming to see us in the next few days. The remaining members of the society

---

[1] Freud's second son Oliver, b. 1891.
[2] *I.e.*, by the military authorities.
[3] *I.e.*, Freud's daughter Anna.
[4] Jews were not allowed to enter Tsarist Russia.

will be meeting in a café tomorrow, Wednesday. My news of Federn is that he was on the *Kronprinzessin Caecilie*, which turned back off the coast of France after receiving a warning and took him back again to New York.

At last I have the marvellous leisure in my study that I always longed for. But see what happens when wishes come true. I find it completely impossible to make proper use of the opportunity. Like everyone else, I live from one German victory to the next, and torment myself meanwhile with fear of fresh complications, breaches of neutrality, etc. The tremendous feats of our allies seem actually already to have saved us. These are great and terrible times.

Of all my plans for the summer and autumn there is one only to which I propose to adhere. As soon as travelling becomes tolerable again I shall go and see my grandson in Hamburg, and so I shall also be coming to Berlin. This is likely to be early in September. Recent experiences of course put one off making plans and projects for the future.

> *Was sind Hoffnungen,*
> *was sind Entwürfe,*
> *die der Mensch, der vergängliche macht!*[1]

Or something of the sort.

I am delighted to hear that you and your family are well, and only hope that correspondence between the allies will be facilitated again. But perhaps *et haec olim meminisse juvabit*, in the words of Virgil.

Cordially in the name of us all,

Yours,
Freud

*

Berlin,
29.8.14

Dear Professor,

You have evidently not received various letters I sent you. I am glad to hear from you at last and at some length. Your

---

[1] 'What are the hopes, what are the plans, made by frail and transient man?' A quotation from Schiller's *Braut von Messina*.

letter and postcard took only three days to get here and I hope mine will take no longer.

I am so pleased that everything is well with you all. I have often wondered what your youngest would do in England, and correctly assumed that van Emden would be the intermediary.

All is well with us here. I have volunteered for hospital work, either here in Berlin, or elsewhere, or on hospital trains. I very nearly went off to Dirschau on the mouth of the Vistula a week ago. But it was decided otherwise and I remain, for the time being at least, at the military hospital on Grunewald racecourse. I have plenty of work, mainly surgical, but later on I am possibly to take over the Psychiatric and Neurological Department. The practice is now very small. I still feel too unsettled for any writing. The need to help in the common cause and the uncertainty of the first weeks of war overshadowed everything else. Now, however, the news is excellent. The German troops are barely 100 kilometres from Paris. Belgium is finished, England defeated on land. The same is true for Russia. The Austrian successes came at the right moment during the days when we were very worried about East Prussia.

My kindest regards to Sachs, Rank and Ferenczi, as well as to all our other friends in Vienna. I have heard nothing about Hitschmann. What is he doing?

None of us has news of Jones, I take it? Do you also find it strange to think that he belongs to our 'enemies'?

I am very eager to hear when you are going to Hamburg. The express train connection with Vienna seems to be fairly reliable again. It does, of course, go through Berlin and we shall be pleased to see you, rather than the Cossacks, marching in; they, according to some frightened rumours, were due to arrive soon. Your visit, however brief, would be a small compensation for Seis. My wife and I offer you our cordial welcome in advance.

With kind regards to you and yours.

.   Yours
                                             Abraham

Berggasse 19,
Vienna IX,
3.9.14

Dear Friend,

At last a proper letter from you, and with a charming postscript from your wife as well. It has been on the way since August 29th until today, so Berlin is still a long way away.

Thank you very much indeed for your offer, which has fortunately been overtaken by events, and for the news of your family, which I shall do my best to reciprocate. We are all well; the only invalid (my sister-in-law) has almost completely recovered. Martin is at Innsbruck, where I shall go and see him over the week-end; he expects to leave by the middle of the month. My son Ernst will probably be taken at the call-up on the ninth. To the young this means nothing but wish fulfilment. The barriers between army and civil population have practically disappeared, and only the barriers of age remain.

The German victories have provided a firm basis for our morale, and we have been badly shaken in expectation of victories of our own. Things seem to be going well, but there is nothing decisive yet, and we have given up hope of a rapid end of the war by catastrophic strokes. The chief virtue will be endurance. In these circumstances interest inclines rather towards scientific matters again. Rank, with whom I spend a great deal of time, because he is now arranging my library, will be writing to you about this. We count on a similar 'positive' turn with you. We wish to show that we can do good work while cut off from our foreign colleagues, and we want to produce respectable numbers of the *Zeitschrift* and *Imago*.

Jones is of course our 'enemy'. Unfortunately correspondence with van Emden and hence also through him is very unsatisfactory.

I like to think that I shall be in Berlin and Hamburg this month. In these days we hardly dare express a firm intention.

A paper from the Flechsig[1] clinic in Alzheimer's journal

---

[1] Paul Flechsig, Professor of Psychiatry at Leipzig, frequently mentioned in Schreber's memoirs.

shows the beginning of a changed attitude to psycho-analysis even in Germany.

With cordial greetings,

Yours,
Freud

Write again soon.

Berlin,
13.9.14

Dear Professor,

I must assume that several cards and at least one of my letters have not reached you. Postal services are still difficult. Your letter, dated and stamped September 3rd, arrived yesterday, having taken nine days to get here.

I am glad to hear that you are all well and that your sister-in-law is on the way to recovery. My best wishes go with your two sons. Many thanks, by the way, for the card that you and Martin sent me.

All is well with our family. There are, on the whole, few signs of war here in Berlin. We have been greatly reassured by the complete defeat of the Russians in East Prussia, and are hoping to hear favourable news in the next day or so about the battles on the Marne. Once these are decided in our favour, France is virtually finished; that is to say, the capture of the south-eastern fortifications will only take a relatively short time. This evening we heard of the Austrian withdrawal near Lemberg. The fortifications and the Carpathian mountains are sure to halt the Russian advance.

Now to the smaller world of our own interests. I wrote a card to Rank on Tuesday, promising him a short paper. On the same evening I had news that early the next day a transport of wounded would arrive at our hospital, which is situated a long way out of town. That meant that I had to get up at 4.30 a.m., was standing in the operating theatre without a break till 2 p.m. and then spent some hours in my own practice in the afternoon. As the next few days were just as full, I could not even make the smallest beginning on my paper. Perhaps it will be better this week. I do not feel like starting on the bigger piece of work, an excerpt of which I had planned to present as my Congress paper, and shall be all the more glad to be able to put my ideas to you when you come to Berlin. I shall try to arrange to do as little as possible at the hospital during your visit.

My kindest regards to you, your family and all our friends,

Yours, as always,

Karl Abraham

*

Hamburg,
22.9.14

Dear Friend,

Thank you very much indeed for the preparations you are making for my second stay in Berlin, in particular for those concerning England.[1] Having regard to them, I propose to leave here early on Friday and to arrive in Berlin at 1.10, and to stay until six in the evening. The time is too short for a meeting of the group, and, if you can manage it, I should prefer it to be restricted to the two of us.

This is not the first time I have been in Hamburg, but it is the first time I have been here not as in a strange town. I live with my children, talk about the success of 'our' loan and discuss the chances of 'our' battle of millions, all this with a faint memory of discussions about an earlier battle which after some partial successes ended in nothing.[2] It is like remembering an earlier life according to the doctrine of the transmigration of souls.

My grandson[3] is a charming little fellow who manages to laugh so engagingly whenever one pays attention to him; he is a decent, civilised being, which is doubly valuable in these times of unleashed brutality. Strict upbringing by an intelligent mother enlightened by Hug-Hellmuth[4] has done him a great deal of good.

---

[1] This refers to Anna Freud, who was caught in England by the outbreak of war and stranded for some weeks.

[2] A reference to the dissension with Jung.

[3] Ernst, the son of Sophie and Max Halberstadt.

[4] Hermine von Hug-Hellmuth, Vienna woman lay analyst.

My son-in-law has every now and then to photograph a departing hero or to enlarge the portrait of a dead hero, but otherwise can devote himself to his family, so that the days pass very happily.

I think I shall be arriving straight from the station in time for your lunch, in connection with which I count on your family hospitality as an unvarying factor.

Hoping that this letter will reach you before I do myself, I send my cordial greetings to you, your wife, and your swarm of children, who, I hope, have now fully recovered.

Yours,
Freud

Berlin,
11.10.14

Dear Professor,

Many thanks for your postcard. I have postponed writing until today. Now that Antwerp has been taken and tension has relaxed, I must at least send you a sign of life. I should be glad to hear soon how you all are and, in particular, to know what news you have from Martin.

It is doubtful whether my trip to Vienna will come off. My work at the hospital takes up more time now than when you visited us. I must not conclude without thanking you, also on behalf of my wife, for the time you spent with us.

With kind regards from house to house,

Yours,
Karl Abraham

*

Berggasse 19,
Vienna IX,
18.10.14

Dear Friend,

At last a sign of life from you. The Antwerp news is fine, at any rate a good sign. It is to be hoped that things are going the same way elsewhere, where we do not suspect it. We too breathe more freely because of it.

The volume of the *Zeitschrift* has appeared with your *Korrespondenzblatt*, unfortunately showing signs of serious negligence by the printer's reader. A number of *Imago* is expected daily. I am working on the big and difficult case history for the *Jahrbuch* and on the third edition of the 'Sexual Theory'. I do not enjoy the hack work required for this. It is never like something that comes in a single draught.

I am now doing five and a half hours' analysis daily, but practically nothing lasting, the cases I have are definite only for a few weeks. Also one's heart is elsewhere.

Ferenczi is still here, and is spending his holidays here, he is missing nothing in Budapest.

In these unfriendly times we enjoy making plans for the summer. This year the house at Berchtesgaden is at last really coming off. Sophie will manage it, and bring the child and the servants. It would be an opportunity for once to spend a long time quietly with one's friends. Karlsbad will now be counted one of the extravagances of the 'good old days'.

I send my greeting to you, your wife and both your children, and I always think with unqualified pleasure of the days I spent with you.

Sincerely yours,
Freud

*

Berlin,
28.10.14

Dear Professor,

This letter brings with it the manuscript[1] I have owed you for so long. I am still deeply immersed in hospital work, and the few remaining hours are taken up by the practice. Perhaps Rank will be good enough to undertake the small job of proofreading, to avoid posting to and fro in these uncertain times.

The practice proceeds quietly for three or four hours a day. I recently started treating one of your former patients, Dr V. I have not heard anything more of Mrs A.

[1] Probably refers to the paper by Karl Abraham, 'A Contribution towards the Understanding of the Suggestive Effect of Medicine in the Neuroses', *Clinical Papers and Essays on Psycho-Analysis*, London, 1955.

It is wonderful to dream of peaceful holidays in the future. But I hardly dare think about it. We would also be in favour of Berchtesgaden. Let us wait and see.

I intend to call an informal meeting of our greatly reduced group. There is not much opportunity for scientific activity. These are hard days at the front but people are, on the whole, full of confidence and are even beginning to make jokes again. A shop selling uniforms and fashion goods displays a placard saying: 'Field grey, the fashionable colour for 1914.'

With kind regards, also from my wife, to you, your family and our friends,

Yours,
Karl Abraham

*

Berggasse 19,
Vienna IX,
31.10.14

Dear Friend,

Your letter was like a refreshing breeze. We are very pleased just now at the re-establishment of the Triple Alliance as a result of the Turkish decision. Otherwise we of course read the same things in the newspapers.

Your short paper was welcome; a proof of my next paper for the *Zeitschrift* is on the way to you. I am again hard at work on the big case history, in which I launch extensively into general discussion. I now realise that the only reason why I wrote so concisely in recent years was that I had so little time. (!) How shall I get the paper to you when it is finished? You will have to come to Vienna to fetch it, or I shall have to go to Berlin again if, as I hope, you stay there.

Otherwise I have very little to do, I have not been able to get more than two patients, and subsequently there are likely to be fewer rather than more.

As for Mrs A., I am able to inform you that she is with her husband at Nassau—interned as an Englishwoman. This situation will not be very oppressive to her; on the contrary, she will enjoy being under state supervision. She is, after all, a victim of British perfidy. I have noticed in general that obsessional people feel better now in wartime, we have descended to their level.

Binswanger has sent in a good paper on Jaspers and psychoanalysis, but makes too much of Jaspers.[1]

An Italian, Levi Bianchini, a lecturer at Naples, who works at the *Manicomio*,[2] intends to begin an international psychiatric library in Italian with the translation of the nine lectures. Perhaps I have already mentioned that to you.

Ferenczi—as I have perhaps mentioned to you too—has gone to Pápa in Hungary for local service with a regiment of Hussars. Eitingon wrote recently from Igló (Hungary). Ferenczi's address is the Hotel Griff. That brings me to the end of my news.

I send you my cordial greetings and hope that your wife and children, whom you do not mention this time, are well.

Sincerely yours,
Freud

I have seen Reik only once on Wednesday.

*

Berlin,
19.11.14

Dear Professor,

The proofs you sent showed me that the wheels of science are not completely at a standstill. The paper[3] is very convincing, both as a whole and in all details. However, in the interests of beginners, I should like to suggest that one paragraph be expanded a little: Page-proof 3, lines 7–12 describe an experience which the initiated will immediately understand, while the inexperienced will require a somewhat fuller explanation.

These technical papers always arrive at the right time. This

[1] Karl Jaspers, Professor of Psychology at Heidelberg.

[2] A series of psychiatric publications published by the *Archivio Psichiatria e Scienze Affini*, Nocera Superiore.

[3] Sigmund Freud: 'Weitere Ratschläge zur Technik der Psychoanalyse' (III), 'Observations on Transference Love (Further Recommendations on the Technique of Psycho-Analysis III)', Standard Ed., Vol. XII.

most recent one has proved extremely helpful to me during the last few days in the treatment of a difficult case.

As a rule I work at my practice three or four hours a day. My experience is that at the moment there is only one type of patient who seeks treatment and can afford it: unmarried men who have come into money. This applies to all my patients.

Zeitschrift and *Imago* have arrived, as well as the *Psycho-Analytical Review*,[1] but I have only read a very little of them.

I hope everything will continue well for your two sons at the front. General morale here is pretty high at the moment and people are very optimistic. I would go into some things more fully but it cannot be done by letter. I should like to come to Vienna to go through your long manuscript, but I do not know yet whether I shall be able to travel in the foreseeable future. Perhaps between Christmas and the New Year.

Many thanks for news of our friends.

I am very busy at the hospital with my fifty patients. The work in itself and its results are very satisfying. All is well with us.

Kind regards to you and yours, also from my wife,

Yours,
Karl Abraham

*

Berlin,
6.12.14

Dear Professor,

Your last letter contained much that greatly pleased and interested me. One generally hears of nothing but trenches, numbers of prisoners, etc. and then, for a change, there comes a sign that our science is still alive. I am extremely curious to know what new ideas have matured in the short time since we met and very much hope to come to Vienna between Christmas and the New Year; this is, however, rather doubtful. I do not even know whether I shall remain in my present hospital post.

In the meantime, we may possibly have the pleasure of seeing

---

[1] American psycho-analytical quarterly.

your wife on her return journey from Hamburg. We should be very pleased if she could spend a few hours with us.

It is good to hear that you feel so much like working. I am also doing quite well in this respect. In spite of having had no summer break, I am standing up to the heavy burden of work. My practice still occupies me for three to four hours a day. It is possible though that the call-up of the reserve may make a further inroad into my small group of patients.

What is to happen about the next *Jahrbuch*? So far I have only got Sadger's paper. I assume the long paper you mentioned several times will be forthcoming. Reik told me that nothing will come of his contribution. The reviews could be dealt with, but I think we would be short of original papers. I personally cannot promise to get anything ready in the next few months. The hospital takes up too much time. Besides, this year's volume will not have had much of a sale and Deuticke might make difficulties. What is to be done?

I know that you, dear Professor, have a long manuscript ready. In your last letter you mentioned that Reik had written something and that, moreover, his paper on *Couvade*[1] had not yet been printed. We could ask Jones via van Emden whether he has anything. Ferenczi, Rank and Sachs are sure to contribute. I have this manuscript from Sadger, and I intend to write my paper on *ejaculatio praecox*. Some miscellaneous items could be added to all this. Anything further forthcoming during next year could form the basis of our three periodicals for 1916, when they will be published in the normal way once again. If this suggestion appears reasonable to you, would you discuss it with our friends in Vienna?

Your present pessimism would sadden me had it not followed upon a time of special productivity. Findings such as those you hinted at recently do not drop from the skies every day, and it is equally certain that there will be more. If, as I hope, I see you before very long, you will surely have new ideas and discoveries to tell me about. Not everyone is as lucky as Mrs Salomé with her six big brothers. But, at any rate, you have some six small but loyal colleagues who make a point of cheering you up at such times.

[1] See p. 176, footnote 1.

I believe that the war is going more in our favour than we know. The Russian army in particular appears to be thoroughly demoralised. We often hear that our enemies want peace but one does not know how much importance to attach to this. The present reverse in Serbia is indeed disappointing. It must be assumed that the Serbs have reinforcements from outside.

I hope next time to hear only good news of yourself and your family and also of your sons, and am, with kind regards from my wife and myself to you all,

Yours,
Karl Abraham

*

Berggasse 19,
Vienna IX,
11.12.14

Dear Friend,

Correspondence is now so slow and difficult that it is best to answer straight away. I realise that you are unwilling to hold out the hope of coming to see me at Christmas. Everything is too uncertain. My case history will remain lying here for a long time.

In regard to the *Jahrbuch*, things are difficult. We shall have to abandon the idea of an annual report. The question is whether we have enough papers to form a volume and whether Deuticke will be prepared to bring one out at all in 1915. I have not talked to him yet, but incidentally I also fully expect Heller to propose ceasing publication after the completion of the current year of *Imago* and the *Zeitschrift*. We really have no material, and are hardly in a position to demand anything else.

The situation is one of continual crumbling, in the face of which it is not easy to do what your Kaiser rightly called for, that is, keep 'good nerves'. After some good results, my own work has plunged into deep darkness; I go on because one cannot remain without 'something to do' (*que haceres*, as the Spaniards say), but often without enthusiasm and with only slight expectation of solving the very difficult problems. My way of working used to be different, I used to wait for an idea to come to me. Now I go out to meet it, and I do not know whether I find it any more quickly because of that.

Rank and Sachs have both been temporarily rejected. Rank is making very fine progress with the problem of the epic, which he intends to use for his thesis for admission to the faculty. Reik is also very productive – prior to his imminent call-up. I shall send the reprint to Liebermann.

My sons write cheerfully and indifferently, they are completely taken up in their training.

As you notice, I am not always in a radiant mood; apart from general circumstances, I am tormented by my own particular intestine, which has shaken off the effects of Karlsbad after four months.

Lou Salomé has written a touching reply to a letter of mine. Her optimism is too deeply rooted to be shaken. As you know, she had six big brothers, all of whom were kind to her.

My wife came back without touching Berlin. We now have an influenza epidemic in Vienna and in the family.

I hope you and your family are well.

With cordial greetings,

Yours,
Freud

*

Berggasse 19,
Vienna IX,
21.12.14

Dear Friend,

I should like to hazard the paradox that your letters are always cheering even if you have uncheering things to report, as in your last. I hope you have now fully recovered, as have the patients in my family.

You are right, I need someone to give me courage. I have little left. In your letter I cherish all the qualities our allies impress us with, and on top of them your own personal qualities, your *coraggio Casimiro*. Sometimes I have a horror of the meal to come. If you can really manage to come and see me, you will be doing a great service to my morale, and we shall be able to talk over everything easily. Your proposals about the journals will be discussed by everyone involved as soon as one of the publishers raises the subject. We do not want to take the words out of anybody's mouth.

The only thing that is going well is my work, which at intervals produces respectable novelties and conclusions. I recently discovered a characteristic of both systems, the conscious (cs) and the unconscious (ucs), which makes both almost intelligible and, I think, provides a simple solution of the problem of the relationship of dementia praecox to reality. All the cathexes of things form the system ucs, while the system cs corresponds to the linking of these unconscious representations with the word representations by way of which they may achieve entry into consciousness. Repression in the transference neuroses consists in the withdrawal of libido from the system cs, that is, in the dissociation of the thing and word representations, while repression in the narcissistic neuroses consists in the withdrawal of libido from the unconscious thing representations, which is of course a far deeper disturbance. That is why dementia praecox changes language in the first instance, and on the whole treats word representations in the way in which hysteria treats thing representations, that is, it subjects them to the primary process with condensation, displacement and discharge.

I might manage a theory of neuroses with chapters on the vicissitudes of the instincts, repression and the unconscious if my working energy does not finally succumb to my depressed mood.

Reik has again read a good paper on puberty rites.[1]

It now takes seven days for a letter to arrive from Hamburg. How is it that you are already able to send letters in closed envelopes? We know nothing of such progress towards liberty.

Trigant Burrow[2] yesterday assured me of his deep sympathy because of the plight *of my country*,[3] and seriously offered me his house in Baltimore as a place of refuge. That is what they think of us in America.

---

[1] Theodor Reik, 'Die Pubertätsriten der Wilden. Über einige Übereinstimmungen im Seelenleben der Wilden und der Neurotiker', *Imago*, 1915.

[2] Dr Trigant Burrow, American psychiatrist and psycho-analyst.

[3] These three words in English in the original.

I do not know if I have already told you that Rank has brilliantly solved the problem of Homer.[1] I want him to make it his thesis for admission to the faculty. I still want to see him, you and Ferenczi as university lecturers in order to enable psycho-analysis to survive the bad times ahead.

With cordial greetings to your wife and children,

Yours,
Freud

*

Berlin,
26.12.14

Dear Professor,

Your letter dated 21st and postmarked 22nd December reached me on the 24th. Postal services seem to be improving. Of course, letters from here to Austria must also be sent unsealed. The fact that my last letters arrived in closed envelopes must have been due to the censorship department. Your letters also sometimes arrive sealed with the censor's stamp on them. I am keeping the projected journey to Vienna in mind and shall gladly come as soon as it can be arranged, especially as I know that I may be of some small personal use to you.

I found the scientific content of your letter most illuminating in so far as I could assimilate it. I am, however, not yet quite clear on some points, but assume the remainder will be equally illuminating once I have mastered it. I should like to keep this for our meeting which I hope will take place soon.

Your news about Rank is very pleasant; although I do not yet know how he has solved the Homer problem, I am glad for him, and for all of us, to learn of his perseverance and success. I have no idea yet what will happen about the lecturership. I hope during the war to be able to do some work on psychoses, but the case material has not been suitable so far. The paper I previously began has also come to a standstill through lack of suitable material and I therefore do not yet know what will happen after the war. I gather from your letter that Ferenczi

[1] Otto Rank, 'Homer. Psychologische Beiträge zur Entstchungsgeschichte des Volksepos'.

is well. I have heard nothing from Eitingon for a long time. I had a card yesterday from Jones via van Emden; its tone is as friendly as one could expect coming from enemy territory. He does not write anything new. I find Trigant Burrow's offer touching.

Kind regards to you and all your family,

Yours,

Karl Abraham

*

Berggasse 19,
Vienna IX,
30.12.14

Dear Friend,

I am very sorry to hear that you are not yet well and that your wife is now ill too. These are times in which one should at least be in good health. Our domestic epidemic is over, but Ernst is in bed at Klagenfurt with a severe attack of tonsillitis, from which he will certainly get better only slowly. One can of course do nothing for him. According to his letter today he is back in barracks, though feverish.

Impotence and penury have always been my bugbears and I am afraid we are now approaching both.

Deuticke has told me that he does not want to publish the *Jahrbuch* in 1915, as he has not yet been able to distribute the 1914 edition. He says that people are pulling in their horns everywhere, and quotes the example of well-known German publishers who in many cases have gone out of business for the duration of the war. I suspected something of the sort when I read of your intentions in your last letter but one.

We have not yet heard from Heller, but do not expect anything different from him.

When you come here—I am delighted you have not abandoned the intention—you will at all events be able to have a full discussion with Deuticke. I shall postpone till that happy occasion telling you about Rank's findings on Homer. My own work is at a standstill. I have not got over certain difficulties, and as a consequence of my state of mind I no longer like my previous findings so much. Because of this estrangement I am often completely at a loss what to do with myself. The obvious remedies are of course those that are now generally recommended – patience and determination to see it through.

Jones writes tirelessly in his old tone; I do not know whether he receives my replies.

You will perhaps receive the 'Sexual Theory' sooner than this letter.

Wishing you all a speedy recovery,

Yours most sincerely,
Freud

Berggasse 19,
Vienna IX,
25.1.15

Dear Friend,

Such a long time has passed since your last meagre and unpleasing postcard that I must write to you again.

First about myself. Physically I am well again and in good spirits, but am not working and have dropped everything on which I had started, including some things that were very promising. I still think it is a long polar night, and that one must wait for the sun to rise again. Whether this feeling is part of a progressive development or only the consequence of an organic periodicity that now reveals itself in the deprivation of so much is a question it will be possible to answer only retrospectively. About other things I have good news for you. I was afraid that Heller would decline to continue publication of the two journals, but that has not happened. The final decision will not be made till next Thursday, but we are agreed that the new annual series of both shall begin in rather reduced form, the International Journal with six numbers as before, each of four signatures, and *Imago* with four numbers of six signatures. Thus our expectations in regard to the journals have been reversed. Of course we shall have to rely for contributions on ourselves and those closest to us, and we count to a large extent on you.

I saw my son Martin early last Wednesday morning between

two trains in the guise of a smart corporal before he left for the Galician theatre of war. I thought in all clarity about the doubt there is whether and how we shall ever see him again.

My medical activity is permanently reduced to a quarter; otherwise there is no news. In the last number of his Dutch weekly van Emden printed a letter about the war for which he had asked me, in which I of course let psycho-analysis have its say.[1]

I send my cordial greetings to you and your family and await your news, I hope from Berlin.

Yours,
Freud

Berlin,
30.1.15

Dear Professor,

You have obviously not received my last letter. I have also been expecting a reply from you daily! Let us hope *this* letter will reach its destination.

As to our journals: I have started a small paper about the relation between hunger and libido.[2] Instead of theories à la Jung, it is in the main to contain analytically established facts and conclusions drawn from them. As you know, it does not depend on me when I shall be able to finish it.

The letter you never got contained my thanks for the *Three Essays,* as well as some remarks about them. I am therefore repeating my thanks again.

It is striking in the hospital how few men are affected by actual neuroses. I have seen a number of traumatic neuroses, well known to us from peacetime, in a typical form. They were all men who had had accidents at the front, such as being run over; they had not been wounded. I have also seen several severe cases of hysteria in men knocked unconscious by explosions. They mostly have aphasia-abasia and hysterical attacks.

[1] Letter to Frederik van Eeden, *De Amsterdammer,* I, 1915, Standard Ed., XIV, p. 301.
[2] This must refer to preparatory work on 'The First Pregenital Stage of the Libido', *Selected Papers,* London, 1927.

I am not giving up my plan to go to Vienna but it will have
to wait some time.

With kind regards, also from my wife, to you and yours,
both in Vienna and at the front,

Yours,
Karl Abraham

*

Berggasse 19,
Vienna IX,
18.2.15

Dear Friend,

I received your letter of January 30th on February 12th and
your postcard of February 16th today, so things seem to be
better again. However, a previous letter from you seems to
have gone astray. We were quite disconsolate at being cut off,
we were without news from Hamburg for eighteen days.

I cannot report any further development of my practice. At
the end of this week my daily sessions will be reduced from four
to three. I have finished something new on melancholia,[1] it is
now with Ferenczi, who will forward it to you. The first number
of the *Zeitschrift* is at the printer's; the introductory article is a
technical contribution by me which I am sending you so that
you may kindly let me know what you think of it. I propose to
send as much as possible to the *Zeitschrift*. We know that we can
count on you to send as much and as soon as you can.

Pfister is drawing very close to us, and has contributed a
critical paper on the 'arson' of the notorious Z. Schmid; and
he has also sent us a short essay by a new man who draws an
analogy between our libido and Plato's theory of Eros. (He is a
Dr Nachmannsohn of Zürich.[2])

Rank yesterday showed me a letter from Jones. He is very
well, is doing ten analyses a day, etc. His group has suspended
its meetings, and appears to be seriously split. All interest is
concentrated on events that are to begin on the 18th, that is to

---

[1] Sigmund Freud, *Mourning and Melancholia*, Standard Ed., Vol. XIV.
[2] Max Nachmannsohn, 'Freuds Libidotheorie verglichen mit der
Eroslehre Platos', *Internationale Zeitschrift*, III, 1915.

say, today. May they bring us victory and therewith liberation and peace. This time I incline towards optimism.

I send my cordial greetings to you and to your wife, and now hope to be hearing from you more often again.

Yours,
Freud

*

Berlin,
28.2.15

Dear Professor,

This time I received your letter within three to four days. I hope mine will also reach you without difficulty.

I must first of all thank you for the proofs. I found nothing to criticise from the first word to the last. To my great satisfaction, everything in this paper corresponds with my own experiences. In saying this is your first paper that did not give me anything new, I only mean that–for once–I did not need to do any re-thinking. On the other hand my own observations were not yet so clearly formulated and I therefore learnt quite a lot from the way you structured your paper.

I can only occasionally find time for writing. I am working on the short paper on pleasure from sucking. If I can complete it, I should like to publish it as No. 1 in a small series, which is to deal with the pregenital phases. I recently began treatment of a relatively simple case of obsessional neurosis which over-whelmingly confirms the theory you put forward in Munich. I should like to present this as No. 2 of the series, and No. 3 would then contain some contributions on the symptomatology of anal erotism. I have only just been able to study at leisure the new edition of the *Three Essays*. I have always had a pre-ference for this work and like it just as much in its new form. The findings of the last ten years fit in very well with the earlier ones.

I often think how the war saved us from unpleasant discus-sions with the Swiss members. When it is over we shall go our separate ways.

We too are wondering what our blockade against England

will achieve. There are no authentic reports so far but, in the light of previous experiences, we may expect amazing facts to be disclosed one day. Our new war loan will probably be another complete success.

With kind regards, also from my wife, to you and all your family,

Yours,
Karl Abraham

*

Berggasse 19,
Vienna IX,
4.3.15

Dear Friend,

The means change, but the result is the same. When you say that my last contribution taught you nothing new, it is as gratifying to me as your usual assurance of the opposite. I believe this effort to be the best and most useful of the whole series, so I am prepared for it to evoke the strongest opposition.

Your announcement of a series of articles, which I take as a definite promise, is extremely welcome. After all, we wish to keep the journals alive at all costs while the war lasts and to conduct them in such a way that later we shall be able to produce them with pride. But the authors are very few. We shall have to do everything ourselves. I have decided to publish three chapters of my germinating summary (instincts, repressions, the unconscious[1]) in three successive numbers of the *Zeitschrift*. For *Imago* I am actually writing a piece of topical chit-chat about war and death[2] to keep the self-sacrificing publisher happy. All this of course against inner resistance.

My heart's in the Highlands, my heart is not here. Actually it's in the Dardanelles, where the fate of Europe is perhaps being decided; in the classical country the inhabitants of which will probably declare war on us in the next few days, with the

[1] Sigmund Freud, 'Instincts and their Vicissitudes', 'Repression', and 'The Unconscious', Standard Ed., Vol. XIV.

[2] Sigmund Freud, 'Thoughts for the Times on War and Death', Standard Ed., Vol. XIV.

result that the places which I have most enjoyed being in will be closed to me for my remaining years; and on the North Sea, on which it will be a long time before one can travel again.

Enough!

I send my cordial greetings to you and to your wife, and hope you will be allowed to remain in Berlin, where doctors are also needed, after all.

Yours,

Freud

Allenstein,

13.3.15

Dear Professor,

I arrived here yesterday and shall be doing surgical work, though I hope to have more time for my own work than I had at home. I have brought with me the paper I recently promised you. My address is: Allenstein (Ostpreussen), Garnison Lazarett I, Hohensteinerstrasse. What is your news, and what do you hear from your sons? I hope that here too I shall hear from you frequently.

With kind regards to you, your family and our friends,

Yours,

Abraham

Berggasse 19,

Vienna IX,

15.3.15

Dear Friend,

Our warmest good wishes accompany you in your new work, which I hope will give you opportunity to see your family and sometimes also leisure to do your intended writing.

Please retain the presidency, which in any case is now a sinecure. If you agree, we propose to announce in the first number of the *Zeitschrift* on which we are now working that because of your call-up publication of the 1915 *Jahrbuch* is now doubtful, but that publication of the two other organs will continue. When I have finished this letter I shall begin drafting *Instincts and their Vicissitudes*.

214

You will have heard that we hold peace in the south to be assured. If we ever see San Martino again, we shall be able to visit it only as guests. In any case I preferred the Karersee, which remains with us.

In eager expectation of your news,

Sincerely yours,
Freud

*

Berggasse 19,
Vienna IX,
27.3.15

Dear Friend,

I eagerly await your news from your new abode, but I myself have little to tell you. I am working slowly and steadily on the papers for *Imago* and the *Zeitschrift*, and have found confirmation of the elucidation of melancholia in a case I studied for two months, though without visible therapeutic success, which, however, may follow.

How are you and your work? What do the children say about papa's absence? How is your wife managing alone?

With cordial greetings from us all,

Yours,
Freud

Deutsch Eylau,
31.3.15

Dear Professor,

I have long postponed commenting on your 'Outline of a Theory of Melancholia' – this was not only because I have no real leisure for work. Some years ago I myself made an attempt in this direction but was always aware of its imperfections, and was therefore afraid that my attitude to your new theory might easily be too subjective. I think that I have now got over this difficulty and am able to accept all the essentials in your work. I do think, however, that one element from my earlier work should be more greatly stressed than it is in yours, and should

215

like to put forward a suggestion which may solve the question left open by you. Important questions do of course remain unanswered, and I have no explanation for them at the present time.

I should like to remind you – not to assert my priority but merely to underline the points of agreement in our findings – that I also started from a comparison between melancholic depression and mourning. I found support in your paper on Obsessional Neurosis[1] (The Rat Man) which had just been published, and I stressed that sadism was important because its intensity did not allow the capacity for love to develop; and I traced the depression back to the subject's awareness of his inability to love. I had to leave completely unanswered the question why melancholia develops in one case and obsession in another. At the time, two important papers of yours were still to be written: Narcissism, and Pregenital Organisations. I recently wrote to you how completely convinced I was by this new concept of obsessional neurosis. If therefore, as you will surely admit, there is a relationship between obsessional neurosis and melancholia, the new insight into obsessional neurosis will also shed light on melancholia.

Of the two important factors in the development of obsessional neurosis – sadism and anal erotism – I strongly stressed the importance in melancholia of the former in my paper of 1911.[2] I must still hold to this view – too much violence and criminality was uncovered in the analyses of my melancholic patients for it to be otherwise. After all, the self-reproaches indicate repressed hostile feelings. The complete motor inhibition leads one to assume that strong motor impulses have had to be made harmless. The same tendency is manifest in the way the melancholic torments those around him. Added to this is the reappearance of the most open sadism in the manic phase. These are only a few of the reasons why I still rate this factor as highly as ever.

[1] Sigmund Freud, 'Observations on a Case of Obsessional Neurosis', Standard Ed., Vol. X.

[2] Karl Abraham, 'Notes on the Psycho-Analytical Investigation and Treatment of Manic-Depressive Insanity and Allied Conditions', *Selected Papers on Psycho-Analysis*, London, 1927.

On the other hand, I think, looking back over my earlier cases, that one should not assume that anal erotism is outstandingly important in melancholia. If I am right in this assumption (which still needs to be confirmed, because at the time of the analyses of the 1911 cases I had no knowledge yet of the importance of anal erotism in obsessional neurosis and may possibly have overlooked it in melancholia), then this may well be the point where these conditions, in other ways so closely related, diverge.

To proceed further from here, I must revert to what you say in your paper under (3). Even though I do not yet see that the melancholic displaces on to himself all the reproaches which are aimed at his love-object and which serve to denigrate it, all that you say about identification with the love-object is perfectly clear to me. Perhaps I could not fully grasp this because of the compression of your arguments. It appeared to me in my patients as if the melancholic, incapable of loving as he is, strenuously tries to get possession of the love-object. In my experience, he in fact identifies with his love-object, cannot tolerate its loss and is hyper-sensitive to even the slightest unfriendliness. He often allows himself to be tormented by the loved person in masochistic self-punishment. He reproaches himself for this instead of reproaching the loved person because, unconsciously, he has done far greater harm to that person (omnipotence of thought). That is how I deduced it in my analyses. But as you well know, dear Professor, I am ready to re-learn. I only regret that our discussion has to be carried on by letter.

What harm has the melancholic in fact done to the object with whom he identifies?

The answer to this is revealed to me in one of your recent papers—I think it is the one on Narcissism (?). You here discuss identification and you point to the infantile basis of this process: the child wants to incorporate its love-object, to put it briefly, it wants to devour it. I have therefore strong reason to suspect that such cannibalistic tendencies exist in the melancholic's identification. It may be safely assumed that this identification has an ambivalent meaning—a manifestation of love as well as of destructive impulses.

The first argument I would advance is the melancholic's fear of starvation. Food has taken the place of love. I would assume that the role which the anal zone plays in obsessional neurosis is assigned to the mouth in melancholia. In menopausal depressions in particular, the fear of starvation plays a dominant role. A further important symptom is the refusal of food. In other less severe and more chronic cases, food in the positive sense is of excessive importance.

Also of interest is the classic form of depressive delusions found in earlier times, called lycanthropy. This is the delusion of being a werewolf and of having eaten men. Such delusions are not so rare even nowadays. I should mention here a characteristic and rather curious form of crude questioning which, up till quite recently, some psychiatrists would use towards patients believed to be suffering from delusional self-reproaches they did not wish to reveal. They would say the following: what have you done, have you perhaps devoured small children? Such so-called jokes must in some way be rooted in real experience.

I think that the impoverishment of the ego becomes more comprehensible in this way. The ego does not, as it were, get the food it wants. It has lost its content (that is to say, that which it wanted to incorporate).

It seems to me that we ought to agree easily, unless the above ideas are too much off the rails. The basic points of your exposition: the melancholic has lost something but does not know what; the impoverishment of the ego and all that is connected with it; the identification with the love-object; the localisation of the process of mourning in the ego-cathexes; the undoing of object-cathexes by narcissistic identification – all this should definitely stand. I think sadism and oral erotism should be added.

I should like to ask you, dear Professor, for unsparing criticism, and also for a more detailed explanation wherever I have misunderstood your very condensed arguments.

In the hope of receiving good news from you and yours – such as I have from my own home – I am,

Yours,
Karl Abraham

Allenstein,
26.4.15

Dear Professor,

Your card of the 19th reached me fairly quickly, as did the parcel of proofs. I have cursorily read through the latter once and should therefore prefer to say nothing about them today. At any rate, it is good to know that the concepts we constantly use are being properly clarified. I enjoyed reading the short paper on War; my wife is at present reading it in Berlin. You were wrong when you wrote deprecatingly about this work some time ago. There can scarcely be any disagreement between us concerning our viewpoint in these matters. I shall therefore only add that this paper has my full agreement and that I am very much looking forward to the chapter on Death. While reading your work, I was struck by an interesting parallel. What is forbidden to the individual in normal circumstances, is now demanded of him – and moreover, in company with all other men. Exactly the same applies to the totem meal, where the whole community consumes the animal which the individual is usually not permitted to touch.

One of your letters, dear Professor, which you wrote to me soon after I was posted here, arrived very late because it was inadequately addressed. In this letter you asked me about my children's reaction to my leaving. I have some nice stories to tell about our little boy. And indeed my daughter was also delighted with my uniform which I had been wearing for some time in Berlin. She was particularly impressed by the soldiers' salutes. The little boy took the matter in a very different way in accordance with his sex and age. He was most impressed by my sword, and I promised that I would let him wear it some time. He was speechless with delight when I put it on him, and the impression stayed with him. The next day he said in front of the whole family at dinner: another father wouldn't have done that – given me his sword to wear. This harmless incident must have served to change the child's hostile feelings into their opposite. I imagine that what he said probably means: if I were in possession of this precious weapon, I would not have given it to anyone else. He was obviously struck by my generosity.

During the following days he was extremely affectionate but there was something in his behaviour which illuminated for me the psychology of the subordinate. For example, on one occasion I was pacing up and down the room and, because of my heavy army boots, my gait was different from what it usually is. The little fellow immediately fell into step with me, walked behind me and imitated the length, rhythm and heaviness of every step I took. He has obviously identified with me ever since I knighted him. This is also apparent from the games he is now playing at home.

I send my kind regards to you and your family and to our friends in Vienna.

As always, yours,
Karl Abraham

*

Berggasse 19,
Vienna IX,
4.5.15

Dear Friend,

A fortnight of being cut off from Germany has at last ended. Your letter and twelve postcards from my wife in Hamburg arrived today by the same post. I now hasten to send you my long delayed reply.

Your comments on melancholia are very useful to me, and I unhesitatingly incorporated in my paper those parts of them that I could use. What was most valuable to me was the reference to the oral phase of the libido, and I also mention the link with mourning to which you draw attention. Your request for severe criticism causes me no difficulty; I liked practically everything you wrote. I should like to make only two points: that you do not bring out sufficiently the essential feature of your assumption, that is to say the topical element, the regression of the libido and the abandonment of unconscious object cathexis, but instead put in the foreground sadism and anal erotism as explanatory factors. Though you are correct in this, you miss the real explanation. Anal erotism, the castration complex, etc. are ubiquitous sources of excitation that are bound to play their part in every clinical picture. Sometimes one thing comes of them and sometimes another; it is of course always our duty to find out what has become of them, but the explanation of the disorder can be derived only from its mechanism, seen from the dynamic, topical and economic aspects. I know that soon you will agree with me.

My work is now taking shape. I have finished five papers: that on Instincts and their Vicissitudes, which is rather dry, but is essential as an introduction and is justified by those that follow, then those on Repression and the Unconscious, the 'Metapyschological Supplement to the Theory of Dreams'[1] and 'Mourning and Melancholia'.[2] The first four are to appear in the new series of the *Zeitschrift*, and all the rest I am keeping for myself. If the war lasts long enough, I hope to get together about a dozen such papers and in quieter times to offer them to a non-understanding world under the title of 'Introductory Papers on Metapsychology'. I think that on the whole it will represent an advance. The manner and level will be that of the seventh chapter of the *Interpretation of Dreams*.

I finished the paper on melancholia a quarter of an hour ago. I shall have it typed and send you a copy. You must let me have your comments.

There is bound to be a decision soon in regard to Italy, and the indications are that it will not be a peaceful one. What a pity that this now disturbs the prospects of the victory celebrations for which we have been waiting for so long. Our admiration of our great ally increases daily.

It was very gratifying of you to like even the 'Thoughts for the Times'. You will soon receive the continuation about 'Death'. Your remark about the analogy with the totem meal is absolutely correct. It is interesting to note how the slightest trace of affect restricts the author's view. What you write about your children is very significant. There is always something to see and to understand.

We have all shown unexpected adaptability in getting used to the war, with the result that we too can say we are well. The biggest surprise to me is my ability not to miss my practice and earnings. I fail to see that I shall ever again get used to a

[1] Standard Ed., Vol. XIV.   [2] Standard Ed., Vol. XIV.

working day of six or eight hours–I had grown accustomed to ten. Is one's elasticity equally great in both directions? We like to quote an advertisement that is very common here and says that you quickly get used to the pleasant taste. By the time you read this I shall be fifty-nine years old, which should perhaps give me a right to comfort, but I have no way of staking my claim to it. So C.C., and let us leave something over for the next generation.

I hope that you too will make frequent use of the reopened postal service, and please give your wife my cordial greetings.

Yours as ever,
Freud

*

Allenstein,
3.6.15

Dear Professor,

You are right–it is indeed a long time since I last wrote to you. Your reminder will at least prove effective. I shall first tell you about all that has happened in the meantime. My wife spent the first week of May with me. We had some pleasant days together, though my duties kept me fairly busy. Shortly after my wife's departure your letter arrived, but, almost at the same time, came the news that our little boy had fallen ill with diphtheria immediately after his mother's return. We have had an anxious time.

I shall start by continuing my report of last time, and tell you some more about our small son who really is a pillar of psycho-analysis. I don't think I told you what his parting words were when I left for Allenstein in March. You may remember that I had gained his confidence and admiration through the incident with the sword. When saying goodbye, he only said: Daddy, perhaps you will win the battle. The best he has produced so far came after my wife's return from Allenstein. On the day after her arrival, her brother and sister came to dinner. During the meal, the little chap obviously wanted to say something: Mummy, while you were in Allenstein I kept having a dream

('dream' is what both children call their daydreams). My wife unsuspectingly asked him what he had dreamt. The answer: I kept on thinking when mummy comes back from daddy whether there would soon be a baby growing inside her. I should mention that our children have been told about pregnancy and birth but not about conception. They have never asked about it. I have no idea where the child heard about it, and I think that he must have put two and two together for himself. I have already told you of his jealousy and his wish to have his mother all to himself. This omnipotent position also includes having children with the mother. Our bedroom has always aroused his curiosity and he has often tried in the morning to look through the keyhole. There can definitely be no question of his having observed anything at night. Nevertheless, the following shows that his ideas were the right ones. When he had diphtheria, he was kept in isolation in his room. During the subsequent disinfecting of the room, my wife was obliged to take him into our bedroom for two nights before he could return to the nursery shared with his sister. He was beside himself with delight. Even earlier on he had asked questions such as: Does daddy allow this? And then: Does he allow me to put my hanky under his pillow? (This seems to be an obvious displacement of his real wishes for something 'very small'.) When the night he had waited for at last arrived, the bedside cupboard with the chamber-pot in it had a magical attraction for him. He woke frequently during the two nights only in order to use it. This seems to bear out one of the frequent infantile theories,[1] and I suspect that this is the explanation of the 'dream'. There is other evidence for this but it would take too long to report it all.

As regards the question of melancholia, I am now fully in agreement with you on one point—that I had not sufficiently appreciated the mechanism, that is to say the topographical aspect. One other point remains: the postulation in your short manuscript that the reproaches directed against the melancholic's own ego are really directed against another person. I am not yet convinced of this, and I do not remember your bringing detailed proof in your paper. If it does not involve too

[1] This refers to birth phantasies.

much trouble, I should like to have a letter from you explaining more exactly what you mean and how you account for it.

I read with great pleasure of your plans for further work, especially in connection with your remark about your fifty-ninth birthday. You have, of course, dear Professor, my good wishes on this occasion. Omnipotence of thought is, however, not yet sufficiently established for us to expect much benefit from good wishes alone.

Many thanks for the paper on Death. It has only one fault, that it is not a little longer. I mean this in two ways: firstly, because I would have liked to read more of it, and, secondly, because the extremely condensed summary of the taboo-totem paper may not be convincing to outsiders. I had the impression that writing this paper did not give you the satisfaction you usually get and that this accounts for its brevity. It is different with the Vicissitudes paper. I must agree with your own judgement—that it is somewhat thin but that it makes an excellent basis for what is to follow.

Since June 1st I have been living in the hospital as medical officer on night duty. There is a slight possibility that a Psychiatric Department may be set up some time and I shall probably be in charge of it. However, everything is still uncertain, even whether I stay in Allenstein.

I remain as optimistic as ever about the big events. Morale has not been shaken here by Italy. One would never have imagined what a nation is capable of in war time when attacked from all sides. It reminds one of analogies in the life of the individual. We may expect further rapid progress after the fall of Przemysl.

With kindest regards to you and your family,

Yours,
Karl Abraham

Berggasse 19,
Vienna IX,
3.7.15

Dear Friend,

There is no simple reason for my having failed to answer you for so long; on the contrary, the motivation was highly complicated, and I shall now try to break it down into its component parts. First of all there was an intention to imitate you in your long silence, which had already caused me concern. This was indeed not groundless, as your child's severe illness coincided with that interval. Then there was the impact of our splendid victories, which expressed itself in increased working energy, with the result that today I have already reached the middle of the eleventh of the proposed twelve papers.[1] As a result of the gap I got into a muddle and do not know what I have already sent you. Some of what has already passed the manuscript stage is transmissible. I am in the same state with Ferenczi, who is so much nearer and turns up in Vienna occasionally. Our correspondence undergoes the most remarkable interruptions, and I cannot remember what I have sent him and what I have not. I think I regard the situation as a repetition of the original one, when I was productive and–isolated. All my friends and helpers are now in the army, and have, so to speak, been taken away from me. Even Rank, who is still in Vienna, has not appeared since his call-up. He is serving with the heavy artillery, and Sachs will be going to the army service corps at Linz.

On top of all this there was a third reason, an absence of several days from Vienna while I was at Berchtesgaden. I liked it so tremendously, it so far exceeded the memory of the five summers I spent there, that the only explanation I can offer is that my libido, having been set free by the loss of Italy, wanted to settle there. Our plans for the summer have now taken shape. The two of us will be going to Karlsbad a fortnight today, and from there probably to Königsee or Berchtesgaden, with an interruption in August for a visit to Ischl on the occasion of my

[1] Of these proposed papers on metapsychology only five were eventually published in 1915-17.

mother's eightieth birthday. (My father reached the age of 81/2, and my eldest brother the same age, so there's a gloomy prospect.) Of course in these times all plans are rather uncertain. *Was sind Hoffnungen, was sind Entwürfe, die der Mensch, der Vergängliche baut?*[1]

I should gladly tell you more about melancholia, but could do it properly only if we met and talked. Have I sent you the typed manuscript of 'Mourning, and Melancholia'?

A book by Putnam called *Human Motives* appeared yesterday; it is a popular work forming part of a series, free of Jung but in the service of his own hobby-horse. I enclose half the wrapper, in case the censorship passes it. Otherwise I hear only of neutral (and Hungarian) requests for translation rights.

I shall be very glad to hear that your young hopeful has fully recovered and that you are really working in a psychiatric department. My cordial greetings and good wishes to you and your wife.

Yours,
Freud

*

Allenstein,
6.7.15

Dear Professor,

I was just going to write to you to ask about the reason for your silence, when your letter arrived. I am glad to hear that it was only delayed for psychological reasons. One so easily fears other reasons in these times. I fully understand your feeling of scientific isolation, and am myself one of those who failed to liberate you from it. But it has been weeks since I was able to add a line to my still unfinished paper. The hospital work takes up almost all my time. My duties as psychiatrist are, by the way, only a side-line. In the main, I have become a surgeon—not only an assistant or dresser, but an operating surgeon. The psycho-analyst in me stands amazed while I operate on a hydrocele or carry out a rib resection for empyema. But war is war.

I have recently regained my good spirits. There was a very

[1] See footnote 1, p. 193.

worrying period again between my last letter and this one. About a fortnight ago I had most alarming news from Bremen about my father, had to rush off there and found him very ill. When I arrived the illness had already passed its climax and he recovered so much under my eyes that I was able to leave after a few days. He is now slowly improving. On my return journey, I stayed one day in Berlin. Our boy is still rather weak after his severe illness.

Regarding your new papers—I am amazed at your productivity during recent months. I have only read what has appeared in print in the meantime and only know about 'Mourning and Melancholia' from our correspondence. I look forward to all that is to come. Incidentally, I shall in my virtually completed paper on the oral phase make some allusions to the connection I mentioned to you some time ago. When the manuscript is ready, I shall send it to you and not to Rank. This seems safer at present.

Some more about psychology. My son recently disowned me in a characteristic way. When my wife told him: Hilde is daddy's daughter and you are daddy's son, he strongly denied this. On being asked who he thought he was, he replied: I am daddy's half-brother.

On my journey to Bremen during the night after receiving the bad news, I had a very nice dream about my dog that died —a dream that has recurred since childhood, with all the signs of infantile hostility. You will be interested to hear of a slip of the pen in your letter of today. You mention the forthcoming eightieth birthday of your mother and add that your father reached the age of eight and a half years.

I spend the little free time I have enjoying the beautiful woods of this neighbourhood. East Prussia offers great natural beauties, especially big lakes lying between wooded hills.

We are pleased about the successful defence of the Austrian Alps, and no less about the great victories in Galicia. In spite of the fact that one cannot see the end anywhere in sight, morale remains firm and confident. Many kind regards and good wishes to you all, at home and at the front,

Yours,
Karl Abraham

Dear Friend,

I was delighted to hear from you, though all your news is not pleasing, but as variegated as life itself is now. Fortunately none of it was definitely bad, however. The psycho-analyst may be surprised, but must adapt himself.

We arrived here a fortnight ago and found that this spa still keeps its old charm; the food is good, and the place is much quieter than it used to be. It is full of officers with Iron Crosses instead of ladies in fantastic dresses. Apart from a disturbance caused by my wife's having some tooth trouble, we can say that everything has been satisfactory, and we are actually thinking of staying on for an extra week. In the middle of August we are going to Ischl for grandmother's eightieth birthday (incidentally, 81/2 was not a slip of the pen, but my usual way of writing 81–82, taken over from my dream notes, *e.g.*, 'dream of August 8/9'). Our daughter is already at Ischl.

Ernst should have left for Galicia yesterday. Martin has been through some severe fighting, a bullet grazed his right arm and another went through his cap, both without doing him any harm. He has been mentioned for gallantry in the field. In his last postcard he mentions the possibility of a fortnight's leave. He has been at the front since January 20th.

Since I have been here I have finished my twelve papers, they are war-time atrocities, like a lot of other things. Several, including that on consciousness, still require thorough revision. The censorship seems now to have made the sending of manuscripts much more difficult. What else may fall by the wayside before the book is ever printed is unpredictable.

There is no news from anyone. Lou Andreas has promised a paper on 'Anal and Sexual'.[1] The editors of *Imago* are all in uniform. My house in Vienna is open, and is thus the best address for correspondence.

---

[1] Printed in *Imago*, 1916.

I hope this letter will be forwarded to you in Mecklenburg.
With cordial good wishes,

Sincerely yours,
Freud

*

Allenstein,
24.10.15

Dear Professor,

We neither met at the beginning of September nor have we even been in contact by letter for quite some time. Up till a few days ago, I have done practically nothing but hospital work day and night. At last work has begun to ease off a little. Yesterday afternoon, for the first time, I had a few free hours when I did not have to make up on sleep, and I finally unearthed my manuscript and wrote a few pages. I tell you this today as a good omen and hope to be able to resume our correspondence as well as my writing.

My wife was delighted with your and van Emden's visit, and I want to repeat my thanks – although I thanked you briefly some time ago. It is over a year since we have seen each other and, unfortunately, I do not at present see any possibility of arranging a meeting. I hope that you and your family, both at home and at the front, are as well as one could wish. Our news is also good – even my father, at the age of seventy-three, has recovered from his severe attack of pleurisy, though he is still very weak and suffering from after-effects.

I am very pleased that both journals are continuing. As I mentioned, I hope to be able to send in a contribution soon. I hardly dare say this since I have so often made this promise to you. As soon as I have more leisure, I should also like to contribute something to *Imago*.

The fact that Sachs remains in Vienna and that Rank is also still there, as well as some older members, means that our work has not completely stopped there as it has here. Rank wrote that you will be having the first meeting of the winter about now; meanwhile, I must sit here *in partibus infidelium*, and am developing more and more into a surgeon!

I hope to hear from you again soon, dear Professor. You will be certain, as always, to have a lot of news while I am ashamed to have nothing positive to report as far as our scientific work is concerned. However, it may be different from now on.

With kind regards to you and all your family,

Yours,

Karl Abraham

29th October

This letter was returned to me because I had sealed it.

Dear Professor,

Your letter of the 7th took only three days to get here;[1] the proofs followed yesterday. Many thanks for both. I am particularly glad that so far your sons have safely and honourably survived all dangers.

I have been able to breathe more freely for the last few days. For the past eight months I had the most exhausting job at this hospital but I have now left the Surgical Department for good. I am at present organising an observation ward for psychopathic soldiers and shall probably very shortly be doing only psychiatric and psycho-therapeutic work, as has long been my wish. It is likely I shall have to write a great many reports for the court but I am sure I shall have time for analytical studies. In these few days, during which I have examined about twelve patients, I have already made some interesting findings about the origin of paralyses in the war-wounded. If things go as I wish, many cases of psychosis should pass through my hands and I hope the scientific results will prove useful to us.

You are quite right, dear Professor, when you write in your letter of my 'awakening'. But while I was working ten hours and more every day, often with disturbed nights as well, and with many other things on my mind, I could do no more than vegetate for months on end. If circumstances permit, nothing on my part will prevent things changing from now on.

[1] This and several others of Freud's letters must have been lost by Abraham owing to war-time conditions.

Your short communication[1] gave me much pleasure, even though I was familiar with the case. You told me about it at Lehrter station in Berlin in the winter before the war on your way to Hamburg. In future, I shall make a particular point of tracing this and similar material in my patients.

I am glad to see that our journals keep going in spite of the difficult times. I hope I shall soon be able to re-enter the ranks of contributors. I have read practically nothing for months, with the exception of your papers.

Is there any chance of your travelling to Berlin or Hamburg again? I very much hope to have a week's leave at Christmas which is barely enough for Berlin and Bremen. Should I have a little more time, a meeting in Breslau might be arranged, but everything could of course turn out quite differently.

I have good news from home. My wife stands up bravely to the long separation; the restrictions imposed by the war are also not easy to bear. But that does not matter. In principle, the war has already been won, though the other side do not want to admit it yet. This is similar to what we see in some difficult cases. We are used to these resistances and to seeing them yield in the end.

With kind regards, also to your family and our friends in Vienna,

Yours,
Abraham

*

Berlin,
28.12.15

Dear Professor,

Contrary to all my expectations, I did get leave which I am spending partly here and partly in Bremen and shall use the present free time to write to you.

I can report that I am at last working as a specialist once again. I hope shortly to have a Psychiatric Department of my own, for observation of patients about whose mental state there

[1] Sigmund Freud, 'A Case of Paranoia Running Counter to the Psycho-analytical Theory of the Disease', Standard Ed., Vol. XIV.

is some doubt, for treatment of neurotic patients, particularly those with hysterical paralyses, and for observation of epileptics. My long-promised paper for the *Zeitschrift* is now finished. I only have to add a conclusion and shall send it off to you from Berlin. It will probably amount to two and a half printed sheets.[1]

We are all very well, and I am especially enjoying the children during my short holiday. The little one in particular has developed very well in my absence, and constantly tries to produce nice examples of your theories. I shall be back in Allenstein on January 3rd and hope to hear from you there. With best wishes for the New Year to you and all your family and also to our friends,

Yours,
Karl Abraham

Allenstein,
13.2.16

Dear Professor,

I hope you have fully recovered from influenza, and also that you have good news from all your family.

I am of course very pleased that my paper meets with your approval. On the last reading I personally felt that the work was a success. This is undoubtedly due in part to the slow way in which it matured. In the course of writing it piecemeal over the last seven or eight months, the whole train of thought could be worked through in my mind. In a few days, when I am rid of my official lecture on hysteria, my wife will visit me for a week. After that, I may put pen to paper again, probably first of all something for *Imago*.

I recently received the number of *Imago* with Reik's excellent paper on 'Puberty Rites', and then the *Zeitschrift* with your 'Unconscious',[2] the first half of which I have already read. I would rather wait until I have read the whole work before making any comment. Incidentally, Heller sent one copy to Berlin and one to Allenstein, and I conclude from this sympto-

[1] Karl Abraham, 'The First Pregenital Stage of The Libido'. *Selected Papers on Psycho-Analysis*, London, 1927.

[2] Sigmund Freud, 'Das Unbewusste', *Internationale Zeitschrift für Aertzliche Psychoanalyse*, Vol. III, 1915; 'The Unconscious', Standard Ed., Vol. XIV.

matic action that he would like to sell double the number he does.

You are quite right, dear Professor, in remarking that I could have given more consideration in my paper to hysterical anorexia. I can explain why I only mentioned this condition in passing and did not investigate it in detail by the fact that I have not yet thoroughly analysed such a case. But there must be a deeper personal reason, just as you consider your passion for smoking to be a hindrance in your investigation of certain problems. I know from experience that my reaction to unpleasant events regularly makes itself felt by loss of appetite. Therefore, without noticing this, I have always avoided analysis of this symptom. However, I believe I have analysed it quite fully in myself and would therefore have only been able to cite myself as an example. Instead of this, I favoured repression while working on the paper. Perhaps it will be possible to make a small addition to the text before final printing.

With kind regards to you and all your family near and far,

Yours,
Karl Abraham

*

Allenstein,
1.4.16

Dear Professor,

During the last few weeks I have spent my somewhat limited leisure time studying your new paper on the Unconscious. I am not quite sure how many times I have read it. I had the same experience as with the *Three Essays* ten years ago. Once again I am amazed how you have succeeded in saying everything of importance so concisely and systematically and linked it all up to form a complete structure. As with the earlier work, every subsequent reading uncovered something new for me which I had not assimilated in previous readings. It is probably the most fundamental and important of your papers for a long time; it provides a final and firm foundation for our whole science, leaving none of the familiar concepts unexamined and, at the same time, developing new concepts so naturally from the old ones that one has occasionally to remind oneself how much has in fact been changed. My only regret is that this exceptionally important piece of work should appear in wartime when it cannot attract the attention it deserves. But I take it that the whole series will appear in book form as soon as the war is over?

I hope in the next few weeks to be quite productive myself. Incidentally, in my Department here I am able to make many interesting observations which I should like to use later on; they concern in particular the neuroses following shell-shock, etc.

I hope all of you, including those at the front, are as well as is possible in these times. I have already spent more than a year here. In May I intend to bring my wife and children here and have the chance of taking a furnished flat. Since there are lovely woods in the neighbourhood, Allenstein is to be the place for this year's summer holiday.

With kind regards,

Yours,
Karl Abraham

Allenstein,
1.5.16

Dear Professor,

I have just moved into 'our' new flat and am expecting my wife and children in a fortnight's time. It is a five-roomed, furnished flat on the ground floor of a fairly old house with a garden all round, and is a reasonable substitute for a summer holiday. My first task is to write to you so that these lines will reach you in time. In accordance with your wish, your birthday will be celebrated very quietly. Surely however, I may participate in this celebration—in the absolute silence imposed by distance—by sending my most sincere good wishes to you and all your family. Nevertheless I wanted to give you at least a small sign of my affection and gratitude. Since the birthday number which was originally planned has not materialised, I have taken the liberty of preparing a small issue all on my own and am sending the manuscript[1] by registered post at the same time as

[1] Probably Karl Abraham, 'Ejaculatio Praecox', *Selected Papers on Psycho-Analysis*, London, 1927.

234

this letter. The work was in preparation for a long time, which is all to the good, but it had to be put to paper within a few days during my brief leisure periods. I hope it will contribute to keeping our journals going. (I expect it to cover at least twenty printed pages.) It does in fact contain some new ideas—for instance on narcissism.

When I think, dear Professor, of the abundance of original ideas contained in every one of your new publications, I see all the more clearly the difference between the efforts of your five closest followers as compared with your own. The five of us, however, seem to be able to accept this fact well enough and to be quite immune from the Jungian type of reaction. The undeniable fact that you have passed your sixtieth year appears completely irrelevant to me in the light of the continuous and upward progress your papers have shown over the last few years. Birthdays are a mere convention, rather like putting the clocks forward one hour as we did last night. May you retain for many years the liveliness and delight in creativity which are the envy of many younger people.

My wife asks me to convey to you her sincere good wishes. I send greetings from us both to you and yours, and remain, as always,

Yours loyally and devotedly,
Karl Abraham

*

Berggasse 19,
Vienna IX,
8.5.16

Dear Friend,

I have just got round to answering your letter last of all, though it was the first to arrive. Because of the announcement in the Berlin papers the day could not be kept as secret as I should have wished, and it was just those in the middle distance, who knew nothing about my wishes, who did most and thus gave me a great deal of work. Also I have received so many flowers from Vienna that I have lost all claim to further funeral wreaths, and Hitschmann sent me an 'undelivered speech' which was so moving and laudatory that when the time comes I shall be entitled to ask to be buried without a funeral oration.

The paper with which you presented me is as admirable as – everything that you have been doing in recent years, distinguished by its many-sidedness, depth, correctness, and, incidentally, it is in full agreement with the truth as it is known to me. It is so crystal clear that it seems to cry out for a graphic representation of the intersecting and ramifying mental forces. It shall not, however, remain mine in the sense of being kept from others. Shall we keep it in reserve for a while in case our *Jahrbuch* is resurrected? Otherwise we shall print it in the *Zeitschrift*.

We are all tremendously pleased that you have your wife and children with you again. Give them my cordial greetings and accept my laconic thanks for something you have said to me.

Sincerely yours,
Freud

*

Allenstein,
16.7.16

Dear Professor,

The first part of your 'Lectures'[1] together with your greetings arrived the day before yesterday. I have already read the first three to my wife, and we both sincerely thank you for some stimulating hours. This paper is of particular interest to me in view of the future. Since I now hold an official psychiatric post here, I hope it will be easier for me to be admitted to the University after the war, and I am using your lectures to learn how one does it. I am sorry to have no other news from you but hope you are all well. Did you get my last letter which must have been written some four weeks ago?

After producing two papers in the last few months, I have come to a short stop in my productivity but am using it as the germinal phase for a new paper; in my free hours I am once again studying *Totem and Taboo* and *The Interpretation of Dreams*, always with renewed enjoyment. My medical work

[1] Sigmund Freud: Introductory Lectures on Psycho-Analysis, Part I, Standard Ed., Vol. XV.

offers much of interest, but little that is relevant to our particular purpose. At any rate, I am at present occupied with a court case[1] which is psychologically most remarkable and which may be worth writing up one day.

With kind regards to you and your family at home and at the front, also from my wife,

Yours,
Karl Abraham

*

Hotel Bristol,
Salzburg,
22.7.16

Dear Friend,

The address will tell you everything. After a few days at Gastein, where we wanted to stay, the four of us, my wife and I and my sister-in-law and daughter, left disappointed, and came for a longer stay here, where we are at any rate undisturbed and free of food worries. It is very difficult to find accommodation in the country this year. There are a lot of things that are missing of course, forest for instance, but who can now get all he wants? You will remember the hotel and the rooms; it is a kind of regression; this was where our so hopeful congress took place in 1908.

I received your letter of four weeks ago. Delayed replies call for no apology nowadays. If you are able to cross the frontier in August, we shall certainly not miss the chance of seeing each other again.

Perhaps I shall manage to finish one or two things here. The Dutch translation of the *Everyday Life* arranged by Staercke was forwarded to me yesterday.

Lou still writes the most delightful, intelligent letters. Jones has managed to get in touch again through Emden. Things are different with him, he has eleven analytic sessions daily, and has now bought himself a small car and a cottage just over fifty miles from London.[2] He too has phantasies about our meeting

[1] Karl Abraham, 'The History of an Impostor in the Light of Psycho-Analytical Knowledge', *Clinical Papers and Essays on Psycho-Analysis*, London, 1955.

[2] The Plat, at Elsted, Surrey.

again. I have at last heard again from Brill, who is engaged in several translations, is squabbling with the Jungians, and hopes that we shall win. Putnam has published an excellent rebuttal of Adler in the latest number of the *Psycho-Analytical Review*. Thus interest in our science is not dying out in America.

I am delighted that you are at any rate permanently united with your family, and also tell myself that you are sure to build up everything again.

With cordial greetings to you and your whole family,

Sincerely yours,

Freud

Hotel Bristol,
Salzburg,
10.8.16

Dear Friend,

This time my pleasure in your letter was spoilt by the vexatious news in it. I was counting on your being able to cross the frontier during your leave, because the latest regulations make that quite impossible for me. This year I have to give up seeing even my daughter and grandson. Here I am in Salzburg without being able to go even once to Berchtesgaden, nor shall I be able to do so in September. So what is the use to me of your trip to Munich? Rank writes today that he may attend the congress as a reporter.

Our intentions are still not definite. Perhaps after all we shall go to Gastein from August 20th to September 9th and then probably back to Vienna. Have another look at your plans, bearing in mind that you, belonging as you do to the army in some way or other, are more mobile than I.

We have been having some enjoyable days of family reunion here. My brother[1] and daughter[2] were here for a short while, both with their other halves, as well as both my sons from the front, both proud lieutenants. Ernst is still with us, as lively as ever. Martin we found tired this time. He went through a great deal during the Russian offensive.

Salzburg is still wonderful. We have had unusual luck with

[1] Alexander Freud, 1866–1943, Professor at the Export Academy, Vienna.
[2] Mathilde Hollitscher.

the weather. Also I am writing in my free time; five lectures, thus roughly one third, are finished. The first number of the *Zeitschrift* is said at last to be on the way from Teschen. Sachs will hasten the second.

Otherwise–well, otherwise one tries to achieve a peace that one does not feel. It is a desolate world. There is no prospect of a pleasing, peaceful end, and there are all sorts of dark threats to the necessary victory. C. C.! I hope you still remember. (*Coraggio, Casimiro.*)

With cordial greetings to you and to your wife and in expectation of your news,

Yours,
Freud

Villa Wassing,
Bad Gastein,
27.8.16

Dear Friend,

You see what has happened. I have been here with the two women for a week. My little daughter is at Aussee, both the soldiers are again at the front. Gastein is incredibly beautiful, far more so than San Martino, where we were so peacefully together last time. The baths make me so tired that a rejuvenation of at least ten years is to be expected. We intend to stay here over September 10th unless–unless the spa administration drives out its remaining guests. However, there will be no water shortage at Gastein. When I am very tired I continue with writing the lectures. Seven of those on the theory of neurosis are already finished. Also the printing of the dream is going ahead. Two Chinese porcelain dogs are on my desk, laughing at me, I think, as I write. I spur myself on by remembering my intention to present the fee to my grandson for his student days. My son-in-law is still doing badly. As you can imagine, giving up his studio has done him a lot of harm materially.

I should very much like to see you, but I shall not be going to Munich. I cannot mingle with those attending the congress, and the idea of crossing the frontier by means of some invented pretext is repugnant to me. So *ceterum censeo*: it is *you* that must cross the frontier, and I shall come and join you at Salzburg or anywhere else you like, even if I have returned to Vienna by the middle of September. I hope you will get permission; Ernst went to Hamburg and Berlin while he was on leave.

I think I can congratulate you on Liebermann. The best thing about present conditions is that you are able to have your little family with you. You will be interested to hear (unless I have told you so already) that Ophuijsen[1] has written solemnly announcing that he has come over to us. Eitingon wrote yesterday from Miskolcz and asked about you. I have now re-read your oral paper in print with the greatest pleasure.

Please answer soon.

Cordial greetings to all,

Yours,
Freud

*

Allenstein,
1.9.16

Dear Professor,

I received your letter of the 27th today. How glad I would be to comply with your suggestion but, from enquiries I have made in the meantime, I understand it is not possible to visit you on Austrian soil. The fact that your son had leave to visit Germany means nothing. I have been told that travel from Austria into Germany is far less restricted. There is, however, a strict embargo in the opposite direction with exceptions made only for very special cases such as severe illness in the family. It is therefore quite impossible for me to come to Gastein or anywhere else.

I can understand that you do not wish to come to Munich. But how about our meeting in some other Bavarian town? It is some two years since we last met and I should be so happy to see you again.

I hope I shall have a favourable reply from you, dear Professor. Meanwhile I send you written greetings – also from my wife – to you and your family near and far, including the

[1] Dr Johan van Ophuijsen, Dutch psycho-analyst, later in New York.

Chinese dogs. Letters will reach me here up to September 12th, and after that in Bremen, Uhlandstr. 20.

Hoping to see you looking as rejuvenated as you promised,

Yours,

Karl Abraham

*

Berggasse 19,
Vienna IX,
26.9.16

Dear Friend,

It could not be done. I returned to Vienna on September 16th, and have given up the rest of the travelling season for this year. It could not be done for various reasons, to be discussed when we meet.

Your card from Regensburg was the midwife of this letter, which otherwise would have seen the light of the censorship a few days later. Believe me, I suffer myself under the restriction I have imposed on myself. At my age one should postpone nothing. But there were certain difficulties that I could not overcome.

I have finished nine of the lectures on the theory of the neuroses which I shall deliver this term. After that I propose to give no more lectures whatever.

At Gastein we shared a table every evening with his Excellency Waldeyer,[1] who at the age of eighty is completely sound in wind and limb and seems to be a very fine man.

Please let me have news of you again soon. With cordial greetings to your wife and children,

Freud

*

Allenstein,
12.11.16

Dear Professor,

I have delayed replying to your last letter for some weeks. Pressure of work is certainly one of the reasons; but added to

[1] See footnote 2, p. 131.

this is the feeling of discontent that for a long while I have been able to write about nothing but petty domestic and personal matters. It was quite different when I had the pleasure of writing to you on theoretical developments, and always eagerly awaited your reactions to what I had to say.

There is not much to report about the Congress. Dr Weiss[1] from Vienna was the only acquaintance I met. It struck us during the discussion on neuroses how official neurology is gradually taking over this and that from us, without acknowledging the source either to themselves or to the world. After the Congress I spent one day in Regensburg and enjoyed all that I could of the Roman and mediaeval traces to be found there. Then a day in Berlin and back to Allenstein.

When is the second instalment of your Lectures due? I assume that the first of my two papers will also appear in the *Zeitschrift* soon? And another question: are you going to Hamburg at Christmas as you did two years ago? And is there a possibility of our meeting?

With kindest regards from my wife and myself to you and all your family,

Yours,
Karl Abraham

Allenstein,
10.12.16

Dear Professor,

I have once again just emerged from a period of excessive work. My colleague Liebermann, who has been suffering from severe otitis, is now improving, but I had in the meantime to deal with up to ninety cases of neurosis and psychosis entirely on my own, and feel quite exhausted. Today I can breathe a little more freely as I have been given a temporary assistant. Otherwise, we are well here and I was glad to hear the same of yourself and your family. Your guests from Hamburg will certainly help you over this difficult time. It is most praiseworthy of the little one to try and thank his grandfather for his hospitality by producing 'material'. As regards our six-year-old, I

[1] Dr Karl Weiss, psychiatrist and psycho-analyst in Vienna.

can report that he eagerly enquired today whether one can marry one's sister. Next time I hope to hear more about your sons and sons-in-law and how they are getting on, and hope it will be only good news!

The *Zeitschrift* containing my contribution has not yet arrived. I am particularly pleased to hear that you have finished your Lectures: for your sake, because you are now once more free for something new; and for my sake, because I look forward to reading them; and for all our sakes, because I cannot imagine a better introduction to psycho-analysis. I can sympathise with your wish not to give any more lectures in the future but I regret this, since our science will then be completely cut off from the University and we do not know whether there will be a platform for our views, either in Vienna or anywhere else in the foreseeable future. After the war I shall try my luck but am doubtful of success.

I am particularly pleased that the proposal for the Nobel prize was made by Baranyi,[1] one of the most original thinkers among doctors. Furthermore, this is the realisation of a long-standing wish I have had for you. It is four years since I tried to get Bjerre[2] to contact the leading authorities in Sweden in this matter. There are sufficient reasons why I would now wish more than ever before that this should be realised for you! Ophuijsen is a good acquisition if he now stands firm and does not begin to waver again because of various resistances.

Nothing more for today except kind regards and good wishes, also from my wife, to you and yours, large and small, near and far. Perhaps some more another time,

Yours,
Karl Abraham

What is Reik's present address?

---

[1] Dr Robert Baranyi, later Professor of Otolaryngology in Uppsala; he received the Nobel Prize in 1915.
[2] Dr Paul Carl Bjerre, Swedish psychiatrist.

Berggasse 19,
Vienna IX,
18.12.16

Dear Friend,

No 2 of the *Zeitschrift* with your splendid paper has at last appeared. The dream lectures[1] went off to your address today. Your letter turned up at the right moment. I am delighted to hear that things are going well, or what is called that nowadays, with you and yours. I gladly give you the same assurance about ourselves.

The little boy[2] is charming and amusing; if there were as much good will and understanding on the part of the Entente as there is with him, we should long since have had peace. Meanwhile he has long since passed beyond the early stages that are so instructive to us. It pains me to hear that you are so overworked. I have little to do, so that at Christmas, for instance, I am again faced with a blank. Leisure is not good for me, because my mental constitution urgently requires me to earn and spend money on my family as the fulfilment of my well-known father complex. In these circumstances, entirely against my will, my hopes turn to the Nobel Prize, though we are all aware that we must count on the familiar resistances there too. This makes the conflict very irritating, almost humiliating. (Endurance!) C.C. is often very necessary.

My best wishes for Christmas. I hope I shall hear from you again soon.

Yours,
Freud

Allenstein,
2.1.17

Dear Professor,

I received your letter and the second volume of the Lectures over a week ago and today want to thank you sincerely for both since I have just finished reading the book. I think it will prove

[1] Sigmund Freud, *Introductory Lectures on Psycho-Analysis*, Part II, Standard Ed., Vol. XVI.
[2] Freud's grandson.

of great value to us, partly because it is so simple and clear and yet contains everything essential, and partly because, by omitting all historical and theoretical material, it makes far fewer demands on the reader than the earlier *Interpretation of Dreams*. Furthermore, your perfect method of presentation and the certainty and clarity of the work are sure to make an impression – as soon as general interest turns back to science again. I spent a number of pleasant hours with this book, and my wife is reading it now. Otherwise, there is little stimulation in this small town. That is why I have used the holidays for reading, and am quite put out that the third volume is not yet available. Meanwhile, the new issue of the *Zeitschrift* has arrived and I see myself in print once again after more than two years. Incidentally, what is to happen to the other paper? If only one knew that there would be peace soon and that we could publish our *Jahrbuch* again, I should like to reserve it for that. But since the future is so uncertain, it would be best if I asked you to publish it some time when the *Zeitschrift* is short of contributions.

Not much new to report theoretically. Among my patients I have had two obsessional neuroses; without thorough analysis, both strikingly confirmed your views and those of Jones. They may be useful material later on.

Yesterday I chanced to come across a dream in *Till Eulenspiegel*[1] which is told about the three-year-old Till and which, as far as I know, has not yet been mentioned in our literature. You might publish it under the Miscellany section in the *Zeitschrift* with reference to disguised wish-fulfilment of childhood dreams. It goes as follows: 'One morning Till told his father what he had dreamt the previous night. "Father," he said, "last night I saw a cake in my dream." "That is a good omen, my son," Father Klaus replied. "Give me a penny and I'll explain the dream to you." "Father," answered Till, "if I had a penny, I would not have only dreamt of cake." '

More some time soon! For today, kindest regards to you all, also from my wife,

Yours,
Karl Abraham

[1] German mediaeval stories about a legendary figure whose pranks and simplicity constantly landed him in trouble.

Berggasse 19,
Vienna IX,
13.1.17

Dear Friend,

Many thanks for your letter. The most important thing is that you are well and are able to enjoy having your family about you. In such circumstances the worth of a good wife, in itself inestimable, is immeasurably increased. I can well imagine that your small town offers you nothing but work and more work, yet not the kind that one desires. From another letter that arrived at the same time as yours I gather that Liebermann is again with you. Your second, hardly less admirable paper, is to appear in the fourth number of the *Zeitschrift*. The third is already at the printer's, with a paper by me,[1] which I shall send you in proof as soon as the block that goes with it is ready. The situation in regard to the *Jahrbuch* is uncertain. Deuticke seems to be offended at the lectures being published by Heller, though I warned him a long time ago that his repeated rejections of our periodicals would ultimately have that consequence. I have asked Karger[2] to send you the fifth edition of the *Everyday Life* direct. According to my calculations the book must long since have been ready, but I have not yet received it.

Your praise of the lectures has done me a great deal of good at this moment. Living in isolation as one does nowadays, one has vigorously to remind oneself that there are still a few people for whom it is worth writing. Otherwise one would forget and, though one would go on working for oneself, one would not commit it to paper.

Your Eulenspiegel dream will be used in the *Zeitschrift*.

It is better not to think in advance about the painful experiences that this spring will bring the world. Little Ernst treats me as he does his father at the war, he allows himself to be helped and attended to, but otherwise ignores me, and demon-

---

[1] Sigmund Freud, 'On the Transformation of Instincts, with Special Reference to Anal Erotism', Standard Ed., Vol. XVII.

[2] S. Karger, Berlin publisher of Freud's *Psychopathology of Everyday Life*.

stratively sticks to his mama, aunt, and other young females. He is very amusing.

With cordial greetings from

Yours,
Freud

*

Allenstein,
11.2.17

Dear Professor,

Soon after your letter arrived, I received the new edition of *Psychopathology* from Karger which I have meanwhile read. I find it enriched in many ways. I have one small comment to make: the examples you have taken from other authors do not all appear to be as fully analysed as your own. To give one instance: the slip of the pen on p. 102, *Levitico* instead of *Levico*, does not seem to me to be sufficiently elaborated.

This objection only holds good for certain examples, not for those from Ferenczi, Jones, etc. A question concerning one of your own contributions (p. 96, a slip of the pen in writing about a sum of money)—could this not be due to the old custom of paying tithes? I should like to take this opportunity of telling you about a nice case of mixing up letters (p. 186). I was told about it by a patient who had been under treatment with Dr Riklin in Zürich. After the patient had returned to his home from Zürich, he received a letter from Riklin which the latter had addressed to his bank in Zürich: had they already received the sum of so-and-so many francs? A letter with medical advice had been enclosed in the envelope and sent to the bank. An unusual form of reminder to a patient.

If I succeed in obtaining a copy of Grimm's[1] dictionary here or other relevant literature, I should like to make a small philological contribution on the same subject soon. This would represent my grateful thanks for your book, which I can only express in a few words today.

[1] German dictionary edited by Jacob and Wilhelm Grimm, published 1852.

You too will have been very pleased with the news about Ophuijsen. Van Emden used to have doubts about founding a medical association while some of the members inclined towards Jung. Since Ophuijsen has changed sides, these difficulties seem to have been resolved. In some respects I have great hopes of this new venture.[1]

I have not yet received the last number of *Imago* but saw it at Liebermann's, and am now looking forward to your article[2] in it of which I knew nothing.

With kindest regards from house to house,

Yours,
Karl Abraham

*

Allenstein,
18.3.17

Dear Professor,

Since last writing to you, I have read two of your new publications, written in times so unfavourable to our science. I was very interested in the 'Types'[3] in *Imago*, especially in the Shakespeare and Ibsen analyses which I found completely convincing. The other paper[4] which you sent me in proof gave me special pleasure, because of its train of thought and particularly as a personal document. It is indeed a shame that there is no possibility within the foreseeable future of our meeting and discussing a great many matters. When you have completed your next paper, you might be tempted to come to this furthest north-eastern corner of Germany, if I tell you that your colleague Copernicus lived in Allenstein for many years. The interesting Templars' castle still contains some mementoes of him.

I feel quite ashamed at being able to produce so little. At least I am at present writing a very small contribution for the *Zeitschrift*. It will be concerned with 'The Spending of Money in

[1] This refers to the setting up of the Dutch Psycho-Analytical Society.

[2] Sigmund Freud: 'A Difficulty in the Path of Psycho-Analysis', Standard Ed., Vol. XVII.

[3] Sigmund Freud, 'Some Character Types met with in Psycho-Analytic Work', *Imago*, 4, 1916: Standard Ed., Vol. XIV.

[4] See 13.1.17, footnote 1, p. 246.

Anxiety States',[1] a phenomenon which you too have probably analysed in your patients. I shall, if I find the time, try to make use of some of my old notes.

The children are well and are making good progress at school. Our boy, now six-and-a-half, recently reassured my wife that he would marry her if I should die.

I have heard from Reik from Montenegro but not from anyone else. All these contacts will one day be re-established. The moment normal conditions return, you may be sure that I shall sound the drum summoning everyone together again. Who knows what the next weeks may bring? At any rate we shall do as Casimiro.

With kindest regards from house to house,

Yours,

Karl Abraham

While I was looking something up in the library in Königsberg, someone happened to ask for one of your books. It was strange to hear the librarian giving information about it.

*

Berggasse 19,
Vienna IX,
25.3.17

Dear Friend,

You are right to point out that the list in my last paper is bound to create the impression that I claim a place side by side with Copernicus and Darwin. However, I did not wish to relinquish an interesting idea just because of that semblance, and therefore at any rate put Schopenhauer in the foreground. The printing of the lectures is going ahead well. The book may be in your hands in May or the middle of June, whereupon I shall ask you for your detailed private criticism.

A contribution from you, whether long or short, will be greedily received. Regrettably, things move very slowly with the journals, though Sachs does everything possible.

[1] Karl Abraham, *Selected Papers on Psycho-Analysis*, London, 1927.

Ferenczi is still on the Semmering, his Basedow's disease is improving, though it may leave some permanent effects. We have again had news from Jones. He is holding firm, and personally things are going very well with him. Pfister announces a little book on psycho-analysis in education[1] which is to appear in a few weeks' time in Leipzig. Jung is said to have published something about the unconscious,[2] but I have not yet received it. Stekel has written a big book on masturbation and homosexuality[3] with an introduction that is very endearing to the initiated, etc. We are awaiting from you the official announcement about the Dutch group.

With cordial greeting to your family from

Yours,
Freud

*

Allenstein,
4.5.17

Dear Professor,

These lines bring you first of all my very best wishes for your birthday. Unfortunately, I am not in a position this time to offer you a gift in the form of a more substantial contribution to the journals. The trifle I recently sent you is in your hands and another may follow soon. My military duties are so exacting that they prevent me from undertaking longer papers. I have had one analytic case for some time, and I may shortly send you a dream of his, of the type you were previously seeking examples of. I am able to report in the theoretical field that my psychiatric work has given me excellent proof of the correctness of your theory on paranoia. A few of the cases are so transparent that I should like to write something on them, but service restrictions would make it too difficult to publish them for the time being. As you can see I am not completely stagnating in spite of the war.

[1] O. Pfister, *Psycho-Analysis in the Service of Education*. London, 1922.

[2] C. G. Jung, 'Die Psychologie der unbewussten Progesse, ein Ueberblick über die moderne Theorie und Methode der analytichen Psychologie', Rascher, Zürich, 1917.

[3] W. Stekel, *Onanie und Homosexualität*, Vienna and Berlin, 1917.

I impatiently await Part III of the Lectures. You are, as always, at work putting us younger ones to shame. The three years of war have scarcely impeded your work, while I have been able to produce so little. Yesterday I passed the forty mark. We both start on a new year at the same time and I have great hopes for you, dear Professor, as well as for myself—I need hardly enumerate them.

With kind regards to you and your family in which my wife joins me,

Yours,
Karl Abraham

*

Berggasse 19,
Vienna IX,
20.5.17

Dear Friend,

After your last missive, with which I should not have been in agreement (but why not?), I had to wait a long time for your promised letter. Yesterday it at last arrived, dated the 4th inst. My cordial thanks for your congratulations, though I believe that at this time of life no notice should be taken of such anniversaries, and I think with regret how different your entry into a new decade would have been had not this disaster overtaken us all.

I see with dismay that you depreciate yourself in relation to me, building me up in the process into a kind of imago instead of describing me objectively. In reality I have grown old and rather frail and tired, and have more or less given up work. The lectures were written in the summer holidays, and since then I have done nothing, though some short papers are still being published. Life bears too heavily on me. I talk very little about this, because I know that others would take such statements as complaints and signs of depression, and not as objective descriptions, which would be unfair to me. I believe I have had my time, and I am not more depressed than usual, that is to say, I am very little depressed, and console myself with the assurance that my work lies in the good hands of men such as you and Ferenczi, and perhaps some others, who will carry it on, and that you in particular in these unfavourable conditions have written the two best clinical studies that we possess, and have certainly compiled ample new material.

I have here an almost complete new edition of the lectures, but it will certainly take another three or four weeks before I am able to send you the book. Thanks to Sachs's really astonishing efforts, the two journals are continuing; the printing of the next number of *Imago* was held up by a sudden paper shortage. But it will come out all the same.

I do not expect to be able to travel to Germany in the immediate future. The senseless restrictions make it quite impossible.

We have heard from Jones that he has married a young compatriot, a singer, he is very happy, and regards himself as a *reformed character*.[1] He has also published a translation of Ferenczi's works, but cannot send us the book.

Our inner turmoil here is perhaps nowhere so plainly revealed as it is by the extremely notable trial of F. Adler.[2] He happens to have been born in the rooms in which we live. I once saw him here when he was a boy of two. When we meet again we shall have many things to talk over that are now either not clear or are not communicable at a distance.

With cordial greetings to you and your wife and children,

Sincerely yours,

Freud

*

Allenstein,
28.5.17

Dear Professor,

Your long silence was due to postal delays after all. Your letter of the 20th arrived here yesterday. I was pleased to learn from it that you and all your family are well and I especially hope that you will continue to have good news from your son

[1] These words in English in the Original.

[2] Friedrich Adler, son of the Socialist leader, Victor Adler, had shot Stürgh, the Austrian Prime Minister.

fighting on the Isonzo front. Many thanks for all your news. I very much regret there is no prospect of a meeting yet.

The *Zeitschrift* arrived at the same time as your letter; a particularly good and substantial number – amazingly good for wartime. I can make no comment on your paper,[1] except to agree with it. I was especially pleased with Ferenczi's essay. I read a paper here on the same theme more than a year ago which coincides in every detail with what he writes. I may soon write a short supplementary paper, since it might be possible to add some important points which I have recently come to understand. The variety of his contributions to the last number proves to me that Ferenczi is well on the way to recovery. I shall write to him in a few days. It is a good thing in these difficult times that Sachs, with his characteristic devotion, has dedicated himself to the journals. Who knows what would otherwise have become of them.

In spite of your appreciation of my two recent contributions, which I do not wish to belittle, I nevertheless feel dissatisfied with myself. It represents too small a harvest over three years, particularly since all the material on which it was based was ready before the war. Let us therefore hope that a great change will soon come.

With kindest regards from house to house,

Yours,
Karl Abraham

Allenstein,
17.6.17

Dear Professor,

Very many thanks for sending the book[2] and for the short reprint. I have only read a few pages of the former, but with the greatest satisfaction. You asked me some time ago for my criticism of the whole work. Would you agree if I did not put this in a letter but wrote it for the *Zeitschrift*? I could then write

[1] Sigmund Freud, 'A Connection Between a Symbol and a Symptom', Standard Ed., Vol. XIV.

[2] Sigmund Freud, *Introductory Lectures on Psycho-Analysis I*, Standard Ed., Vol. XV.

it during my summer holiday which I shall probably start on July 20th. Or has somebody else already been given the review?

A second and younger psychiatrist has recently been appointed to my hospital; he is interested in psycho-analysis and may settle in Berlin after the war.

With kind regards from house to house,

Yours,
Karl Abraham

Berggasse 19,
Vienna IX,
22.6.17

Dear Friend,

Have I already had an opportunity of telling you that we shall be leaving on the evening of June 30th for Csorbató in the Tatras (Villa Maria Theresia), Liptau County? The country is said to be magnificent, but there is now a question mark against everything connected with food.

So far my books have never been reviewed in our journals. If you would like us to start a different régime with the lectures, you would be troubled neither by objections nor competition. Your observations will be just as valuable to me whether you make them publicly or by letter.

I can promise you a number of the *Zeitschrift* and also of *Imago* within the next few days. Everything now takes a long time. When one has any energy and spirit nowadays, one uses them up raging and grousing.

Enjoy your leave with your family thoroughly, but write to me first.

Yours,
Freud

*

Csorbató,
13.7.17

Dear Friend,

This place is situated on the Csorba Lake 4,000 feet up in magnificent surroundings and with beautiful forests, but it rains and storms mercilessly and we are as cold as if it were winter. I do not know whether we shall put up with it for long. Ferenczi is expected to arrive here on leave on the 24th.

A woman patient of Jung's has sent me his new paper on the psychology of the unconscious processes with a view to making me change my mind about that noble character. It bears the date 1917. But he seems theoretically not to have gone beyond the crude statement of the fact that he came across myself and Adler. We are in contact on 'fundamentals'.

Shortly before we left my sister's twenty-year-old son[1] was killed in action. Her grief surpassed description. There is no news about my warriors.

Hoping that your well-earned leave will do you nothing but good and looking forward to news about yourself and your family,

Cordially yours,
Freud

*

Csorbató,
21.8.17

Dear Friend,

What you supposed has happened. The bad weather came to an end, and splendid summer weather set in, with the result that we have been having an undeservedly delightful holiday, which my wife and daughter have also been enjoying as they have seldom enjoyed holidays before. The Hungarians are uncouth and noisy but obliging and hospitable and friendship and loyalty are taking the form of generosity, with the result that we are able to wallow in a superfluity of bread, butter, sausages, eggs, and cigars, rather like the chief of a primitive tribe. The hotel alone would not have been able to do so much, though in present circumstances it cannot be blamed. I am even able to indulge in my passion for hunting for mushrooms in the woods here. I have done no work, but have been able for hours and for whole half days to forget the wretched state of the world, aided by the fact that during this period my three war-

[1] Herrmann Graf, son of Freud's sister Rosa.

riors have been away from the front. Shortly before our departure my sister's only son, a boy of twenty, was killed on the Italian front.

There is no news on the scientific front. Heller has received a good fee for the Dutch translation (of the lectures). You know that I now need money, and nothing so urgently as money, for my family. Binswanger has sent me part of the manuscript of his book,[1] which is to deal with the position of psycho-analysis in relation to psychology.

So now your leave is behind you. I hope that it has invigorated you and your family for a long time to come. We are thinking of leaving for Vienna on the 30th or 31st. Sachs is hard at work trying to change the standstill in the production of our journals into movement.

With cordial greetings to you and your wife,

Yours,
Freud

*

Allenstein,
23.9.17

Dear Professor,

I assume that you have been back in Vienna for some weeks —just as we have been back here in Allenstein. My wife and children benefitted from the holiday and I at least had a good rest, though my old bronchial trouble somewhat spoilt my holiday.

On the scientific side I have hardly anything of my own to report, except perhaps that several cases of obsessional neurosis, only superficially investigated, have given me striking confirmation concerning sadism and anal erotism. The other faithful members of our small circle had the opportunity of meeting you this summer. Unfortunately I have had to forego this pleasure for exactly three years, since three years have passed since you and your brother were in Berlin in 1914. I constantly plan to make up for lost time, as far as possible, immediately the

---

[1] Ludwig Binswanger, *Psychoanalyse und Klinische Psychiatrie,* 1921.

war is over. But as long as 'thoughts are not omnipotent', I shall be confined to wishing.

Since I shall be unable for the time being to review your Lectures for the *Zeitschrift*, I should like to say a few words here. The third part is so excellent that I find it difficult to pick out any examples. So much has been placed in a new context and so many new ideas and vistas open up, that I shall have to read it again to be able to judge it as a whole. As I have very little time, I can only read it chapter by chapter but I shall savour it more fully that way. In my opinion, the nineteenth chapter[1] is the climax of the whole and I would say it has made a stronger impression on me than most of your papers. The same could be said of the last lectures. Only after the war is over shall we be able to feel properly grateful that it was in fact the war that gave you the leisure to write up the Lectures. We may then expect a rapid advancement in our prestige and new followers will at last have the kind of introduction that was lacking before (though I believe that the initiated will gain far more from your Lectures than beginners).

During the heavy fighting on the Italian front my wife and I often thought of your sons. I sincerely hope that they have remained unhurt and that all of you at home are well too. Many thanks for your report on all our friends who visited you at Czorbató. Unfortunately one loses contact through such a long separation. I should like to know where Reik is (still in Montenegro?) and how Ferenczi is. Do you still hear from Jones? I secretly hope that one of the Dutch members will come to the Congress in Bonn.

With kind regards and good wishes to you all, also from my wife,

Yours,
Karl Abraham

---

[1] Sigmund Freud, 'Resistances and Repression', Lecture XIV, *Introductory Lectures on Psycho-Analysis*, Standard Ed., Vol. XV.

Berggasse 19,
Vienna IX,
5.10.17

Dear Friend,

Your letter gave me great but painful pleasure. How much has changed since we last saw each other, and not everything for the best. When I think of the time when you told me that it was no longer an act of martyrdom to be called my pupil. The enclosure with this letter, unless it remains in the hands of the censor, illustrates one of these changes. If you find me cross and out of sorts, you will know why.

After a few days I got a great deal of work, and am now working for eight or nine hours a day with nine patients. It amuses me and, strangely enough, has done a great deal of good to my health, to which the certainty of avoiding the otherwise inevitable bankruptcy substantially contributes. My income is now the same as before the war, but the value of money has changed greatly. My writing–I had some little things in progress–will be held up for only a short time.

Your praise of the lectures gave me uncommon pleasure, though my opinion of them does not coincide with yours. I hope you will still discover their great deficiencies and not leave them unmentioned in your review.

Jones wrote in real English fashion a few weeks ago that German resistance was still too strong, so the war was bound to last for a few years yet.

As I write to you so seldom, I do not know whether I have yet mentioned the paper on Lamarck,[1] the point of which is to be that even the 'omnipotence of thoughts' was a reality once.

I do not know where this letter will reach you. I hope it will reach you, and soon produce as cheerful an answer as is possible nowadays.

With cordial greetings to you and your wife,

Yours as ever,
Freud

[1] Jean Baptiste A. P. de Lamarck, 1744–1829, French naturalist.

Dear Professor,

The great events of the last few days often drew my thoughts towards Vienna. Today I want first of all to express the hope that your sons have remained unhurt; they must have been through a gruelling time. May we at last be able to gather the fruits of this outstanding success in the form of favourable peace terms!

Now I have to thank you for your last letter and for the enclosed photograph. Just to show that I do not always see only the good side of things, I want to stress my impression that three years of war have not passed you by either without leaving their mark. Hardly any of us will have remained completely unscathed in body and soul. You would find me too with many grey hairs and, in spite of sufficient food, much reduced in weight. I find your photograph–apart from the changes for which the photographer cannot be held responsible–otherwise good. Perhaps I shall have an opportunity of sending you a photograph of myself. Many things have changed of course. What for instance might have happened to Casimiro's courage during the last few days?

How is your son Ernst, who was at home recovering when you wrote, and how are you and all the others? Your letter contained some pleasant news: that you are back at work with your old vigour, that Ferenczi is looking forward to a wish-fulfilment and that our Dutch colleagues are eagerly at work. I did not quite follow your hint about a paper on Lamarck. What did you mean? You have not mentioned it before, but must have thought you had done so. I am curious about Tausk's remarks on my last paper.[1] So far I do not like his paper on Deserters,[2] it is too verbose, not concise enough. Incidentally, I shall make use of my experiences in legal psychiatry over the last two years for this topic of desertion–not for a psycho-analytic paper but in order to try my luck with my lecturership thesis after the war.

---

[1] Victor Tausk, 'Bemerkungen zu Abraham's Aufsatz Ueber Ejaculatio Praecox', *Internationale Zeitschrift*, Vol. IV, 1916–17.

[2] Victor Tausk, 'Zur Psychologie des Deserteurs', *Internationale Zeitschrift für Aertzliche Psychoanalyse*, Vol. 4, 1916–17.

I forgot to tell you last time of an interesting *lapsus* of Bleuler's. In his paper 'Physisch und Psychisch' he incorrectly reproduced several things from the *Interpretation of Dreams*. I referred him to the newly published *Lectures on the Dream*. After reading the latter Bleuler wrote, *inter alia*: 'As I have shown, Freud has for many years directed his attention only to the psychological aspects of dreams and has deliberately and consciously ignored everything else. I finished reading his latest publication only yesterday. Admittedly in this he pays more attention to other aspects which partly serve to supplement his former theories and which partly weaken them; but I must say that his previous ingenious and vigorous one-sidedness has hindered (impressed) me more than his present reserve . . .' (The letter was typewritten; the correction in brackets was handwritten in the original. Don't you think the correction very revealing? Impressed instead of hindered! In fact he was hindered since it obstructed his ambition!)

I recently received a very interesting paper by Fliess; it contains brilliant new observations about a pituitary syndrome. Would you be interested? If so, I could send it to you.

Our life here is not subject to any great changes. My wife and the children are well. Hoping to receive good news about all of you soon, I am, with kindest regards from my wife and myself,

Yours,
Karl Abraham

Berggasse 19,
Vienna IX,
11.11.17

Dear Friend,

I have today been able to overcome a certain reluctance to answering your letter because we have just had the first news of Martin since the beginning of the offensive (October 23rd), and he is well. Ernst is still with us, and Oli is helping to build a bridge across the Dniester.

I am very busy with eight or nine analyses a day and some on the waiting list, and am very pleased at being able to avoid brooding and worrying in this way. It is still very interesting. But I am ageing rapidly all the same, and occasionally feel doubtful whether I shall live to see the end of the war, whether I shall ever see you again, etc. During the war travelling to Germany is practically out of the question. The next blow that I expect is the stoppage of our journals; Heller is not threatening this, but with the continuation of the war it will become inevitable. At any rate I behave as if we were faced with the end of all things, and in the last few days I have got ready for publication in the *Zeitschrift* two papers of the 'metapsychological' series[1] ('Supplements to the Theory of Dreams', 'Mourning and Melancholia'). I originally intended to use these and other papers, with some that have already appeared ('Instincts and their Vicissitudes', 'Repression', 'The Unconscious'), for a book. But this is not the time for it. It will also be a good thing for your promised review of the lectures to see the light of day before this particular end of the world that is to be expected. With the cessation of the journals our role will for the time being have been played out.

As you see, I do not believe that the events in Russia and Italy will bring us peace. I think one should take the British assurances about their intentions seriously and also admit that the U-boat war has not achieved its object. In that case our future is pretty dim.

What you say about Bleuler's statement again shows how hard it is to satisfy these people. I hope you have not received the impression that I have weakened or taken anything back. I have heard about Fliess's book; things are too uncertain to send it to me, unless you have two copies I shall try to hunt up a copy here.

Have I really not told you anything about the Lamarck idea? It arose between Ferenczi and me, but neither of us has the time or spirit to tackle it at present. The idea is to put Lamarck entirely on our ground and to show that the 'necessity' that according to him creates and transforms organs is nothing but the power of unconscious ideas over one's own body, of which we see remnants in hysteria, in short the 'omnipotence of thoughts'. This would actually supply a psycho-analytic

[1] See footnote p. 225.

explanation of adaptation; it would put the coping stone on psycho-analysis. There would be two linked principles of progressive change, adaptation of one's own body and subsequent transformation of the external world (autoplasticity and heteroplasticity), etc.

I am not sure either whether I have drawn your attention to a book by Groddeck[1] in Baden-Baden (*Psychologische Bedingtheit und psychoanalytische Behandlung organischer Leiden*, S. Hirzel, 1917). You will not have missed Lou Andreas's paper in the *Zeitschrift für Sexualwissenschaft*.[2] It is full of subtleties, but hardly intelligible to the general public.

Enough for today; I send my cordial greetings to you and your family. *Poveretto Casimiro*!

Yours,
Freud

Allenstein,
2.12.17

Dear Professor,

I found it somewhat distressing to receive such a gloomy letter from you. It would not be psycho-analytic were I to attempt to dispel your mood with counter-arguments and I shall therefore only take up one of your worries. You think that our journals will soon cease publication. I have written to Sachs today asking him to inform you of a suggestion that seems appropriate to me. If you both agree, a solution could be found.

I hope you have further good news from the front and that all of you at home are well too. I have been very preoccupied with the theoretical content of your letter (Lamarck). You will remember that for several years I worked on the history of evolution and theories of heredity, and therefore have a particular interest in these problems. I can hardly comment on your theory on the basis of the brief hints you have given me, but I feel extremely envious of those who have the opportunity

---

[1] Dr Georg Groddeck, German writer and psycho-analyst.
[2] Lou Andreas Salomé, 'Psychosexualität', *Zeitschrift für Sexualwissenschaften*, 1917.

of frequently exchanging views with you, while I can only write my *Epistulae ex Ponto*.

The most recent political events in Russia seem to me well worth noting, however sceptical I may be regarding an early peace. When it comes, our science will be sure to rise to unprecedented heights. After these years when interests have inevitably been focussed on the war, on politics and on getting enough to eat, people will be most eager for intellectual activity and I think quite a few prejudices will disappear.

I cannot help saying it—we are, after all, better off than Casimiro.

For today, only greetings in haste from house to house,

Yours

Karl Abraham

Berggasse 19,
Vienna IX,
10.12.17

Dear Friend,

I am using the leisure of a Sunday to reply to your letter of the 2nd of this month (and I am so cold as I do so that I wrote 'the 7th' instead of the '12th' by mistake.) The newspaper sellers in the streets have just been shouting the news of the armistice with Russia, and if one had not grown so blunted one would be glad at having survived the end of half the war.

Sachs has told me of your proposal. It is impracticable, since it involves Deuticke, who has blocked everything since the beginning of the war, and also is very ill and angry besides, because the lectures are being published by Heller. Meanwhile what I feared has rapidly come true. The last number of *Imago* (No. 2) which has been in print for a long time, cannot be distributed because no wrapping paper is obtainable, and Prochaska has announced that he has no paper for Rank's 'Artist', of which Heller wanted to produce a second edition. Officially we have not ceased publication, and perhaps we shall be able to drag on for some time yet. Sachs still hopes to avoid the ignominy of having to stop before the last number of the

Zeitschrift (No. 6) without being able to complete the annual series. I wanted to print in that number the two papers belonging to the metapsychological series about which I have already written to you.

I should gladly tell you more about the Lamarck idea, but it would have to be on a walk. I am at daggers drawn with writing, as with many other things. Included among them is your dear German fatherland. I can hardly imagine myself ever going there again, even when it again becomes physically possible. In the struggle between the Entente and the Quadruple Alliance I have definitely adopted the viewpoint of Heine's Donna Bianca in the disputation at Toledo:

Doch es will mich schier bedünken. . . .[1]

The only thing that gives me any pleasure is the capture of Jerusalem and the British experiment with the chosen people.[2]

I am very busy, and for nine hours a day on six days of the week I can exercise patience and aloofness. On the seventh both generally fail me.

With my cordial greetings to you and your wife,

Yours,
Freud

Allenstein,
16.12.17

Dear Professor,

These days mark the tenth anniversary of my first visit to you in Vienna just after I had started my practice. It has in recent times looked rather more likely that I shall be back in Berlin in the foreseeable future and that I shall then also be able to visit Vienna. Plans for the future are thus beginning to assume a somewhat more definite shape.

A week ago I had to escort a sick officer from my hospital to Bremen, and therefore had the opportunity of spending two

---

[1] 'But I rather suspect . . .' (The quotation from Heine that Freud leaves incomplete continues: *Dass der Rabbi und der Mönch / Dass sie alle beide stinken*, 'that both the rabbi and the monk stink alike'.)

[2] The reference is to the Balfour declaration.

days with my mother. I made use of a short stay in Berlin to visit Bonhoeffer and to discuss with him the question of my lecturership. I knew that Bonhoeffer is easy to get on with and that he has kept apart from all attacks made against us. He was personally pleasant to me, drew my attention to all the obstacles and, although he was honest enough to make no promises, was not in principle opposed to the idea. He said that he would enquire of Bleuler, among others, about my scientific qualifications and he also asked me for a list of my publications. The matter does not seem completely hopeless to me. One point was not discussed but it is of some importance. Bonhoeffer may well be afraid that a follower of an extremist school of thought would use his lectures to wage war against the established view. It would have been appropriate to re-assure Bonhoeffer beforehand in this respect, but I said nothing of this, neither in our discussions nor in a letter I wrote to him today, because I was afraid of giving a wrong impression. The thought has occurred to me that a letter from you, dear Professor, mentioning not only my scientific qualifications but also my personal qualities, might be helpful and reassuring in this respect. I am, however, not quite sure whether this would be the best way and I shall leave it to you to decide whether to write or not. I think a reassurance that there would be no reason to fear unpleasant incidents from my side would be appropriate. Perhaps you can think of a better way to allay such a fear. The work on my thesis is progressing slowly. It has just occurred to me that it might be better to write such a letter to Kraus with whom you have had correspondence about me before. You might ask him to talk to Bonhoeffer on this point. At any rate I give you both addresses: Professor Dr Bonhoeffer, Director of the Psychiatric Clinic of the Königliche Charité, Berlin NW., and Professor Dr Kraus, Director of the Medical Department of the Königliche Charité.

No news from us. I hope all is well with you too, both at home and at the front. With many thanks in anticipation and kind regards,

Yours,
Karl Abraham

Berggasse 19,
Vienna IX,
21.12.17

Dear Friend,

I am glad to hear that you are able to make any plans for the future at all. If I can do anything to help, I shall gladly do so. But a strong feeling warns me against writing to Bonhoeffer. If I try to justify this, the argument runs as follows. I find nothing particularly hopeful in your account of your conversation with him. I doubt whether personal intervention by me will do more good than harm, and I am reluctant to get in touch with a stranger from whom I am not sure even of receiving the usual courtesies. Even Kraus, who is perfectly amicable towards me, could not bring himself to answer one of the two letters I sent him. My relations with him at the time of my contribution to his handbook, even though I let myself be guided by consideration for his relations with you, can have had only a cautionary effect on me.

For these reasons I think it far preferable to write again to Kraus, with whom the ice is already broken, and, picking up the thread of my pre-war letter to him, to try to persuade him to back you with Bonhoeffer. I shall do so this week, though I do not think it will help much. I shall write to the effect that I know you not to be one of those who turn scientific opposition into personal animosity and thus damage the dignity of science (at any rate in our sense of the word).

Otherwise I have no news. Is it really ten years? They were significant and rich in substance enough, though not always pleasant. My greetings to you and yours.

Sincerely yours,
Freud

Berggasse 19,
Vienna IX,
26.12.17

Dear Friend,

I am afraid you may have concluded from my last letter that I was unwilling to write to Kraus and hence may be worrying that because of obscure obstacles the promised letter would never be written. So let me reassure you by telling you that the letter has already gone off as planned.

It certainly cost me some gnashing of teeth. Part of the complex was a reluctance against which I had to struggle, and there was another part that overcame the reluctance. On the one hand there was anger at being in the position of having to ask a favour of the hostile world, and on the other there was the consideration that it might perhaps be useful to you. I hope that the latter may turn out to be correct.

Rank came to see me yesterday. He is now a prisoner of the editorial department of the *Krakauer Zeitung* and is in very low spirits.

If this letter reaches you in time for the New Year, may it bring you the end of exile and a new beginning of independent existence.

Sincerely yours,
Freud

Allenstein,
6.1.18

Dear Professor,

Many thanks for your two letters and for complying with my wish concerning Kraus. I gathered from your *first* letter that you found it difficult to come to a decision, but I did not doubt for a moment that you would in fact write to Kraus, and it was therefore unnecessary to set my mind at rest with the second letter. I am very sorry that my request made you feel so uncomfortable Perhaps we shall both be rewarded by a favourable result.

There is nothing new to report from here. Today I received the reprints of the trifle, 'The Spending of Money in Anxiety States'. My work on the thesis progresses slowly. On the scientific front, I might mention that I am getting interesting results from the analysis of a case of obsessional brooding which will be suitable for publication later (contributions to its anal-sadistic genesis).

I am enclosing with this letter the promised review of

Pötzl.[1] I am very disappointed with the paper. The author's attitude to psycho-analysis is ambivalent, in that he agrees with everything theoretically but, at the same time, robs the concepts of their real content; thus his acceptance becomes meaningless and in practice he is very far from using our method. I have therefore written a review which is moderate in tone but unequivocally unfavourable. Has Pötzl become a member in the meantime? After this paper I should find that difficult to understand.

I am sorry to hear that Rank is not well. Sachs on the other hand seems to be in top form. As soon as I feel there are real hopes of peace, I personally am ready for anything and I already have a number of plans for a scientific meeting! That does not mean to say that the war years have passed me by without trace. Just like everyone else, I have lost some of my vigour, hair pigmentation and weight. But I hope for a quick regeneration and not for myself alone.

Since you do not mention any details about your family, I assume that you are all well, including those at the front.

With many good wishes for 1918 (Casimiro!) and kind regards from house to house,

Yours,
Karl Abraham

*

Berggasse 19,
Vienna IX,
18.1.18

Shivering with cold

Dear Friend,

I am very glad you did not take my recent difficulties more seriously. Your equable temperament and indestructible vitality stand up well to my alternations between cheerfulness and resignation. The resistances against which it was written were evident in my letter to Kraus. The handwriting changed at

[1] Dr Otto Pötzl, 'Ueber einige Wechselwirkungen hysterieformer und organisch zerebraler Störungsmechanismen', *Internationale Zeitschrift für Aertzliche Psychoanalyse*, Vol. V., 1919.

least four times in two pages. But at any rate the contents were straightforward; I have not received an answer this time either, but gladly put up with this if only it helps you.

Your criticism of Pötzl did him great honour, because it was completely honest. He has now become a member, and his reply to such reproaches is that he has since gone much more deeply into analysis. Also he is soon to go to Prague as successor to Pick; this too will be no drawback to us.

The Dutch are now doing things in earnest. We recently received from them a pile of reviews of Dutch papers and polemical writings, and a quite admirably clear and definite rebuttal of Jung's latest product on the psychology of the unconscious process (1917). A new local group is about to be formed at Warsaw.

Otherwise there is little news. I am reading about Darwinism without any real aim, like someone with plenty of time in front of him, which may be appropriate in view of the paper shortage. The practice is still very busy, and also interesting. Successes have been good. One of my sons (Ernst) is at present nearer to you than to me, he should be visiting his sister at Schwerin today. We receive occasional news of the other two, none of it bad. If the war lasts long enough, it will kill off everybody any way.

Farewell, and go on being a brave Casimiro to me, and accept the most cordial greetings from

Yours,
Freud

*

Allenstein,
4.2.18

Dear Professor,

Although there is not much new to report, I do not want to delay my reply any longer. I have in the meantime studied the issue of the *Zeitschrift* that has been published. The really good paper is by Ferenczi.[1] I could contribute a great deal in

---

[1] Sandor Ferenczi, 'Ueber Zwei Typen der Kriegsneurose', *Internationale Zeitschrift für Aertzliche Psychoanalyse*, Vol. IV, 1916/17.

confirmation of his main paper and might perhaps do so later on. This may well be the best paper that Ferenczi has written so far. Apart from his smaller papers in this number, his review of Schultz[1] is excellent.

Pötzl's paper on dreams,[2] which Sachs has promised me for reviewing arrived today. I shall write the review as soon as I can. I use most of my spare time for preparing my thesis. I had a letter from Bonhoeffer which does not hold out very much hope, but does not completely bar the way and I shall at any rate make the attempt. I want to thank you again for overcoming such great resistances in yourself.

Our Dutch colleagues do indeed deserve much appreciation for what they are achieving in these times. This increase of interest in the west, in spite of the war, promises well for peace time. But when will peace come? You, dear Professor, are mistaken if you think that I remain completely untouched by the years. At times I too feel depressed but so far have always succeeded in accepting the inevitable.

With kind regards from house to house,

Yours,
Karl Abraham

*

Berggasse 19,
Vienna IX,
17.2.18

Dear Friend,

I received a brochure from Germany a few days ago that is bound to be of special interest to you. I cannot send it to you, because I want it to be generally known here, but you will be able to get it easily. It is called '*War Neuroses and Psychical Trauma*. Their reciprocal relations presented on the basis of psycho-analytical and hypnotic studies by Dr Ernst Simmel,[3]

---

[1] Schultz, I. H., S. Freud's 'Sexualpsychoanalyse', *ibid.*

[2] Dr Otto Poetzl, 'Experimentell erregte Traumbilder in ihnen Beziehungen zum indirekten Sehen', *Internationale Zeitschrift für Aertzliche Psychoanalyse*, Vol. V, 1919.

[3] Dr Ernst Simmel, psycho-analyst, founder of the Tegel Sanatorium, near Berlin; later in Los Angeles.

now medical superintendent of a special hospital for war neurotics, with an introduction by Dr Adolf Schnee, Verlag Otto Nemnich, Leipzig-Munich, 1918.'

This is the first time that a German physician, basing himself firmly and without patronising condescension on psychoanalysis, speaks of its outstanding usefulness in the treatment of war neuroses, backs this with examples, and is also completely honest on the question of sexual aetiology. It is true that he has not gone the whole way with psycho-analysis, bases himself essentially on the cathartic standpoint, works with hypnosis, which is bound to conceal resistance and sexual drives from him, but he correctly apologises for this because of the necessity of quick results and the large number of cases with which he has to deal. I think a year's training would make a good analyst of him. His attitude is correct.

The brochure was written in the military hospital at Posen,[1] and is probably intended to be only the preliminary communication of a more detailed work. I think you should read and review it for us; it will be easy for you, and I suggest it to you as a relief from your thesis, which does not seem to me to be very promising of success.

I hope we shall be able to continue with our journals. Heller seems to be well disposed. We have ample material.

The world is surely in a chaotic state.

With cordial greetings to you and to your family,

Sincerely yours,
Freud

*

Allenstein,
12.3.18

Dear Professor,

I sent for the book by Simmel and Schnee and have just read it. I too am amazed at their achievement and even more by the courage of their convictions—that of the author as well as of Schnee. I shall get in touch with Simmel and may thus be able to contribute something to winning him completely over to our interests. I find many of my own hospital experiences confirmed

[1] Now Poznan in Poland.

271

in the book. Perhaps a meeting with him may be possible as Posen is on the Allenstein–Berlin railway line.

Our journals are continuing after all. Since we have managed to keep them going for so long, they will probably stay alive until peace comes. Whenever there is a small spark of hope making one think of peace, plans automatically seem to start up in my mind. I must confess to you that I am already preparing a paper for the next Congress on the prognosis for patients under psycho-analytic treatment. I do not have sufficient material for other theoretical papers but think I can speak definitively on a practical problem of this kind on the basis of my seven years' experience before the war. There are other reasons too for choosing such a subject.

Hoping to have good news from you and your family soon, I am with kind regards from house to house,

Yours,
Karl Abraham

*

Berggasse 19,
Vienna IX,
22.3.18

Dear Friend,

There is no need to explain the slip of the pen on the envelope.[1] As the great offensive has now begun, I assume your spirits will have been raised, if not by the hope of peace, at any rate by that of victory, and for that reason you will think my confession to being tired and weary of the struggle all the more irresponsible. As you see, I can hardly write legibly any more. Perhaps, as I have always been a carnivorous animal, the unaccustomed diet contributes to my listlessness.

If travelling were not now forbidden and subject to all sorts of penalties, I should very much like to go and see my daughter and grandson at Easter, and Schwerin is not too far from Allenstein. But it cannot be done.

If you were free now, a vast field of work would be open to you as the natural intermediary with German neurology. To-

---

[1] Instead of *Kasino*, officers' mess, Freud had written *Kaserne*, barracks.

day—following in the wake of Simmel—I received a monograph from Lewandowsky's collection (Vol. 15), called *Wahn and Erkenntnis* by Paul Schilder[1] (Leipzig), which is quite analytic in its conclusions, though it dutifully ignores the Oedipus complex. Schilder of course writes as if these gentlemen had discovered everything, or most of it, by themselves. That, in short, is the way in which our findings will be 'adopted' by German medicine. Not that it matters.

I recently sent you the proofs of the last number of the *Zeitschrift*, both because of my metapsychological efforts and because of the—not exactly distinguished—reaction of Tausk to your paper on premature ejaculation. We are continuing to print the journals, but Heller is ill and inaccessible, so that we are uncertain about the future. I wanted to persuade him to publish a fourth volume of my *Sammlung zur Neurosenlehre*, and would have given him for that purpose a long case history that has been in store since 1914.[2]

My cordial greetings to you and to your wife,

Yours,
Freud

*

Allenstein,
16.4.18
(Please address letters to: Reservelazarett
Artillerie-Kasino).

Dear Professor,

I have to thank you for your letter and the proofs. I have only just been able to read the latter. I wanted to read the first of your two papers[3] through twice before letting you know my reactions. It is very difficult and I had first to adjust myself to this new way of thinking. I believe I have now achieved this and can say that I have no serious objection to make. I shall now re-read the whole series of articles and after that let you

[1] Dr Paul Schilder, member of the Vienna Psycho-Analytical Society, later Professor of Psychiatry at Vienna University.

[2] Sigmund Freud 'From the History of an Infantile Neurosis', Standard Ed., Vol. XVII.

[3] Sigmund Freud, 'Lines of Advance in Psycho-Analytic Therapy', Standard Ed., Vol. XVII.

know again what I think. I already knew the draft of your Melancholia paper[1] so that it was less of a surprise to me. I am pleased to note that my 'incorporation phantasy' could be fitted into the wider framework of your own theory. I haven't any important criticisms of this paper either, and can only admire your ability to complete a theoretical structure of this kind at such a time. One very minor criticism is the following. The so-called ideas of inferiority found in the melancholic only seem to be such. Sometimes they in fact represent delusions of grandeur, as for instance when the patient imagines that he has committed all the evil since the creation of the universe. Even though the self-reproaches may be aimed at the love-object, they signify at the same time a narcissistic over-estimation of the patient's own criminal capacities (similar to obsessional neurotics who think themselves capable of monstrous crimes).

Next week I am going (in an official capacity) to the Psychiatric Congress at Würzburg. Afterwards I shall visit my mother and also stay a short while in Berlin. If time permits I may visit Simmel in Posen on my return journey.

Kindest regards from house to house,

Yours,
Karl Abraham

*

Allenstein,
19.5.18

Dear Professor,

Your birthday has passed without your receiving a sign of life from me. My good wishes are no less sincere for being belated. At the beginning of May I went from the Psychiatric Congress at Würzburg to Bremen, where I found my mother gravely ill, so gravely that I dared not risk leaving for days on end. I still receive news of her progress every day by telegram or express letter. You will not be angry with me that in these circumstances I postponed writing.

Otherwise we are getting on well here. We have settled down in our very primitive new flat. The big garden is a paradise for

[1] Sigmund Freud, 'Mourning and Melancholia', Standard Ed., Vol. XIV.

the children. My private work has recently increased,–I do two hours of analysis daily and shall shortly be doing three. One of them, a case of obsessional neurosis, is improving satisfactorily.

I spent a few wonderful days in Würzburg enjoying art and natural scenery to the full. Apart from its architecture, Würzburg offers exceptional beauties of mediaeval and later sculpture. One evening, incidentally, I made the acquaintance of our critic Isserlin[1] in a small circle of colleagues. He sat opposite me and at once paid tribute to psycho-analysis by upsetting his glass. In other ways too I found him rather neurotic; I was also surprised to find he is of our race.

I have not yet managed to get around to writing the reviews on Pötzl and Simmel for the *Zeitschrift*; perhaps soon.

What news have you from your sons at the front and how are you all at home? Kindest regards to you and your family from my wife and myself,

Yours,
Karl Abraham

Berggasse 19,
Vienna IX,
29.5.18

Dear Friend,

You are passing through a bad patch, I can tell. How could I take amiss your not writing more often? I know that you like writing when you have anything cheerful to say, but obviously that cannot be all the time.

My mother will be eighty-three this year, and is now rather shaky. Sometimes I think I shall feel a little freer when she dies, because the idea of her having to be told of my death is something from which one shrinks back.

So I have really reached sixty-two, still unable to achieve that quiet, firm resignation that so distinguishes you as a German, though you use an Italian motto. My prevailing mood is powerless embitterment, or embitterment at my powerlessness. Perhaps you yourself will remember a recent instance of this.

---

[1] Max Isserlin, Professor of Psychiatry at Munich.

A fortnight ago Reik read us an excellent paper on Kol Nidre;[1] he has hit on Bible exegesis, and will remain with it for a long time. But on Thursday morning he left for Mount Asolone, where violent fighting is taking place. He is one of our hopes. My three sons are at present out of the firing line. Ferenczi is taking a great deal of trouble to fix us up again in the Tatras, where he can spend the holidays with us. He is likely to succeed for half the holiday period, we have no plans yet for the rest. I am very busy, but my heart has already gone out of my work.

A remarkable feature of these times which I have not yet mentioned to you is the way in which we have been victualled for the past year or so by patients and friendly followers. Actually we live on gifts, like a doctor's family in the old days. Our Hungarians, with Ferenczi and Eitingon at their head, as well as some Budapest families who believe in psycho-analysis, keep us supplied with cigars, flour, lard, bacon, etc., either free of charge or at incredibly low prices, and I have also found other such quartermasters. Thus the world shows me I have not lived in vain. I am now having my portrait done by a patient who has been restored to art; it is the last that I am willing to have done for posterity.[2]

I send my cordial greetings to you and your wife, and ask for nothing better than that you in turn should write to me about yourself.

Yours,
Freud

*

Allenstein,
21.6.18

Dear Professor,

I received news practically at the same time from yourself and from Sachs, and am now once more well informed about everything that is going on in Vienna. I shall therefore write about myself again today.

[1] Theodor Reik, 'Das Kol Nidre', in *Probleme der Religionspsychologie*, Leipzig, 1919.
[2] Pencil drawing by Kriser.

276

Concern about my mother is less acute at present. She is no longer in immediate danger but still suffers from persistent oedema. I feel very much in need of a rest. My military duties continue to be rather exhausting and, in addition, my psycho-analytic practice has developed during the last few months. I am pleased about this from a financial point of view but it is an extra burden of three to four hours daily. These cases are also theoretically quite productive.

After my return from leave, the hours I have available are already filled. Thanks to your recommendation, Miss X. has written to me and we have arranged that she will arrive here at the beginning of August. She is also bringing her nephew aged eleven for treatment. From your letter written in January which she enclosed, I have already acquainted myself with the difficulties of this case. Strangely enough, I had intended to write to you in this letter that I should like to do some special work on this form of resistance (on patients who do not associate during the session but do so at home instead). I've had a small number of cases of this kind – they appear rather difficult and theoretically less favourable. It is reassuring to hear that you too have had difficulties with this kind of resistance. I am always afraid that this is due to my lack of technique.

What you write about the return to the system of payment in kind in your practice is quite familiar to me. These are strange times.

I was extremely pleased with your report on Reik's scientific achievements. I think highly of him.

I have not yet quite abandoned the hope of seeing you this year, dear Professor. It would be a great joy after almost four years.

With kind regards from house to house,

Yours,
Karl Abraham

Csorbató,
27.8.18

Dear Friend,

You are right, I have not seen you since the beginning of the war, correspondence has been no compensation for that, and so I am quite specially looking forward to our meeting at the congress at Breslau,[1] and hope that I shall have no difficulty in getting there.

I did not answer your last letter, I think because I was then too angry and too hungry. Here I have recovered and regained my composure. The reception in Budapest by my new friends[2] was charming, the mountain air of the Tatras did the rest, and so for a time I can venture to join again in

der Erde Lust, der Erde Leid zu tragen.[3]

I ascribe a good share of my better spirits to the prospects that have opened up in Budapest for the development of our cause.[4] Materially we shall be strong, we shall be able to maintain and expand our journals and exert an influence, and there will be an end to our hitherto prevailing penuriousness. The individual whom we shall have to thank for this is not merely a wealthy man, but a man of sterling worth and high intellectual gifts who is greatly interested in analysis; he is in fact the sort of person whom one would have to invent if he did not already exist. Bad faith on his part is out of the question. He is a doctor of philosophy and a brewer, and I think his youthful model was Jacobsen[5] in Copenhagen.

I think Sachs has already told you something about Dr. von Freund, whom I am here describing. I shall have more to tell you when we meet. It is to be expected that Budapest will now become the headquarters of our movement.

Two of my sons are near us here in the Tatras, and there is no bad news of the other one.

With cordial greetings to you and yours,

Freud

---

[1] The psycho-analytic congress originally intended for Breslau was eventually held in Budapest.

[2] Dr Anton von Freund and family.

[3] 'Bearing the world's pleasure and the world's pain.' A quotation from Goethe's *Faust*, Part I.

[4] Dr von Freund had promised an endowment of 1m. crowns for the development of psycho-analysis.

[5] J. P. Jacobsen, 1847–85, Danish novelist.

Allenstein,
2.9.18

Dear Professor,

Your letter gave me two-fold pleasure – because it brought me a sign of life from you after a long break and because it contained good news. I am eagerly looking forward to everything I shall hear in Breslau about Dr von Freund and his plans and, even more, to our meeting after such a long time. The programme already seems very full. I think the participants will exceed the number originally anticipated.

No news from us. Greetings to all your family and also to those who signed the card I recently received. Kind regards to you from my wife and myself.

Hotel accommodation in Breslau seems to present no difficulty.

Yours,
Karl Abraham

*

Allenstein,
27.10.18

Dear Professor,

Exactly a month has passed since our pleasant days in Budapest. The opportunity for discussion we had there made correspondence superfluous for a while, but I should now like to resume it.

In the meantime, the meeting on Neurosis has taken place in Berlin and, as I already foresaw in Budapest, I was delegated to it. The political situation made it impossible for Simmel and me to intervene successfully for our cause. Since an early peace was then anticipated, one could hardly expect a receptive mood towards new ideas. Moreover, I was able to convince myself that hostility from psychiatric circles has remained unchanged. I cannot even say that I am unhappy about this, for I did not like the idea that psycho-analysis should suddenly[1]

---

[1] This refers to the interest suddenly taken by the authorities in psychoanalysis as a means of restoring soldiers to health and thus to active service.

become fashionable because of purely practical considerations. We would rapidly have acquired a number of colleagues who would merely have paid lip service and would afterwards have called themselves psycho-analysts. Our position as outsiders will continue for the time being.

On the return journey from Budapest, and also more recently in Berlin, I have become more closely acquainted with Simmel. He has not yet in any way moved beyond the Breuer-Freud point of view, has strong resistances against sexuality which he is not yet clearly aware of, and, unfortunately, actually stressed at the Berlin meeting that, according to his own experience, sexuality does not play an essential part, either in war neurosis or in analytic treatment. Perhaps he will develop further. But we must not overrate him. The letter you showed me in Budapest does not give a complete picture.

Political events absorb so much of one's interest at present that one is automatically distracted from scientific work. All the same, some new plans are beginning to mature. I am making progress with Miss X., but it remains to be seen what the therapeutic success will be. I have also discovered something new about obsessional counting. I shall only say for now that the connected compulsion to establish symmetry is directly linked with the hands (fingers). In these, as in some cases I have previously analysed, the hands are an important erotogenic zone. So far nothing has been written in our literature about patients who at times of libidinal excitation get congestion in their hands. Miss X., for instance, during an infantile vision of an approaching large body (father) had the feeling that her fingers were swelling. There seems to be complete success with the patient's young nephew.

I hope you are not suffering too much from the general deprivations in Vienna about which we now constantly read. Here in East Prussia we are tolerably well off in this respect. But the political future is dark.

With kind regards to you all,

Yours,
Karl Abraham

Berggasse 19,
Vienna IX,
2.12.18

Dear Friend,

I received your letter of a few weeks ago, but did not answer it immediately because there was something that I wanted to let mature first, and meanwhile I wanted to send you the statutes to have your opinion on them. When the latter failed to appear for such a long time, I also postponed the other news I had for you.

You will have seen from the rules that I have undertaken the administration of the Barczy fund. From the revenue I propose to award two annual prizes, as an honour to the winners, of course, not for their enrichment or financial recompense. One prize is to be for an outstanding medical paper, and the other for one of the *Imago* type. Provision is made for the division of the prize money if it is desired to draw attention to two works of outstanding merit, but the greater or smaller cash value of the prize should not be connected with any greater or smaller estimation of the value of the work for which it is awarded. Each prize is of 1,000 crowns, which nowadays means very little. I chose the period up to the Budapest congress as the first for which prizes are to be awarded; subsequently they will be awarded annually. In order not to have to exclude the best of you from the potential prize-winners, I did not appoint a panel of judges. Thus the counterpart of the statutes is that they leave to me an act of unmitigated dictatorship.

On this occasion I have decided to award the medical prize for two papers: your investigation into the earliest pre-genital stages of development of the libido (1916) and Simmel's familiar pamphlet (500 crowns each). The *Imago* prize is to go to Reik for his work on the puberty rites of savages. You will already have noted that the prizes go, not to authors, but to their works. I must ask your forgiveness for the small scale of the whole arrangement. I did not want to put a heavier burden on the fund until its potentialities and the demands that will be made on it have grown clearer. Actually the revolution has limited it for the time being to a total of 250,000 crowns, and Freund is now trying to reinforce it by associating it with the bigger, already existing, fund for the city of Budapest. The interest on a quarter of a million amounts only to 10,000 crowns, and the foundation of the publishing house will rapidly whittle the capital away. It is extraordinary how much money you have to have before you can do anything decent with it. Thus the prizes are only honours, an encouragement for the younger men and recognition for the mature.

A direct letter arrived from Jones by way of Zürich, with the news that he has lost his young wife, apparently under an operation.

My son Martin has not come home, and all the information points to his whole unit having been taken prisoner without a battle. This would not be the worst. But we have had no news about his personal fate since October 25th. Ernst is at Munich, and Oli reached home unrobbed.[1] The restrictions are serious here, the uncertainties great, and my practice naturally minimal. The society has not yet met.

Meanwhile my cordial greetings to you and yours.

Sincerely yours,
Freud

*

Allenstein,
15.12.18

Dear Professor,

Your letter of December 2nd has been a long time getting here. Before taking up its contents, I should like to express the hope that your son Martin has in fact suffered no worse fate than being taken prisoner with his unit. Perhaps you will have had news of him meanwhile, or at least have found out more about the whereabouts of his regiment.

Now, my thanks for your award for my 1916 paper.[2] I had not expected, as one of the older men, to be considered at all.

---

[1] In the revolutionary disturbances of the period officers were frequently robbed of their kit.

[2] Karl Abraham, 'The First Pregenital Phase of the Libido', *Selected Papers on Psycho-Analysis*, London, 1927.

However, compared with us, our younger colleagues were in fact less able to produce any scientific work during the war. Apart from your own work, there have been very few contributions to clinical psycho-analysis during these years. The sum of money, though it has little value at present, will be used for a long-postponed wish-fulfilment—a visit to Vienna—as soon as circumstances permit. I shall write to Simmel today. The money has already been paid into my Berlin bank and I shall pass half of it on to Simmel as soon as I have his present address.

I was discharged from the army yesterday, but shall stay here with my family over Christmas, partly because of my practice – three analytic cases – and partly for other practical reasons. I was in Berlin at the beginning of last week and took a furnished flat on a temporary basis.

When you write again, dear Professor, please write to the Berlin address where I hope to arrive on the 30th. With kindest regards from house to house and with the wish that 1919 will be better than previous years,

Yours,
Karl Abraham

*

Berggasse 19,
Vienna IX,
25.12.18

Dear Friend,

So I can write to you in Berlin again, and the nightmare of war has ended for you too. I feel convinced that your practice will quickly regain its old level, and my only wish is that your health will improve to the same extent. What you say about the prize was not without a certain sting in the tail for me. Having suddenly acquired wealth, I have simultaneously to admit how inadequate it is in relation to my intentions. I did not want to make any distinction between the beginners and the masters of analysis, because in this case I should not have found the models to hold up for aspirants to follow.

The publishing house has not yet been established; like everything else one sets about nowadays, it is meeting with great difficulties, but I think that we shall succeed. We have appointed you and Hitschmann to be among the editors of the *Zeitschrift*, and wish you in particular to concern yourself with the preparation of the annual report, which will be published as a supplement. Hitschmann's special task will be to look after the reviews, which are intended to be models of seriousness and thoroughness. I am already in direct touch with Jones by way of Sachs, but we cannot yet get material from him.

I have no news of Martin, and still do not know where he is. That contributes to the depression of these times. Deuticke today advised me of the payment for the Danish translation of the five lectures; thus a minor victory. One of these days I shall be entrusting to the post the fourth volume of my *Kleine Schriften* directed to your new address.

Cordially wishing you all the luck you deserve in the new life you are beginning, Sincerely yours,

Freud

Berggasse 19,
Vienna IX,
5.2.19

Dear Friend,

First, let me state that it is bitterly cold here in this room, and then let me add that I have heard with pleasure from various sources about your improved state of health and the arrival of your review. But I have nothing yet from E. Simmel; I have had no word from him, and you do not mention him in your letter.

The preparations to set up the publishing house are going forward very well. Rank is really outstandingly competent and keen. The second number of the *Zeitschrift* is almost completely in type, the first is on the way from Czechoslovakia, and paper has been bought. There is talk of Rank's going to Switzerland to meet Jones there and perhaps build up the organisation a little further. We are delighted to be able to work in our *jardin secret* while the storm lays waste everything outside.

The societies here, in Budapest and in Holland, are active. We hope the same will soon be true of yours in Berlin.

The last few weeks have brought me several new editions and translations, of which the most recent is the Leonardo. The first half of the Dutch translation of the lectures has appeared, and a Danish translation of the American lectures is assured.

I have been lingering not unintentionally on the bright side of things. Depicting the other side would take us too far afield. I am very busy, but .... Of Martin, who is at Genoa, we have since had no news. In any case he would not be missing any work here. I was recently visited by an American belonging to Wilson's staff. He came accompanied by two baskets of provisions and exchanged them for copies of the *Lectures* and the *Everyday Life*. He gave us confidence in the President.

My cordial greetings to you and your wife.

Yours,
Freud

*

Berlin-Grunewald,
23.2.19

Dear Professor,

In spite of the unquiet times, there seems to be a lot of scientific activity in Vienna. I was glad to hear about the development of the *Verlag*, the new editions and the work of your Society. There is, of course, only a very modest amount of scientific life to report about from here. Our group now has three meetings a month, two of them on medical subjects and one on an *Imago* topic.

I am writing a short paper about patients who persistently avoid free association[1] and hope to send the manuscript to Rank in a week or two. It is a paper I read in our first meeting this year. This week I shall speak about animal totemism in dreams. My health is fairly good now so that I am able to cope easily with my work. My practice is growing and has recently provided me with various new findings which I hope to make use of soon; among others, some contributions to the theory of the

[1] Karl Abraham, 'A Particular Form of Neurotic Resistance against the Psycho-Analytic Method', *Selected Papers on Psycho-Analysis*, London, 1927.

erotogenic zones, with special reference to the eye. A most instructive case of writer's cramp gave me some nice material about the hand as an erotogenic zone.

Rank sent me the table of contents for the second volume of the *Zeitschrift*. I find in it a heading 'Putnam✝'. Do you know any details about this?

The first two months of my practice have proved it is possible to live as well as to practise away from the centre of town. I should not like to return to the centre but it is very difficult to find a suitable flat out here. Our present one is only a temporary solution and, after three years of Bohemian existence, we should like to live comfortably again.

Have you any news from Genoa? And how are you all? It is quite like spring here already. If the weather is the same in Vienna, at least you need not suffer so much from shortage of coal. In this respect we are well off, but in others living conditions are still pretty difficult. You are right that it is as well for the time being to bury oneself in science. It is good that our work gives us such hopeful prospects for the future.

With kindest regards from house to house,

Yours,
Karl Abraham

*

Berggasse 19,
Vienna IX,
13.4.19

Dear Friend,

It still cannot be called a proper postal service if a letter takes eleven days to arrive.

In regard to the over-estimation of Pötzl, it is not as bad as all that here. We rather enjoy the piquancy of the situation of the first assistant of the psychiatric clinic's associating himself with psycho-analysis, but we made him spend years winning us over, and are very well informed about his ambivalent character. His very notable intelligence and scientific training are in his favour; if he does nothing for us, we shall put up with the situation very well. We did not wish to reject him so long as he

286

was enthusiastic. Optimism in regard to academic circles has no place with us.

Rank is back; in view of the uncertainties of the recent situation in Hungary, he did not commit himself in any way, but he made many contacts. He found Jones as devoted to us as ever. He wants a congress, or at any rate a meeting of the committee, in Holland in the autumn. I hope it will be possible. Your two contributions have been received with many thanks. The technical paper is particulary good and topical. What is missing is only that the whole attitude derives from the father complex. Printing is going forward. The state of our affairs is in conformity with the troubled times. Ernst is cut off from us in Munich, and from the prisoner we have rare but not unsatisfactory news.

With cordial greetings to you and your wife,

Yours,
Freud

*

Berlin-Grunewald,
5.5.19

Dear Professor,

This letter was meant to reach you on May 7th, but it will arrive some days later after all. My good wishes are nonetheless sincere. I had hoped to be able to send you a scientific contribution in honour of the day, as I have done several times previously. The paper in question will however be more extensive than I had anticipated and, because of my limited leisure, will not be ready for some weeks. It uses your recent publication on 'The Taboo of Virginity' as a point of departure and deals with the castration complex in women;[1] I think it contributes something new. Some days ago I spoke in our Society about this topic. We have had regular meetings since the end of the war and they are far more productive than they used to be.

For myself, I can report that my health is now fairly satisfactory. The practice is lively and will become more lucrative in

---

[1] Karl Abraham, 'Manifestations of the Female Castration Complex', *Selected Papers on Psycho-Analysis*, London, 1927.

due course. I have the impression from my analyses that I have made progress in technique in spite of the long interval. My handling of neuroses and psychoses at the military hospital was certainly less intensive in each single case but gave me much insight and extended my experience. You may be interested to hear that I have recently begun the analysis of a case of *paranoia querulans*–most instructive and fully confirming your views.

We are still without a permanent home, and living conditions are altogether pretty difficult. My family are well. I hope you and yours are the same.

We shall soon have to decide whether there is to be a Congress and where it should take place. Holland seems to be the most suitable country, although the exchange rate makes this journey very difficult, particularly for the Austrians. I would be in favour of writing round to the Societies immediately in order to find out whether there would be enough participants for Holland.

Is there no hope, dear Professor, that you will be coming to Germany (Hamburg)?

With kind regards from house to house,

Yours,
Karl Abraham

*

Berggasse 19,
Vienna IX,
18.5.19

Dear Friend,

The period of my birthday brought me a great many congratulations, dotted about all over the place from the 1st to the 7th; my own brother settled for May 3rd, though he should have known better. The uncertainty in the matter is a highly pertinent criticism of a practice which, like so many other things, should now be ripe for abolition. I read with much satisfaction in your letter the news about your health and your practice.

The first book published by the International Psycho-Analytic Press now lies ready before me, that on the war neuroses. I do not regard it as an outstanding performance, but perhaps for that very reason it will make an impression on our honoured contemporaries. The second, by Ferenczi, is soon to follow. We are completely cut off from Budapest; we know only that Ferenczi has become an official teacher of psycho-analysis. The embassy here has paid us out one-fifth of the fund; the remainder does not seem to be endangered. A congress this year is still out of the question, as Emden agrees, it might perhaps be possible to organise a meeting of the members of the committee or of presidents of the societies, but that too is still doubtful. Just as the war deprived us of the activity of the Berlin headquarters, so is the revolution now depriving us of that of the Budapest group. Actually a change in organisation seems to be indicated.

Kraus and Brugsch have again reminded me of my promise to produce an article on the psycho-analytic theory of the neuroses for their handbook by April 20th. The recognition of psycho-analysis in their first synzygiology[1] is very meagre.

F., a real medical 'subject' in Heinrich Mann's sense of the word, has sent us his character-study of Wilhelm II from the *Umschau*. I conclude from this symptom that the Hohenzollerns are finally done for. Of all the rats this F. is the most disgusting.

With cordial greetings to you and your family,

Yours,
Freud

*

Berlin-Grunewald,
5.6.19

Dear Professor,

Two very full days have prevented me from writing my letter. Apart from work in the practice, which now fills the whole of my day, I have tried almost daily during the last five months to find a permanent home. These last months have proved that patients do not mind coming out as far as Grunewald, and I have now rented a place very near our present refuge.

[1] Synzygion, in Greek a two-horse team; here a jocular reference to Kraus and Brugsch.

Meanwhile, the publication on War Neuroses has arrived. Jones's contribution interests me particularly but I have not been able to read it yet.

As you know, Dr S. is one of my patients. He is definitely making progress and I may soon be able to give a final favourable report on him. I do not know whether I mentioned in my last letter that I have taken on the analysis of a *paranoia querulans*. It is progressing very successfully. The patient has lost interest in those things about which he complained, has utterly changed and is making a surprising switchover away from men towards women. He is a complete and brilliant confirmation of the theories you develop in the Schreber case. It is the sort of case where one would least expect to achieve a therapeutic success. This man, who two months ago had no thoughts or words but those of complaint, said to me today: 'I'm feeling damned well.' The speed of the improvement can probably be accounted for by only one factor – the patient's homosexuality had been very little repressed and its significance became evident to him very rapidly.

It is weeks since I have written anything. The paper I promised on the female castration complex got stuck right at the beginning. Now flat-hunting is over, I hope to become productive once again.

What do you think at your end about a Meeting or a Congress in the course of the year? The Hague is hardly feasible while going abroad is so difficult. We here would be very pleased if a German town were considered and our Society asks that this proposal should be given some thought.

I have not heard any more from Reik. He was supposed to come to Berlin some time ago.

In conclusion, I once more send my best wishes for your wife's speedy recovery.

With kindest regards from house to house,

Yours,

Karl Abraham

Berggasse 19,
Vienna IX,
3.10.19

Dear Friend,

There is already something dream-like about the times behind us, when friendly solicitude kept the seriousness of life
away from us.[1] The dreadful conditions in this city, the impossibility of feeding and keeping oneself, the presence of Jones,
Ferenczi and Freund, the necessary conferences and decision-
making, and the hesitant beginnings of analytic work (five sessions = 500 crowns) result in a vivid present in the face of
which memories quickly fade. Let me tell you briefly the outcome of the committee meetings, which unfortunately had to
take place in your absence. Because of the uncertainty of the
situation in Hungary, Ferenczi handed over the presidency to
Jones until the congress, at which the latter is to be installed
definitely. Jones is also undertaking to produce a *journal of
psycho-analysis*[2] for Britain and America; this will remain in the
closest contact with the *Zeitschrift*, and the contents of the latter
will be freely available to it. The technical production will take
place in Vienna, and it will be imported to London; two numbers have already been assembled. I have handed over administration of the fund to Jones, and he will take the money back
with him to England. Ways and means of transferring funds
from London for our work in Vienna have already been found.
It was Rank's idea to arrange for the fund to produce commo-
dities (the products of the publishing house) here which would
then be sold in England and America. In other words, the
orientation towards the west proclaimed by our Chancellor!
Another point on which your opinion will be decisive is the
following. It is proposed on the occasion of the foundation of
the Berlin clinic to admit Eitingon to full membership of the
committee. If you too agree with this, please mention it to him
without further delay. In any other eventuality please let us
have your views on the proposal immediately.

[1] The reference is to Freud's visit to Abraham during the previous month.
[2] These words in English in the original. The *International Journal of
Psycho-Analysis* was first published in 1920.

I send my cordial greetings to you and your family, and again thank you all for all the proofs of friendship you gave us during our visit.

Yours,
Freud

Dear Professor,

Many thanks for the joint card from Kobenzl,[1] for your letter and for your photograph which I received from Hamburg. It is excellent, true to life and technically perfect.

I have naturally not the slightest objection to Eitingon becoming a member, and he has been glad to accept. I am only too pleased to have someone here with whom I can discuss everything, should the need arise.

Everything contained in the Committee report interested me very much and meets with my approval. There seems a general wish for a Congress in the spring. Since most of the participants live in Germany and Austria and will therefore be unable to afford a journey to Holland just at present, the Congress will probably have to take place either in Germany or Austria. Eitingon and I should like to propose to the Committee that the Congress be held in Berlin and should further like to suggest that our closed scientific meetings be followed by a number of lectures on medical and general subjects. We would ask you to pass on this suggestion with our comment that there would certainly be a considerable number of participants for such a project.

After I discussed this with Eitingon, I met Federn who broke his journey in Berlin. He said the Vienna Society was declining and expressed the hope that a Congress in Vienna would revive interest there. What do you think about this? We naturally do not want to stand in your way. The previous objection raised against university towns is no longer valid. Berlin is clamouring for psycho-analysis and a week of explanatory lectures would be of great service to us.

[1] Restaurant on a hill overlooking Vienna.

Simmel recently gave an excellent report in the Society here on the psycho-analysis of a gambler. He has been coming on very well lately.

A word about your last paper.[1] I am most enthusiastic about it. It seems to me that you have never before penetrated so deeply into the uttermost depths of a problem. Moreover, the presentation is so beautifully comprehensible and lucid that reading it is in itself an outstanding intellectual and aesthetic pleasure.

Kindest regards from my wife and myself to you and yours,

Yours,

Karl Abraham

How did you like Boehm's Paper?[2] It sounded very good when he presented it.

Berggasse 19,
Vienna IX,
2.11.19

Dear Friend,

My congratulations on your new address, which means the re-establishment of a home of your own.

I put your and Eitingon's proposal to call a congress in Berlin in the spring to a committee meeting attended by Ferenczi, Freund and Rank. At first they were all greatly taken by the idea, but slowly they began to share the doubt which had prevailed with me from the first. Finally we were all in agreement. The chief objection was that, particularly in view of our new orientation towards the west, we could not decide anything without consulting Jones. But Jones attaches importance to some Americans being present this time, and has already said that arrangements for their trip have to be made many months in advance. We also think that it would undoubtedly be better for several numbers of the British journal to have been published before the congress discusses it. So it was decided to write

[1] Sigmund Freud, *The Uncanny*, Standard Ed., Vol. XVII.

[2] Dr Felix Boehm, 'Beiträge zur Psychologie der Homosexualät', *Internationale Zeitschrift*, Vol. VI, 1920.

to Jones and ask his opinion. Moreover, I thought it better that the congress week should fall in the autumn instead of the spring. In my opinion we should not forget that we have received an invitation to Holland and, as the last congresses were necessarily restricted to the Central Powers, it seemed appropriate that the next should be closer, even geographically, to our Entente members. There is absolutely nothing to be said in favour of Vienna, no good is to be done here; Federn's description is correct, but nothing can be done about it. Everyone liked very much the idea of the week of lectures you would like to associate with the congress. We should like to know whether your proposal is that these should be independent of the congress or a continuation of it. This is an idea of which something should come.

Rank is very vigorously at work here. My daughter has begun work as an assistant in the English department of the publishing house. Ferenczi is staying until the eighth, and Freund for an indefinite period, his condition now permits certain perhaps misleading doubts. I am analysing nine hours a day and cannot manage anything else. Dr Forsyth,[1] who is still under analysis with me, turns out to be a very notable personality; he talks a great deal about the great interest in analysis in England. Boehm's work is now being read by Ferenczi. I liked it. As it is too long for the *Zeitschrift*, we are now considering whether we could make a supplement of it.

The first meeting of the society takes place today.

With cordial greetings to you and your wife and children,

Sincerely yours,

Freud

Berlin-Grunewald,
23.11.19

Dear Professor,

I agree that it would be desirable if some Americans were to attend the Congress. It does, however, seem impossible to me to hold a Congress in Holland until the German and Austrian exchange rates greatly improve. This can hardly be expected

[1] Dr David Forsyth, British psycho-analyst.

by the autumn, but by then the Americans should have no difficulty in travelling to Germany. At the moment, a journey to Holland plus a few days' stay there can hardly be managed for 1,500–2,000 marks and there are very few who can afford this. Things are even worse in Austria and most people from there would find the journey alone far beyond their means. A Congress which excludes most of the Austrians, Hungarians and Germans would be no Congress. Therefore, everything seems to speak in favour of Berlin. Let us wait and hear what Jones has to say about the Congress before arranging the week of lectures.

As co-editor of the *Zeitschrift*, I should like to repeat my objection against making it top-heavy. I still think it was a mistake to discontinue the *Jahrbuch*. Now that we have our own *Verlag*, there should be, alongside the *Zeitschrift* to which one subscribes, a *Jahrbuch* which one can buy to get information about the development of our science. It seems an unnecessary weighting to include reviews in the *Zeitschrift*. Extra numbers containing longer articles do not seem practicable to me, and I think we should once again consider the question of resuming publication of the *Jahrbuch*.

A short paper of mine ('The Narcissistic Evaluation of Excretory Processes in Dreams and Neurosis'[1]), which is now being typed, will be sent to Rank within a few days. The paper about the female castration complex, which has been completed for some time, needs revising. I discovered, while I was churning out the reviews, that the literature already contains material which I had believed to be new. During the war I was unable to follow the literature in detail.

Reik's book[2] is excellent. The paper on the Shofar in particular is convincing and extremely penetrating. Rank sent me his book on Myths.[3] His achievements are truly amazing. I am just starting on those articles that I do not yet know.

The necessity for working very long hours unfortunately leaves me too little time for theoretical work. You, dear Professor, are in the same position. Added to this is the fact that I

---

[1] Karl Abraham, *Selected Papers on Psycho-Analysis*, London, 1927.

[2] Theodor Reik, *Probleme der Religionpsychologie*.

[3] Otto Rank, 'Psychoanalytische Beitraege zur Mythenforschung', *Internationaler Psychoanalytischer Verlag*, 1919.

have not yet had a break this year and am therefore less keen on writing than I might otherwise have been. I shall probably take one or two weeks off at Christmas.

Hoping to have good news from you, I am, with kind regards – also from my wife, to you all,

Yours,
Karl Abraham

Berggasse 19,
Vienna IX,
1.12.19

Dear Friend,

I do not turn a deaf ear to the weight of your arguments against Holland and in favour of Berlin, and I am actually afraid that they may turn the scale, but I must confess that to me there is something unsatisfactory about such a congress. Also I do not know whether it will really be possible to get British and Americans to come to Berlin next autumn. Hostile prejudice is stronger than you suppose. In any case Rank, who is now at The Hague, and is travelling to London tomorrow with Emden and Ophuijsen, will be coming to see you in the course of this month, and he will tell you Jones's attitude in the matter; and what the two of you then decide will be acceptable to all of us here. I am almost of the opinion that with $3\frac{1}{3}$ crowns to the mark either journey will be just as difficult to most of the Viennese.

Your proposal to resuscitate the *Jahrbuch* will be carefully considered, and should have a place in your discussions with Rank. For the time being I feel that the difficulties outweigh the demand. Because of the tremendous costs of printing, the publishing house already feels the maintenance of two journals as a serious burden. Moreover, a third publication would be restricted to the purely psycho-analytic public, which has not a great deal of buying power. Deuticke might be persuaded to revive the *Jahrbuch*, but I am afraid that the material produced by us in the course of a year might not be sufficient to keep it going. We have not exactly a superfluity of material even for the *Zeitschrift*. A far deeper interest by a much wider public would be necessary to create a real demand for the *Jahrbuch*. Also we must not forget that what Britain (and America) produce is henceforward to be diverted to the *British Journal of Psycho-Analysis*.

The papers you announce will be given the usual welcome. It is astonishing how much work you are still able to do in a situation in which, as I am well aware myself, all one's energy is required to maintain one's economic level.

I now have all my three sons together for a short time. Martin is marrying on the 7th inst., and next day Ernst will be leaving for Berlin, where you will certainly see him more often. There has been hardly any news from Ferenczi since his departure, and Freund, who is here, is in a bad way. He will not leave Vienna alive, it seems metastases have now been confirmed beyond doubt.

With cordial greetings to you and your wife,

Sincerely yours,
Freud

*

Berlin-Grunewald,
7.12.19

Dear Professor,

Your letter of the 1st reached me by the 5th. Is this a sign that conditions are improving?

I want to start my reply with best wishes for your son's wedding. We hope to see Ernst here shortly and Rank too before long.

I am terribly sorry to hear about Freund's serious illness. If metastases are already present, one must be prepared for the end to come soon. Does he himself know about his condition?

I shall discuss the question of the Congress and the *Jahrbuch* with Rank.

Your praise for my productivity is not justified. In the few free hours the practice leaves me I have a marked disinclination for work. Otherwise there would be more to show. The small contributions of the last few months can be explained by the fact that I am unwilling to start on anything more extensive.

You may have already heard from Eitingon that there is a possibility of suitable premises for our Clinic. We shall rent it if the price is within our means. Simmel will be an excellent personality for the Clinic.

I have some additions to make to Reik's papers which I may write quite soon. I shall take a holiday from December 24th to January 4th but shall not go away.

With kind regards from house to house,

Yours,
Karl Abraham

*

Berggasse 19,
Vienna IX,
15.12.19

Dear Friend,

Thank you for your congratulations. The wedding was a small family affair and passed off very well.

Your contribution on the omnipotence of excreta[1] amused me greatly. After all, they really are creations, just as ideas and wishes are. At the same time I read something on the interpretation of dreams at the subjective level, and once more had a strong impression of what a superfluous addition that is to the understanding of dreams. Of course one destroys the father only because he is the 'inner' father, that is, has significance for one's own mental life.

Rank has sent a telegram from London. At last! But, as he had to waste a whole week in Holland waiting for his entry permit, he will have to come back by the shortest route on a Swiss special (pre-Christmas) train without touching Berlin. I have therefore to report that he is definitely against Berlin and still favours Holland in the autumn. I do not even know whether that will be possible. There is no question of any improvement in communications. (Your letter of the 7th reached me today, the 15th.)

Freund knows everything; he has, for instance, directed that

[1] Karl Abraham, 'Zur narzistischen Bewertung der Excretionsvorgänge', *Internationale Zeitschrift für Psychoanalyse*, 1920.

the ring he wears is to be restored to me after his death. He has also sensed that it is intended for Eitingon.

So far as work is concerned, things are no better with me than with you. Only I think that in my case it is not a phase of short duration. I think I have finished with sowing and shall not get to the reaping.

Captain Schmiedeberg,[1] who was Eitingon's guest, gave me a piece of news that is so good that I cannot believe it, namely that you are about to get a professorship of psycho-analysis. As you have not mentioned this in your letters, I can no longer contain my curiosity. I shall of course keep the secret if there is anything in it.

Sincerely yours,
Freud

*

Berlin-Grunewald,
29.12.19

Dear Professor,

Your letter of the 15th reached me yesterday, which hardly permits the assumption that the postal services are improving! Meanwhile, your son Ernst has turned up here as a live source of news.

I very often think of poor Freund. I would like to write to him but do not want to remind him unnecessarily of his fate. Yet it does seem wrong to me to take no notice of his life and suffering, especially as he showed me so much friendship in Budapest. Could you advise me what to do? You are sure to know whether he is sensitive to his illness being mentioned.

I was afraid that Schmiedeberg would talk prematurely in Vienna. Eitingon had told him something in confidence and I only heard about it after Schmiedeberg had left, so that I could not ask him to keep it secret. Now I shall, of course, tell you the whole story and you will appreciate why I did not want to count my chickens before they were hatched.

Through his political activities Simmel has some contacts with the Ministry of Education. Some important people there told

[1] Walter Schmiedeberg, lay analyst in Berlin, later in London.

him, partly as a result of his article in the *Vossische Zeitung*, that the Ministry would be very favourably disposed to the founding of a Chair of Psycho-Analysis. Simmel first discussed the matter with Eitingon and thought that I, Eitingon and he himself might be considered. Eitingon firmly declined and said that no one but me should be considered. Simmel allowed himself to be persuaded, spoke to me about it and then with the official concerned in the Ministry. The latter thereupon asked me to call on him, which I did at the beginning of December. In the meantime, the very disagreeable incident occurred in Parliament concerning the Chair in Tuberculosis for Friedmann and for this reason the Ministry had to proceed far more circumspectly with the Faculty than would otherwise have been the case.[1] After a long discussion, I was asked to get our Society to send in a detailed and scientifically based document on the introduction of psycho-analytic teaching. The outlook is therefore by no means as favourable as one might have assumed when the matter was first mooted, but it is not hopeless. If the Ministry brings a certain amount of pressure to bear and even if only a few of the professors are definitely in favour, the chances are not too bad. Interest in academic circles is visibly increasing. The Clinic, which will certainly be opened in January, is arousing great interest on the part of the Ministry. Of the professors I hope to win over at least Kraus and His. Even if the whole operation should prove unsuccessful, the hope still remains that there will be a change in the Faculties' right of appeal.

The document must contain all the facts that serve to demonstrate the increasing interest in and need for psycho-analysis. I would need Rank's consent to plagiarise – I find a great part of the introductory article[2] in the first number of *Imago* eminently suitable as a basis for our document, and I expect he will be

[1] Dr F. F. Friedmann had used his political affiliation to enlist the Ministry's help to obtain a Chair. Between 1904 and 1912 he had published numerous papers on preventive and therapeutic vaccination of animals and men with tortoise tubercle bacilli. Well-known scientists examined and subsequently discredited his claims and the Faculty prevented his nomination. This gave rise to a scandal.

[2] 'Entwicklung und Ansprueche der Psychoanalyse' by Dr Otto Rank and Dr Hanns Sachs, *Imago*, No. 1, Vol. 1, 1912.

pleased to agree to this. I would further ask him on this occasion to let me have news of Sachs's whereabouts and state of health.

I should like to ask both of you not to discuss this matter for the time being. It would be very nice if it came off. I am sure the lectures would be well attended.

[The remainder of this letter is missing in the original.]

*

Berggasse 19,
Vienna, IX,
6.1.20

Dear Friend,

I had my first business conference with Rank today, and promised to write to you immediately. All your arguments in favour of holding the congress in Berlin are sound, and yet I had to decide in favour of Holland. You neglect the most important factor in the situation, the pressing need of the publishing house to win over the Americans to the *British Journal of Psycho-Analysis.* Failing that, we shall not be able to keep the German journals alive for more than a year. Jones now assures us that there is no chance of getting the Anglo-Saxons to come to Berlin, and that is decisive. Obviously we have no correct picture of these people's state of mind. What is at stake in this re-orientation is no question of scientific precedence, but of practical advantage. In comparison with that, our own travel and exchange difficulties dwindle into nothing; they will in any case be partly met by arrangements made by the Dutch. I hope you will not turn a deaf ear to these considerations, and will not allow the war that is soon to be wound up to flare up again in the bosom of the committee.

Perhaps there is an underground passage connecting this subject with my next. So far as I know, Schmiedeberg was directly charged with telling me the secret of your chances, and I do not see why I should not have my share in the forepleasure when the end-pleasure will perhaps not materialise. I too say that it would be a splendid thing, and that it would cause the whole of Germany to collapse, but I am afraid it is too good

301

to be true. It is too reminiscent of Ferenczi's ephemeral professorship in Budapest. For my part I shall be happy if a lecturership comes out of it for you. In the long run the faculty would not tolerate anyone imposed on them.

Yes, you did ask for the Spanish journal for review. Delgado[1] announces a new work *El psicoanalisis*, that is perhaps already afloat on the ocean.

It is a pity that conditions are so unfavourable to your intention to hold the congress in Berlin. Certainly your own prospects would be improved thereby. Jones knows nothing of such a possible advantage for you stemming from the congress.

Now at last to private matters. Rank today unpacked the provisions bought in Holland. We have received advice of boxes of gifts from Britain and America, but of course they do not arrive. The most surprising people have congratulated me on my 'nomination'[2] on December 31st. The republic has brought about no change in the greed and respect for titles that prevailed under the monarchy.

I hope that your wife has already recovered, and that the children are growing up as happily as when we saw them in September. There are now only three of us, and we are fairly well.

With cordial greetings and New Year wishes to you and your family,

Yours,
Freud

P.S. Freund is slowly withdrawing into himself. It is perhaps more advisable not to stir him up.

Berlin-Grunewald,
28.1.20

Dear Professor,

I have just heard that neither you nor your wife will be able to travel to Hamburg. As it is therefore impossible to express my sympathy to either of you personally, I feel compelled to send you and your family a few words of deepest sympathy.

---

[1] Dr Honorio F. Delgado, psychiatrist in Lima, Peru.
[2] Freud had been made a titular professor.

Your sad news[1] has affected us as deeply as if our own family had to mourn the loss of a young life.

My thoughts are with you and I remain, as always,

Yours devotedly,
Karl Abraham

Berggasse 19,
Vienna IX,
3.2.20

Dear Friend,

I am not yet very well able to write, but I shall not delay any longer thanking you, your wife, and all the members of your group for your heartfelt telegram of condolence. My wife, though very shaken, appreciated all these signs of sympathy.

Meanwhile our work goes ahead under ever-increasing difficulties. We are now threatened with a paper shortage. You will soon be receiving a circular letter concerning reviewing in which apologies will be made to you because of the setting up of a central editorial office in Vienna. The post between Vienna and Berlin is so bad at present that we were forced to decide on this simplification. I hope that you will be left with enough to do.

How are the prospects for the professorship?

With cordial greetings,

Yours,
Freud

*

Berlin-Grunewald,
13.3.20

Dear Professor,

Our correspondence has come to a complete standstill. I kept silent for some weeks since I did not wish to put you under the obligation of replying to me so soon after your sad loss. As I have been in constant touch with Rank, you will in any case have heard what has been happening with us. Besides, two

[1] The sudden death of Freud's daughter Sophie during the big influenza epidemic.

of your children have been able to bring you news from here. Both my wife and I were very pleased to welcome them. We are expecting Ernst back here soon and hope he will be a frequent guest. He has won lasting recognition for himself in his designing of the Clinic, which is admired by everyone. It is a good thing that everything is now completed. One cannot tell, after the changes[1] that took place so quietly this morning, what will happen next and whether it will be at all possible to realise our plans in the near future. I have just finished the detailed document on the teaching of psycho-analysis at the University, and we must wait and see whether such a move is now feasible.

The Clinic is well attended. I have already written to Rank about this: my own lecture course, which was not sufficiently advertised, only had ten participants, but the quality was very satisfactory on the whole. I hope that all the teaching will soon be well organised. We have other plans as well. Eitingon wants to arrange one room of the Clinic as a reading room where all our literature will be available. For the more distant future there is a project to start a special department for the treatment of neurotic children. I should like to train a woman doctor particularly for this. All our plans depend on having enough new followers and so far we unfortunately have not got them. We have no young people fresh from University and I want to try in every possible way to gain such workers.

I found 'The Uncanny' very gripping. I have had a few similar cases in the last few months and came to the same conclusions, although I did not formulate them so concisely.

At our last meeting Boehm read a paper on 'Homosexuality and Polygamy' which enlarged on some known points but also introduced one new aspect. Our small circle here is so unproductive that I am pleased if anything new emerges once in a while. Our activities, by the way, have recently been very much restricted.

If possible, I shall write to Rank and Reik today. I add in haste kind regards from my wife and myself to you and all your family,

Yours,
Karl Abraham

[1] Attempted overthrow of the Government by General Kapp.

Berlin-Grunewald,
4.4.20

Dear Professor,

That was really a disappointment. I could now have been with you and all our closest friends, were travelling not so beset by countless difficulties; I must at least send a few lines to follow up my telegram. Unfortunately, the telegraphic invitation arrived too late. Now we shall probably not meet till the autumn.

I have done a lot of writing during recent weeks. While it lasted, the general strike cut my practice down to half and so I had sufficient free time. The article for the *Neue Rundschau*, amounting to some twenty pages, has now been sent off and will be published in June or July; its title is 'The Cultural Significance of Psycho-Analysis'.[1] The document for the Ministry of Education is completed and will go off after Easter.

My course for doctors is nearing its end. Attendance was not good because it was advertised too late (ten participants). I have, however, made two valuable acquisitions which are, in effect more important than large numbers. One young colleague, Dr Alfred Gross,[2] an assistant of Bonhoeffer's, has become an enthusiastic follower and will probably soon start his training at the Clinic. Another colleague attending the course, a woman just about to take her finals who was already well informed before she started, wants to take up psycho-analysis with the particular aim of treating children. It is imperative for me to enlist younger colleagues and I hope the next course will be more successful in this respect.

With kind regards, also to those members of the Committee who may have stayed on in Vienna,

Yours,
Karl Abraham

[1] Karl Abraham, *Clinical Papers and Essays on Psycho-Analysis*, London, 1955.

[2] Dr Alfred Gross, emigrated to England and settled in Manchester; he later accepted a position at the Menninger Clinic (Topeka) and finally at Yale University where he died in 1957.

Berggasse 19,
Vienna, IX,
22.4.20

Dear Friend,

I answer your letter of the 4th inst. only today because in these last weeks my energy for work and writing has been unusually disturbed. I too cannot get over the disappointment about Easter. It would have been so delightful to see you all together for once and to reinforce the harmony between you that guarantees the future of our cause.

The holidays, for which I have a big work project in mind, will probably be at Gastein to begin with. There are still nearly three months to go, and I have already lost my pleasure in work.

All the difficulties of life here make one feel very blunted. But even in Vienna interest in psycho-analysis has grown livelier. I have got into communication with Havelock Ellis again. There would be a great many things of interest to discuss, let us hope we shall be able to catch up.

I send my cordial greetings to you and yours, and my lively regrets that I hear from you so seldom, certainly partly through my own fault.

Sincerely yours,
Freud

*

Berlin-Brunewald,
1.5.20

Dear Professor,

This time I'll not keep you waiting long for a reply. There is a holiday today and therefore less work and, having finished the reviews for the Annual Report, I want to resume 'contact'[1] with you and to begin by wishing you as much happiness for the sixth as can be expected in these difficult times. The burden

[1] The word used in German is 'Nervenanhang' and is an expression quoted from Schreber's Memoirs (Denkwürdigkeiten eines Nervenkranken von Dr jur. Daniel Paul Schreber, Oswald Mutze, Leipzig, 1903).

of my other duties made it impossible for me to present you with a psycho-analytic contribution this year, but I want at least to give you some news about which I now feel reasonably optimistic. Four months ago I was asked by the head of the department concerned in the Ministry of Education to submit a document drawn up by our Society on the introduction of psycho-analysis as a subject to be taught at the University. He advised me to use our first experiences at the Clinic concerning the number of patients attending for treatment and the number of participants for our lecture courses. I did this but, just when the document was completed, the military uprising and the ensuing chaos made conditions unfavourable for consideration of our case. Therefore I only visited the Ministry yesterday to deliver the document and to discuss the matter once again with the same official. I was very pleasantly received, which you will be able to understand when I tell you that we have now, since the revolution, some younger senior civil servants, aged 30–40, working alongside the older ones. The head of the department will hand the document directly to the Minister. In the middle of next week, after he has read it, I shall ask for an interview with him. The Minister[1] (Haenisch) is very interested in all new ideas. He will pass the matter on to the Faculty for their views. I shall go and see the relevant specialists – Bonhoeffer, Kraus and His. The Ministry will only turn our application down if the Faculty puts forward irrefutable objections. The assurance I was given leaves room for hope that a merely unfriendly and negative attitude on the part of the Faculty will not have any effect on the decision; and there is a certain probability that the outcome might be favourable. The question to be decided is not my personal admission as a lecturer but the setting up of a Chair in Psycho-Analysis, that is to say of an extraordinary Professorship. Almost too good to be true! (It is possible, dear Professor, that the Ministry might send an official enquiry to you concerning the person suitable for the Professorship.[2] I hope I shall not founder on this rock!)

[1] Konrad Haenisch, 1876–1925, Minister of Education under the Weimar Government.

[2] These hopes never materialised since the Ministry was ineffectual and the Faculty remained hostile. Subsequently, the question was taken up

I too deplore the bad luck that prevented me from travelling at Easter. You are now making me curious to hear about your work project for the holidays. There is probably no hope of a meeting before the autumn, that is at the Congress. Until then one must be content with correspondence which nowadays is so slow.

With kind regards, also from my wife,

Yours,
Karl Abraham

*

Berggasse 19,
Vienna IX,
14.5.20

Dear Friend,

Must I be put into the position of a pampered old man to whom everyone brings a beautiful present on the occasion of his birthday (the 6th inst.)? Eitingon brought a magnificent American endowment for the fund and you the marvellous announcement about the imminent acceptance of psycho-analysis at Berlin University. If only the second gift were as assured as the first. I am waiting impatiently to answer the Ministry's enquiry. Can you not force the privy councillors there to write to me at last?

All that is fixed about the summer is Gastein until the middle of August. Then there is a gap until the congress, which this time we wish to arrange comfortably.

At Gastein I want to work up my paper on group psychology[1] into a short book. With nine hours of analysis daily that is impossible.

With cordial greetings to you and your wife,

Yours,
Freud

---

again and Abraham was told he had reasonable chances if he were to be baptised and became a Protestant. He refused to consider this. Such a move was however the accepted passport to official positions before the Weimar Republic.

[1] Sigmund Freud *Group, Psychology and the Analysis of the Ego*, Standard Ed., Vol. XVIII.

Berlin-Grunewald,
25.5.20

Dear Professor,

What a pity we had to do without you at Ernst's wedding. I want at least to tell you that the young couple made so pleasant an impression on the day that one felt justified in giving a favourable prognosis for this union. Once more, all best wishes. We were sorry to have had no more than a glimpse of your wife and daughter. The latter will bring you my collection.[1] Many thanks for thinking of me. I shall send on the preface later. I have not found time to write it today. I wrote to Rank some days ago that I should like to add a few non-medical papers, but I have since decided to omit them as they would be out of tune with the rest.

My business with the Ministry is still pending and I hope to hear tomorrow how it stands. I have reason to assume that the opinion of the Faculty, that is to say of Bonhoeffer, will not be completely negative. As soon as I hear more, I shall let you know.

What about the programme for The Hague?[2] Do you intend to speak there about group psychology? I am considering the female castration complex as a possible theme.

With kind regards,

Yours,
Karl Abraham

*

Berlin-Grunewald,
10.6.20

Dear Professor,

In spite of certain reservations, I answered positively to your question about Urban and Schwarzenberg.[3] As far as our cause is concerned, it makes a difference whether you yourself or someone else contributes to a comprehensive work of this kind, and it may even happen that the publisher will decide to omit

[1] Karl Abraham, *Klinische Beiträge zur Psychoanalyse*, 1921.

[2] The 6th International Psycho-Analytical Congress.

[3] Freud had asked Abraham to write in his place a contribution for a text-book by Kraus and Brugsch.

any presentation of our view on the theory of neuroses. On the other hand, I should be glad to relieve you of this burden. It is better for all of us if you are free to do your own work. It would hardly be a holiday task for me since my vacation will only last for three weeks from July 15th to August 5th and I very much need this short spell--which incidentally, I shall spend at home--for a rest. If the publishers commission me for the work, I shall spread it over some time and shall postpone other plans. To conclude, I want to assure you that I do not simply regard it as a burden but am pleased that you entrust me to do this in your stead.

Our memorandum is now with the Medical Faculty. Some days ago I had a longish discussion with Bonhoeffer who is the most influential person concerned. Bonhoeffer is no friend of psycho-analysis; but he is not an enemy on principle, and certainly not an unfair one. He openly admitted to me that his arguments against are emotional and 'completely unscientific' but that he accepts much of it. He has no essential objection to a Chair in Psycho-Analysis but only a technical one which needs discussing. There is a tendency in Berlin to change all Professorships in special subjects into Chairs, thereby making such subjects obligatory for students and also examination subjects. In his opinion, psycho-analysis is not ready for this yet. On the other hand, he does not object to my being personally entrusted with the teaching. I replied that, in our view, psycho-analysis would gradually establish itself and that for the time being we were not concerned with making it a compulsory subject but only teaching it to such students who were interested, of whom there were many. He conceded this point at once and promised to contact me again after reading the memorandum, which he had not yet seen. I believe that his opinion will not be entirely unfavourable, especially as his personal attitude to me is very friendly. With the Faculty on our side, the whole matter would of course be much easier than if we had either to do without their agreement or act against it. Besides, we would then be independent of political hazards, since the socialist Prussian Minister of Education may fall overnight and a great deal would then become problematic. Therefore, *Coraggio*, *Casimiro*.

Yesterday we had a business meeting of our Society in order to draw up an autumn and winter programme. We are very enterprising and have planned the following:

1) August–September, a course for teachers by Mrs Hug-Hellmuth.

2) Following the Congress, there will be lectures in Berlin which in addition to you and me, will include Jones, Ferenczi, Ophuijsen and possibly Rank and Sachs.

3) A course for doctors each term.

4) Lectures for doctors.

5) Lectures for laymen (Sachs).

6) Analyses of medical colleagues for the purpose of learning psycho-analysis (Sachs). I hope you agree with these plans and especially with item 2.

Did you know that I have been treating Mrs N. for several weeks? The analysis is progressing wonderfully but one cannot tell yet what the final therapeutic result will be. There is much to be learned from her. She is as great an authority on obsessional neurosis as Schreber on paranoia.

I am enclosing a general review on all the Spanish literature I have received. It is meant for the Annual Report. I hope Rank will find room for this small contribution. I am prepared to review for the *Zeitschrift* the new Spanish and Portuguese publications mentioned in Number 2 of the *Zeitschrift*, of which I have the proofs.

I am still undecided what to talk about at The Hague–either 'The Female Castration Complex' or 'Contributions to the Theory of the Anal Character'. There is ample new material for both subjects. Which would you prefer?

Kindest regards to you and your family, also from my wife,

Yours,
Karl Abraham

Berggasse 19,
Vienna IX,
21.6.20

Dear Friend,

What an example of real Berlin energy again. Heavens, what a programme, and how many flies are going to be hit by these repeated swipes. I am tremendously pleased that things are so active in Berlin, and that you too are now beginning to be convinced of the impossibility of restricting psycho-analysis to the doctors. Best of all is the installation of Sachs. If he retains his health, you will have a great and lasting gain in him. We could do nothing for him.

Now comes the grit in the oil. I shall not be able to undertake the prominent role you intended for me. I shall probably not be present at the Berlin week at all. The first and external reasons for this are as follows. Between Gastein (the end of August) and the congress (September 8th) there is one week left with which I can do nothing except travel to The Hague *via* Berlin and Hamburg. After the congress I shall either stay in Holland and meet a friend from London (Lou Jones, now Mrs Herbert Jones) or leave quickly to meet Ernst and his Lucie somewhere in the south. The deeper reason is this: I am getting old and undeniably lazy and indolent, as well as being spoilt by the many gifts of food, cigars and money that are made to me, and that I have to accept because otherwise I could not live. But for the time being I am still working harder than is good for me. This year I have prolonged my working season by a fortnight, and am taking with me to Gastein a job (the group psychology) that is germinating with difficulty. Another week of the thus shortened holiday period has to go to the congress, and for the remaining time I shall have to rest from psycho-analysis, otherwise I shall not be able to get down to hard work again in October. If at all possible, I do not propose to read a paper at the congress. I think I have talked enough. Do you know the story of the doctor and the patient who clings so obstinately to life which ends in the doctor's saying: 'Have you pissed enough now?' Things were near enough to that with me, except that in that respect I am unexpectedly well.

Also it will do no harm if all of you slowly get used to the situation of my not being present. What is the committee for except to make me more and more dispensable? So far as you are concerned, I think that you should choose the subject of the female castration complex as the richer. I shall enjoy following your excellent expositions.

I am still sceptical about your cause with the Ministry. It is going too slowly for my liking, and you were certainly right in fearing that political and personal changes are a serious threat to your chances. Even then it will be no great misfortune, psycho-analysis will go ahead all the same. The only thing is that I should have liked you to have the position. Ferenczi has now been excluded from the Budapest Medical Society as a penalty for his Bolshevik professorship. As a consequence of the still existing letter censorship I could only congratulate him on the honour.

Look after yourself and grant yourself too some rest with your family.

Sincerely yours,
Freud

*

Berlin-Grunewald,
27.6.20

Dear Professor,

You misinterpret the purpose of the Committee. It is not meant to put you out of action but to make your work easier, particularly within the psycho-analytic circle. Even though I cannot speak for all the Committee members, I am certain that none of them would agree to your staying away from the Berlin meetings. Your absence would make these pointless since nobody in local medical circles knows anything about Jones, Ophuijsen and Ferenczi. You alone are the focus of both positive and negative interest: therefore, to make the whole matter acceptable to you, I suggest the following changes. We arrange the lectures, which incidentally will not take up a week but only two evenings with three papers on each, not after the Congress but before it. This seems to be the best way of using the time at your disposal before The Hague. Please do agree! We shall then try to get the other speakers for the earlier dates as well. I am hoping for your 'yes'!

My views about bringing in non-medical people have not really changed. The papers planned by Sachs deal with non-medical matters, and I have always been in agreement with extending this part of our science to lay circles and have tried to further it with my own writings.

As regards the question of a Professorship, the delays are due to the fact that the Faculty must first ask the holder of the Chair of Psychiatry to give his opinion and they then have to decide about the matter in a subsequent meeting. Without undue optimism, I do not view the matter as hopeless. I should also like to give you some further news, which may not be of much importance in itself but is a pleasant sign of the times. I am going to Halle at the end of the week to read a paper to the staff of the Medical Clinic of the University. The Director of the Clinic, Professor Volkhardt, has invited me, through a colleague who is a mutual acquaintance, to read a psycho-analytic paper and I have chosen as my subject 'The Neurotic Disturbances of the Intestinal Tract'. The staff of the Psychiatric Clinic are to be invited.

Our conditions for working at the Clinic are: first, sufficient neurological and psychiatric training; second, sufficient knowledge of psycho-analytic literature; third, personal analysis of the candidate, which Sachs will undertake. I am very much looking forward to Sachs coming here, for it is not pleasant always to be the one to stimulate others without receiving any stimulation in return. I have not yet heard from Urban and Schwarzenberg. I have registered my paper (Female Castration Complex).

With kind regards from house to house,

Yours,
Karl Abraham

Berggasse 19,
Vienna IX,
4.7.20

Dear Friend,

We have now known each other for about thirteen years and have always got on excellently. It will be the same this time, but for this purpose you must give in, and admit that what you are asking is no small thing. If some day you reach the age of sixty-four and have behind you ten months of a working year such as this has been, the claim to an undisturbed break will not seem to you to be an unwarranted act of stubbornness, and the possible effect on Berlin medical circles will seem a matter of indifference in comparison. So leave me out of it, because I shall speak in Berlin neither before nor after the congress. You have no need to alter your programme because of that. In any case my rest will be by no means complete. In August I have a difficult subject to write that requires complete concentration, and in September there is the congress, which again leads back to analysis. But more than that is impossible.

You say your arrangements are useless unless I co-operate. That is precisely the attitude that I want to oppose. Only try, and you will see that you will manage without me. Tomorrow or the next day you will have to make do without me in any case, so better begin today.

Your summons to Halle seems to me to be very gratifying. In Germany and England things are very active in general. Even with us interest in psycho-analysis is growing, probably as a result of foreign influence. The society is at present trying to obtain a psycho-analytical department in an extension of the general hospital. This is very much against my wishes, because if we got it, it would have to be in my name, I could devote no time to it, and there is no-one in the society to whom I could entrust its management.

You will all have great pleasure from Sachs if only his health stands up.

With cordial greetings to you and to your wife,

Sincerely yours,
Freud

Berlin-Grunewald,
16.7.20

Dear Professor,

Of course I must give way to your arguments. I would not have made the second proposal – that you should speak in Berlin before the Congress – had you given your reasons for declining the first time. You wrote to me at the time that the dates we had originally proposed were not convenient. Your first letter did not contain a definite refusal. I am not so very much at fault after all. We have in the meantime given up the whole project. It would have involved considerable expense in the form we planned and this could only have been met with your name to arouse interest in medical circles. But you will be speaking at The Hague?

Now I want to tell you about Halle. The paper was read on July 10th, and was very successful. I spoke before thirty doctors, most of them from the Medical Department. The psychiatrists stayed away for all kinds of reasons. Only one doctor from the municipal mental hospital turned up. My listeners were at first inclined to be sceptical and negative but, in the course of the paper, their supercilious smiles gave way to the utmost attention. The discussion yielded far more agreement than disagreement. One lecturer spoke very definitely in favour of psycho-analysis. A second followed. Others put factual questions, including some concerning the possibility of studying psycho-analysis. One of the senior physicians of the Clinic told me afterwards that he had up till now completely rejected psycho-analysis but, through my paper, he had come to see there was something in it. One young assistant definitely declared that he wanted to know something about psycho-analysis and that he would come to Berlin for this purpose. The only psychiatrist present said that the youngest generation of psychiatrists 'inclined strongly towards Freud'. I came away well satisfied. I may possibly be asked to speak in the autumn before the Medical Association of Halle which has about two hundred members. Such invitations are becoming more frequent. Today, for instance, I was asked whether I would speak this winter to the *Monistenbund*.[1] I did not refuse as I wanted to keep such a possibility open for Sachs.

With kindest regards to you and your family,

Yours,

Karl Abraham

Berggasse 19,
Vienna IX,
31.10.20

Dear Friend,

I never thought that the circular letters[2] would put an end to our private correspondence, only I am afraid that my writing will have to be restricted to Sunday. Nine analytic sessions daily have become a greater strain because of the shift to English in five of the sessions; I note with surprise how greatly the effort of listening and inwardly translating uses up one's free energy. Besides, my English is not by a long way as good as your wife's, and my earnings are still only two-thirds of what they were before the war. But one has to put up with it.

I got over the Nobel Prize passing me by for the second time excellently, and have also realised that any such official recognition would fit not at all into my style of life. On an occasion when I had to appear as an expert witness before a commission investigating neglect of military duties arising out of a charge against Wagner,[3] I once more had occasion to note the concealed animosity of the psychiatrists here. But of course they dared show it only after I had left. In my presence they were as friendly as sh..t, as one says in the language of the erogenous zones.

I have of course read your article in the *Rundschau*, it is clear and correct and to us particularly worth reading. The general public will miss phrases and flourishes, it is not likely to have an affective impact.

We are all proud of the upsurge in Berlin. Nothing similar

[1] See footnote 4, p. 49.
[2] Regular correspondence between Freud and the members of the Committee.
[3] Julius von Wagner-Jauregg, Professor of Psychiatry in Vienna and a Nobel prize-winner, was accused of having ill-treated soldiers by electric shock.

317

is to be expected here. Nunberg[1] will not get a visa, at any rate that is the rationalisation. But here he will probably get no patients. Conditions here are quite appalling, and nobody knows what will happen.

We are well and lonely.

With cordial greetings to you and your whole family,

Sincerely yours,

Freud

Berggasse 19,
Vienna IX,
28.11.20

Dear Friend,

In view of your agreement I have spoken to Reik and offered him the position of a literary director, with responsibility for reviews and the annual report. I did not conceal the criticisms that have been made of his work in the publishing house, and in reference to his psychology expressed the hope of a better performance by him in an independent position. He agreed to accept the post with effect from January 1st, 1921, and appreciated that personal considerations will not prevent his being removed if it turns out that he does not measure up to the job. His salary remains the same as before, that is to say very modest, but he has four analyses which will enable him to keep his head above water.

Now another point arises. He is also willing, even keen, to move to Berlin, where his task would be facilitated in all sorts of ways by association with the clinic; and the position of the clinic itself as the headquarters of the psycho-analytic movement would be only strengthened thereby. The question I now wish to ask you is whether in addition to Sachs, whose activities must not be impaired, you also have room for Reik for analysing doctors and giving lectures. If that is the case, he can move very quickly, the publishing house here will take over his flat, and we shall have extricated one more of our people from the Vienna quagmire. As Reik has a small family, he would have to be found a roof over his head in Berlin. Please let me have your views about this.

[1] Dr Herrmann Nunberg, Vienna psycho-analyst, now in New York.

I am as usual very busy, but the special feature now is that I have to speak and listen to a foreign language for from four to six hours a day, and it is to that that I attribute my complete incapacity to work. It is an exhausting business. You will receive *Beyond the Pleasure Principle*[1] in a few days; when my daughter returns I shall be able to devote myself to the 'Group Psychology' again.

Your book will be ready very soon, and you will have heard of other plans from the circular letters, which may be a nuisance, but are certainly very useful.

My cordial greetings to you and to your wife, and I hope the children enjoy 'life in the country' in winter too.

Yours,
Freud

*

Berlin-Grunewald,
6.12.20

Dear Professor,

Eitingon, Sachs and I are in full agreement regarding your enquiry on Reik's behalf—that for the time being the answer must be negative. We prepared for Sachs for months in advance and lined up for him all the doctors who wanted analysis. At the moment there are no cases or, at the most, one possible one; however, since the colleague in question is badly off, he is virtually non-existent as far as Reik's financial interests are concerned. Sachs' time is fully occupied. If new analysands turn up, we could keep them for Reik but that will take rather a long time. There is sufficient scope for one lecturer but at present there is not enough for two. We feel that all of you in Vienna have a mistaken idea about conditions in Berlin. You write about Reik that he is keeping his head above water in Vienna. He could not expect more here for it is no different for any of us. Expenditure on necessities completely runs through even a large income. We are very pleased that Sachs, for instance, has sufficient income to live comfortably. Reik, who would naturally for some time earn less than Sachs, has a wife and child

[1] Standard Ed., Vol. XVIII.

to support and would have great difficulties. You must consider that I, for instance, can only just earn enough for our needs. The only thing that Reik might find better here is that food is easier to get. I shall keep the whole matter in mind. The gratifying progress of our science in Berlin may offer a better opening at a later date. Incidentally, it is not clear to us how the person responsible for our literature could work at such a distance from the publisher. Correspondence is too difficult at present.

We have decided to include something about conditions in Berlin in our next Committee letter so that, for instance, Ferenczi and his colleagues are informed as well and are prevented from expecting too much.

I have very good news to report about my introductory course. The participants remain as keen as ever and there is already pressure for an advanced course.

You, dear Professor, will be interested to hear that your gift of one hundred guilders has found its use.[1] With the help of a patient, I shall get bicycles for both children and there will soon be double rejoicing.

With kind regards, as always,

Yours,
Abraham

Berggasse 19,
Vienna IX,
3.1.21

Dear Mrs Abraham,

Your children's letters were too delightful – I hope they did not cost them too much trouble or even tears, were not several times rewritten, etc. I should have answered them myself, but I was afraid of undermining their morale, because I should certainly have had to confess that the finest gifts are spoilt by having to say thank you for them. Also it would have embarrassed me to have had either to have gone on playing the part

---

[1] Because of the inflation in Austria and Germany, Freud had received Dutch currency for his Congress expenses. He gave the remainder to Abraham to buy a present for his children. See Freud's letter below.

of a munificent patron or to admit that I had made them happy by means of the resources of others. When the opportunity arises, please tell them the true state of affairs, to which the moral can be attached that it is possible, though rather late in life, to acquire a few Dutch guilders of one's own even by such work as the practice of psycho-analysis.

I conclude from your letter than your husband is now at last well again. We were very distressed about his illness. Here too we are haunted by more illness than is actually indispensable.

Wishing you all a Happy New Year, richer in fulfilment and entirely devoid of anything disagreeable,

Sincerely yours,
Freud

Berggasse 19,
Vienna IX,
4.2.21

Dear Friend,

My hearty congratulations on the appearance of your book,[1] which is generally appreciated by analysts as a collection of classical, model papers. Incidentally, Deuticke is willing to publish a second edition of *Dreams and Myths* if you care to get in touch with him.

With warmest greetings from

Yours,
Freud

C.C.!

Berlin-Grunewald,
9.2.21

Dear Professor,

My most sincere thanks for letting me know with such warm congratulations about the publication of my book. You know best how much of the book stems from ideas you first put forward. I may say that, as I wrote each separate paper over all these years, I wanted to make my readers aware of my gratitude and loyalty towards you. And because I thought that these

[1] Karl Abraham, *Klinische Beiträge zur Psychoanalyse*, London, 1921.

sentiments were clearly recognisable, I omitted dedicating the book as a whole to you. Rank will present you with a copy on my behalf as postal restrictions prevent my sending it from here. I know no better way to respond to the encouraging 'C.C.' on your card than by unchanging and loyal participation in our common work.

I shall get in touch with Deuticke about *Dreams and Myths* as soon as I have a more exact idea about the amount of revision that will be needed.

My wife was particularly pleased with the letter she received from you some time ago and sends her belated thanks. It is virtually impossible to separate the children from their bicycles. If you have ever made anyone happy, dear Professor, you have certainly succeeded here.

With kind regards from house to house,

Yours,
Abraham

*

Berggasse 19,
Vienna IX,
6.3.21

Dear Friend,

Ungrudging congratulations on your well-earned convalescence leave. I hope your 'hand luggage' (the two Glovers[1]) will not disturb you. Unfortunately I cannot think of coming to see you in the beautiful south. I am glad to be tolerably well, to be able to make money and write the 'Group Psychology'.

Recently I have quite frequently been giving your address to people who applied to me for treatment, including on one occasion, on a suggestion from America, a lady at Königsberg. In this respect your absence from Berlin is an embarrassment to me. Normally I count on your handing on to others the cases you cannot deal with yourself.

With best wishes for weather and well being,

Yours,
Freud

[1] Dr James and Dr Edward Glover, psycho-analysts in London.

Berlin-Grunewald,
2.5.21

Dear Professor,

Our good wishes were expressed in the Committee letter which has just gone off, and Eitingon will certainly repeat what we wanted to say when he presents you with the bust.[1] This does not prevent me, however, from sending my personal and special good wishes in this letter, naturally on behalf of my wife as well. I very much regret that I do not have Eitingon's freedom of movement; otherwise, nothing would have stopped me from visiting you on the occasion of your birthday and expressing my good wishes to you personally. I hope we shall spend some pleasant days together in the autumn.

I take this opportunity of thanking you, dear Professor, for the various patients you recently referred to me.

With the *Corragio Casimiro* so appropriate nowadays and with kindest regards,

Yours,
Karl Abraham

Berggasse 19,
Vienna IX,
8.5.21

Dear Friend,

Please be satisfied with this short letter of thanks and with Eitingon's report. I am short of sleep and am trying to get rid of a mountain of correspondence.

The many congratulations remind one of how old one is, and being given presents makes one infantile, and the two go very well together.

Your proposal for the committee meeting is approved by us Viennese.

With cordial greetings to you and your family,

Yours, .
Freud

[1] A bust of Freud by the sculptor Paul Königsberger.

Berlin-Grunewald,
21.7.21

Dear Professor,

I have to ask you today for some information I need for a quotation. I am busy writing a short paper on Rescue Phantasies.[1] It deals particularly with the phantasy in which the neurotic sees a carriage approaching along the road, with the emperor or some other father-substitute in it, and with the horses out of control. He throws himself at the horses reins and thus rescues the emperor. I think you have mentioned this particular phantasy somewhere. In the *Contributions to the Psychology of Love I*,[2] I can only find a general reference to the rescue of a high-ranking father substitute. Even Eitingon, with his almost unfailing knowledge of the literature, cannot help me and I therefore ask for your assistance. I have come across this phantasy in several analyses, but feel that I first heard about it from you. Many thanks in anticipation.

Secondly, could you let me know now approximately when and for how long we shall be meeting in September?[3] I must know this as soon as possible because of other arrangements. An approximate date would, of course, be sufficient.

I hope, dear Professor, things are going well with you and you will fully recuperate so that in September we shall find you as fit as you were last year.

With kind regards, also from my wife,

Yours,
Abraham

Bad Gastein,
24.7.21

Dear Friend,

You are right, the phantasy comes from me, even though it refers only to an imago, an important man, not to father or

[1] Karl Abraham, 'The Rescue and Murder of the Father in Neurotic Phantasy-Formations', *Clinical Papers and Essays on Psycho-Analysis*, London, 1955.

[2] Sigmund Freud, 'A Special Type of Choice of Object Made by Men (Contributions to the Psychology of Love I)', Standard Ed., Vol. XI.

[3] This refers to a meeting of the members of the Committee in the Harz mountains.

emperor. But where is it? It is difficult to trace it here, as I do not take my collected works with me on my travels. But I think you will find it in the *Everyday Life*, among the paramnesias, where I explain why I call the day-dreamer in *Le Nabab* Jocelyn, though his real name is Joyeuse. If that is not where it is, this hint will be sufficient to guide your or Eitingon's memory to the right place. (*The Interpretation of Dreams?*)

It will also interest you to hear that a few months ago a young woman student sent me a Hofmann booklet in which such a rescue is described; because of the verbal coincidence it must have been the cryptomnesic source of my Paris phantasy. You surely know those pearls of the high school libraries? I of course read and forgot many of these booklets in my time, because whenever one gave oneself airs and applied for a serious book one was always thrown back into one's childhood by one of these Hofmann booklets, which were innumerable.

Here I am enjoying rest and idleness, and I send you my cordial greetings.

Yours,
Freud

*

Berlin-Grunewald,
6.8.21

Dear Professor,

Just as I was about to write to you 'Group Psychology' arrived. I am looking forward to reading it for the second time during the next few days and, for the present, only want to thank you very much indeed.

At the same time I am sending you the short manuscript on Rescue Phantasies. Rank has already received a copy. I prefer to send you a copy before it goes to print, firstly, because I do not wish to introduce something as new when it may already have been said; and secondly, because I should like to know whether you agree with the content. Since the paper is only a short one, I hope you will not be angry with me for sending it to you during your holidays. If anything that I assumed to be new is already contained in one of your papers,

I would ask you to return the manuscript with a short comment. Otherwise, I should be grateful if you would briefly let me know that you agree—(in that case the manuscript can be destroyed).

Furthermore, I have to thank you for the reference you gave me. I am sure the section in the *Interpretation of Dreams* is the one I was looking for without success.

With kind regards, also from my wife,

Yours,
Karl Abraham

Bad Gastein,
8.8.21

Dear Friend,

I have no corrections or criticisms, I fully agree with your deeper interpretation of the rescue phantasy, and I wish only to draw your attention to an awkward feature of the Oedipus passage which has already caused me a great deal of trouble.

You write of a 'hollow way' as the place of meeting, and that is just as suitable to us as a symbol of the genitals as it is suitable as a spot for giving way. L. Frank, who has retold the story of the psycho-analytic parricide in the 'Ursache', also makes his hero engage in phantasies about a 'hollow way' which he cannot properly remember. But the Greek text known to me talks of a ὁδὸς σχίστη, which means, not 'hollow way' but 'cross-roads', at which one would suppose giving way would not be difficult. Would it not be as well to consult a scholar before you publish?

I cannot decide the date of our congress alone. I was thinking of the last week in September, so that I could be in Vienna on the 30th. The question of the date should soon be settled. A great deal depends on Jones's arrangements.

My cordial greetings to you and yours,

Yours,
Freud

*

Dear Friend,

I invite you in my wife's name to be our guest when you come here at the New Year for your lecture. We have arranged a room as a guest room, and it is at present occupied by Frau Lou Andreas. She praises it highly, we know it to be not ideal, but still it is as good as a hotel room–hotels are now terribly dear–and it is well heated.

With cordial greetings to you and to your wife and children,

Yours,
Freud

Berlin-Grunewald,
25.12.21

Dear Professor,

This card brings you my most sincere thanks for your delightful Christmas gift.[1] You must know how beautiful the *Introductory Lectures* look in this binding and I therefore do not need to say any more about it. If no *vis major* (strike ?!) intervenes, I hope to be with you on January 3rd. For your wife's information, I shall be having dinner on the train. There is no need whatsoever for any preparations for my arrival and I would expressly ask that no one should bother to meet me at the station. A taxi will take me to Berggasse in a few minutes.

Oliver, who has just left us, has told me everything a foreigner needs to know. I am very much looking forward to seeing all of you in Vienna once again after such a long interval and hope to find you well. With best regards to you and all your family,

Yours,
Karl Abraham

[1] A leather-bound pocket edition of the lectures, published by the *Internationaler Psychoanalytischer Verlag.*

Berlin-Grunewald,
13.3.22

Dear Professor,

It is a long time since I was in Vienna and you have not had any direct news since then. I only wrote to your wife after my return home to thank you all for the pleasant days in Vienna. The circular letter told you everything that has happened since. In Vienna I once again had the opportunity of seeing how your correspondence keeps you busy far into the night and I feel even more reluctant than before to add to your burden. At other times, however, my wish to report to you gains the upper hand and I am today giving into this for a change.

My load of work is frequently so overwhelming that it prevents me from going as thoroughly into certain problems in my spare time as I should like–particularly manic-depressive states. My two analyses in this field throw quite a lot of light on this in their daily sessions, and some of the questions we discussed in the autumn are beginning to take a more definite shape. The parallels to kleptomania interest me very much, since this also goes back to the oral phase and represents the biting off of penis or breast. The regression of the melancholic has the same aim, though in a different form.

Incorporation of the love-object is very striking in my cases. I can produce very nice material for this concept of yours, demonstrating the process in all its detail. In this connection I have a small request–for a reprint of 'Mourning and Melancholia' which would be extremely useful to me in my work. Many thanks in anticipation.

One brief comment on this paper. You, dear Professor, state that you find nothing in the course of normal mourning which would correspond to the swing-over from melancholia to mania. I think, however, I could describe such a process, without knowing whether this reaction is invariably found. My impression is that a fair number of people show an increase in libido some time after a period of mourning. It shows itself in heightened sexual need and appears to lead relatively often to conception shortly after a death. I should like to know what you think about this and whether you can confirm this observation. The increase of libido some time after 'object-loss' would seem to be a valid addition to the parallel between mourning and melancholia.

I can fully confirm what you told me about *pseudologia phantastica*. My patient's quite fantastic lies do in fact correspond to a psychic reality.

I should like to mention briefly that I shall in the near future speak in our Society on a special form of parapraxia. I shall soon be dictating this short paper[1] and shall send it off to Rank. It is about those slips which, like obsessional actions, do not permit the repressed impulse to break through but which overcompensate it.

Another small comment. At a recent meeting, one of our members drew our attention to an interesting misprint in your *Kleine Schriften IV*, 'History of the Psycho-Analytic Movement', in the footnote on p. 74 – 'discredit' instead of 'discrete'. This misprint does not occur in the original (*Jahrbuch der Psychoanalyse*). The interest lies in the fact that it was overlooked in proof-reading and not that it was a type-setting error. The intention of discrediting Jung comes to the fore in a most amusing way.

With many kind regards to you all, also from my wife,

Yours,
Karl Abraham

*

*Berggasse 19,
Vienna IX,
30.3.22*

Dear Friend,

After more than a fortnight I decided to re-read your private letter, and came across your request for a reprint, which for some reason made no impact on me when I first read it.

I plunge with pleasure into the abundance of your scientific insights and intentions, only I wonder why you do not take into account my last suggestion about the nature of mania

[1] Karl Abraham, 'Mistakes with an Overcompensating Tendency', *Clinical Papers and Essays on Psycho-Analysis*, London, 1955.

after melancholia (in the 'Group Psychology'). Might that be the motivation for my forgetting about the 'Mourning and Melancholia'? No absurdity is impossible for psycho-analysis. I should like to discuss all these things, particularly with you, but it is impossible to write about them. In the evening I am lazy, and above all there is the inescapable 'business' correspondence, declining invitations to give lectures, go on journeys, write articles, and so on and so forth, that stands in the way of a decent exchange of ideas with one's friends. I am now doubly glad that we instituted the circular letters. With eight and sometimes nine hours work daily I do not manage to achieve the concentration required for scientific work. At Gastein, between July 1st and August 1st, I hope to be able to commit to paper some little things that I told you about in the Harz mountains.

The rest of the summer, from August 1st until the middle of September, is still as blank as the map of Central Africa was in my school days. The Austrian summer is going to be a hard problem. Meanwhile even the spring is appalling.

I find character analysis with pupils more difficult in many respects than analysis with professional neurotics, but admittedly I have not worked out the new technique.

My cordial greetings to your wife and your two rapidly growing children. I did not know your wife had acquired such an obstinate sciatica.

And give in to the impulse to write privately again to

Sincerely yours,
Freud

*

Berlin-Grunewald,
2.5.22

Dear Professor,

Your forthcoming birthday gives me a welcome excuse to write to you once again outside the framework of our circular letters. As far as I am aware, I have no need to compensate for bad wishes and a few words will therefore suffice to assure you once more of the sincerity of my affection for you.

330

As on several former occasions, I am once again enclosing a small contribution[1] for the *Zeitschrift* as a birthday present, in the hope that it will interest you and meet with your approval.

Your letter of March 30th is still waiting for a reply, but I have already thanked you for your reprint of 'Mourning and Melancholia'. I fully understand your forgetting it. Your failure in sending the paper I asked for was meant to indicate that I should first of all study the other source (Group Psychology). I am, however, quite familiar with its contents concerning the subject of mania and melancholia but, in spite of going through it once again, I cannot see where I went wrong. I can find no mention anywhere of a parallel reaction after mourning in normal cases which can be compared to the onset of mania (after melancholia). I only know from your remark in 'Mourning and Melancholia' that you were aware of something lacking and I referred to this in my observation. The increase of libido after mourning would be fully analogous to the 'feast' of the manic, but I have not found this parallel from normal life in that section of 'Group Psychology' where this 'feast' is discussed. Or have I been so struck by blindness that I am unable to see the actual reference?

My family joins me in sending kindest regards to you and all your family,   Yours,

Karl Abraham

Berggasse 19,
Vienna IX,
28.5.22

Dear Friend,

With Eitingon's help I discovered to my amusement that I completely misunderstood you through no fault of yours. You were looking for a normal example of the transition from melancholia to mania, and I was thinking of the explanation of the mechanism.

With many apologies,   Cordially yours,

Freud

[1] Probably Karl Abraham, 'An Octogenarian's Mistake', *Clinical Papers and Essays on Psycho-Analysis*, London, 1955.

Dear Professor,

We have been here for a fortnight and are thoroughly enjoying our stay in the mountains, in spite of very uncertain weather. My old passion for mountaineering has gripped me again and my son is proving a good companion on these excursions. I have not heard from you for a long time but hope you and your family are well. I am in frequent communication with Jones and Eitingon, and yesterday revised the programme for the Congress.[1] Could you not let me know what the 'undisclosed' subject of your paper is going to be. I am starting to prepare my own paper today.

With kind regards and good wishes for your holiday to you all from all of us,

Yours,
Karl Abraham

Berggasse 19,
Vienna IX,
26.12.22

Dear Friend,

I have received the drawing[2] that is supposed to be your portrait. It is abominable.

I know what an admirable person you are, which makes it the more shattering that such a cruel penalty should have to be exacted for such a trivial blot on your character as your tolerance or sympathy for modern 'art'. I hear from Lampl that the artist said that that was how he saw you. People like that should be the last to have access to analytic circles, because they are all too unwanted illustrations of Adler's theory that it is just individuals with severe innate defects of vision who become artists and draughtsmen.

Let me forget this would-be portrait in sending you and yours the very best wishes for 1923.

Cordially yours,
Freud

[1] The seventh International Psycho-Analytical Congress in Berlin.
[2] A charcoal drawing of Abraham by the deaf-mute artist Tihaniy.

Berlin-Grunewald,
7.1.23

Dear Professor,

I have to thank you, dear Professor, for your amusing lines about my portrait, though I cannot completely agree with you. The painter is certainly very gifted. I had seen a number of brilliant and lifelike drawings in his studio and decided to ask him to sketch me. I did not know that these drawings dated from an earlier period and that he had in the meantime switched over to the most modern school. I do not in the least subscribe to this abstract school. However, since the picture was finished, I did not wish to withhold it from our circle. If one looks at it often over a period of time, more and more characteristics become apparent. In order to make good the injury I have done you, I intend to give myself over to another artist some time soon. At the end of February I am to read a paper[1] in Hamburg and intend to call on an artist of whom you approve.

In the next few days I shall write to Rank more fully about the *Kindersammlung*.[2] The day's work leaves little time for other matters. At present I am writing a short paper containing some contributions on the vicissitudes of the Oedipus complex.[3] If possible I shall enclose it in my letter to Rank. In that case, dear Professor, I should like to have your opinion and to know whether you agree with the conclusions. Reading this paper will not take up more than ten minutes of your time and no special letter is necessary. A comment in the circular letter will be sufficient. The subject I spoke on at the Congress is growing into a longer paper and I intend to write it up in the next few months. Perhaps it can appear as a supplementary number.

I was pleased to hear yesterday from Storfer that suitable accommodation has been found for the Verlag; a good beginning at least in such difficult conditions. Our Clinic received from

[1] 'Die Wiederkehr primitiver religiöser Vorstellungen in Phantasieleben des Kindes.'
[2] Probably the part of the *Internationale Zeitschrift* called 'Aus dem infantilen Leben'.
[3] Paper read to the Berlin Society.

Miss van der Linden, who is here with Ophuijsen, a present of one hundred guilders, at the moment worth 330,000 marks, which is useful even in present times. We shall have to expand somehow in the course of the year. The consulting rooms are no longer adequate and we do not have big enough lecture rooms for our courses.

Developments here are satisfactory. Yesterday a young doctor from Leipzig came to see me. He has taken a house appointment in Berlin in order to undergo a training analysis. Such events are becoming increasingly frequent.

With kind regards from house to house,

Yours,
Abraham

Berggasse 19,
Vienna IX,
4.3.23

Dear Friend,

I return the newspaper cuttings[1] with thanks. Some of them I have had from other sources. My chief feeling is of annoyance at not being able to be there, and above all at the prospect of descending to the Styx without having sailed on the Nile.

It now seems certain that they will soon find the mummy of the king and perhaps also that of his consort, a daughter of our analytic Pharaoh. According to a rumour spread by the Swiss here, Jung's Frau X has announced she knows she was this queen. Personally I hope Tutankhamen had better taste. What a crazy hussy.

In Vienna things are pretty quiet, as Berlin has taken the wind out of our sails. Also the times are too wretched. A charming letter from Romain Rolland[2] recently arrived here like a breath of fresh air; he mentions incidentally that he was interested in analysis twenty years ago.

[1] About the discovery of the tomb of Tutankhamen.

[2] Romain Rolland, French author, 1866–1944. (Freud's reply appears in *Letters of Sigmund Freud, 1873–1939*, Hogarth Press, London, and Basic Books, New York, 1961 (Letter 200).

I hope that things are well with you and your wife and children and send my cordial greetings to you as well as the Ophuijsens.

Cordially yours,
Freud

*

Berlin-Grunewald,
1.4.23

Dear Professor,

The Berlin circular letter has just been sent off but, since it is no substitute for personal contact with you, I am using the free time of the Easter holidays to send you direct news once again. I have received the newspaper cuttings about Egypt and your letter. I will not have it that a trip to Egypt is quite out of the question for you. It would naturally be expensive and time-consuming but, if you cut your summer holiday by a month, you could surely be absent for a few months at the beginning of next year and enjoy Egypt. I do not consider it right that you should simply resign yourself. I had an uncle who, at the age of seventy-five, celebrated his golden wedding by travelling with his wife to Egypt and who even took camel rides in the desert. And you say you cannot take a boat up the Nile!

A further question about your plans for the summer. The invitation to Oxford[1] affects my arrangements. After this Congress (in August) I should like to go to some place not too far from where you are based so that we could meet. I should be grateful if you could let me know some time.

In the circular letter I mentioned my recent lecture on the history of the development of object-love.[2] It has brought me an unusual amount of appreciation from our circle and I myself feel it is an important addition to the theory of sexuality and, at the same time, my best work to date. I shall try and write

[1] International Congress of Psychology, Oxford, July 1923.

[2] Karl Abraham, 'A Short Study of the Development of the Libido, viewed in the Light of Mental Disorders. Part II. Origins and Growth of Object-Love', *Selected Papers on Psycho-Analysis*, London, 1927.

it up as a paper soon. At the same time I feel that this whole idea coincides with your own views and will meet with your approval. Apart from the main finding (explanation of the developmental process from narcissism towards object-love), the paper makes a not unimportant contribution to the understanding of paranoia and other forms of neurosis such as pseudologia, etc., which have so far received little attention. If travelling were not so very difficult, I would come to Vienna in the near future in order to hear your views.

With kind regards from both of us to you, dear Professor, and your family,

Yours,
Karl Abraham

*

Berggasse 19,
Vienna IX,
8.4.23

Dear Friend,

Every letter of yours bears the mark of the lively and successful Berlin constellation and of your own optimism. May it be long preserved.

It is extraordinary how much you still overrate me, both materially and physically. Though I am still eight years short of your uncle's age at the time of his camel ride in the desert, I cannot imitate, but only envy him. I am neither rich nor well enough. You must gradually get used to the idea of my mortality and frailty.

I am very glad to note that my paladins, you, Ferenczi, and Rank, always tackle fundamentals in your writings instead of decorative incidentals of any kind. That is the case now with your object love. I am very much looking forward to reading it, but cannot tell how far you have got with it.

With most cordial greetings to you and your wife and children,

Yours,
Freud

Berlin-Grunewald,
3.5.23

Dear Professor,

I am combining my reply to your letter with my most sincere wishes for your birthday. But please do not be angry if I straightaway draw your attention to a contradiction in your letter. You express the hope that I will retain my optimism and you advise me in the very next sentence to get accustomed to the idea that your vitality is limited. How am I to reconcile these two things? Well, since it is impossible I shall choose the former, and am firmly determined to take my stand on the omnipotence of wishes and to express my conviction that the new year will give you all possible energy and health compatible with your years. If you are a psycho-analyst (as Stekel would say), you will have to permit me to point out the over-determination of conviction. I am just reading your book,[1] for which many thanks; it shows evidence of such unchanged vitality that can only delight all of us who hold you in affection. The second reason stems from myself since, as in many previous years, my own birthday is the day when I write to you to congratulate you on yours. Thus, I fill this letter with the maximum amount of confidence and only ask you to introject it for suitable use!

We too are thinking of the southern Tyrol for August and are particularly interested in the Groedner valley (St Ulrich or Wolkenstein). I wonder what our meeting at the end of August will be like.

Good news from here. Our courses have started and are very well attended. Our young members and the guests of our circle are extremely keen; among them, Lampl[2] is shaping well. My analysand from Vienna, Dr X., presents no easy task, but I expect good results. The same is true of Radó.[3]

It is impossible for me to write today about recent theoretical results. I am working on the manic depressives (my Congress paper) and might wish to publish this, possibly together with

[1] Sigmund Freud, *The Ego and the Id*, Standard Ed., Vol. XIX.
[2] Dr Hans Lampl, psycho-analyst in Berlin, Vienna and Amsterdam.
[3] Dr Sandor Radó, psycho-analyst in Budapest, Berlin, later New York.

the history of the development of object-love, as an extra number of the *Zeitschrift*. I should like to put the basic ideas about object-love before our small circle in August. In Oxford I shall probably speak about something on the Psychology of the Early Infancy.[1]

To conclude for today, dear Professor—my thanks for all your kind and appreciative words in your last letter.

E tanti buoni auguri—for a new year and may it bring you, your family and all of us—your growing analytic family—many good things, not to forget a reviving drink for you from the Fontana di Trevi![2]

Yours,
Karl Abraham

Berggasse 19,
Vienna IX,
10.5.23

Dear Friend,

I must shamefacedly ask you to accept this wretched card in reply to your long, warm letter. Because of the visits and celebrations of the last week I am behind with all my obligations. I can again chew, work and smoke, and I shall try your optimistic slogan: *many happy returns of the day and none of the new growth.*[3]

Cordially yours,
Freud

Berlin-Grunewald,
7.10.23

Dear Professor,

During the last few weeks I have been in continuous and lively contact with you in my thoughts, which were certainly charged with affect though not expressed in a letter. I knew

[1] Karl Abraham, 'Psycho-Analytical Views on Some Characteristics of Early Infantile Thinking', *Clinical Papers and Essays on Psycho-Analysis*, London, 1955.

[2] Fountain in Rome.

[3] These words in English in the original.

you would not interpret my reserve in any other way than it was intended. After having heard, however, about your own attitude to your illness and operation, I cannot stand it any longer and am therefore writing to you. But I promise beforehand that this letter will not say anything about your health and will not even contain any good wishes except those which you read between the lines.

I think there is only one thing I can do for the time being to give you pleasure and that is to let you have good reports about our position in Berlin. And, always providing that political conditions do not paralyse our work, I hope to be able to carry out my intentions. Some days ago I reported in the circular letter on our first two meetings and there has been more good news since then. We are just about to start our lending library which will give our younger members access to psycho-analytic literature. Apart from the courses already announced, a further one will be arranged – by Mrs Klein[1] – for kindergarten teachers on Infantile Sexuality.

I have something pleasant to report in the scientific field. In my work on Melancholia,[2] of which Rank has the manuscript, I have assumed the presence of an early depression in infancy as a prototype for later melancholia. In the last few months Mrs Klein has skilfully conducted the psycho-analysis of a three-year-old with good therapeutic results. This child presented a true picture of the basic depression that I postulated in close combination with oral erotism. The case offers amazing insight into the infantile instinctual life.

I am pleased to see that my assumptions about the two stages in the anal-sadistic phase are confirmed by new material. I had a remarkable experience with one of my melancholics who is still in treatment with me. On my return from holiday, I found him at the beginning of a new depression following a disappointment connected with his fiancée. The depression had not set in with the same intensity as on previous occasions, but the rejection of the love-object was visible in its characteristic

[1] Mrs Melanie Klein, psycho-analyst, a pioneer in the field of child-analysis.

[2] Karl Abraham, 'A Short Study of the Development of the Libido, viewed in the Light of Mental Disorders', *Selected Papers on Psycho-Analysis*, London, 1927.

form. Quick intervention resulted in the melancholia changing within a fortnight, and more clearly on each subsequent day, into an obsessional neurosis with the main obsessional idea of strangling the mother (fiancée). In contrast to previous times, no cannibalistic-oral sadism, but manual sadism. The patient has already resumed work and my impression is that it has been possible to divert a melancholia *in statu nascendi* into a relatively more favourable form of illness.

May I go on talking about my work? What I said in Lavarone[1] about the stages of object-love, and particularly about partial incorporation, is being very nicely confirmed at present. I had assumed that in paranoid and related psychoses regression to this phase could be demonstrated. The analysis of a psychosis which was presented at our first meeting supplied excellent confirmatory material. The patient had, among other delusional ideas, the idea that a monkey was inside her. This monkey could be shown with absolute clarity to be her father's penis.

This is all for today. But I would just like to add a word about the general impression made by our first two meetings. Keenness among our slowly growing circle continually increases and I feel I am keeping our members together as never before. Registration of papers for the Congress are already coming in to the extent that one will have to try and curb them.

Now only one more remark, and that is that I naturally do not expect any reply. I have my own sources from which I get the news I want. Perhaps I shall come myself in November or December to see that things are going well. I conclude in haste in order not to break the promise I gave at the beginning of this letter, and am, with kind regards to you and your family,

Yours, as ever,
Karl Abraham

[1] A village in the South Tyrol where Abraham visited Freud in August 1923.

Dear Professor,

During the last few days, Rank, Lampl and Deutsch[1] have virtually competed with each other in keeping me informed about your state of health. Lampl came back today and gave me a full report. This is indeed a day of joy and now that I know there is every cause for optimism, I want to congratulate you and your family with all my heart. I do not tend towards pessimism as you know, and I was therefore able during these anxious days to hold on to the impression of undiminished vitality which I had so recently observed in you. And the confidence I felt did not deceive me. But I breathe more freely again now that I know my hope has become a reality. From the reports it appears that you are not suffering too much from the direct consequences of the operation. All of us who are devoted to you may permit ourselves to enjoy the great gift which fate has granted us. I have been asked by my wife, my daughter and my son to convey all their good wishes to you.

It is customary to send convalescents of all ages pictures to look at and pleasant things to read. That is why I am sending under separate cover a number of new Egyptian photographs which you may already be fit enough to enjoy, or at any rate will be able to enjoy soon, and I should also like to tell you about some pleasant events.

Last night – and I was unable to report about this in my circular letter – Sachs began his course on psycho-analytic technique; the rest of us do not start for another fortnight. He had an audience of about forty, a very satisfactory number for a course of this kind. My own course of introductory lectures which had eighty to ninety participants last autumn, will no longer be held in the limited accommodation of the Clinic, but across the road in the *Zentralinstitut für Erziehung und Unterricht.*

You will be pleased to hear that Dr Deutsch[2] has now got far enough to be able to do a lot of theoretical work and that she is working on her investigation into the psychology of

[1] Dr Felix Deutsch, physician and psycho-analyst in Vienna, later in Cambridge, Mass., and Freud's personal physician for some time.

[2] Dr Helene Deutsch, psycho-analyst in Vienna, now in Cambridge, Mass.

women.[1] She has also completed a short article which will probably go off to the *Zeitschrift* soon.

We shall have our meeting on Saturday. Sachs and Radó will give a review of 'The Ego and the Id'. There is no better proof of the keenness in our Society than the fact that members from outside Berlin – Foerster from Hamburg, Dr Happel[2] from Frankfurt and possibly Dr Benedek[3] from Leipzig – will come to Berlin especially for the occasion.

I shall continue to get news from Deutsch about your health, dear Professor, and shall write again myself as soon as there is anything to tell you.

In the confident hope of further good news,

Yours,
Karl Abraham

Berggasse 19,
Vienna IX,
19.10.23

Dear Incurable Optimist,

Today the tampon was renewed, I got up, and put what is left of me into my clothes. Thank you for all the news, letters, greetings, and newspaper cuttings. If I can sleep without an injection I shall soon go home.

Cordially yours,
Freud

*

Berlin-Grunewald,
26.11.23

Dear Professor,

It was very painful for me to hear that you had to undergo a second operation and have therefore still some way to go to final recovery. The last reports sound reassuring and I there-

---

[1] *Zeitschrift*, 'Psychologie des Weibes in den Funktionen der Fortpflanzung', *Internationale*, Vol. XI, 1925.

[2] Dr Klara Happel, psycho-analyst practising in Frankfurt, Hamburg and later in Detroit, where she died.

[3] Dr Therese Benedek, psycho-analyst in Leipzig and Berlin, now practising and carrying out research in Chicago.

fore hope that this episode will soon be over and well behind you.

I must now thank you most sincerely for giving time and trouble to going through my paper[1] in spite of your poor health. I had wanted to ask your opinion for a long time, but did not wish to burden you with such matters. You have immediately pounced on the weak point–the chapter on Mania. I have revised it in the meantime and I think that the whole work has gained by this. During this revision I came to understand the reasons for the initial failure. I am glad, however, that you had no criticism of large sections of my manuscript and I was indeed touched that you tried to make your criticism of some parts more acceptable by your appreciative remarks at the end. The day before yesterday I sent Rank a short addendum to the problem of mania which I had just met with. It strikingly confirms your concept of the 'feast' content of mania and also the ceremony of the liberation of the ego by an act of cannibalism. My patient told me at the end of a short hypomanic episode of barely three days that during that time he had felt the wish to gorge himself silly on meat; a kind of meat intoxication.

A short paper on An Infantile Sexual Theory[2] will go off to Rank soon. A paper on a Pathological Impostor[3] is to follow. There are always a few small matters in hand which one has to write up.

Dr Benedek of Leipzig was elected a member after her paper on the Development of the Organisation of Society, which was very good indeed.

With many kind regards and all good wishes,

Yours,
Abraham

---

[1] See footnote 2, p. 345.

[2] Karl Abraham, 'An Infantile Theory of the Origin of the Female Sex', *Selected Papers on Psycho-Analysis*, London, 1927.

[3] Karl Abraham, 'The History of an Impostor in the Light of Psycho-Analytical Knowledge', *Clinical Papers and Essays on Psycho-Analysis*, London, 1955.

Berggasse 19,
Vienna IX,
4.1.24

Dear Friend,

I have left so many of your friendly letters unanswered that today I am delighted to have to write you about a factual matter, though there is nothing pleasing about the fact itself. I have to report that nothing whatever can now be based on the psycho-analytical fund.

Because of the numerous Christmas visitors from Berlin, I have heard and talked a great deal about you recently. I was delighted to hear only good things about you, so at any rate your optimism is not unfounded. I declined all purely personal Christmas visitors on the ground that you yourself suggest; only my son Oliver was with us here with his young wife. I did not wish further to postpone making the acquaintance of my new daughter.

I am by no means out of trouble or released from treatment, but I resumed my analytic work on the 2nd and hope to be able to manage.

With cordial greetings and New Year wishes to you and your family,

Yours,
Freud

Berggasse 19,
Vienna IX,
15.2.24

Dear Friends,[1]

I have heard from various sources, not without surprise, that the recent publications of Ferenczi and Rank, I mean their joint work[2] and that on the birth trauma,[3] have caused some unpleasant agitation in Berlin. On top of this I have been called

[1] This circular letter and that beginning on p. 349 are included in this correspondence because of their importance for the understanding of what follows.

[2] S. Ferenczi and O. Rank, 'Entwicklungsziele der Psychoanalyse'.

[3] O. Rank, 'Das Trauma der Geburt'.

upon by one of our immediate circle to make a statement to you on the pending situation in which he sees a germ of possible dissension. Thus I am complying with his wishes, but not out of any desire to impose my views, my purpose being rather to exercise as much restraint as possible and to allow each of you freely to follow his own path.

When Sachs was last here, we exchanged some comments on the birth trauma book, and perhaps the impression that I regard its publication as an oppositional move or am in complete disagreement with its contents is based on that. I think, however, that the circumstance that I accepted its dedication to myself should have made this view impossible.

The fact of the matter is this: our harmony, the regard for me that you have so often demonstrated, should not hamper any of you in the free exercise of his productivity. I do not want you to be guided in your writings more by their pleasingness to me than their conformity with observation and your ideas. Among half a dozen men of different characters complete agreement on all matters of scientific detail and all questions that break new ground is neither possible nor even desirable. The only condition on which our fertile co-operation depends is that none of us should leave the common ground of psycho-analytic assumptions, and of this we ought to be certain in the case of every individual member of the committee. On top of this there is a circumstance that is not unknown to you and that makes me particularly unsuitable for the role of tyrannical and ever-alert censor. I do not find it easy to feel my way into unfamiliar trains of thought, and generally have to wait until I have found a point of contact with them by way of my own complicated paths. So if every time you had a new idea you insisted on waiting for my approval, it would run the risk of growing very old first.

My attitude to the two books concerned, then, is the following. I value the joint book as a corrective of my view of the role of repetition or acting out in analysis. I used to be apprehensive of it, and regarded these incidents, or experiences as you now call them, as undesirable failures. Rank and Ferenczi now draw attention to the inevitability of these experiences and the possibility of taking useful advantage of them. Otherwise the book

345

can be regarded as a refreshing intervention that may possibly precipitate changes in our present analytic habits. In my opinion it has the fault of not being complete, that is, it does not work out the changes of technique that the two authors have at heart, but only hints at them. Certain dangers are associated with this departure from our 'classical technique', as Ferenczi called it in Vienna, but that does not mean they cannot be avoided. So far as questions of technique are concerned, my view is that the two authors are entirely justified in enquiring whether for practical purposes different lines should not be followed. We shall see what the outcome is. At all events, we should guard against condemning any such undertaking as *a priori* heretical. Meanwhile certain doubts need not be suppressed. Ferenczi's active therapy is a dangerous temptation to ambitious beginners, and they can hardly be prevented from making such experiments. I shall make no secret of another impression or prejudice of mine. During my illness I found out that a beard that has been shaved off takes six weeks to grow again. Three months have now passed since my last operation, and I am still suffering as a result of the changes in the scar tissue. So I find it rather hard to believe that it is possible in a slightly longer time, four or five months, to penetrate into the deep layers of the unconscious and bring about lasting changes in mental life. But I shall of course bow in the face of experience. Personally I shall certainly continue with 'classical' analysis, because in the first place I hardly take patients now but only pupils, and it is important that the latter should learn as much as possible about the inner processes–training analyses cannot be conducted exactly like therapeutic analyses–and in the second place I am of the opinion that we still have a great many new things to discover and cannot yet base ourselves only on our assumptions, as is necessary in the case of shortened analysis.

Now to the second and incomparably more interesting book, that of Rank on the birth trauma. I do not hesitate to say that I think it a very important book, that it has given me a great deal to think about, and that I have not yet formed my final opinion about it. What I see plainly is this. We have long known and recognised the importance of womb phantasies, but with the position that Rank gives them they assume a far greater role and at once show us the biological background of the Oedipus complex. To recapitulate in my own language. The birth trauma must be associated with an instinct that desires to re-establish the former state of affairs. This might be called the instinct to seek happiness, bearing in mind that the concept of happiness is generally given an erotic significance. Now Rank goes beyond the neurotic into the general human field and shows that men change the external world in the service of this instinct, while the neurotic spares himself this labour by taking the short cut of returning in phantasy to the womb. If one superimposes upon Rank's view Ferenczi's idea that the male is represented by his genitals, one can for the first time get a derivation of the normal sexual instinct that fits in with our conception of the world.

Now comes the point at which my difficulties begin. The return in phantasy to the womb is opposed by obstacles that produce anxiety, namely by the incest barrier, the origin of which then remains unexplained. Its representative is obviously the father, reality, the authority that forbids incest. Why did the latter set up this incest barrier? My explanation was historical, social, phylogenetic. I deduced the incest barrier from the primordial history of the human family and thus saw in the actual father the real obstacle that re-creates the incest barrier in each new individual. Here Rank departs from me. He refuses to enter the phylogenetic field and makes horror of incest a direct repetition of birth anxiety, so that neurotic regression is inherently checked by the nature of the birth process. This birth anxiety is transferred to the father, but he is only a pretext for it. The attitude to the womb or the genitals is assumed to be *a priori* ambivalent. That is where the contradiction lies. I find it very difficult to make up my mind here, nor do I see how the question can be settled by experience, because in analysis one would always hit upon the father as the representative of the ban. But that is of course no argument. For the time being I must leave the question open. I can also adduce as a counter-argument that it is not in the nature of an instinct to be associatively inhibited, as here the instinct to return to the maternal body would be by association with the shock of birth. Actually any instinct in the form of an impulsion to re-establish an earlier state of affairs presupposes a trauma as the cause of the change,

347

and so there could be none but ambivalent instincts, that is, instincts accompanied by anxiety. There is of course a great deal more that could be said about this in detail, and I hope that the idea conjured up by Rank will be the subject of numerous and fruitful discussions. But we are faced here, not with an upheaval, a revolution, a contradiction of our established knowledge, but with an interesting contribution, the value of which should be recognised by us and by the outside world in general.

When I add that it is not clear to me how prematurely informing a patient that his transference to the physician represents attachment to the mother can lead to a shortening of his analysis, I have given you a true picture of my attitude to the two books in question. Thus I value them highly, in part accept them, have my doubts and hesitations about a good deal of their content, look forward to clarification in the matter from more reflection and experience, and should like to recommend all analysts not to form an opinion about the questions raised too quickly, least of all a negative one.

Forgive my discursiveness, which may perhaps deter you from rousing me to express an opinion on matters which you are just as well able to decide for yourselves.

Freud

Berlin-Grunewald,
21.2.24

Dear Professor,

You hardly need to be told that your letter made a deep impression on me. It was, as everything else you write, a document which leaves its mark. I too owe you a debt of gratitude for it. What you say and the way in which you say it has made me review once again my attitude to the three books by Ferenczi and Rank.

The criticisms which Sachs raises in his letter coincide with yours on the important points, dear Professor. Now Jones's letter has arrived and contains similar comments. I agree with all these objections and also with those that go beyond your own criticism. But I am troubled about the importance of specific implications contained in these new books and my concern has increased in weeks of constant self-examination. Your letter and the discussion I had yesterday with Sachs have reassured me somewhat on certain points. To start with, there is no question of hunting heretics. Results of whatever kind obtained in a legitimate analytic manner would never give me cause for such grave doubts. This is something different. I see signs of an ominous development concerning vital issues of psycho-analysis. They force me, to my deepest sorrow, and not for the first time in the twenty years of my psycho-analytic life, to sound a warning. When I add that these facts have robbed me of a good deal of the optimism with which I observe the progress of our work, you will be able to gauge the depth of my disquiet.

I have one request to make, dear Professor, which you must not refuse. Please call a meeting of the Committee just before the Congress and give me the opportunity to speak my mind freely. The time allowed for the necessary exchange of opinions should however not be too short. Your agreement to this proposal would reassure me greatly.

Yours, as ever,
Abraham

Berggasse 19,
Vienna IX,
25.2.24

Dear Friends,[1]

I am delighted that my circular letter reassured you on some points. But obviously it did not reassure you on all of them. I am ready to do anything to bring about further clarification. Perhaps you will come earlier to Vienna, so that we can travel to Salzburg together and so use the travelling time to continue the exchange of ideas. Jones has asked for a day of discussion at Salzburg to avoid having to come to Vienna. This must be taken into account. The day for further discussion can only be Easter Sunday.

Rank has been confined to bed, I have not seen him for a fortnight, and have not been able to talk to him.

[1] See footnote 1, p. 344.

As my letter showed, I am far from having come to a definite opinion, and am myself not free of an inclination to be critical. But I should like to be told what the danger is that I do not see. The matter may be further clarified in the interval until we meet.

I am very sorry to think that your unity would vanish immediately on my disappearance, but in any case I am selfish enough to wish to prevent it as long as I am still here.

With cordial greetings,

Yours,
Freud

*

Berlin-Grunewald,
26.2.24

Dear Professor,

I can scarcely tell you how much gratification your second letter gave me. Since I see that you are prepared to listen to criticisms even though they go beyond your own and concern persons who are particularly close to you, I begin once again to hope for a solution of the difficulties. Your words regarding the preservation of the Committee fully coincide with my own ideas and wishes and I therefore look forward to further developments with somewhat greater confidence. You, dear Professor, ask me to tell you what dangers I alluded to. If I tell you, you may well shake your head and refuse to listen further. But it is no longer possible to keep them back and I shall therefore state briefly what I intend to put before our meeting, giving full and detailed reasons for my opinion.

After very careful study, I cannot help but see in the *Entwicklungszielen* as well as in the 'Trauma der Geburt' manifestations of a regression in the scientific field, the symptoms of which agree in every small detail with those of Jung's secession from psycho-analysis.

This was not easy to say. I am glad to be able to add that I am not blind to the differences in personality: Ferenczi and Rank with all their pleasant qualities on the one side; Jung's deceitfulness and brutality on the other—I have by no means overlooked these. This must not prevent me, however, from stating that their new publications are a repetition of the Jung case, which I was initially loath to believe myself. This is one great danger I can see. Two of our best members threaten to stray from psycho-analysis and will therefore be lost to it. Their turning away from what we have up till now called psycho-analytic method is closely connected with the signs of falling apart within the Committee, and this falling apart represents the second danger. The third one is the damaging effect on the psycho-analytic movement to be expected from the new books.

Before I continue, I must ask your forgiveness, dear Professor, if I have given you pain just now when you are so much in need of friendly and encouraging impressions. How much I should like to be able to give you these today! But I have no choice if I wish to protect you from worse to come. The discussion I suggested for our meeting appears to me the only means of preventing what you yourself have seen coming: the breaking up of our most intimate circle. It almost fell apart last autumn. I may say it was I in the first place who prevented this at the time. I shall now use all my influence once more to avert these dangers, as far as is still possible. I promise you, dear Professor, in advance, that it will be done on my part in a non-polemic and purely factual manner and only with the wish to serve you and our work, which is identical with your person.

Do you remember that at the first Congress in Salzburg I warned you about Jung? At the time you dismissed my fears and assumed that my motive was jealousy. Another Salzburg Congress is before us and once more I come to you in the same role—a role which I would far rather not play. If, on this occasion, I find you ready to listen to me despite the fact that I have so much to say that is painful, then I shall come to the meeting with hope of success.

With kind regards,

Yours,
Karl Abraham

Dear Friend,

You certainly made my heart heavy by the reawakening of Salzburg memories. I regretfully conclude from your letter that you feel that there are certain personal and factual differences that it is not easy to discuss with me. I know that is what my opponents proclaim to the world, but my nearest friends should know better. Nor is there any reason for you to make any such assumption, because, though my personal intimacy with Rank and Ferenczi has increased because of geographical reasons, you ought to have complete confidence that you stand no lower than they in my friendship and esteem.

Let me assure you that an apprehension of the kind that you expressed is not so far from my mind. When Rank first told me about his findings, I said jokingly: 'With an idea like that anyone else would set up on his own.' I think that the accent is on the 'anyone else', as you yourself admit. When Jung used his first independent experiences to shake himself free of analysis, we both knew that he had strong neurotic and selfish motives that took advantage of this discovery. I was then able to say with justification that his twisted character did not compensate me for his lopsided theories. Incidentally, I conclude from a case that came to me from him that he has been tempted into tracing back a severe obsessional neurosis to the conflict between individualism and collectivism.

In the case of our two friends the situation is different. We are both confident that they have no evil motives other than those secondary concomitants of scientific work, the ambition to make new and astonishing discoveries. The only danger arising out of this is of falling into error, which is hard to avoid in science. Let us assume the most extreme case, and suppose that Ferenczi and Rank came right out with the view that we were wrong to stop at the Oedipus complex, and that the really decisive factor was the birth trauma, and that those who did not overcome this later broke down also on the Oedipus complex. Then, instead of our sexual aetiology of neurosis, we should have an aetiology determined by physiological chance, because those who became neurotic would either have experienced an unusually severe birth trauma or would bring an unusually 'sensitive' organisation to that trauma. Further, a number of analysts would make certain modifications in technique on the basis of this theory. What further evil consequences would ensue? We could remain under the same roof with the greatest equanimity, and after a few years' work it would become plain whether one side had exaggerated a useful finding or the other had underrated it. That is the position as it strikes me. Naturally I cannot in advance diminish the force of ideas and arguments that you may produce, and therefore I am in full agreement with the proposed discussion.

Now to the practical side, as you say. You want us to begin the discussion on the Friday before Easter, which would give us plenty of elbow-room until Sunday evening. Here I must make an objection. Two or two and a half days' debate would be practically equivalent to a doubling of the congress time, and that is too much for my weakened capacities. I must once more fly in the face of your incurable optimism and point out that I really am no longer the beast of burden that I used to be. Efforts I should not have noticed before my illness are now obviously too much for me. I even doubt whether I shall be able to listen to all the fifteen papers to be read at the congress, and in a corner of my heart, to quote our Nestroy,[1] there actually lurks a desire to be spared the whole bother of the congress. I hope that between now and then my state of health will improve, and thus extinguish this impulse, but it is still quite certain that I shall not be able to read a paper or attend the dinner. Those two injured functions permit no exhibition.

I therefore take the view that all the free hours of Saturday will have to be sufficient to settle the matter. Our all meeting in Vienna is excluded by Jones's urgent request to be spared the journey to Vienna.

With cordial greetings to you and your whole family,

Yours,
Freud

---

[1] Johann Nestroy, 1801–1862, popular Austrian dramatist.

Dear Professor,

I knew that my last letter would cause you pain. I shall not try to describe how difficult it was for me to write all this. My doubts on how you would accept my point of view referred exclusively to the fact that I had once more put you in the position of having to listen to very serious criticisms of two colleagues who are so close to you. Neither in my letter nor at any time previously have I suggested it is difficult to discuss factual differences with you. My opinion is exactly the opposite and I can only admire over and over again your readiness in this respect. Further, I have never at any time felt myself slighted by you. On the contrary, at our meetings in the Harz mountains and in Lavarone, I felt that you gave me your very special confidence. It is seventeen years, dear Professor, since I first met you, and in all these years I have always felt happy that I could count myself among those closest to you; and this has not changed till now. I do not wish you to feel the slightest doubt about this.

Concerning the factual aspect, I find it gratifying to know that my opinion and yours are not irreconcilable. When I speak in more detail in Salzburg, I hope we shall achieve full understanding. Wherever I see a possibility of *rapprochement*, I shall, as always, be glad to seize on it. I do not want to worry you any further today. There is only one point I wish to stress once again: it is not at all difficult for me to assimilate new discoveries if they have been arrived at in a legitimate psychoanalytic manner. My criticisms are not directed at the results achieved by Ferenczi and Rank but against the methods they used. These seem to me to lead away from psycho-analysis and my criticisms will refer solely to this point.

I am glad to agree that we should meet on Saturday afternoon in Salzburg. My suggestion that we should meet a day earlier was not intended to prolong our discussions by another day but, on the contrary, to have more time for rest in between.

This letter will go first to Sachs who will probably add a few lines.

In unchanged (and unchangeable) loyalty,

Yours,
Abraham

Dear Friend,

This letter is to inform you of a possibility that you have perhaps not yet taken into account.

As the result of a possibly influenzal nasal catarrh at the beginning of this month, my health has progressively deteriorated so much that last Saturday and Sunday for the first time in my medical career I had to stop work over the weekend. The short visit to the Kurhaus at Semmering obviously did me good, but just because of that there is a possibility that I foresee. Unless between now and Easter my general condition improves in quite extraordinary fashion–your seasoned optimism will immediately assume that it will, but I remain doubtful–I shall not be able to attend the Salzburg congress, but shall again go to the sanatorium, where I may recover sufficiently to enable me to continue the essential part of my work.

In that case neither my meeting with the former committee nor the speech in which you proposed to warn me of the threat represented by the new movement would take place. I think you should get used to the idea of such a possible course of events, and I take it that in such circumstances there will be nothing for it but for all of you to thresh out matters between yourselves, which is really what you should have done in the first place. For to whatever extent your reaction to Ferenczi and Rank may have been justified, quite apart from that, the way you set about things was certainly not friendly, and it has become completely clear to me on this occasion that the committee no longer exists, because the state of mind is lacking that would make a committee of this handful of people. I think that it is now up to you to prevent a further deterioration, and I hope that Eitingon, whom I expect here on the 13th, will help in this. It cannot be your intention because of this anxiety of yours to cause the collapse of the international association and everything that depends on it.

I am selfish enough to feel it an advantage that because of my frailty I am at least spared having to listen to and to form an opinion on everything connected with the new squabble. I am

355

neither very pleased about this advantage nor about the situation from which it derives. As a cautious question-mark still hangs over my decision, I shall wait till the week before the congress before letting you know definitely.

With cordial greetings,

Yours,
Freud

Berggasse 19,
Vienna IX,
3.4.24

Dear Friend,

I promised to write to you again as soon as I had made up my mind. I am therefore now writing to let you know that I shall not be attending the congress, but at Easter shall be on the Semmering, seeking out the peace and good air that I have needed so urgently since my influenza. I am simultaneously informing Jones and Eitingon, who is expected at Meran.

With cordial greetings,

Yours,
Freud

Berlin-Grunewald,
4.4.24

Dear Professor,

My first reaction to your letter which I received yesterday was deep concern that your health is troubling you again. I was particularly sorry—both for your sake and for ours—to hear that you think you may have to stay away from the Congress. My next thought was that the discussion before the Congress could be held among ourselves and, on your arrival, we could just report the result to you. You would thus be spared anything that might be detrimental to your health. If you agree to this suggestion, everyone else will as well. In the meantime, I shall continue to hope that your indisposition will soon pass so that we may at least expect you for the Congress itself.

For the rest, your letter expresses a distrust of me that I find extremely painful and, at the same time, strange. I had believed

356

that the correspondence we had some time ago had been concluded in a satisfactory manner and now I suddenly receive the most serious reproaches from you. I must however state that your letter has not evoked even a shadow of guilt in me. It is easy for me, dear Professor, to show you that I am the victim of a lapse of memory and that all your accusations rest on a displacement of facts in my disfavour.

Your main reproach is that I should have tried to obtain a direct understanding between myself and the others. By avoiding this, I failed in my friendship to Ferenczi and Rank. This reproach would have been justified if I had written spontaneously to you, dear Professor, to tell you of my objections. The facts are exactly the reverse. You yourself on February 15th sent a long circular letter to us all, and each one of us replied in his own way, as I also did and as I had a right to do. At your express desire, I then wrote more extensively. There was, therefore, no behaviour on my part which could give the impression of bypassing the others or of making a surreptitious approach – there was only a legitimate reaction to your circular letter. This 'guilt' does therefore not exist.

The further lapse in your memory concerns the purpose of our meeting before the Congress. You write that I wish to make a speech in order to warn you. It is true that two of my letters contained a warning; but the purpose of the meeting was, as I explained in detail in my letter, to have a free discussion amongst all of us in order to re-establish the unity of the Committee. You understood me correctly at the time and replied: 'I am therefore in full agreement with the suggested discussion.' Only afterwards did a misinterpretation of my intention creep in and I now appear as the disturber of the peace and even as the destroyer of the Committee.

Now to the third point. Last year in San Cristoforo[1] the Committee would certainly have disintegrated had I not kept it together. During those days I worked with great devotion to preserve the Committee which is so important to me, and to save you, dear Professor, from seeing it break up. You will also remember that at Lavarone I tried hard to smooth out disagreements and to effect a conciliation. We said goodbye to each

[1] San Cristoforo on Lake Caldonazzo near Lavarone in the South Tyrol.

other on the Postplatz in Lavarone, glad to have achieved that much at least; and now you say that I want to destroy the Committee. This can only have been due to a blotting out in your memory of all that speaks in my favour. Your reminder that it is up to me to prevent the disintegration of the Committee does in fact perfectly correspond with what I considered my foremost task when I last wrote to you.

And finally: it could not be my intention to cause a split in the International Association. I can truly say of myself, dear Professor, that in my twenty years' adherence to our cause there has never been one day of uncertainty in my attitude towards it. I do not exaggerate if I state that I have devoted myself to the work of organising the Berlin Society and also the International Association. During the last few months I have borne practically the whole burden of preparation for the Congress, in the hope of making it particularly harmonious and thereby giving you a pleasant and encouraging experience. And I was quietly occupied with plans for the Association which I hoped would give you pleasure at the Congress–and now you suspect me of wishing to dissolve the Association!

I am well aware of what I have done. I have plainly put before you the dangers that face psycho-analysis, for mutual understanding in our closest circle and for the whole of our work. I knew how painful all this would be for you. You also know from my letters how hard I found it to do this. I added that I was exposing myself to a similar reaction from you as in the past, when I first drew your attention to unwelcome facts. You, dear Professor, vigorously asserted that I need not expect any kind of affective reaction, admitted that my objections were not too far removed from your own and agreed to my suggestion for discussion. But now, four weeks later, the reaction has set in after all!

I feel with complete assurance that a talk with you, dear Professor, would disperse your suspicions within a few moments. This solution is impossible at present. But I know well enough that in the long run you cannot possibly misconstrue my feelings and intentions in this way. On the contrary, I am certain that you will change your opinion some day. For the moment, just the assurance once again that I shall approach a meeting, even if you do not take part in it, without any polemic intent. I take into account that at the meeting some of the Committee members may also treat me with the same distrust as you. Discord stemming from certain sources is readily directed against the man who frankly indicates these sources. But just because I am fully aware and conscious of having behaved with loyalty towards everyone, I can calmly face these reactions. I continue to go along with my friend Casimiro and am therefore,

Yours, as ever,
Abraham

Berggasse 19,
Vienna IX,
28.4.24

Dear Friend,

This letter, which is to congratulate you on the presidency, would have been sent several days earlier had not the wash of the congress thrown up on my shore so many callers whom it was impossible to turn away. I think with regret that you allowed yourself to be deterred from coming to Vienna, and yet I must be selfish enough to regard it as a relief for which I thank you. The good Casimiro will have appreciated that this time it is not a matter of a passing indisposition on my part, but of a new and much reduced level of life and work.

I have heard with pleasure that the congress passed off without any disturbing clashes, and I am very glad to acknowledge your services in this matter. As to the affair itself, I am, as you know, in an uncomfortable position. I am in fact very close to your standpoint, or rather I am growing closer and closer to it, but I still cannot take your side personally. I am fully convinced of the correctness of your behaviour, but I still think you might have done things differently. On the question of nuance of attitude I agree with Eitingon.

Now let me wish you an active and successful period of office, and I send my greetings to you and yours with unruffled cordiality.

Yours,
Freud

Berggasse 19,
Vienna IX,
4.5.24

Dear Friend,

Your very conscientious report has completed my knowledge of events at the congress in the most desirable manner. My heartfelt thanks. Also it did me a great deal of good to hear that real difficulties stood in the way of your coming to Vienna, so that it did not depend on my will alone. It is very painful to me to think that of all people it was you, my *rocher de bronce*, whom I had to keep away, while I had to see and speak to Emden, Jones, Laforgue[1] and Levy.[2]

You must make a real effort to put yourself in my position if you are not to feel ill-disposed towards me. Though apparently on the way to recovery, there is deep inside me a pessimistic belief in the closeness of the end of my life, nourished by the never-ceasing petty torments and discomforts of the scar, a kind of senile depression centred on the conflict between irrational pleasure in life and intelligent resignation. Accompanying this there is a need for rest and a disinclination to human contacts, neither of which are satisfied, because I cannot avoid working for six or seven hours a day. If I am mistaken and this is only a passing phase, I shall be the first to confirm the fact and again put my shoulder to the wheel. If my forebodings are correct, I shall not fail, if sufficient time remains, to ask you quickly to come and see me.

The idea that my sixty-eighth birthday the day after to-morrow might be my last must have occurred to others, because the city of Vienna has hastened to grant me on that day the freedom of the city, which is normally not given until the recipient's seventieth birthday. I have been informed that at mid-day on the sixth Professor Tandler,[3] representing the burgo-master, and Dr Friedjung,[4] the children's specialist and a mem-

[1] Dr René Laforgue, French psycho-analyst.
[2] Dr Lajos Levy, head of the Jewish Hospital in Budapest.
[3] Julius Tandler, Professor of Anatomy in Vienna.
[4] Dr Josef K. Friedjung, a member of the Vienna Psycho-Analytical Society.

ber of the council, who is one of our people, are to pay me a ceremonial visit. This recognition is the work of the Social Democrats, who now control the Town Hall. Dr Friedjung shares my birthday but not, of course, my age.

Though during the worst period I was able to write a few small things that you will see in the *Zeitschrift*, I am now quite inactive and without ideas. I am moving further and further away from the birth trauma. I believe it will *fall flat*[1] if it is not criticised too sharply, and Rank, whom I value because of his gifts, his great service to our cause, and also for personal reasons, will have learned a valuable lesson. Your reconciliation with Ferenczi seems to me to be particularly valuable as a guarantee for the future. Of course the whole episode has had an unfavourable effect on my spirits in these difficult times.

And now I send you my very cordial greetings and wish you and your wife and children a happy time that will justify your optimism.

Yours,
Freud

*

Berlin-Grunewald,
7.5.24

Dear Professor,

Our letters crossed. In order to prevent this happening a second time I postponed writing until I got your reply concerning America and only sent you a congratulatory telegram for your birthday yesterday. Now you have rewarded me so generously with your two letters, particularly with the second, which actually arrived yesterday making me feel as if it were my birthday. I find it difficult to put into words my thanks for all the warmth and cordiality expressed in your letter. I feel infinitely relieved now I know there is no factual discrepancy. For the last six months I have been very seriously worried. I cannot, of course, in principle refute the possibility of having made an error in procedure. If I were to try and give a fuller explanation of my behaviour, I would have to go into many things that I

[1] The words in English in the original.

have so far intentionally left untouched in our correspondence. I believe it is better to leave them unsaid; instead, I promise in future to show every consideration necessary in this far from simple situation. I was glad, dear Professor, to receive your good wishes for my Presidency. If I on my side repeat my good wishes for your new year, I feel I am justified in being far more confident about the future than you are yourself. I can well imagine how the constant discomfort from the scar keeps painful thoughts alive. Even the necessity of having to think about one's health is a burden, and I never doubted the gravity of last year's illness. On the other hand, six months have now passed since your operation without any new objective reasons for concern, and the latest news from my various sources—the most recent being Jones and Hitschmann—is that they found you better and stronger than expected. If my informants are correct and the discomfort from the scar is gradually receding, I look forward to the immense pleasure of visiting you fairly soon and of congratulating you on your recovery. I am not to be easily put off from seeing the future in this light. As far as the citizens of Vienna are concerned, I give them two years to think of a better way of honouring you on your seventieth birthday.

I have already written about my work plans. At Deuticke's suggestion, I am preparing the second edition of Segantini. It is a pity, I think, that this small *opus* was not taken over by the *Verlag* along with so many other papers.

Some time ago we rented a small flat for the summer months at Sils-Maria (Engadine) where we shall do our own housekeeping—that is if we can get an exit permit. Travelling difficulties are still very considerable.

I do not expect a reply to this letter, dear Professor! Neither visits nor correspondence should become a burden to you. I shall write again soon if there is anything to report.

With all my very best wishes and with kindest regards from house to house,

Yours,
Karl Abraham

*

Sils-Maria, Engadine, Haus Gilly,
30.6.24

Dear Professor,

I was distressed to hear that you had to give up your journey to Switzerland. I have no idea where you will spend your holidays, but must naturally agree with you that it is better not to be too far away from Vienna. Since travel restrictions in Germany have been lifted, I could come at the end of my vacation to wherever you are staying. I therefore hope to hear some time where you will be spending the first half of August.

It is eighteen years since I was in the Engadine and I am again as enchanted with it as on all previous occasions. Especially now in the spring there are more flowers in bloom here than anywhere else in the Alps. It is well before the season and everything is rather empty, enabling us to enjoy to the full all the splendours of the mountains.

Some daily analytic work—for the time being only one patient—keeps me in contact with my customary activities. Besides I am writing the new edition of Segantini for Deuticke and am going over my Congress paper.[1] If you, dear Professor, should wish to read it, I could send you the manuscript some time (but you are not to say yes just to please me!).

There is nothing else to report from the quietness of Sils-Maria. I wish you and your family very enjoyable holidays and am, with kind regards from house to house,

Yours,
Karl Abraham

Berggasse 19,
Vienna IX,
4.7.24

Dear Friend,

There are circumstances in which one can be altruistic even in old age. So I take pleasure with you in the Engadine, although I myself cannot go there. I have too clearly recognised

---

[1] Karl Abraham, 'The Influence of Oral Erotism on Character Formation', *Selected Papers on Psycho-Analysis*, London, 1927.

my dependence on my doctor's[1] consulting room to put such a distance between him and me, and have taken the Villa Schüler, next to the Südbahnhotel at Semmering, from where I can comfortably get to Vienna and back in a day. The rent is so high that I cannot think of a second stay anywhere else. So, if you want to come and see me in August, you need make no other journey. This time I too have brought a patient with me as hand-luggage who will keep me in practice. I have recently been having *ups and downs*,[2] according to whether the prosthesis, the nose or the ear chose to torment me more or less. I hope we shall now find a *modus vivendi* with each other.

If you wish to send me your congress paper, it is exceedingly probable that I shall read it with the greatest interest. We intend to move to Semmering on July 8th.

With cordial greetings to you and your family and best wishes for the summer,

Yours,
Freud

Semmering,
31.7.24

Dear Friend,

It is good to hear that you are so thoroughly enjoying Sils-Maria. There is no question of my saying no to your coming to see me, if the small extra journey does not put you off. I am having a good rest here, I am no longer so withdrawn, and I am looking forward greatly to seeing you again. I have read your manuscript with the interest it deserves. Forgive me one small comment of secondary importance. You charge Adler with responsibility for the connection between ambition and urethral erotism. Well, I have always believed it was my discovery.

Until we meet again, then. With cordial greetings to you and your wife and children,

Yours,
Freud

---

[1] Professor Hans Pichler, oral surgeon, who worked on Freud's prosthesis.
[2] These words in English in the original.

Dear Friend,

In re 7[1]

I am putting at your disposal an idea the value of which I cannot judge myself because of ignorance.

I should like to take a historical view and believe that the significance of the number 7 originated in a period when men counted in sixes. (Here ignorance sets in.) In that case seven would not be the last of a series as it is now in the week, but the first of a second series and, like first things, subject to taboo. The fact that the initial number of the third series, that is to say, 13, is the unluckiest of all numbers would fit in with this.

The origin of my idea was a remark in a history of Assyria that 19 was also one of the suspect numbers, which the author explains with reference to the length of the month by the equation $30 + 19 = 49$, or 7×7. However, $19 = 13 + 6$, the beginning of a fourth series of sixes.

This system of sixes would thus be pre-astronomical. One should now investigate what is known of such a system, of which enough traces remain (dozen, gross, division of the circle into 360 degrees).

Moreover, it is notable how many prime numbers appear in this series:

1

7

13

19

25 is an exception, but is followed by

31

37

43

49 which is again 7×7

The craziest things can be done with numbers, so be careful.

Cordially yours,

Freud

[1] This refers to a remark of Abraham's in a letter of 26.4.24 that he wanted to investigate the significance of the number 7 in myths, customs, etc. He never carried this out, however.

Berlin-Grunewald,
23.8.24

Dear Professor,

I have been home for just a week and cannot wait any longer to send you a few lines to let you know at least some of my feelings. First of all, the great and incomparable pleasure of finding you, dear Professor, in spite of all you have gone through, so well, lively and energetic, as I had scarcely dared hope from all written accounts. I left you with the wish that the comfortable days spent on the Semmering would further contribute to your recovery. Moreover, I must thank you and all your family for all the kindnesses shown me. The days I spent with you made a particularly pleasant end to my holidays. I very much hope that your health will permit me to repeat my visit fairly soon.

I spent a day and a half in Vienna. At the *Verlag* I spoke to Storfer about the publication of my paper. You already know that he intends to print it together with an earlier paper. It is just possible that I may rapidly add a short supplementary chapter about character formation at the genital level.[1]

25.8.24

I had got so far the day before yesterday when your letter arrived. In the meantime I have studied your suggestions and want first of all to thank you for your stimulating ideas. I was so pleased that you immediately took up the problem of the number seven and made it yours. I have meanwhile studied the ethnological and other relevant literature, but with very meagre results. Either the 'seven planets' or the 'quarter of the lunar month'–that's all anyone knows.

The idea about the system of the sixes is very interesting and undoubtedly an important contribution, especially in connection with thirteen, nineteen, etc. and with the taboo on one, first things. But this on its own is not enough, apart from the fact that I have so far only found some confirmation of a primitive system of fives not of sixes. Here is one of the many arguments:

[1] Karl Abraham, 'Character-Formation on the Genital Level of the Libido', *Selected Papers on Psycho-Analysis*, London, 1927.

not only the seventh day, the seventh month, etc. are taboo with the Jews, Babylonians, etc., but all dangerous things representing a taboo, such as evil spirits, are seven in number. Most important, there are strong psychological grounds which make irrefutable the connection between the number seven and the unconscious. I am convinced that these psychological sources are linked with others, among which the one you suggest may well be of great importance. One must ask oneself why this idea has not occurred to any of the orientalists.

Your communication encourages me to report to you as soon as I have any new findings. But I cannot promise anything as the literature has let me down and I am still waiting for analytic material.

Perhaps something soon about another project. For now, only many thanks and kindest regards from house to house,

Yours,

Abraham

Berlin-Grunewald,
17.9.24

Dear Professor,

You have not heard from me for some time even though I promised to report everything that might be of interest to you.

At present, the projected meeting at Würzburg is of prime importance for us. It promises to be reasonably satisfactory and I am very pleased that participation of a number of non-Germans will dispel the suspicion of our wishing to isolate ourselves. We already have a good selection of papers. Moreover, the question of training will be fully discussed, as Simmel will report on the organisation of our Institute with special reference to the teaching syllabus, and Sachs will talk on training analyses in particular. You will have heard that the latter will be giving a course on technique in London. We had, incidentally, to postpone our meeting until October 11th and 12th.

The courses scheduled for our winter term will be similar to those of last year. The only change is that Radó will give the introductory course in my stead and I shall probably speak on character development to an audience of doctors and teachers.

The following little story may amuse you. A few days ago I found this announcement in an antiquarian's catalogue: 'Freud, S., "*Ueber Spinalganglien und Rückenmark des Petromyzon,* 1878".' I did not know this work but remembered that I had recently come across a reference to it in your manuscript ('An Auto-biographical Study').[1] I have now obtained the paper—it belonged to a Dr Langerhans, who died here some time ago and to whose work on a similar theme your paper refers. I found it very interesting to recognise your later style in this, your earliest paper. Up till now I have been the only one in psycho-analytic circles to own a copy of your dissertation on the coca plant and now that I also possess your second earliest paper, I am *hors de concours*.

I am at present dictating a third paper for the Character book (the Genital Level of Character-Formation). There is a good essay on Stereotyped Attitudes of Catatonic Patients in the Peruvian *Revista de Psiquiatria*. I am having it translated and shall then send it to Ferenczi for inclusion in the *Zeitschrift*.

Hoping that you and your family will spend pleasant autumn days on the Semmering, I am, with kind regards,

Yours,

Karl Abraham

Semmering,
21.9.24

Dear Friend,

Thank you for so conscientiously keeping your promise. But when were you not conscientious?

There is little to report from here. I am waiting with curiosity for the return of Rank, who will probably not be in Vienna before the end of next month. I have been in lively correspondence with Ferenczi, and hope that you too will not lose contact with him. His behaviour in the 'affair' was vacillating, but he is now retreating from his partisanship for Rank.

I am thinking of breaking off my stay here in a week's time. Not without great regret, because the last few days have been

---

[1] Sigmund Freud, 'An Autobiographical Study', Standard Ed., Vol. XX.

magnificent. I, that is to say, my prosthesis, is again under treatment to adapt it to changed conditions.

It is making severe demands on the unity of the personality to try and make me identify myself with the author of the paper on the spinal ganglia of the petromyzon. Nevertheless I must be he, and I think I was happier about that discovery than about others since.

In the autumn I shall have to give up the leadership of the Vienna group, because I am too tired in the evening to be able to follow a meeting lasting several hours, and my hearing works on one side only. I do not yet know what the group will do.

My best wishes for the German meeting.

With cordial greetings to you and your family,

Yours,
Freud

*

Berlin-Grunewald,
15.10.24

Dear Professor,

Your telegram arrived at the end of the Würzburg meeting and I want to begin by thanking you for it. I had planned to send you a detailed report about the proceedings but I think you will already have heard personally from van Emden and perhaps from others as well, so I can be briefer.

Attendance was quite satisfactory; the list shows about forty-eight names. Most of the papers were of a remarkably high standard. I think all the participants were pleased with the way the meeting went. Besides, those two sunny autumn days on the river Main were delightful and it was a great pleasure to visit the lovely old town.

In the Spanish language, which I like so very much, one puts the question-mark at the beginning of the sentence and I shall therefore precede a piece of news received today with a question mark. ?Are you, dear Professor, really coming to Berlin quite soon and is it true that you will read a paper. This interests me, first of all because I would see in it an extraordinary sign of objective improvement and subjective well-being; and besides . . . but I do not need to say this!

I have just received the final proofs of my small book on character-formation.[1] The investigation into the number seven has been completely put aside for the time being – that is to say, I have not found any literature referring to it. But I have come to believe that the idea I put to you on the Semmering is fundamentally correct. I see that one cannot attack the problem either from the angle of astronomical significance or from that of numerical systems. The basic psychological phenomenon seems to me to lie in the ambivalent attitude of mankind to the number seven. This must represent the thing to which one is most ambivalent and I thus come back once more to the Oedipus complex. Seven is the number of abstinence (Sabbath, etc.) everywhere, it expresses the taboo and is at the same time the number of many rites compulsively performed. I see in this double significance the justification for assuming a fusion of two other numbers in this one, and believe that the significance of the three equalling father and the four equalling mother (three patriarchs and four matriarchs mentioned in the Bible, etc.) will have to be retained. I hope I shall soon be able to look for further material. (The above requires no reply!) Another thing which has occupied me recently is the subject of fear in an enclosed space, a phenomenon which, as far as I know, has not yet been dealt with in detail. A few observations made recently have provided me with some interesting findings and, at the same time, demonstrated the very slight significance of the birth process in the formation of this neurotic symptom.

With kind regards from house to house,

Yours,
Abraham

---

[1] Karl Abraham, 'Studien zur Charakterbildung', published 1925.

Berggasse 19,
Vienna IX,
17.10.24

Dear Friend,

How ambivalent can rumour be! In Vienna it pronounces me to be dead about once a fortnight and in Berlin I am expected to arrive to deliver a lecture. Neither is true, the truth lies in between. I am still alive, as you see, but I have no desire to lecture, and shall be able to think of travelling again only if Pichler succeeds in making a good and stable foundation for my prosthesis, which so far is not the case. My condition, that is to say, my capacity to speak and chew, is still so variable that there is ample room for the optimism of all the Casimiros.

I have heard only good things about Würzburg, but you are certainly the most competent reporter about that. The whole thing is very gratifying.

Emden is here, as you know. He wanted to have an hour's analysis daily for four weeks, but I had to decline. I am now miserly with my work, alien as that may be to my previous nature, and am unwilling to do more than five hours. Nevertheless a sixth is almost invariably added, because of consultations and having to see people. Apart from that, I am correcting proofs, beginning the revision of the *Interpretation of Dreams* for the complete edition, and so on. The *Autobiographical Study*, which you have read, has already been set and corrected. I shall turn the fee into reprints and distribute them generously.

Rank is expected at the end of the month. You are right, we too must wait, but I think that nothing good lies ahead. I should like to separate his personality from the birth trauma and to have evidence about what may be valuable in the latter. The *Psycho-Analytical Review* has a paper by him on the significance of the birth trauma for analysis; I have not received it.

I am sending a proposal in writing to the next meeting of the society that I should retain the presidency for a time and be represented by a deputy at the meetings. It would be a semi-miracle if I were ever able to resume my functions, and I do not believe in it. So it is only putting it off.

The prospect of getting a house for a clinic has evaporated.

The wealthy lady who wished to build it is now behaving as if she were offended and is withdrawing. I was thinking of arranging a flat in the house for Ferenczi, who would then have moved to Vienna as the head of the institute. But now nothing has come of it, and I have one more confirmation that nothing will grow on Vienna soil.

With cordial greetings to you and your family,

Yours,
Freud

*

Berlin-Grunewald,
20.10.24

Dear Professor,

The resistance of a patient, who presents me with an hour of undisturbed peace, gives me the chance of replying to you at once. I had not expected such a long letter and was therefore doubly pleased to find you, if not keen to talk, at least keen to write. But to reassure you straight away—this letter requires no reply. It merely contains some news which I could have sent you a fortnight later, but it gives me pleasure to be in contact with you in this way.

The 'rumour' had already been dispelled before your letter arrived. The speaker, who is to talk to a Zionist organisation here, is a schoolteacher from Vienna who bears your name. However, the invitation to the lecture went out with the name 'Professor Freud from Vienna'. Probably a slip on the part of the President of the organisation which will have the effect of providing your namesake with a larger audience than anticipated.

I have started to read the book by Levy-Brühl[1] (Sorbonne) on thought in primitive people, the first work I have found useful in my investigation into the number seven. More about this later.

I am immensely sorry, dear Professor, that you may experience further worry because of Rank's return and that nothing can be done to spare you all this. I also do not see anything good coming out of it and can scarcely imagine the possibility of col-

[1] Lucien Levy-Brühl, French philosopher and ethnologist, 1857–1937.

372

laboration with him. The other question – how we are to replace such an exceptionally capable worker – is, by comparison, less important; after a detailed discussion with Sachs and Eitingon, I feel that all difficulties can be overcome. We have also discussed the future of the *Verlag*.

In spite of everything, coming events make me feel somewhat hopeful. If a complete break should come about between Rank and yourself, there would be nothing to prevent the rest of us from re-establishing the Committee. Looking back over the past, I would say that the neurotic process in Rank developed over the course of several years. At the same time as he tried to compensate for his negative tendencies by over-conscientious work, his need for friendly co-operation with others lessened and his arbitrary and tyrannical behaviour became more striking in many ways. Added to this, there was an increased emphasis on money and, simultaneously, increased irritability and hostility. Thus, an undeniable regression to the anal-sadistic phase. The disappearance of all friendly feelings towards you recently became very clear once again. When I consider all this, I can only take an analytic point of view – I do not feel a trace of hostility towards Rank. My reaction is one of infinite regret that you have to suffer this trial, and particularly with Rank, and that Rank himself seems to have become involved in an apparently irreversible pathological process.

With kindest regards from house to house and all good wishes for your health,

Yours,
Karl Abraham

*

Berlin-Grunewald,
12.11.24

Dear Professor,

The evening paper reports that rail traffic in Austria is to be resumed tonight and I take this as a signal for writing to you at last. But the letter will need no reply.

After Eitingon's return, we three[1] had a discussion to which

---

[1] Abraham, Eitingon and Sachs, the three Berlin members of the Committee.

we invited Radó. We are all of the opinion that the solution is as favourable as it could possibly be under present circumstances. The sad feeling remains that after two years of first latent and then open conflict ending in the break with Rank, we have to accept it as quite definite and yet make it appear as unobtrusive as possible to outsiders.

We have lost one of our best members, but he is, after all, only one. During that same time we were threatened by another loss from which we were fortunately spared. We of the old guard who remained round you, dear Professor, shall certainly not slacken in our endeavours to provide you with some gratifying experiences after so much trouble.

I shall today follow my old custom of raising in my letters theoretical matters which occupy me. You, dear Professor, will certainly remember the conversation we had on the Semmering on the way home from the strawberry hunt, when you spoke to me of an idea you had. It referred to the origin of predicting the future from entrails. I was recently reminded of your theory in an analysis—certain cannibalistic phantasies of my patient led to the probable roots of the Jewish prohibition against eating milk and meat together. In this analysis the milk proved to be an allusion to the mother and the meat an allusion to the typical biting castration phantasy directed against the father. It made me reflect about this prohibition; its origin is the biblical law, repeated several times and enigmatic in meaning: Thou shalt not seethe a kid in his mother's milk.[1] This law prohibits the killing and eating of even an animal shortly after its birth, obviously with the intention of preventing the same action in the case of a human child, particularly before birth. This would make it a direct prohibitory law against the primitive customs you suggest.

With kind regards,

Yours, as ever
Karl Abraham

---

[1] Exodus, Chapter XXIII, verse 19.

Berlin-Grunewald,
3.12.24

Dear Professor,

All your news interested me greatly, particularly the expert opinion[1] you were asked to give.

I saw your handwriting quite unexpectedly today, Mrs O. brought me your introduction and I shall try and fit her into my day. A difficult case like all drug addictions, but probably one from which something new can be learned.

I cannot remember where the kid and the mother's milk was mentioned but I must not of course—which is always dangerous when one thinks one has found something new—rely on my memory.

I have at last got hold of some clinical material for the investigation into number seven. First of all—something that had also been forgotten!—the dream about the wolves in the History of the Infantile Neurosis; and secondly, in the analysis of a new patient. I think I shall soon have collected sufficient material. Despite careful searching, I have not been able to find any proofs for the numerical system with the six which you, dear Professor, suggest, and certainly not among the Babylonians. Did you know, by the way, that the Babylonians had a five-day week? The taboo on the seventh day seems to be completely independent of this. I hope to have time for further research at Christmas.

I have another theoretical question but there is no urgency for a reply and you should not write or dictate a letter for this purpose alone. The question concerns a point in the theory of sexuality. Your concept of a change of erotogenic zones in the woman at puberty has always proved correct in practice. I have recently wondered whether in early infancy there may be an early vaginal awakening of the female libido, which is destined to be repressed and which is subsequently followed by clitoral primacy as the expression of the phallic phase. A number of observations seem to bear this out. If my assumption is correct,

[1] Freud was asked to give a written opinion on the question of lay-analysis. This request arose from Reik's difficulties in practising as a lay-analyst.

it would have one advantage for us: we would be better able to understand the female Oedipus complex as the result of an early vaginal reaction to the father's penis (possibly in the form of spontaneous contractions) and the change of the erotogenic zone in puberty would then be a resumption of the original position. One could justifiably follow up this idea some time, since it is based on a number of observations. It could be fitted into our present theory which it does not contradict in any way and to which it might make a small addition. If it seems worth your while, I could report some of my observations which gave me the idea. It has not yet been clarified and the relationship to the phallic phase in particular is so far unclear.

Yesterday we had a meeting (short contributions) and among others heard an excellent short clinical paper by Dr Benedek from Leipzig on erythropobia (this has already been accepted for the *Zeitschrift*). She is of great value in her ability to attract young people as well as in her excellent practical work. I shall save up any other news from Berlin for the next circular letter. For now, only many good wishes for your health and kindest regards from house to house,

Yours,
Karl Abraham

Berggasse 19,
Vienna IX,
8.12.24

Dear Friend,

My obscure memory in regard to the subject of the newborn lamb and its mother's milk is not connected with you personally. I have the impression that this dietary ban was pointed out to me by someone to whom I mentioned the idea. It may have been Rank. In any case your memory is not at fault.

The problem of 7 still interests me greatly. I have not got any further with it, or got any closer to the interpretation at which you hinted.

Finally, your latest theme, the assumed vaginal share in the early infantile flourishing of the libido, interests me greatly. I do not know anything about it. As I gladly admit, the female side of the problem is extraordinarily obscure to me. If your ideas and observations on the subject already permit communication, I should very much like to hear about them, but I can wait. According to my preconceived ideas on the subject, the vaginal share would tend to be expressed anally. The vagina, as we know, is a later acquisition by separation from the cloaca.

With cordial greetings to you and your family,

Yours,
Freud

*

Berlin-Grunewald,
26.12.24

Dear Professor,

I owe you a reply to your letter of the 8th and am glad to take advantage of the quiet of the Christmas holiday to write to you.

The suggestions about the female erotogenic zones that I made in my last letter are far from ready to be incorporated into our theory of sexuality as it stands. In recent months I have felt that some of our theories about the erotogenic zones appeared incomplete. I have for a long time questioned whether the displacement from the clitoris to the vagina could have occurred in an earlier version though in an inverse direction. We have had to convince ourselves in so many other contexts that the psycho-sexual processes of puberty are repetitions. This assumed sexual stage would have to have as a sexual aim the reception of the penis. The opening intended for this seems to me, too, to have cloacal characteristics; that is to say, one has to assume vaginal sensations are conducted from the anal zone and that pleasurable contractions of the vagina must somehow be linked with contractions of the anal sphincter. The ease with which little girls can be seduced to coitus-like actions, as well as the tendency to vaginal masturbation and, in particular, the introduction of foreign bodies, must all rest on such processes. Two neurotic symptoms have forced me to assume something which we could call an early vaginal-anal stage: frigidity and *vaginismus*. In the light of all my psycho-analytic experience, I cannot

377

believe that frigidity is merely based on the failure of the libido to pass from the clitoris to the vagina. There must be a prohibition which has an immediate and local basis; this is even more valid for *vaginismus*. Why should the vagina react so negatively to the first attempts at coitus unless something positive has preceded this? Similarly, hysterical vomiting is preceded by a positive and pleasurable experience in early infancy.

As I mentioned last time, such an assumption would also throw light on the obscure origin of the female Oedipus complex.

My investigation into the number seven is progressing, though a great deal still remains unclear. The significance of seven has already become far more comprehensible. The second problem—why seven is suitable for expressing certain things in the psychological life of the human species—is certainly far more difficult, but here too a few points have become clearer. I may shortly be able to tell you something about it. To return once more to your assumption of a numerical system with the six; there seems nothing of that kind, though you are right in one sense. The mysterious sequence does not, however, start with six but with the number three. If one is added, we have four (which dominates American mythology), seven (for which I know several explanations but am looking for some more), ten, thirteen and nineteen (Babylonian).

Enough for today. Perhaps I may soon be able to let you have some news of importance to the psycho-analytic movement, but it is still too uncertain. May it come true in 1925, dear Professor, just as everything else I wish for you, your family and for all of us!

With kind regards from my family and myself to you all,

Yours,
Karl Abraham

Berggasse 19,
Vienna IX,
29.12.24

Dear Friend,

That you would be conciliatory in the Rank affair was something that I only expected from your kindness and correctness, and I cannot be surprised about your reserve in the matter.

The explanation is that you do not know all the circumstances of the case, and cannot have got from the letter a proper impression of the individual concerned and his transformation. I know all about it, know the whole sad story, and can say that I am confident that he has been cured of his neurosis by this experience just as if he had gone through a proper analysis. Moreover, he is still very depressed, understands the whole difficulty of his position, and in the next few weeks wants to go to America to make good the harm he has done there, and he has no illusions about how much greater his difficulties will be than on the occasion of his first visit.

As for the two scientific questions mentioned in your letter, my attitude is different in each. In the first, the question of the female leading zone, I am eager to learn, look forward to your novelties in the matter, and have no preconceived ideas. In regard to the problem of the number 7, I cannot suppress my scepticism. I am very ready to believe that my idea will lead to nothing, but I doubt whether you are on the right track. *Vedremo*.

It will only make our letters richer and livelier.

The date reminds me to send my heartfelt good wishes for 1925 to you, your wife and children, though the New Year only plays the role of a commonplace *agent provocateur* in the matter. Sincerely yours,

Freud

*

Berlin-Grunewald,
6.2.25

Dear Professor,

I should like to let you have some good news without waiting for the circular letter. In all my seventeen years of work in Berlin, no medical society has asked me to speak on psychoanalysis. I have now been invited, and have accepted the invitation, to speak to the Berlin Society for Gynaecology and Obstetrics on March 13th. Subject: 'Psycho-Analysis and Gynaecology.'[1] If the paper meets with a favourable reception,

[1] Karl Abraham, 'Psycho-Analysis and Gynaecology', *Clinical Papers and Essays on Psycho-Analysis*, London, 1955.

379

this will have a very positive effect since other specialist societies will follow suit and this will mean the first official recognition of psycho-analysis in Germany.

Some other good news will be found in the circular letter.

Now I want to say a few frank words about another matter. Ferenczi's article on Sexual Practices[1] is to be the first in the new volume of the *Zeitschrift*. As far as wealth of ideas is concerned, it is perhaps his most mature and best work but I have grave doubts about its technical content. At the end of 1923 his *Entwicklungsziele*[2] appeared, outlining the technical rule of setting a time limit and, in general, advocating a strong active tendency. It has taken only one year for the time limit rule to be modified, but a new activity is now recommended in its stead which can hardly have been tested for more than a year in this form and the rules of which are somewhat vague and undefined. It might have been better not to have been in such a hurry with a new set of technical innovations and with their publication. Eitingon has already suggested to you that it would be preferable if it were to follow after your short paper on the 'Wunderblock'[3] (which I read with the greatest pleasure since one feels so secure in the clear and unassailable structuring of your thoughts!) Eitingon's suggestion has my full support. If Ferenczi's paper were placed before yours, this would imply that it virtually had official sanction; otherwise it is, like any other paper, the author's own responsibility.

This leads to another question. We cannot in the long run avoid discussing technical problems. What would you, dear Professor, prefer: to arrange a symposium at the Congress or to have an exchange of opinions in several numbers of the *Zeitschrift*? And, in the latter case, would you yourself wish to participate?

I am very glad to have continued good news about your health. With kindest regards from house to house,

Yours,
Abraham

[1] Sandor Ferenczi, 'Zur Psychoanalyse von Sexualgewohnheiten', *Internationale Zeitschrift für Psychoanalyse*, Vol. XI, No. 1, 1925.

[2] *Sandor Ferenczi und Otto Rank*, see footnote 2, p. 344.

[3] Sigmund Freud, 'Notiz über den Wunderblock, 'A Note upon the Mystic Writing Pad', Standard Ed., Vol. XIX.

Berlin-Grunewald,
4.5.25

Dear Professor,

Your birthday is imminent and, as it is not possible for me to bring you my good wishes in person this year either, it has once again to be done by letter (and no reply is required!). Even though your state of health often leaves much to be desired, I firmly believe you have made good progress since your last birthday. May this progress be accelerated in the new year.

In order to give you some news on your birthday about the growth of psycho-analytic activity in Berlin (about which Eitingon will also inform you) I wish to tell you that, apart from three lectures on crime in Berlin, I have to give three further papers in Holland this month: one in The Hague to the Medical Association on the 'Hysterical Symptom', and two in Leyden to psychiatrists on the 'Psycho-Analytic Treatment of Schizophrenic States'.

If all goes according to plan, I hope to see you, dear Professor, and your family in exactly four months' time in Hamburg. Kindest regards to all of you from all of us,

With many good wishes,

Yours,
Abraham

Berggasse 19,
Vienna IX,
10.5.25

Dear Friend,

In spite of your waiver of a reply, herewith my heartfelt thanks. And please pass them on to the society. It was splendid, though rather tiring, in fact it was a test to which I did not stand up very well. As the annual general meeting happened to have been arranged for the same afternoon, Ferenczi was present as well as Eitingon.

The good news about your family and work gave me great pleasure. If one is a hopeless (I mean incurable) optimist, one should at least have good reason to be so.

In contrast to your travel plans, we propose to spend the summer quietly at the villa on the Semmering that you know. With cordial greetings to you, your wife and children,

Yours,

Freud

*

Dear Professor,

This time I am writing from my bed; I brought back a feverish bronchitis from Holland which appears persistent.[1] Just before I went to bed, the day before yesterday, an unexpected question was put to me about which I must tell you.

The director of an important film company came to see me and told me of his intention to produce a popular, scientific, psycho-analytic film[2] with your authorisation and with the collaboration and supervision of your recognised colleagues. With regard to the latter, I am to have the right to make suggestions.

I need hardly mention that this kind of thing is not really up my street; nor that this type of project is typical of our times and that it is sure to be carried out, if not with us then with people who know nothing about it. We have so many 'wild' analysts in Berlin–if only to mention Kronfeld, Schultz and Hattingberg[3] who would be only too keen to grasp at such an offer should we decline. In that event, they would have the financial gain and our work would be damaged.

The difference between this straightforward offer compared

---

[1] This apparent bronchitis was the first manifestation of Abraham's fatal illness. It in fact started with an injury to the pharynx from a fishbone and was followed by septic broncho-pneumonia, lung abscess and terminal subphrenic abscess. The illness took the typical course of septicaemia, prior to the introduction of antibiotics, with swinging temperatures, remissions and euphoria. Abraham's previous emphysema had doubtless made him susceptible to such infection.

[2] 'Geheimnis der Seele', KulturAbteilung der Ufa (Secret of the Soul, produced by the Educational Unit of Ufa).

[3] Dr Hans von Hattingberg, psychiatrist in Munich.

with that of the American Goldwyn[1] is obvious. The plan for the film is as follows: the first part is to serve as an introduction and will give impressive examples illustrating repression, the unconscious, the dream, parapraxis, anxiety, etc. The director of this company who knows some of your papers is, for instance, very enthusiastic about the analogy of the invader used in the lectures to illustrate repression and resistance.[2] The second part will present a life history from the viewpoint of psycho-analysis and will show the treatment and cure of neurotic symptoms.

Furthermore, Mr Neumann suggests the publication of an easily comprehensible and non-scientific pamphlet on psycho-analysis. My idea is not to describe psycho-analysis systematically but to give examples from every-day life and to develop the theory around them. Neumann would like to publish this pamphlet, which should be sold at 2–3 marks, either through a large publishing firm which would ensure the widest circulation, or through our *Verlag*. This may present an opportunity of helping the fortunes of the *Verlag*.

I assume, dear Professor, that you will have no great sympathy for the plan as a whole but that you will come to acknowledge the force of the practical argument. Our influence should extend into every detail in order to avoid anything that might discredit us in any way.

Tomorrow I shall discuss the whole matter with Sachs, if my voice has returned by then. I shall, with his and Eitingon's help, choose some suitable young colleagues from our circle. I shall naturally be grateful to you for any kind of advice.

I am limiting myself today to this one subject; writing in bed is rather uncomfortable. I shall tell you about Holland and any other matters in the circular letter on the 15th. In the hope that your reply will also bring very good news about your health,

I am, with kind regards,

Yours,
Karl Abraham

[1] Samuel Goldwyn had, some years before, suggested to Freud that a film be made and Freud had refused.

[2] Sigmund Freud, *Introductory Lectures on Psycho-Analysis*, Lecture XXII, Standard Ed., Vol. XVI.

Dear Friend,

First of all let me express the hope that by the time you receive this letter – written an hour after receiving yours – you will be out of bed and have the use of your voice again. My news is not bad, I have my usual small complaints to put up with, but on the whole I am better. I stop work on the 27th inst.

I do not feel happy about your magnificent project. Your argument that if we do not do it, it will be done by others at first seemed irresistible. But then it struck me that what these people are willing to pay for is obviously the authorisation. That they can get only from us. If they do something completely wild because we refuse, we cannot stop them and are not implicated. After all, we cannot stop anyone from making such a film without obtaining our consent.

After settling this argument, the matter can at least be discussed. My chief objection is still that I do not believe that satisfactory plastic representation of our abstractions is at all possible. We do not want to give our consent to anything insipid. Mr Goldwyn was at any rate clever enough to stick to the aspect of our subject that can be plastically represented very well, that is to say, love. The small example that you mentioned, the representation of repression by means of my Worcester simile, would make an absurd rather than instructive impact.

I am of course completely confident that you yourself would never approve of anything susceptible to such or similar objections. As you seem not disinclined to engage in the matter, I suggest that you do the following. Tell them that I do not believe in the possibility of anything good and useful coming of the project and therefore for the time being cannot give my authorisation. But if examination of the script should satisfy you, and me also, of the opposite, I shall be willing to give it. I do not deny that I should prefer my name not to come into it at all.

If, contrary to expectation, everything turned out satisfactorily, we should need no judge, as they say in Vienna, in regard to the ten per cent. If anything came of it I should gladly give my share to the publishing house.

I am retaining the letter to the company.

With cordial greetings and in the hope that your wishes may quickly come true,

Yours,
Freud

Berggasse 19,
Vienna IX,
21.6.25

Dear Friend,

I hear from Sachs to my surprise, and also to my dismay, that your illness is still not a thing of the past. That does not fit in with my picture of you. I like to think of you only as a man continually and unfailingly at work. I feel your illness to be a kind of unfair competition, and appeal to you to stop it as quickly as possible. I look forward to news about you from your family and meanwhile send you my cordial good wishes.

Yours,
Freud

Berlin-Grunewald,
25.6.25

Dear Professor,

Your letter arrived some days ago, and, almost simultaneously, Dr Deutsch telephoned to enquire about my health. My wife gave him detailed information and asked him afterwards by letter to pass this on to you, dear Professor. This morning an unsigned telegram arrived from Vienna; my wife assumed that it was from you and telegraphed the reply to your address. I am however dictating this to her in order to give you detailed news.

The illness itself had run its course by the beginning of this week—the bronchial pneumonic *foci* have healed but part of the pleura is still sensitive, so that I shall have to stay in bed for the time being. In about a fortnight I am to go to the mountains to recuperate, but still feel somewhat exhausted from my illness, though I hope everything will clear up satisfactorily.

Thanking you very much for your sympathy and wishing you and your family an extremely enjoyable summer, I am, with kindest regards in which the writer of these lines joins me,

Yours,

Karl Abraham

Villa Schüler,
Semmering,
1.7.25

Dear Friend,

It was not I who sent you the telegram, at the time I had been reassured by Deutsch on the telephone, but I was glad to have your telegram. I was delighted to hear that you are convalescent again – but be a conscientious convalescent, for your own sake as well as ours.

We arrived here yesterday; it is delightful to be here in spite of the gales and the modesty of the natural surroundings. Everything is so comfortable and quiet, as is only appropriate to the old, it is a kind of *Austragstüberl*,[1] if you know that Alpine expression.

My own state of health, which unfortunately is still a matter of interest to my friends, promises well. With truly angelic–or asinine–patience, my worthy physician dealt with all the complaints that disturbed the peace of my prosthesis until he got a tolerable result. Finally he paid me the parting compliment of saying that, considering my age and the troubles that I had been through, I was in pretty good condition.

I have written a memorial for J. Breuer[2] which will appear in No. 2 of the *Zeitschrift*. I exchanged cordial letters with his family, and so brought my fateful relations with him to a dignified conclusion.

---

[1] Room set aside in peasant's house for parents who have retired from work.

[2] Dr Josef Breuer, 1842–1925, paternal friend of Freud's during his student days and joint author with him of *Studies on Hysteria*, 1895.

Do not fail to keep me informed of the progress of your recovery. With good wishes to you and your family,

Yours,

Freud, who has been worrying

Berlin-Grunewald,
6.7.25

Dear Professor,

This is to show you that I am making good progress; at the same time I want to tell you how pleased I was with your warm and fatherly letter. I was glad to hear that your health continues to improve. Although I am twenty-one years younger than you, I shall have to spend just as quiet a holiday. We have decided on Wengen in the Bernese Oberland. It is 1,270 metres high and has the advantage of a mountain railway for riding up if one cannot climb much. Address from July 17th: Hotel Victoria.

Eitingon came to see me yesterday. He has, during my illness, made excellent preparations for the Congress. The programmes are already in print.

If you, dear Professor, are not coming to Homburg, I am afraid that I shall not see you for some time as I cannot do very much for a while. It's only now I realise how much strength this month has cost me and I shall therefore not be able to help you with raspberry picking.

With kindest regards from my family and myself to you all,

Yours,

Karl Abraham

Villa Schüler,
Semmering,
9.7.25

Dear Friend,

Anna with her telepathic sensitivity remarked yesterday that it was time we had news of you. We lacked confirmation that on the occasion of your recent exertions you had coughed up all the noxious substances.

Now I am delighted to have that confirmation. Just because of the twenty-one years' difference in our ages, your illness means more to our cause than mine. But the quiet holidays must be doing you good, I myself am feeling the good effect. If I did not have a capriciously sensitive spot – Pichler seriously assures me that there is no disease of the tissue and that it is only hyper-aesthesia – I should feel very well, and the bits of writing I have started would go ahead quickly. Before he left, the good man attacked the bad spot with a galvano-caustic 'horse-cure', as he called it, and so I now have the burn to complain about instead of the spontaneous sore. Strangely enough, however, this is a gain.

For your amusement, let me tell you that a copy of the *Matin* arrived today with a leader on psycho-analysis. Nothing remarkable about that, you may say, but this *Matin* is published at Port-au-Prince in Haiti, with which one does not have correspondence every day.

It is now the strawberry season on the Semmering; with the raspberry season I shall certainly remember your help.

Accept my warmest and most genuine – because fundamentally selfish – wishes for a quick and complete recovery, and give my kindest regards to your certainly delighted wife and children.

Sincerely yours,
Freud

*

Wengen,
Hotel Victoria,
18.7.25

Dear Professor,

Here are my first greetings from Wengen where I am conscientiously resting in a deck-chair to recover my health. I have weathered the long journey well and am pleased with the choice of place and hotel. The situation of Wengen, exactly opposite the Jungfrau, is extraordinarily beautiful; besides, the peace here is unique considering present conditions. Wengen can be reached from Lauterbrunnen only by funicular or on

388

foot and there is no road, no cars or dust. We are also very lucky with the weather and all prerequisites for my recovery are thus fulfilled. But, for the time being, the patient's egocentric mode of thinking remains with me owing to the unaccustomed necessity of having to consider myself at every step. Until now I did not even know that one could walk so slowly or that a lift could become one of the necessities of life. In other words, my breathing is not yet easy but I confidently hope that the high mountain air will have a good effect.

So much about myself. My wife, who nursed me until it became impossible to go on without an outside nurse, is also rather exhausted, but I hope she too will benefit from our stay here.

I should like to know whether you are still suffering from the discomforts you mentioned in your last letter. I hope to hear about it soon. If writing is a nuisance for you, dear Professor, I shall be well content with a few lines from Miss Anna.

Before my departure there were discussions about the question of the film. Today I only want to say that Sachs and I believe that we have every guarantee that the matter will be carried out with genuine seriousness. In particular, we think we have succeeded in principle in presenting even the most abstract concepts. Each of us had an idea concerning these and they complemented each other in the most fortunate way. More about this another time.

Otherwise, I am completely inactive scientifically and intend to remain so for some time. Instead, now that I can read again, I am enjoying my old favourites, Aristophanes[1] and Heine, and as a semi-invalid have learned to value the game of patience.

With kindest regards from my wife and myself to you and all your family,

Yours,
Karl Abraham

[1] Which Abraham read in Greek.

Dear Friend,

No, writing is really no burden to me. I was delighted to have news of you so soon, because my thoughts often stray to other objects of love from an ego the claims of which have become burdensome. When you describe how much you are occupied with the unaccustomed 'needs of your own poor Conrad'[1] I am consoled, being experienced in the matter, by the certainty that you are having to practise this adaptation only for a short time. A permanent re-adaptation is far more difficult.

The unexpected eventuality has occurred that on looking through the list of congress papers I was glad to see that your name is not among the speakers. With such a task ahead it would be difficult to rest the intellectual faculties. But we all hope that by the first week of September our president will have re-acquired his freedom of respiration and of action.

We are very comfortable this year in the Semmering surroundings that you know. This summer has a different, friendlier character, and with prolonged familiarity the modest charms of the neighbourhood make a strong impact. The women find the housekeeping very convenient, and living in this well-equipped house can be called almost ideal.

The day goes by without one's really knowing what one has done with it. If one thinks about it in the evening, one has done very little. Giving some free play to one's phantasy at the writing desk, an hour with the crazy American who is supposed to pay the high rent, some adventures with Wolf,[2] whom you have not met yet—with his passionate affection and jealousy, his mistrust of strangers, and his mixture of wildness and tractability he is an object of general interest. Also writing a few letters, some proof-correcting, family visitors from America, etc. The energetic intervention with which my doctor took leave of me three weeks ago has changed the character of my complaints thoroughly for the better. All the paraesthesias that

[1] A reference to the personification of the body used by the Swiss writer Karl Spitteler (1845–1924) in his novel *Imago*, published in 1906.
[2] Anna Freud's alsatian.

390

tyrannically forced themselves upon my attention have disappeared, and have left behind an individual free to complain, if he feels like it, about his awkward speech and never-ending nasal catarrh. So life is admittedly tolerable, but after this spoiling and weaning process what will regular work taste like in October?

I have written a few short papers, but they are not meant very seriously. Perhaps, if I am willing to admit their parentage, I shall tell you about them later. Their titles I can reveal to you: 'Negation,'[1] 'Inhibition and Symptoms,'[2] and 'Some Psychological Consequences of the Anatomical Distinction between the Sexes.'[3]

Now get well quickly and may you find in Wengen whatever you need to bring your period of illness to an end. Our heartfelt thanks are due to your wife for her contribution to your recovery. I have cause to remember that sort of thing.

With our very best wishes to you all,

Yours,
Freud

*

Hotel Edelweiss,
Sils-Maria,
14.8.25

Dear Professor,

I am improving from week to week but certain residues of my illness remain—for instance, my breathing which is not yet quite easy. The results of the examination are very favourable and promise a complete re-establishment of the *status quo*. My wife has just left for home; I shall stay until the 31st of the month in this, my favourite spot, which is unequalled by anything else in the Alps.

I am sorry to hear that there has been some upset to do with the film though I do not know what it is about. But the work is progressing well and I feel sure that one day you will come round to agreeing with Sachs and myself.

Yours most sincerely,
Abraham

[1] Standard Ed., Vol. XIX.
[2] *Inhibition, Symptoms and Anxiety,*' Standard Ed., Vol. XX.
[3] Standard Ed., Vol. XIX.

Sils-Maria,
20.8.25

Dear Professor,

I am so glad to hear continuing good reports of you. Ferenczi too found you well and energetic. However it is painful for me that I see no chance of coming to convince myself in person of this for some time. A year has passed since I had my last glimpse of you on the Semmering.

Of myself, I can give increasingly good news. Yesterday I had a particularly good day and walked for several hours – very slowly of course and with breaks – and climbed about four hundred metres. Certainly a good sign. Other days leave much to be desired and, particularly for the first hour after getting up, I cough and have difficulty in breathing. I still feel all the time how weakening my illness has been but have every confidence that the Engadine air will have helped me even further by the end of this month.

My stay at Sils suits me far better than the first weeks in the Bernese Oberland. The level woodland paths along the shores of the lakes, the valleys and slopes have greater variety than I have ever found anywhere else. My wife and I are toying with the phantasy of building a holiday cottage here. This dream will probably be shattered by lack of money, especially as these months of my illness have not done anything to help me financially.

The work on the film is progressing well. Sachs is devoting himself to it and is proving very competent, and I am also trying to do my share. All the same, I agree with you, in view of their advertisement, that one should not have anything to do with these people. Our attitude in the matter is very far removed from theirs.

This letter needs no reply. Whatever you, dear Professor, may think or intend to do about this matter, would you please inform Sachs only, so that you are spared the trouble of writing twice.

I shall try and follow your advice not to tire myself too much at the Congress but should like to know how to do this successfully.

With kindest regards to you and yours,

Yours,
Abraham

Berlin-Grunewald,
8.9.25

Dear Professor,

I started writing a report in Homburg about my impression of the Congress which I intended to send to you, but hundreds of things claimed my attention and I could not finish it. Meanwhile you have already received first-hand reports about all that happened, and the photograph, which turned out well, is also in your possession. So I prefer to start anew and only to emphasise what I may see somewhat differently from your other informants. To begin with, the assurance that the Congress was scientifically of a good standard and that what I have to report is mainly favourable. It was better attended than Salzburg and more international. America was strongly represented and – to my satisfaction – some of the American colleagues proved more capable and better informed than we had expected. Coriat[1] made the soundest impression on me. Papers given by the others were less good though Pierce Clark's[2] had at least some interesting content to it. Among the other papers, there was only one which was really bad and that was Groddeck's; when one first met him he seemed full of brilliant ideas, but this time he was incredibly platitudinous and monotonous. Reik, Ophuijsen, Reich,[3] Alexander[4] and Róheim[5] all spoke very well indeed. Ferenczi's new attitude to the problem of therapy implies a *rapprochement* which gave me much pleasure, but this time his paper was not as rich as usual in original ideas. Rank tried in a commendable way to come closer to us and we, on our part, have – I believe – helped him in this. On the evening of the dinner I had a lengthy discussion with him which should certainly have a good effect on our future relationship. One thing, however, I could not say to him – that even now he seems really ill to me. He read his paper at a furious

[1] Dr Isadore Henry Coriat, American psycho-analyst.

[2] Dr L. Pierce Clark, American psycho-analyst.

[3] Dr Wilhelm Reich, Viennese psycho-analyst.

[4] Dr Franz Alexander, Hungarian psycho-analyst, practising in Budapest, later Berlin, then in Chicago, died recently in Los Angeles.

[5] Dr Geza Róheim, Hungarian anthropologist and psycho-analyst, died in U.S.A.

speed so that no one could follow and, once again, all his statements were without foundation and completely unproven. Add to this, his euphoric mood and another trip to America. For me all this means a new manic phase, this time however with more euphoric than irritable behaviour. That is why I could not really get any pleasure from our meeting.

His trip to America is very unwelcome to the Americans and it would have been better for him not to go. One of my main efforts at the Congress was to establish good personal relations with the Americans, not only in order to provide a counterbalance to the painful incidents of the past year, but also to counteract all ideas about secession. I think the business meeting greatly contributed to this. As regards lay analysts, a *rapprochement* has been reached. The appeal that training should be as uniform as possible was sympathetically received, and it would be far more effective to lay down strict conditions about this rather than issue printed rules about the acceptance of candidates. Federn's open admission of the mistakes made in Vienna had a favourable effect, as did my own plea for considering the different circumstances in other Societies. The question of discussions at future Congresses was also settled in a satisfactory manner. My re-election took place in a form which I can certainly regard as a vote of confidence. The replacement of the Council, consisting of all the Presidents of societies by only two representatives, gave me the welcome opportunity of getting Hitschmann nominated to the Executive.

But now I come to the best part of the whole Congress. The news that Miss Anna would read a paper of yours[1] evoked spontaneous applause at the beginning of the Congress which I wish you could have heard for yourself. Her extremely clear way of speaking did full justice to the contents. But it was not only its scientific content that gave the Congress its brilliant send-off; the personal note in certain trains of thought aroused strong emotion in all of us. The impression that, in the three-and-a-half years since the last Congress, there has been immense improvement in your health and vitality was intensified by the distribution of the latest number of *Imago*, containing three of your papers.

[1] See footnote 3, p. 391.

Immediately before the Congress, the *Frankfurter Zeitung* published an article by Drill who was highly appreciative of psycho-analysis provided it left religion undisturbed.

On the whole, therefore, I am satisfied with the Congress. I quite understand, incidentally, why you kept away. I really had some exhausting days. All the people who only wanted to speaks to me for 'half a minute' exacted such an amount of talking from me that I found it a very great strain and I shall need several days to get my breathing right again. I shall in any case have to undergo some treatment for my nose and throat from Fliess. If this letter were not already unduly long, I would tell you how my illness has most strikingly confirmed all Fliess's views on periodicity.[1]

I am gradually resuming work, starting with a few hours each day. After these months of scientific sterility, I want first of all to write a short paper on a criminal psychological theme (The History of an Impostor).

And now, only all good wishes for the remainder of your stay on the Semmering to you and your family, and kindest regards,

Yours,
Karl Abraham

*

Semmering,
11.9.25

Dear Friend,

So what I feared has happened. The congress was a great strain on you, and I can only hope that your youth will soon get the better of the disturbance.

Many thanks for the trouble you took in compensating me for my absence by your detailed report. To me the only fully enjoyable thing was your pleasure at the appearance of my paper on the programme. I had not thought of it myself, it was a last-minute idea of my daughter's. There are many other things I should like to discuss with you; in writing, differences stand out too luridly.

[1] *Der Ablauf des Lebens*, by Wilhelm Fliess, 1923.

395

I am staying here until the end of September. The weather is unfortunately very bad, but I hear that you are just as cold in Berlin.

Let me hear of your complete recovery, and with cordial greetings from

Yours,
Freud

Berggasse 19,
Vienna IX,
16.10.25

Dear Friend,

Hearing from you direct[1] of course gave me more pleasure and was more reassuring than all the indirect news. I hope you will soon be able to write and say that in this respect you have become completely uninteresting again.

Your short paper[2] is excellent. I think you should not wait for your turn in *Imago*, but that it should be used as the introductory article in the next annual series of the *Zeitschrift*. The subject is interesting enough for physicians too. In one respect I should have stated the idea rather differently, I should not have emphasised the deprivation of pleasure, but the fact that he could form no super-ego because he had been unable to achieve an Oedipus complex. The fact that in these circumstances he was able to establish an unconscious need of punishment instead of a normal conscience could be the point of departure for further reflections.

We have almost forgotten the summer, though the weather is now more summer-like than it was at the end on the Semmering. I have interesting and not too much work, and am still struggling with my usual minor complaints.

With cordial greetings to you and your family,

Yours,
Freud

[1] Abraham's letter has not survived.
[2] Karl Abraham, 'The History of an Impostor in the Light of Psycho-Analytical Knowledge', *Clinical Papers and Essays on Psycho-Analysis*, London, 1955.

Berlin-Grunewald,
19.10.25

Dear Professor,

Your letter has just arrived. You probably already know from the circular letter that I am very much better. The diseased lung appears to be healing: I did not completely get over the infection when it occurred the first time in June. The very disagreeable addition of gall-bladder colics has also disappeared and, according to the last examination, the liver enlargement seems to have gone down. I still need to be careful and shall probably resume work at the end of the month, providing no further trouble occurs.

I am so sorry to hear that you are continuously troubled by certain discomforts. As far as I know these are due to a disturbing amount of secretion and I have been wondering whether a stay in a very dry climate might be beneficial. But I do not know whether you still need to be near your surgeon. You may be interested to hear that Fliess, who heard about your illness two years ago, has repeatedly asked after your health with the warmest interest. As far as I am concerned, I must repeat here once again that I owe him the utmost gratitude.

I gladly accept your suggestion about the one point in my manuscript on the Impostor. I have, after all, mentioned elsewhere the failure to form an ego-ideal and need only put it more precisely in the place you mention.

With kindest regards from house to house,

Yours,
Abraham

*

Berlin-Grunewald,
27.10.25

Dear Professor,

Our last letters referring to the publication of my short paper (The Impostor) were overtaken by events. I received the proofs for correction some days ago so that in any case nothing could be done about its publication in *Imago*. It seems it was needed to fill a gap there. I am now writing an essay of similar length–'Psycho-Analytical Notes on Coué's System of Self-Mastery'[1]–which is based on your Group Psychology. Radó wants to include it in the first number of 1926 and I shall therefore appear in that number at any rate.

You know, dear Professor, that I am very unwilling to enter once again into a discussion of the film affair. But because of your reproach of harshness (in your circular letter), I find myself once more in the same position as on several previous occasions. In almost twenty years, we have had no differences of opinion except where personalities were concerned whom I, very much to my regret, had to criticise. The same sequence of events repeated itself each time; you indulgently overlooked everything that could be challenged in the behaviour of the persons concerned, whilst all the blame–which you subsequently recognised as unjustified–was directed against me. In Jung's case your criticism was that of 'jealousy'; in the case of Rank 'unfriendly behaviour' and, this time, 'harshness'. Could the sequence of events not be the same once again? I advanced an opinion which is basically yours as well but which you did not admit into consciousness. All the unpleasure linked to the relevant facts is then turned against the person who has drawn attention to them.

It gives me pain to have aroused your displeasure once again, although I am certain that this time, as on previous occasions, you will one day reconsider your judgement of me; but I on my part wanted to do everything to get the facts clear. I am, with kindest regards to you and your family, in unaltered and unalterable sincerity,

Yours,
Karl Abraham

---

[1] Karl Abraham, *Clinical Papers and Essays on Psycho-Analysis*, London, 1955.

Berggasse 19,
Vienna IX,
5.11.25

Dear Friend,

I note with pleasure that your illness has not changed you in any way, and I am willing to regard you as having again recovered. That takes a great load off my mind.

It does not make a deep impression on me that I cannot convert myself to your point of view in the film affair. There are a good many things that I see differently and judge differently.

Let us not give too much play to repetition compulsion. You were certainly right about Jung, and not quite so right about Rank. That matter took a different course, and would have passed over more easily if it had not been taken so very seriously in Berlin. It is still quite possible that you may be even less right in the matter with which we are concerned now. You are not necessarily always right. But should you turn out to be right this time too, nothing would prevent me from once again admitting it.

With that let us close the argument about something that you yourself describe as a trifle. Such differences of opinion can never be avoided, but only quickly overcome.

What matters more to me is to hear whether you intend to stay in Berlin or spend the winter in a milder climate. I am not quite sure in my mind what to wish for you, but in any case let the outcome be that you cause us no more worry.

With cordial greetings to you and your wife and children.

Yours,
Freud

Berggasse 19,
Vienna IX,
17.1.26

Dear Mrs Abraham,

Since my telegram on receiving the news of your husband's death I have put off writing to you. It was too difficult, and I hoped it would become easier. Then I fell ill myself, became feverish, and have not yet recovered. But I already see that putting it off was useless, it is just as difficult now as it was then. I have no substitute for him, and no consolatory words for you that would tell you anything new. That we have to submit with resignation to the blows of fate you know already; and you will have guessed that to me his loss is particularly painful because, with the selfishness of old age, I think he could easily have been spared for the probable short duration of my own life.

The only consolation is the news that in your brother you have found a helper who will enable you to watch over the development of your daughter and son free of crippling cares. May you find a new and rich meaning in life from your motherhood. I have no prospect of travelling, so I do not know whether I shall see you again. Trusting that you will keep me too in your memory, and with heartfelt sympathy,

Your devoted
Freud

INDEX

A

Abraham, Karl, ix–xvi

Abraham, Karl

Publications:

'On the Significance of Sexual Trauma in Childhood for the Symptomatology of Dementia Praecox', 1

'A Screen Memory Concerning a Childhood Event of Apparently Aetiological Significance', 16

'Psycho-Sexual Differences between Hysteria and Dementia Praecox', 25, 83, 103

'The Psychological Relations between Sexuality and Alcoholism', 42

'The Significance of Intermarriage between Close Relatives in the Psychology of the Neuroses', 42

Dreams and Myths, 53, 54, 57, 73, 74, 115, 321

'Hysterical Dream States', 81, 82, 84

'Remarks on the Psycho-Analysis of a Case of Foot and Corset Fetishism', 85

'On Neurotic Exogamy', 89, 150

'Giovanni Segantini; a Psycho-Analytical Study', 97, 101, 106, 107, 362, 363

'Notes on the Psycho-Analytical Treatment of Manic Depressive Insanity and Allied Conditions', 107, 216

'A Complicated Ceremonial Found in Neurotic Women', 109

'Amenhotep IV', 112, 118–19, 124

'Some Remarks on the Role of Grandparents in the Psychology of Neuroses', 130

'A Screen Memory Concerning a Childhood Event of Apparently Aetiological Significance', 130

'Mental After-Effects produced in a Nine Year Old Child by the Observation of Sexual Intercourse between its Parents', 133

'The First Pregenital Stage of the Libido', 136

'Restrictions and Transformations of Scopophilia in Psycho-Neurotics', 138, 147, 161

'The Ear and Auditory Passage as Erotogenic Zones', 150

Review of C. G. Jung's *Versuch einer Darstellung der Psycho-analytischen Theorie*, 152

'A Constitutional Basis of Locomotor Anxiety', 159, 168

'The First Pregenital Stage of the Libido', 178, 210

'The History of an Impostor in the Light of Psycho-analytical Knowledge', 237

'The Spending of Money in Anxiety States', 249, 267

'The First Pregenital Phase of the Libido', 282

'A Particular Form of Neurotic Resistance against the Psycho-Analytic Method', 285

'Manifestations of the Female Castration Complex', 287

'The Narcissistic Evaluation of Excretory Processes in Dreams and Neurosis', 295, 298

'The Cultural Significance of Psycho-Analysis', 305

Klinische Beiträge zur Psychoanalyse, 309, 321

'The Rescue and Murder of the Father in Neurotic Phantasy-Formations', 324

'Mistakes with an Overcompensating Tendency', 329

'An Octogenarian's Mistake', 331

'A Short Study of the Development of the Libido', 335, 339, 343

'Psycho-Analytical Views on Some Characteristics of Early Infantile Thinking', 338